ORIGIN

Jack Gallaway began his literary career with the *Graziers Journal* when World War II was at its height. As soon as he was old enough, he joined the RAN and took part in campaigns in the Pacific. At war's end he joined the Australian Regular Army, and went to Korea with 3 RAR. Returning to civilian life in the late 1950s, he joined the Commonwealth Department of Primary Industries for a time before returning to journalism. He did not make a clean break from the army, but continued to serve with the reserve, and spent more than seven years as a senior NCO with Queensland's only cavalry unit, the 2/14 Queensland Mounted Infantry. He has worked in both the print and the electronic media, and is the author of three books, *The Last Call of the Bugle: The Long Road to Kapyong*, *The Odd Couple: Blamey and MacArthur at War* and *The Brisbane Broncos*.

*This book is dedicated to the memory of
Ron McAuliffe and to his early heroes,
the legendary players of the 1920s*

ORIGIN

Rugby League's Greatest Contest 1980–2002

JACK GALLAWAY

UQP

First published 2003 by University of Queensland Press
Box 6042, St Lucia, Queensland 4067 Australia

www.uqp.uq.edu.au

Typeset by University of Queensland Press
Printed in Australia by McPherson's Printing Group

Distributed in the USA and Canada by
International Specialized Book Services, Inc.,
5824 N.E. Hassalo Street, Portland, Oregon 97213–3640

Cataloguing in Publication Data
National Library of Australia

Gallaway, Jack, 1926–   .
    Origin: Rugby League's greatest contest 1980–2002.

    Includes index.

    1. State of Origin (Australia) — History. 2. Rugby League
    football — Queensland — History. 3. Rugby League football —
    New South Wales — History. I. Title.

796.33380994

ISBN 0 7022 3383 8

Contents

Foreword

I AM SOMEWHAT casual with my association of dates and events from my past. I am very much a plan-and-dream-ahead, live-for-today person. But when first approached by Jack Gallaway and queried about my twenty-odd years involvement with Queensland State of Origin teams, and when I observed his obvious enthusiasm for the task and his bare-faced 'them and us' attitude that makes Queenslanders different, I readily agreed to help where I could and I have no regrets that I did.

Jack Gallaway took me back to the beginning of an incredible journey in sport, an association and participation as part of a team that ultimately became an Australian icon and changed the attitude of Queenslanders and of Queensland sporting teams forever.

My role in the book's preparation was a requirement to agree or disagree with passages of play in various games and to verify or otherwise deal with the author's thinking on some of the teams and great player personalities and to provide some of the background emotion and passionate resolve to win that was always an essential ingredient of our annual crusades. That Jack Gallaway has been able to understand that and to capture with his written word some of the great moments and personal triumphs of the Queensland team certainly identifies him to me as a True Believer in the Queensland cause and any contribution that I have been able to make has given me a great deal of pleasure.

To the Rugby League purist, Gallaway's book will provide an excellent reference guide to games, results, players and all manner of information pertinent to questions and answers relative to the twenty-three years of Origin Rugby League that it records. The author's easy speak, slightly Maroon-tinted view will appeal to most Queenslanders as his story unfolds. His brief description of the foundation of the Queensland Rugby League and of how it first broke the shackles of subservience to New South Wales will be an eye-opener to many, and he gives a potted history of the triumphs of the 1920s when giants like Thompson, Potter, Dempsey, Madsen, Steinhort and others bestrode the Rugby League scene clad in Maroon guernseys.

The detail the author offers is the result of an enormous amount of research, endless hours viewing tapes of all of the games played, and personally interviewing those men who, by virtue of their performance for Queensland, became household names, heroes to schoolboys and sporting legends in every sense of the word. Their names are the centre point and the heart of the team that made us all proud to be associated with them.

The author has also captured the 'Love Queensland, hate New South Wales' attitude that was so much a part of our most successful State of Origin teams. I am happy to report that, from observation of our success in 2002, the present team is generously endowed with this same philosophy.

There are always those who are seen to lead the way and dominate in any sport, be they coaches, players or administrators. They are the ones who guide their sport to success and Gallaway's work clearly identifies the men who provided the leadership that inspired the Maroons to rise to such great heights in State of Origin.

Arthur Beetson was one of Australia's all-time great players long before State of Origin and he brought to the fledgling concept an enormous knowledge of what was required at the top level of Rugby League. His popularity with the players, and his ability to lead without driving, laid the foundation for Queensland's unique success in the experiment that became State of Origin and the rallying point for that group of footballers and officials who would become known over time as the 'Origin Family'.

Wayne Bennett inspired loyalty and he maintained the comfortable, happy and attractive nature of 'in-camp' life that Artie had first established, but when Wayne first became coach he also introduced a degree of discipline which was needed to get the Maroons back on track. The Broncos' coach made good players better and delivered to Queensland the ultimate prize — a 3–zip whitewash of the enemy, the first in almost seventy years. How sweet it was!

Wally Lewis was there from the start. He played in 31 games and captained the Maroons in 30 of them. His influence, the respect in which he was held by the players and his dominance over the game for more than a decade are almost incalculable.

These three men were the major factors in Queensland fulfilling a destiny that had lain dormant since the early 1930s, and their opportunity to do this came about through the efforts of the administrator who was their leader. Senator Ron McAuliffe grew to manhood in the halcyon days when Rugby League teams led by Duncan Thompson ruled the land. Jack Gallaway has provided us with a permanent written memorial to the Great Gunsynd and he tells the story of what inspired him when he convinced New South Wales president, Kevin Humphreys, of the merits of the State of Origin concept. The author has dedicated the book to the man who will always be remembered as the father of State of Origin Rugby League.

The preparation of this work has been a huge undertaking and I hope that you, the reader, enjoy the book to the same degree that Jack Gallaway enjoyed writing it.

RICHARD (TOSSER) TURNER

And a Word from the Bosun ...

MY LIFETIME involvement with the game of Rugby League earned me the privilege of reading Jack Gallaway's work in manuscript and I am grateful to him for thinking of me. Jack's writing carried me back through history to all of those games of State of Origin which I have attended since 1980, his coverage reminding me of the game descriptions that I used to read by great sporting journalists like Lawrie Kavanagh and the late Tom Goodman. He recalls past glories in great detail, even Jack Reardon's role in sparking debate on State of Origin. A native of Lismore, my home town, Jack Reardon was lured to Queensland to play with Brisbane Norths, the highlight of his career being a Kangaroo tour in 1936–37 as vice-captain of Australia. As a journalist, he was the first to suggest that the Queensland Rugby League ought to have access to its expatriate players in Sydney. This is ironic, of course. Had State of Origin been the rule in Jack Reardon's day, he would never have been captain of the Maroons, since he would have been eligible only for the Blues.

Jack Gallaway's ability to describe a game and hold one's interest is remarkable. His coverage is even-handed and in writing this foreword I have no intention of sullying his achievement by descending into interstate politics.

The writer describes in great detail the process that brought State of Origin Rugby League into being, and in doing so he brings the reader to a realisation of the contribution that it has made to the modern game. Followers of the game will gain a new appreciation of the wonderful games that have been played over the past two decades and look forward with confidence to many more yet to come. The passion that both sides bring to the annual State of Origin contest produces the best football played by any code anywhere in the world. Here in Australia, this view is backed by the television ratings that are achieved each year and the coverage that the game and its stars receive in the daily press.

Reading Jack's manuscript brought back personal visions of past games and performances. Queenslanders such as Arthur Beetson, Wally Lewis, Allan Langer, Chris Close and Darren Lockyer and famous Blues such as Michael O'Connor, Steve Mortimer, Laurie Daley, Andrew Ettingshausen, Steve Roach and the Blues' most recently retired captain, Brad Fittler, are all there in this book.

It must be said that playing Rugby League is not for the faint-hearted, and only the strong survived in the great games that we witnessed at Lang Park, the Sydney Cricket Ground, the Sydney Football Stadium and Telstra Stadium.

Jack Gallaway and I have crossed paths many times. We both served in the Royal Australian Navy in World War II. Post-war, I was a member of the RAN and Jack served in the Regular Army, and we both played Rugby for our respective services. Yet it needed this book to occasion our first verbal encounter. Our first conversation revealed that we share a deep love for our country, for life in general and for Rugby League. I believe that our game owes a debt of gratitude to Jack Gallaway for his in-depth research into State of Origin and into the ninety and more years that Rugby League has been played in Australia. Many thanks, Jack, for allowing me to write this Foreword. Well done, mate.

ERIC ('BOSUN') COX
Vice-President,
New South Wales Rugby League

In the Beginning ...

RUGBY LEAGUE was first played in Australia in the city of Sydney in 1908 and a team of Queenslanders wearing maroon guernseys met a New South Wales side whose members wore sky blue in the first interstate clash in Sydney in that same year. The visitors were comprehensively defeated, 43 points to nil. That initial defeat was the first of three that they suffered that year, but the Maroons would become accustomed to that.

In 1922 the Queenslanders travelled to Sydney to meet a New South Wales team for the twenty-third time, and for the first time since the game was introduced to Australia the Maroons defeated the Blues. What is more, they did so convincingly, by 25 points to 9.[1] They came back the following year to prove that it was no accident. Rugby League's influence had spread from Brisbane and tapped deep wells of talent in Queensland's regional centres. When the Maroon squad of nineteen for Sydney was selected in 1923, it smelt very strongly of gum leaves. Fourteen players from the country were picked and only five from the Queensland capital.[2]

The Maroons whitewashed the Blues that year when they beat them three times, 23–14, 18–13 and 25–10. In 1924 they did it again, 22–20, 20–7 and 36–6. Then in 1925, the two state teams met five times. The opening clash drew more than 30 000 fans to the Brisbane Exhibition Grounds to watch the Maroons win, 23–15. Two days later, at the Sydney Sports Ground, the Queenslanders were again victorious, 27–13. The Blues won a third game, played at the Sydney Cricket Ground, 27–16. The Queensland team broke its journey home to play an additional fixture against a New South Wales side at Newcastle. The Maroons scored 12 tries in a 56–23 flogging of the Blues.

The Queenslanders played a touring New Zealand side twice that season. They won 43–19 on the first occasion and 29–20 on the second. Later in the season, the New South Wales team journeyed to Brisbane for a two-game series. The Maroons won the first encounter 26 points to 8, and immediately after this game twenty-two Queenslanders left for a seven-week tour of New Zealand. What might well be called Queensland's 'thirds' met the Blues a few days later and scored 32 points to their opponents' 13.

The Maroons tour of the Shaky Isles was no less successful. Three 'tests' were played and although the visitors lost the first 14–25 they won the second by 35 points to 14 and the third 44–20. They were also undefeated in seven matches played against provincial teams and their record for 1925 stands unique in Rugby League history. The Queenslanders played eighteen representative games that season and they lost only two. The Maroons were the undisputed Australasian Rugby League Champions.

A Kangaroo touring party was due to leave for England at the end of the 1925 Australian season and Queensland's Rugby League community awaited the announcement of the selected team in a state of euphoric anticipation. In three tours of England undertaken since 1908, a grand total of just eight Queenslanders had gained selection. Any Australian touring party picked in 1925 would have to be dominated by Maroons. There was a sensation at season's end. Instead of announcing the names of twenty-six Kangaroos to tour, the Australian Rugby League Board of Control informed the media that the English Rugby League had decided that the Kiwis would provide stronger opposition than the Australians. The Poms had withdrawn the longstanding invitation to the Australians and a party of New Zealanders would tour in their place.

In the light of the Maroons mauling of the Maorilanders in the season just completed, both at home and abroad, no Queenslander believed the story for a moment. No Queenslander ever would. The disappointed Maroons were certain that the cancellation of the Kangaroo tour had been a New South Wales initiative, and it was a blow to Queensland pride which could never be forgotten and would certainly never be forgiven. Descendants of Maroons who ought to have won Green and Gold blazers[3] still recalled their families' anger almost eighty years later. To Queenslanders, the true reason for the cancellation was plain to see. The New South Wales Rugby League simply could not tolerate the thought of an Australian team that contained a majority of Maroons.

In Queensland, this gross act created a distaste for everything for which the Blue guernsey stands. Eighty years later, the cancellation of the Kangaroo tour is a faded footnote to the game's history, but the attitude of the New South Wales Rugby League toward Queensland and Queenslanders has remained constant. To those Southerners who control the code, Queensland is a relatively unimportant Rugby League satellite, a casual by-product of the main game which is concentrated in metropolitan Sydney.

In the 1970s, a cheeky and battle-scarred Maroon half-back, a 22-test veteran of vast international experience, discovered years ahead of biological science that anything that wears a Blue guernsey is, in fact, a Cockroach.[4] Although he was overlooked for the Nobel Prize for science that year, Barry Muir is revered for his discovery, his iconic status among Queenslanders celebrated by their universal adoption of the term he chose to describe any and all New South Welshmen. Generation after generation of Queenslanders have maintained the rage that first surfaced with that cancelled Kangaroo tour in 1925, and a ritual based on this tribal animosity erupts three times each year. Of course, there is rich irony associated with Barry Muir's role in this, since he is, by birth, a Cockroach.[5]

CHAPTER 1

Decline and Fall

T HE ACTIONS of the forebears of Barry Muir's 'cockroaches' were the foundation of a rivalry so deeply based as to be eternal. It is a rivalry which was shaped in its modern form, then fostered and nursed to maturity, by a gentleman who set out to return Rugby League in Queensland to the pre-eminence that it had enjoyed in that star-studded decade when the Maroons ruled.[1]

In 1971 Mr Ron McAuliffe was elected to the Australian Senate to represent Queensland in the interests of the Australian Labor Party. In that same year, Senator Ron McAuliffe was elected President of the Queensland Rugby League. His ten years of service in the Australian Parliament were some of the most tumultuous in Australia's political history. The Labor Party won office after a record period in the wilderness. There were two double dissolutions of the parliament, the Governor-General sacked the prime minister and his government and Ron's party was routed in the subsequent election. However, Ron McAuliffe's name is unlikely to be found among those of the movers and shakers during these turbulent political times in Canberra. A newly elected senator's role hardly went beyond putting his hand up to vote in Caucus and being present for divisions whenever parliament was sitting. This left Senator McAuliffe ample time to attend to the day-to-day affairs of the Queensland Rugby League.

Ron McAuliffe's family had strong ties to the working-class tradition that produced the game of Rugby League, and Ron grew to manhood in what was by far the most exciting period of the early history of the game. He was born in July 1918 and was just four years and one month of age on 25 September 1922 when the Queenslanders won that first historic victory. Few events remain so vivid in a sportsman's memory as do the stirring deeds of the heroes of his childhood. The Maroons went on to win eight more matches unconquered and it was 1925 before New South Wales won another game against them.

Ron grew up at a time when Maroon-clad giants roamed the land. Queenslanders such as Eric Fraunfelder and Billy Paten, Norm Bennett and Nigger Brown, Duncan and Colin Thompson, Herb Steinhort, Dan Dempsey, Cyril Connell and 'Mick' Madsen were household names. During the years that Ron McAuliffe spent at school, Queensland Rugby League ruled. Between 1922 and 1934 the Maroons were victorious in the interstate series on nine occasions and the Blues won just four times. It was a time when Australian Rugby League test teams were dominated by Queenslanders. A fourteen-year-old member of the Gregory Terrace firsts in 1932,[2] Ron McAuliffe was present at the Brisbane Cricket Ground to see the second test against the visiting English team. The Cricket Ground became a battlefield that day during one of the bloodiest international encounters ever staged. Under the rules of the day, head-high tackles were the norm, there were no replacements allowed for injured players, and eleven Australians, many walking wounded, defeated Jim Sullivan's thirteen Englishmen in the fabled Battle of Brisbane by 15 points to 6.

Herb Steinhort captained the depleted side. With two more magnificent Queenslanders, Mick Madsen and Dan Dempsey, he packed a three-man scrum and won the ball from six English forwards for most of the game.[3] Memories of such heroes of his youth were embedded deep in the McAuliffe psyche.

Ron McAuliffe played senior Rugby League with Brisbane's Northern Suburbs club in 1939, but when World War II broke out he joined the AIF. Five years later, Warrant Officer McAuliffe was discharged from the army after honourable service in the Middle East and in New Guinea with the 2/2 Casualty Clearing Station, a front-line medical unit. He returned to his civilian job with the

Queensland Railways Audit Office and took up residence at New Farm, adjacent to Brisbane's Fortitude Valley.

. The war had stolen Ron's best football years and he no longer played the game, but he retained a passionate interest in Rugby League and he formed close social ties with officials and players from the famous Valley Diehards. When former Queensland captain Duncan Hall played with the club in the late 1940s, he shared a flat with former international front row forward Roy Westaway in Brunswick Street, right in the heart of the Valley's social life. Ron McAuliffe was one of the first people he met. According to Duncan:

> [Ron] was just one of the blokes who was always around the place. There were at least five or six SP bookies around the Valley in those days, and Ron loved the punt. He turned up at all the games; he knew everyone worth knowing and everyone knew him. He drank at the Valley pub with us every night after work. In fact, he was one of these blokes who was the life of the party and who never seemed to want to go home. He was always around.

It wasn't long before McAuliffe became well known to a wider circle. He was elected to Valleys' committee in 1951, and was appointed club delegate to the Brisbane Rugby League in the same year. His rise was rapid, for in 1952 he was elected Chairman of the Brisbane Rugby League, and 1952 was a year of great change in the structure of Rugby League in Queensland.

In the beginning the game had been controlled by the Queensland Rugby League but there was friction between the Brisbane clubs and the then full-time secretary of the Queensland Rugby League, Harry Sunderland. While Sunderland was overseas as manager of the Australian team in 1922, the Brisbane clubs severed their close relationship with the Queensland body. They formed the Brisbane Rugby League, an affiliated autonomous body with a committee of management and a secretariat separate from and independent of the Queensland Rugby League.

There was no love lost between the two bodies and friction between them plagued the game for the next thirty years. In 1953, peace was declared. The Brisbane Rugby League ceased to exist and was replaced by the Brisbane division of the Queensland Rugby

League. For the purposes of administration, the two bodies came under the conjoint control of a single, well-paid secretary. When he was offered the appointment, Ron McAuliffe resigned from his position with the Queensland Railways Audit Office and accepted.

Rugby League was first played in Brisbane at Davies Park, on the riverside at West End, and the League hired the Exhibition Grounds for representative matches. Later, the Brisbane Cricket Ground at Wooloongabba became the game's headquarters, but the Gabba always was, and always would be, the home of Queensland Cricket. Rugby League could never be more than a rent-paying poor relation. Cricket Club members always had free access to their seats in their own stand and these freeloaders were always a visible thorn in Rugby League's side, especially at the highly profitable representative games against New South Wales and visiting international sides. In any case, the wide open spaces of a cricket ground are not wholly compatible with a game that is played on a rectangular field that occupies less than forty per cent of the oval's surface area.

The amalgamation of the Queensland Rugby League and the Brisbane Rugby League provided the joint secretariat with a much wider base of operations and gave the combined leagues a much stronger case to argue for the provision of its own ground. One of McAuliffe's first acts as secretary was to open the negotiations with the Brisbane City Council which resulted in the two Leagues being granted a 21-year lease of Lang Park to commence in the 1954 season.

The Queensland Rugby League's contribution towards the future development of Lang Park was £17,000.[4] At that time, the ground lacked any but the most basic facilities, but in 1957 Lang Park hosted its first game of first grade football. In 1958, improvements were at a sufficient level for the Queensland Rugby League headquarters to host its first Brisbane Rugby League Grand Final, when Brothers defeated Valleys 22 points to 7. Lang Park had arrived.

During Ron McAuliffe's busy watch as Secretary to the Queensland Rugby League, there were many improvements made to Rugby League in Queensland, but unfortunately this did not extend to the Maroons' performance in the annual interstate series played against New South Wales. In the 1950s, New South Wales won five series,

Queensland won two, and three were drawn.[5] Winning only two series out of ten was hardly brilliant success, but that was as good as it was going to get for Queensland for a long, long time.

The interstate competition was cancelled in 1942 when a Japanese invasion of Australia seemed possible. In 1945, with the end of World War II in sight, an 'unofficial' interstate series was played, just two games. Although New South Wales won both of them fairly easily, everyone was talking about a brilliant young second-rower from Brisbane's Southern Suburbs. Yet to reach his twentieth birthday, Harry Bath was the outstanding forward prospect in Australia. When the first post-war season commenced in 1946, he was wearing the gold and black of Balmain, and later that year he wore the sky blue of New South Wales. Harry Bath was the finest Australian forward never to represent his country. He represented both Queensland and New South Wales before his twenty-first birthday and was the first forward picked to play against the touring Englishmen in the first test in 1946. When he hurt his knee in a club game, the injury kept him out of all three tests, but he went to England in 1947 where his record with Warrington over the next ten years gained him immortality.[6]

The trickle south of Queensland talent that started with Harry became a flood a few years later when the New South Wales government legalised poker machines. By the mid-1950s Sydney Rugby League clubs had become the pacemakers in what was the state's most volatile growth industry. Club committees suddenly found that they had access to funds that were unlimited by Queensland standards. In 1946 Harry Bath signed with Balmain for what was little more than a comfortable living wage. Ten years later, senior executives with major national corporations were earning less than Sydney's top footballers. The kind of loyalty to club or state which would ignore such offers was rare indeed.

The table of results of interstate matches reflects this drain of talent to the south, and it shows that by the 1970s, the competition had become embarrassingly lopsided. In Sydney, the annual games were being played before smaller crowds than those attending unimportant club fixtures. The major Sydney clubs begrudged the allocation of weekend fixture dates for the interstate contests. They complained bitterly about the risks that their highly priced players ran of injury, and in 1971 the interstate competition was reduced from four games annually to three. In years in which an international Test series was played, the two state sides met only twice. So as not to interfere with the Sydney competition, interstate games were downgraded to mid-week fixtures, and to emphasise Sydney's lack of interest most of them were played in Brisbane. The final humiliation for Queensland came when the single game each season in Sydney was played mid-week at suburban Leichhardt Oval where fewer than 7,000 turned out to watch. In 1977 the New South Wales Rugby League declined to host a Queensland team in Sydney at all. Just two games were played, both in Brisbane.

In that same year, the makers of Winfield cigarettes were persuaded to sponsor Queensland's state league competition. The comedian Paul Hogan was guest speaker at the corporate function held in Brisbane to launch the company's involvement with the Queensland Rugby League. In a speech that probably amused his employers more than it did the local audience, he said, 'Every time Queensland produces a good footballer, he finishes up being processed through a New South Wales poker machine.

CHAPTER 2

1980–1981

The Union Whiz Kid

NO ONE in the history of the game in Queensland ever worked harder or more effectively for Rugby League than did Senator Ron McAuliffe. He introduced live-in training schemes, he pioneered the employment of sports medicine specialists and physiotherapists, and he coaxed, cajoled and bullied sponsors to find money for a retention fund — anything to keep young Queenslanders of promise in Queensland. But he was like the little Dutch boy with his finger in a very leaky dyke. With no thought for the game of Rugby League outside Sydney, the New South Wales Rugby League was concerned only for the local clubs. The southern media decried the interstate series as a waste of time and the evidence was on their side.

The year before McAuliffe assumed the presidency of the Queensland Rugby League, the Maroons defeated the Blues by a single point, 16–15, in just one of the four games played. In 1975 they won another, but between that win in 1970 and the end of the 1979 season, New South Wales won 25 games. However, the decade of the 1970s wasn't entirely bereft of good news. It is unlikely that the journalist who wrote the headline 'UNION WHIZKID IN FOR VALLEYS' and the report that followed had the slightest idea of the importance to Rugby League of its content.

The 'Union Whizkid's' involvement with the game of Rugby Union was both fortuitous and temporary. The youngster was a student at Brisbane State High School, where Rugby Union was the only code of football played. Captain of the school Firsts, he was selected in 1977 to tour Great Britain with the Australian schoolboys team, which returned undefeated. But this was no Union whizkid. Walter James Lewis's father, Jimmy Lewis, played First Grade Rugby League as wing and fullback for both Wests and Souths in Brisbane. Wally's mother, June, was a sports champion in her own right, a Queensland netball representative. Wally and his brothers were sportsmen from birth and they were steeped in the Rugby League tradition. As a teenager at State High, Wally lived a double life. At weekends he was the captain of Valleys Under-18 Rugby League side. In 1977 he locked the Valley's scrum and led his team to a premiership. In 1978 he skipped the Under-20s, the Under-23s, the Cs and the Bs. He went straight into Valleys First Grade side and won the award for Brisbane's Colt of the Year. As the whole world knows, for more than a decade Wally Lewis's name would be the most important one in Australian Rugby League.

But that was for the future. In 1979 Queenslanders were no happier about the Rugby League situation than were the southerners although for different reasons. In Brisbane, the Rugby League community was calling loudly for a halt to the pirating of their top footballers by Sydney clubs. It was obvious that, regardless of any form of control that might be attempted, no Queensland footballer of better than average ability with any thought for his financial future could afford to turn down the lucrative offers that came from the south. In 1979 the winds of change began to blow. It was only the slightest of zephyrs at first, but the breeze carried a voice that would not be stilled.

At the start of the 1979 series it was four years since the Maroons had won a match, and they hadn't won a series for nineteen years. A pattern for change had been mooted by former Queensland captain Jack Reardon as far back as 1964, when he suggested that expatriate Queenslanders playing in Sydney be made eligible to play for their state. In the south he was laughed out of court.[1] Jack's suggestion may have been the first that appeared in print, but under various guises the principle of a player's place of origin being the basis for the selection of Queensland and New South Wales Rugby

League teams had been bandied about for years. It wasn't revolutionary. In the United Kingdom, birthplace of all the major sports played in Australia, it is the rule for most of them.

The 24,653 dedicated Queenslanders who assembled at Lang Park to watch the first game of the 1979 interstate Rugby League series trudged wearily homeward after witnessing a game that was won by a New South Wales team that hardly got out of a canter: the Southerners 30, Maroons 5. The Queensland selectors made some changes for the second game and hoped for the best. Lawrie Kavanagh described the result in the *Courier-Mail* of 30 May.

> The Sydney Harbour Bridge would not have spanned the gap between New South Wales and Queensland in the return interstate Rugby League match at Lang Park last night ... New South Wales beat Queensland 31–7 to take the interstate series after winning the first match 30–5 last week ... Queensland supporters showed last night that they are not prepared to roll up to what appears to be a stacked deck ... A major suggestion now is a State of Origin series. That would be an interesting series although only three former Queenslanders, Kerry Boustead, Rod Reddy and Rod Morris, represented New South Wales last night. But there are enough former Queensland players playing top grade in Sydney to fill two NSW teams.

This was the clincher. Only during Rugby League's first decade had the Maroons suffered more at the hands of the Blues than they did in the 1970s. On accepting the presidency in 1971, Senator McAuliffe had proudly announced a three-year plan to beat New South Wales. As he looked back from the end of the decade during which he had occupied the chair, he could count just two victories and two drawn games against twenty-six losses to the New South Welshmen. The natives were restless, and who could blame them. Lawrie Kavanagh's suggestion raised a tidal wave of support. Letters to editors, talk among officials and discussions in pubs were all unanimous — Queensland needed access to its talented sons in the south if it was ever to become competitive again.

Former first grade cricketer and footballer Barry Maranta was a sports consultant who had entered into partnership with Wayne Reid, a Melbourne establishment figure with wide sporting interests. They formed International Sports Management with a view to taking a commercial interest in a wide range of sporting activities, although the company's main concern lay with tennis. Tennis was the only Australian sport that was then considered a full-time professional occupation by its participants, but Maranta took a lively interest in all sports.

Leon Larkin, a Western Australian, was also involved in International Sports Management and he invited Maranta to watch a unique game of Australian Rules to be played in Perth.[2] The Australian Rules situation in Western Australia was analogous to that of Rugby League in Queensland. The local competition struggled while being bled white of talent by wealthy Victorian clubs. In an attempt to instil some competitiveness into the annual interstate games, a match was to be played at the end of the 1978 season with Western Australians who played in Victoria eligible for selection for their home state.

Beyond his involvement during his playing days, and his acting as agent for one or two footballers who had sought his advice, Barry Maranta had no connection, official or commercial, with Rugby League. But he subscribed to the view that was being freely expressed that Rugby League could not survive as a major sport without a robust interstate competition. Maranta had taken part in discussions of the State of Origin principle on numerous occasions and was interested to see its application in another code. With his partner, Wayne Reid, he travelled to Perth and was one of more than 40,000 people who attended Subiaco Oval to watch the Western Australian team defeat the Victorians in the first state of origin football match of any code played in Australia.[3]

Maranta could see no reason why a similar Rugby League initiative would not succeed, and through contacts developed in his playing days he was able to arrange an appointment with Ron McAuliffe. However, although McAuliffe remained interested, he was unconvinced.

Author, journalist and Gregory Terrace old boy, Hugh Lunn wore the same old school tie as Ron McAuliffe, and in November that year chance placed them in adjacent seats on a plane flying to Canberra. Inevitably they discussed Rugby League, and equally inevitably the possibility of a state of origin game arose. McAuliffe asked Lunn: 'Why should we reward the fellows who leave us? Why should we take the jersey away from a loyal Queenslander?'

Lunn reminded the senator of a view often expressed by southerners in their criticisms of those who lived north of the Tweed: 'You can take the Queenslander out of Queensland, Ron, but you can't take Queensland out of the Queenslander.'[4]

Another Queenslander who spoke to McAuliffe and argued for the introduction of a 'state of origin' series was asked, 'But what if we recall our boys from Sydney to play, and we are beaten. Where would we go from there?'[5]

Barry Maranta took the matter further when he sought the assistance of his partner. Wayne Reid was a member of the Confederation of Sport, and so was Kevin Humphreys, president of the New South Wales Rugby League. Reid spoke to Humphreys and proposed that Maranta's concept — that a state of origin game be promoted as a 'one-off' test selection trial — be tried the following year. Kevin Humphreys was cut from different cloth from most Sydney Rugby League club officials. He was an innovator and a publicist who could sense an opportunity and he believed that the time was ripe for a new initiative. Humphreys was sold on the idea of 'state of origin' and when McAuliffe approached him to discuss a trial of the concept, he convinced the New South Wales Rugby League to give it a chance.

The plan was that the 1980 series would consist of two games played under traditional rules, one game in Brisbane and a second in Sydney. A third match, a 'state of origin' match, would be played at Lang Park in Brisbane, but only if the series had already been won 2–nil by one side or the other. Traditional selection procedures, and not 'state of origin', would be used if the game was to decide the series.

Humphreys laid down another condition:

That the expatriate Queenslanders would at all times be under the supervision of a representative of the New South Wales Rugby League whose duty it would be to protect the interests of both the New South Wales Rugby League and the clubs to which they were contracted.

In 1980, and for several years thereafter, this role was filled by Mr

Bob Abbott, a Cronulla official and a close associate of Kevin Humphreys and his later successor, Ken Arthurson.

There were still three Sydney clubs implacably opposed to the plan. St George, Easts and South Sydney all threatened to refuse to release their players for the 'state of origin' game. Humphreys was a step ahead of them. He informed the recalcitrant officials that, if they persisted, he would declare the game to be an official Australian Rugby League trial match, and make the release of players mandatory. The reluctant clubs caved in, but there was no long-term commitment to the principle of 'state of origin'. The 1980 game was designed to be a trial, a one-off promotion believed by most New South Wales supporters to be largely a sop to quiet the whinging Queenslanders. The Sydney media took a similar view, suggesting that it would be a 'three day wonder' whose attraction would quickly disappear once the New South Welshmen had again thrashed the Maroons regardless of their origins. Most took the view that Sydney footballers on both sides would hold back when opposed to club mates on the field. Rugby League 'immortal' Bob Fulton described it as the 'non-event of the century'.[6]

There were no half measures with McAuliffe. Once convinced, his commitment was total and the senator threw himself into promoting State of Origin with immense enthusiasm. Queenslanders Rod Morris, Kerry Boustead and 'Rocket' Rod Reddy ran out in blue guernseys at Lang Park for the first of the interstate games in 1980 and the New South Welshmen handed out their routine annual flogging to the Maroons, 35 points to 3. A week or two later, in Sydney, Queensland did a little better, but they still lost, 7–17. Then on a glorious July night, in a Lang Park packed to the rafters with an over-capacity crowd, the three rebels wore Maroon, Rod Reddy for the first time, and they weren't the only expatriates to return. Balmain's half-back, Greg Oliphant, the Tigers' star front-rower, Rod Morris, Norths' five-eighth, Alan Smith, and Easts' and Australian hooker, Johnny Lang, also donned Maroon.

And there was a seventh Queensland expatriate who played that night. Artie Beetson starred for Redcliffe when the club won the Brisbane Grand Final in 1965. A talent scout spotted him and signed him for Balmain, and in 1966 he represented both New South Wales and Australia. By 1980 his career had run the whole gamut of Rugby League, through three Sydney clubs, seventeen games for New South Wales and fourteen Test matches for Australia. But he had never worn the Maroon guernsey and at age thirty-five it seemed certain that he never would. This was 1980 and Artie was in his sixteenth year of grade football. His race was considered to be just about run when the Queensland Rugby League selectors called on him to lead his state. Wearing the Maroon guernsey for the first time, Artie was the proudest man at Lang Park that night, and he demonstrated clearly what Hugh Lunn had told MacAuliffe on that plane ride to Canberra: 'There's no such thing as an ex-Queenslander.'[7]

In taking the census a quarter of a century later, the inclusion of the question 'Were you present at Lang Park for the first State of Origin game in 1980?' would probably reveal that a quarter of a million loyal Maroon followers would claim to have been present. Over 200,000 of them would not be telling the truth!

If a follow-up question was asked, 'What do you most remember about the game?', the odds are that at least half of them would say, 'When Big Artie started the game off by belting his mate Mick Cronin'

In fact, they'd be 'remembering' something that didn't happen. But what would it matter? It has become Rugby League folklore that Arthur Beetson rallied the disparate elements of this first Queensland State of Origin team by selecting his Parramatta team-mate Mick Cronin for a whack over the ear during the 'softening-up period', those opening minutes of the game during which it was once the habit of referees to take a tolerant view of a reasonable measure of organised brutality. The softening-up period was then considered by some to be as essential to a game of Rugby League as grace before meals is to a Christian household, or an overture to an opera. Strangely for the time, there was no softening-up period in that first State of Origin game. Neither did Artie open the proceedings by belting his club mate.

The quality of Artie's leadership that night is unquestioned and it needed no theatrical gestures on his part to encourage his troops. To a man, the Queenslanders idolised Arthur Beetson; they considered him to be a living legend and they were proud to be playing in the

1ST STATE OF ORIGIN GAME
LANG PARK, 8 JULY 1980

Queensland	New South Wales
Colin Scott	Graham Eadie
Kerry Boustead	Chris Anderson
Mal Meninga	Mick Cronin
Chris Close	Steve Rogers
Brad Backer	Greg Brentnall
Alan Smith	Alan Thompson
Greg Oliphant	Tom Raudonikis
Wally Lewis	Jim Leis
Rod Reddy	Graham Wynn
Rohan Hancock	Bob Cooper
Arthur Beetson [c]	Craig Young
Johnny Lang	Steve Edge
Rod Morris	Gary Hambly

Reserves:

Norm Carr	Steve Martin
Bruce Astill	Robert Stone

Coaches:

John McDonald	Ted Glossop

Referee: Billy Thompson (UK)

same side. They were prepared to follow him through hell and high water. Their natural ability, their commitment to the Maroon guernsey, and an early penalty which saw them leading 2–0 after just two minutes of play gave the Maroons all the lift they needed. Then in the 13th minute of the game, a penalty from a scrum on the 22-metre line saw Mal Meninga kick his second goal and it was Queensland 4, New South Wales 0.

The New South Welshmen had started the game full of confidence, and it was probably for this reason that there had been no significant resort to violence in the early stages. There was a brief encounter about six minutes after the start of play when the two half-backs, Tommy Raudonikis and Greg Oliphant, exchanged a punch or two, but this was a private matter. They had a minor score to settle from a recent encounter in a club game in Sydney.

A sound kicking game and powerful defence enabled the Maroons to bottle the Blues up in their own half for the first quarter-hour of the game, but in the 18th minute the Southerners broke their bonds when Graham Eadie made a strong run from full-back, broke the line and sent Mick Cronin away. Mick was backed up by hooker Stephen Edge who found Greg Brentnall running free and unmarked outside him. The winger scored in the corner. Mick Cronin's kick was astray, so Queensland still led, but only by a single point, 4–3.[8]

At some point early in the game, Greg Oliphant had become upset at the behaviour of Graham Wynn. In the 23rd minute he was part of a gang tackle on the Blues second-rower. While Wynn was secured under the weight of the two forwards who had assisted in the tackle, Ollie seized the moment. He administered a brief but vigorous facial massage to the recumbent New South Welshman. Ollie stood as marker as the 190-centimetre Wynn rose from the ground, played the ball, and then threw a well-timed left hook to the little half's jaw. Like all good half-backs, Greg Oliphant was quite prepared to pursue the matter despite being considerably over-matched in both height and weight, but he didn't need to. A front-rower is honour-bound to defend his half-back. Artie Beetson prized honour above pearls and before the Oliphant v Wynn contest had time to develop, the cavalry arrived. Artie came in swinging and a free-for-all developed. Wally Lewis and other Queenslanders punched New South Welshmen's heads with warm enthusiasm wherever they appeared. Rod Morris and Graham Eadie staged a private boxing match on the side and the picture of Chris Close fighting at least three New South Welshmen at once will live forever in the memory of those who saw it. The officials took a couple of minutes to sort it out but the English referee, Billy Thompson, was quite broad-minded about the affair. He restarted play with a scrum and gave the feed and loose head to the Maroons. Shortly afterwards, Ted Glossop took Graham Wynn out of the game and replaced him with Robert Stone.

The Maroons seemed to gain in stature after the fisticuffs. Two minutes after the game settled down, Rohan Hancock made a break which saw him pulled down only millimetres short of the line. In the 27th minute Mal Meninga got within a metre of scoring, and from a ruck just two minutes later Ollie Oliphant sent the ball to Alan Smith who passed to Meninga. Mal beat his man, and gave the ball to Chris Close who drew both centre and winger before sending it on to an unmarked Kerrie Boustead. Boustead scooted away, crossed in the right corner and then improved his position to score halfway between corner flag and goal post. Mal Meninga made the conversion and it was Maroons 9, Blues 3.

Apart from the dust-up midway through the first half, there had been little rough play. Both half-backs were showing some signs of wear and tear, particularly Ollie Oliphant, but this was due more to their private disputation than to any tactical employment of violence. When the Maroons were penalised for a scrum infringement in the 30th minute, it was the first chance that Michael Cronin had to convert a penalty into points. He made it 9–5, still in Queensland's favour, and that remained the score at half-time.

The Maroons were on the attack four minutes into the second half when they were awarded a penalty right in front of the posts. Mal Meninga kicked his fourth goal from four attempts, his team led 11–5 and the Blues were becoming desperate. They began to play 'catch-up' football. Such desperation breeds mistakes and the New South Welshmen made a lot of them. Breaking early from a scrum, front-rower Craig Young threw out a desperate leg and tripped the Queensland half-back. Billy Thompson awarded a penalty well within Mal Meninga's range and fourteen minutes into the second half Mal made it 13–5 for Queensland. Just two and a half minutes later Greg Brentnall had a rush of blood to the head and attempted to knee Kerry Boustead as he played the ball. From the restart of play that followed the penalty-line kick, Greg Oliphant worked a set move and gave the ball to Chris Close. With a magnificent burst of speed and evasiveness, Close beat in turn Alan Thompson, Tommy Raudonikis, Chris Anderson, Graham Eadie and Stephen Edge to touch down close to the posts. With Mal Meninga's conversion the Maroons were away to a thirteen-point lead, 18–5.

Visits to the Maroons half by the New South Welshmen were rare, but in the 21st minute of the second half Arthur Beetson was penalised for a high tackle on Gary Hambly some thirty-five metres out from the Queensland try line. Shortly afterwards, there occurred the tackle by Arthur Beetson on Mick Cronin which later became famous.

Mick's progress had been stopped but his arms were free to unload the ball when Arthur came into the tackle to lock up the ball. His left arm went around Mick's neck in what was no more than a smothering tackle. Mick went to ground, arose and played the ball.

That was it. There was nothing in the tackle to attract the referee's criticism and the game went on.[9]

A little later, Tommy Raudonikis ran from dummy half and scored a try under the posts. Cronin's simple conversion brought the teams closer together but the Maroons still held an eight-point cushion of safety. The Blues would need to score two tries to win. When Mal Meninga kicked a penalty goal, his seventh two-pointer for the evening from seven attempts, he placed the Maroons on even safer ground: two converted tries clear with the score at 20–10.

From the commentary box, former Queensland, New South Wales and Australian front-rower Mick Vievers still couldn't see a Queensland victory.

'They'll need more than that,' he told his listeners.

But they didn't.

The New South Welshmen threw everything at the Maroons in the final ten minutes. Desperate to score, they tried every trick, and there were a couple of brief rounds of boxing too, as the Queenslanders desperately protected their lead. The frenzied crowd chanted 'Queensland, Queensland, Queensland'. Then as Arthur Beetson threw himself into ferocious defence and the clock ticked down, the cry changed to 'Artie, Artie, Artie ...'

In what was the most significant promotion in the history of the game of Rugby League in Australia, Queensland won the match, and they won the fight, such as it was. They thrashed New South Wales by 20 points to 10 and changed the course of Rugby League history forever. Lang Park went wild and a disease called State of Origin Fever manifested itself for the first time, an affliction which would flare annually in Queensland and long endure as a totally new concept of Rugby League took form.

Final result

Queensland 20 defeated New South Wales 10.

Tries for Queensland: Kerry Boustead, Chris Close. Goals: Mal Meninga (7).

Tries for New South Wales: Greg Brentnell, Tom Raudonikus. Goals: Mick Cronin (2).

Crowd: 33,210.

Man of the Match: Chris Close.

Arthur Beetson moved back to Queensland at the end of the 1980 season to play a farewell season for Redcliffe, the club that first gave him a chance in A Grade. He was selected as captain–coach of the Queensland residents' side which was again defeated twice by New South Wales. Unfortunately, an injury suffered in a club game kept him out of the State of Origin side for its second clash with the Blues but he stayed on as coach.

The southern media maintained that the New South Wales team had taken the Queenslanders too cheaply in the 1980 game. Proof of this seemed to lie in their failure to 'soften them up' right from the start. If this was the team's view, then they made no similar error in the 1981 State of Origin game. The opening exchanges of the match were a reprise of what occurred halfway through the first half of State of Origin, 1980. For the first six minutes chaos reigned. Rod Morris and Les Boyd traded blows. The Blues had chosen a noted thumper in five-eighth Terry Lamb and he engaged Wally Lewis in an interesting bout. Chris Close and Les Boyd staged a powerful exchange but no single Blue was ever enough for Chris and he was quickly involved with numbers as he cheerfully distributed left and right hooks while his Maroon guernsey hung in rags about his waist. Meanwhile Rod Morris and Craig Young took up from where they had left off in Origin I. All of this drew a general warning from referee Kevin Steele which had little effect until he put Steve Bowden and Rod Morris in the sin-bin for ten minutes. The New South Welshmen were then the first to settle down to play football. With Queensland on the attack deep in the New South Wales

STATE OF ORIGIN, 1981
LANG PARK, 28 JULY

Queensland	New South Wales
Colin Scott	Phil Sigsworth
Brad Backer	Terry Fahey
Mal Meninga	Mick Cronin
Chris Close	Steve Rogers
Mitch Brennan	Eric Grothe
Wally Lewis (c)	Terry Lamb
Ross Henrick	Peter Sterling
Chris Phelan	Ray Price (c)
Paul McCabe	Les Boyd
Rohan Hancock	Peter Tunks
Rod Morris	Ron Hilditch
Greg Conescu	Barry Jensen
Paul Khan	Steve Bowden

Reserves:

Norm Carr	Gary Dowling
Mark Murray	Graeme O'Grady

Coaches:

Artie Beetson	Ted Glossop

Referee: Kevin Steele (NZ)

half, Parramatta winger Eric Grothe picked up a loose ball and galloped eighty metres to slide over in the corner in Brad Backer's covering tackle. Mick Cronin's kick from the sideline added the extras and it was 5–0 to the Blues. They then proceeded to score two more converted tries in the next twenty minutes. Down 15–nil after only 27 minutes, the Maroons could see the game slipping away, but they settled to solid defence before a break by the forwards saw Brad Backer get on the end of a Paul McCabe pass and score a tearaway try in the corner. Mal Meninga's kick from the sideline was good and the teams went to oranges with New South Wales leading 15–5.

Coach Artie Beetson read the riot act at half-time, and the Maroons returned in aggressive mood. Captaining his state side for the first time, Wally Lewis showed the world what he could do when he scored a try that has been replayed on television more times than 'I Love Lucy'. He took the ball on his opponents quarter-way line and then, with a dazzling, determined diagonal run, he beat and fended three opponents before diving over the line. Meninga goaled and the score was New South Wales 15, Queensland 10.

Just four minutes after the restart, Colin Scott was caught centi-metres short of the line after a 45-metre run. When Eric Grothe, the tackler, attempted to impede the play-the-ball by lying in the ruck, Chris ('Choppy') Close gave him a backhander which lifted him clear of the ground and shifted him a metre and a half sideways before Choppy[10] grabbed the ball and dived over for a try alongside the posts.

New South Wales lock Ray Price hated to be beaten by anybody, and, like most New South Welshmen who had become accustomed to flogging Queensland teams, he had a particular aversion to losing to the Maroons. With the score 15 all, Queensland attacking, and the game quickly going down the toilet, an indignant Price head-butted Queensland lock Chris Phelan, leaving him unconscious on the ground. He was penalised for this social error and Meninga's ultra-reliable boot made it 17–15 with just five minutes to go.

There was less than two minutes remaining on the clock and with their supporters going wild in the stands, the Maroons were again on the attack, with New South Wales defending desperately, when Mal Meninga toed a ball through and gave chase. He appeared to be about to dive and ground the ball in goal when he was tackled by a Blues' defender. Traditionally, Australian officials are reluctant to award penalty tries, but New Zealand referee Kevin Steele had no such inhibitions. He blew the whistle and pointed to the spot. Since the conversion of a penalty try is taken from in front of the posts, this was a further gift of two points to Meninga. When the siren blew shortly afterwards, Queensland had convincingly defeated New South Wales and Queensland's supporters were loudly demand-ing that the whole basis of the interstate competition be changed.

The State of Origin principle had a Force 6 gale behind it now and the Brisbane *Courier-Mail* asked:

Final result

Queensland 22 defeated New South Wales 15.

Tries for Queensland: Brad Backer, Wally Lewis, Chris Close.
Penalty try: Mal Meninga. Goals: Mal Meninga (5).

Tries for New South Wales: Eric Grothe (2), Mick Cronin. Goals:
Mick Cronin (3).

Crowd: 25,613.

Man of the Match: Chris Close.

Should the Interstate Series be changed to a State of Origin basis? That's the question that many people are asking after Tuesday night's brilliant win by the Queensland team which gives them the perfect record of two out of two in this type of match.

The writer provided the view of the president:

Chairman of the Queensland Rugby League, Ron McAuliffe, believes that State of Origin is the answer and he'll be having talks with the New South Wales league very shortly with that idea in mind ...'[11]

Being in the unusual position for a Queenslander of having a 2–nil win under his belt, the senator was able to initiate the talks from a position of some strength. Of even greater interest to the Australian and New South Wales Rugby Leagues than the result were the television ratings, which went off the top end of the Richter scale and not just in Brisbane and Sydney. State of Origin rated its socks off in the southern state capitals where Australian Rules was king. The Rugby League hierarchy were quick to understand that they had struck it rich and that Queensland Rugby League had at last found its place in the sun. In the last decade of 'traditional' interstate rivalry, the Queenslanders won only two games out of thirty played. The Maroons were now two out of two in the new format, and it was inevitable that State of Origin Rugby League would tilt the axis upon which the Australian Rugby League world rotated. This would so offend the New South Wales sense of football propriety that the game could never be the same again.

CHAPTER 3

1982

A Friendly Referee

NINETEEN EIGHTY-TWO marked the seventy-fifth anniversary of the introduction of Rugby League to Queensland and Senator Ron McAuliffe's eleven years of stewardship had paid a considerable dividend to the Queensland Rugby League. The acquisition of Lang Park had been a masterstroke, and McAuliffe and his committee had worked hard to improve the venue. Little more than a derelict public reserve in the 1950s, the advent of the 1980s saw it transformed. The first structure provided at the time of the takeover had housed a licensed club and in 1982 it was completely encompassed and covered by the Frank Burke stand where supporters could watch their favourite team in comfort from a perch as close as twenty metres from the western touchline.

Concrete terraces had been built to provide for twenty thousand spectators or more and bars and refreshment stalls were adequate to deal with the biggest crowds. On the eastern boundary, a massive two-storey steel and concrete structure honoured the man responsible for most of this change. The Ron McAuliffe stand provided seats for more than five thousand, and unmatched facilities and conveniences within its bulk. Above all, McAuliffe had convinced the Australian Rugby League to adopt the State of Origin principle. It would apply to the 1982 series and to all interstate games from that day forth. Rules that clearly defined the meaning of the term were formulated. A player's state of origin would be deemed to be that state in which he first played Rugby League with a club team at Under-16 level or higher.

But unrecognised, even unsuspected at the time, Queensland's immediate future in this new format had been decreed by a number of quite unrelated events that had taken place back in the 1950s and 1960s.

Always a passionate Queenslander and a spiritually devout man who was punctilious in his attendance to his religious duties, there is no doubt that Ron McAuliffe had always reinforced his hopes and plans for the future of Queensland football with the appropriate prayers. It is also likely that after watching yet another Maroon defeat, on yet another Saturday afternoon, at the hands of the despised Blues, many another Queenslander attended mass or service the next morning and raised a voice to heaven asking for an end to the sporting torment. If this was indeed the case, then it is strong evidence to support the ancient Christian belief in the power of prayer. During the 1950s and 1960s, maternity wards all over Queensland echoed to the lusty cries of infant boys who would grow to manhood and wreak vengeance on the Blues. In Townsville, the Dowlings, Scott and Miles families were blessed, as were the Shearers in Sarina, the Closes in Rockhampton, the Meningas of Nambour and the Hancocks in Warwick. In Ipswich, Mrs Langer produced a future hero whose lack of inches and modest demeanour would belie his status as the most enduring giant of the game. Mrs Walters went two better, contributing no less than three boy babies to the future State of Origin talent pool. In Brisbane the McCabe, Jackson, Currie, Ribot de Brissac, Vautin, Murray and Conescu families celebrated new arrivals of great future potential, and then, on 1 December 1959, Mrs Lewis of the Brisbane suburb of Cannon Hill gave birth to the boy who would be king. These babies and others like them would grow to adulthood and between them they would appear more than two hundred times for Queensland. They would become the solid core of sides that would raise Queensland Rugby League to the kind of eminence that it had enjoyed sixty years earlier, and in various combinations they founded an undying legend.

The first two games played under the State of Origin format were experimental, and few diehard supporters of the Blues took the results seriously. New South Wales honour was not at stake since, in each case, the annual series was already in the Blue bag. The Sydney media was unanimous in assuring its listeners, viewers and readers that 1982 would be different. With the series result on the line, the outcome was a foregone conclusion and Southern punters could take the short odds-on that bookies demanded with confidence. The Blues would win and win handily.

There was controversy almost immediately. Inclusive of the time spent training together for the annual City versus Country game, the Blues who ran on to Lang Park for the first of the State of Origin games had enjoyed a two and a half week preparation under the state coach, Frank Stanton. In contrast, the Queensland team had been very hastily assembled. Sydney clubs refused to release their players from club duties on the weekend before the game, and Queensland coach Artie Beetson had just four days in which to meld a team from a group of players when, in football terms, some of them were total strangers to each other. Because the Sydney recruiters had been busy, there were more expatriates to choose from in 1982, but most of them were virtual unknowns at that point in their careers. However, the New South Wales side was, as usual, stacked with internationals. Then, before the Queensland side took the field, there was trouble in the camp.

Despite the new order which saw expatriates made available to play for their state, McAuliffe never wavered in his determination to retain as many young Queenslanders as he could. The Queensland president had used sponsorship money held in the procurement and retention fund to secure Wally Lewis's future with Queensland as far back as 1979, but there were other young stars, products of that magnificent natal harvest of the 1950s and 1960s who were attracting southern interest.

The Queensland team was in camp at the Gazebo Hotel on Brisbane's Gregory Terrace. Seven of the fifteen players chosen were already lost to Sydney, but there were several youngsters among the other eight who were coming off contract with Brisbane clubs. They were prime for the offer of a Sydney contract. The Sydney vultures were circling but the senator took them by surprise. All of the resident Queenslanders were presented with contracts to sign, contracts which made their selection for Queensland conditional on their agreeing to remain in Queensland for another year. Several of the players had already had lucrative offers from Sydney clubs and others were hoping to receive them, so McAuliffe's documents were as welcome as a taipan at a tea party. Fullback Colin Scott, half Mark Murray and centre Gene Miles refused to sign.

In this, his first year in the job, team manager Richard 'Tosser' Turner was not quite the father figure which he later became to State of Origin players. McAuliffe had entrusted Tosser with the task of obtaining the players' signatures on these documents, a task made no easier by the presence in camp of a Trojan Horse. One of the senior members of the Queensland side, an expatriate bush lawyer from Sydney, was acting as legal adviser to the recalcitrant trio. Late on the evening before the game, Tosser rang the senator to tell him that the three players flatly refused to sign the contracts.

The Senator was adamant:

> Listen to me, Richard. You tell those bloody lads that we are not kidding. Tell them that replacement players have already been selected and if they don't sign the contracts, then they won't be playing for Queensland now or probably ever.[1]

Dick Turner was nothing if he wasn't persuasive. Eventually they signed, although, and again on the advice of their bush lawyer, each of them made a note on his contract that it had been signed 'under duress'. When told of his agent's success and made aware of the signatories' qualification, McAuliffe snorted, 'Under duress? I don't care if they signed them under water so long as they spell their names right.'[2]

The reluctant trio had signed with only hours to spare and more than 27,000 people watched them run out with the Maroons to do battle in the first game of the first State of Origin series.

Having agreed to a three-game series, the New South Wales administrators were still unconvinced that it was of such importance that it ought to be allowed to interfere with their precious club competition. The New South Wales Rugby League stipulated that the first two games of the series would be played at Lang Park. If the result after Game 2 was one game each, then, and only then,

STATE OF ORIGIN I, 1982
LANG PARK, 1 JUNE

Queensland	New South Wales
Colin Scott	Greg Brentnall
John Ribot	Chris Anderson
Mitch Brennan	Mick Cronin
Mal Meninga	Steve Rogers
Kerry Boustead	Ziggy Niszczot
Wally Lewis (c)	Alan Thompson
Mark Murray	Steve Mortimer
Paul Vautin	Ray Price
Paul McCabe	John Muggleton
Bruce Walker	Tony Rampling
Paul Khan	Craig Young
John Dowling	Max Krilich (c)
Rohan Hancock	John Coveney

Reserves:

Gene Miles	Royce Ayliffe
Bob Kellaway	Brad Izzard

Coaches:

Artie Beetson	Frank Stanton

Referee: Kevin Roberts (NSW)

the third game would be played in Sydney. Although the administration might have had its doubts, the players had none. They were wholehearted in their determination to regain the ground lost to the Maroons in this new format. To prove it, they laid on two tries in the first seven minutes of the game, and they were almost carbon copies of each other.

Steve Mortimer put up a bomb at the end of only the second set of six tackles of the game. The Queenslanders failed to take the ball on the full and it bounced around inside their twenty-metre line until it was picked up by the Blues' fullback, Greg Brentnall. Steve Mortimer had chased his own kick. He took a neat pass from his fullback and then passed it to second-rower, John Muggleton. Winger

Ziggy Niszczot backed up inside to take Muggleton's pass and head for the corner to score. The always reliable sharpshooter Mick Cronin converted. The Blues led 5–0.

From the re-start of play, the Blues went on the attack and once again Muggleton and Niszczot were the destroyers. John Muggleton ran off a pass from Ray Price and fed the ball to Ziggy who planted it on almost the same spot that it had occupied a couple of minutes earlier. Mick Cronin reprised his conversion and New South Wales was 10–0 after just seven minutes of play.

The fiery clashes that had enlivened the earlier State of Origin games were absent in this first game of the 1982 series, and the Maroons offered the capacity Lang Park crowd solid defence rather than spectacular attack. Cronin landed a penalty, but Mal Meninga's three successful penalty kicks kept the Queenslanders in touch, and when they trooped off at half-time only six points separated the two sides: New South Wales 12, Queensland 6.

Scrums were both competitive and more frequent in the early 1980s than they became later, and Blues' captain and hooker, Max Krilich, starved the Maroons of possession when he won seven scrums straight to open the second half. Steve Mortimer made it even tougher fourteen minutes after half-time when he scored a brilliant individual try. When Mick Cronin converted to make the score 17–6, New South Wales seemed to be home and hosed. But the Queenslanders weren't done. Five minutes later, with the Maroons in possession on the halfway line, a magnificent burst by Mal Meninga brought the Lang Park crowd to its feet. Johnny Dowling ran from dummy half and served Meninga who was coming through on the charge. Mal drove through tackle after tackle, beating in turn Alan Thompson, legendary defender Ray Price, John Coveny and Steve Mortimer before being caught by Steve Rogers. Mal got a pass away to Kerry Boustead who tore down the touchline. Bowie was cornered inside the Blues ten-metre line but got the ball to his opposite winger, John Ribot, who had backed up. Ribot put his head down and charged at the line to score with two defenders clinging to him. Mal Meninga converted and maintained his perfect record.

With only eleven minutes to go, the Maroons scored again, and once more Mal Meninga was heavily involved when he ran on to a pass by Mitch Brennan. Steve Rogers' attempt at a tackle was brushed off, Steve Mortimer was swatted away, and when the heavy cavalry arrived in the form of cover defence, Mal had Mitch Brennan running free on his outside. Mitch accepted the pass and sped away to score. Mal's conversion took the Queenslanders to within a point of equalising: New South Wales 17, Queensland 16.

The dramatic comeback had the Lang Park crowd almost hysterical as they chanted Meninga's name and the Maroons responded with equal fervour, but it was not their night. The Blues held on, and close to full-time a try by Brad Izzard in the corner sealed their victory.

Final result

New South Wales 20 defeated Queensland 16.

Tries for New South Wales: Ziggy Niszczot (2), Steve Mortimer, Brad Izzard. Goals: Nick Cronin (4).

Tries for Queensland: John Ribot, Mitch Brennan. Goals: Mal Meninga (5).

Crowd: 27,326.

Man of the Match: Mal Meninga.

The Queenslanders were far from disgraced, a fact borne out by the Man-of-the-Match award going to Mal Meninga, but a loss is a loss, and after seeing his team beaten Senator McAuliffe blamed the New South Wales Rugby League and the selfishness of their clubs. The *Courier-Mail* reported him as saying:

> I can see I was too generous in agreeing to the Origin series while not asking for defined rules regarding team preparations. I will ask for wider access to our selected Sydney players next year. They should be available to us in a live-in situation for a week before the match and allowed to return home for their club matches at the weekend.[3]

For Origin II, the New South Wales team remained largely unaltered, although the selection of ex-Union utility Tony Melrose to replace the injured Chris Anderson on the wing was something of a surprise. Queensland made several changes. Mal Meninga was

out, injured, and so was Mitch Brennan, but Kerry Boustead was a
surprise omission. Gene Miles and Graham Quinn came into the
back line and Brad Backer took Bowie's wing spot. Bruce Walker
was dropped and Fatty Vautin moved to accommodate Brisbane
Western Suburbs' Norm Carr who was called in to bolster the side's
cover defence capability. Rod Morris was one of the southern-based
heroes of the first two State of Origin games, but he had been
overlooked for Origin I in 1982, possibly because he was no longer
playing in Sydney. His brother, Des, was coaching Brisbane's Eastern
Suburbs, and when Rod's contract with Manly ran out at the end
of 1981 Des had asked the front-rower to return to his old club,
which was short of forwards. He was picked as a reserve in the

---

ORIGIN II, 1982
LANG PARK, 8 JUNE

Queensland	New South Wales
Colin Scott	Greg Brentnall
John Ribot	Tony Melrose
Graham Quinn	Brad Izzard
Gene Miles	Steve Rogers
Brad Backer	Ziggy Niszczot
Wally Lewis (c)	Alan Thompson
Mark Murray	Steve Mortimer
Norm Carr	Ray Price
Rod Morris	John Muggleton
Paul McCabe	Tony Rampling
Paul Khan	Craig Young
John Dowling	Max Krilich (c)
Rohan Hancock	John Coveney

Reserves:

Paul Vautin	Royce Ayliffe
Greg Holben	Brett Kenny

Coaches:

Artie Beetson	Frank Stanton

Referee: Barry Gomersall (Qld)

announced team, but coach Artie Beetson wanted Rod Morris back in the Queensland pack from the kick-off for this vital game. Already moved from lock to make way for Norm Carr, Paul Vautin was displaced in the second row to accommodate him.

The biggest selection surprise of all was the referee. An unknown North Queenslander called Barry Gomersall got the nod. Unknown then, perhaps, but Gomersall was destined to become famous as 'The Grasshopper'.[4]

Queensland's loss in the first game did nothing to boost the gate for the second. There is always a fickle percentage in any football crowd, and there was a sharp drop in attendance at the return Brisbane game. However, 19,435 faithful Maroon supporters were at Lang Park on 8 June and they were rewarded early when the Maroons totally dominated both possession and territory in the initial exchanges.

Their first points came shortly before the halfway mark of the session when New South Wales front rower, Craig Young, provided an offside penalty in easy kicking distance. Colin Scott kicked the goal and Queensland led 2–0. As the 25-minute mark approached, Mark Murray took the ball at first receiver, dummied to pass wide and then handed it off to Paul Khan who charged down the middle to draw the defence before he passed to Johnny Dowling. Gene Miles came on the burst to take a pass from the hooker and steamrollered the unfortunate Tony Melrose as he drove over the line to score wide out. Scotty missed the conversion and Queensland led 5–0.

Ten minutes before half-time, the Blues' five-eighth, Alan Thompson, ran from first receiver and passed to Steve Rogers. Rogers drew two defenders before passing to the big, powerful Penrith centre, Brad Izzard. Izzard took Mitch Brennan on, fended him off and then beat the cover defence with pace to score in the corner. Tony Melrose's conversion attempt failed and the resultant scoreline, 5–3, remained the tally when the half-time hooter suspended play.

Four minutes after the resumption, John Ribot beat Tony Melrose with a simple sidestep and scored in the corner. The Queenslanders had a five-point lead, but, as play continued, Melrose redeemed himself to a degree by landing two penalty goals to bring the Blues to within a point of the Maroons, who led 8–7. The nineteen thousand Queenslanders in the stands made sufficient noise for a crowd of twice that number as the game settled into a fierce defensive battle that took its toll on both packs of forwards. Replacements were made on both sides, and just ten minutes before full-time Fatty Vautin finally got into the game, replacing Paul Khan. His first touch came when Rod Morris took the ball up and was tackled only metres short of the New South Wales try-line. He tried to unload in the tackle but a Blues' hand knocked the ball out of his grasp. There was a confused scramble by Queensland forwards. Rohan Hancock emerged with the ball and stumbled towards the line before passing it to Fatty who galloped delightedly across the stripe and touched down.

It was a fitting finale to a game that had been fairly scrappy in many respects, and the 11–7 result hardly told the story. Colin Scott missed several penalty attempts, and when Wally Lewis relieved him of the duty the King did no better. In total, two conversions and six penalty kicks sailed wide of the posts. A three tries to one victory really deserved a better scoreline.

Final result

Queensland 11 defeated New South Wales 7.

Tries for Queensland: John Ribot, Gene Miles, Paul Vautin. Goal: Colin Scott.

Try for New South Wales: Brad Izzard. Goals: Tony Melrose (2).

Crowd: 19,435.

Man of the Match: Rod Morris.

For Origin III, there were changes to both sides.

Heads rolled in all directions when the New South Wales selectors swung their hatchets. Craig Young, John Coveny, Tony Rampling and Alan Thompson were out, and Tony Melrose had played both his first and his last game of State of Origin Rugby League. Brad Izzard was sent to the bench to make way for the return of Steve Rogers from injury, props Royce Ayliffe and Don Mckinnon were recruited, Les Boyd came into the second row, Brett Kenny (sometimes known as the Electric Eel) from Parramatta replaced Alan Thompson, and the selectors reached out to the Western Plains to find a winger to oppose John Ribot. Phillip Duke made the Country side that year from the Moree Boomerangs. He had marked the big Queensland winger in the City versus Country game earlier in the season.

Gene Miles and Mitch Brennan were dropped from the Queensland side as originally selected, but injuries to Colin Scott and Graham Quinn saw them both reinstated. Mitch went to fullback, and for the first time the two giant centres, Miles and Meninga, appeared side by side for the Maroons. Origin II Man of the Match,

ORIGIN III, 1982
SYDNEY CRICKET GROUND, 22 JUNE

Queensland	New South Wales
Mitch Brennan	Phil Sigsworth
John Ribot	Terry Fahey
Gene Miles	Mick Cronin
Mal Meninga	Brad Izzard
Kerry Boustead	Phil Duke
Wally Lewis (c)	Brett Kenny
Mark Murray	Steve Mortimer
Norm Carr	Ray Price
Paul McCabe	Les Boyd
Rohan Hancock	Paul Merlo
Paul Kahn	Don McKinnon
John Dowling	Max Krilich (c)
Rod Morris	Royce Ayliffe

Reserves:

Paul Vautin	Alan Thompson
Tony Currie	Craig Young

Coaches:

Artie Beetson	Frank Stanton

Referee: Don Wilson (NZ)

Rod Morris, was named in the starting thirteen and Paul Vautin on the bench.

At one game each and one to go, the future of State of Origin was assured when the venue for the final game was announced. The sole New South Wales versus Queensland game that had become the norm for Sydney each year had long since been banished to Leichhardt Oval, where the pitiful crowds that attended did not look quite so sub-standard. But on the night of 17 July 1982, interstate Rugby League returned to the Sydney Cricket Ground. The twenty thousand plus crowd was less than half capacity, but it was almost five times the numbers attending recent interstate fixtures in Sydney, and the largest to attend a Queensland versus New South Wales game in Sydney for more than a decade.

Wally Lewis showed why he deserved to captain Queensland. His kicking game kept the Blues on the back foot, while his long torpedo passes sent his outside men deep into his rival's half time after time. Nine minutes after play started, just such a pass landed the ball right on 'Muppet' Murray's chest and put him away. With Sigsworth, the Blues fullback, looming, he sent it on to the unmarked second-rower, Rohan Hancock, who put it under the posts. Mal Meninga had no trouble with the conversion and Queensland led 5–0.

Origin II had been largely free of violence, but there was a good deal of niggle in the first half of Origin III. John Dowling never took a backward step, and when Les Boyd decided that the hooker's face needed a massage, Dowling responded. Kiwi referee Don Wilson gave them both five minutes to seek forgiveness in the sin-bin. Just before half time, Brett Kenny justified his selection when he took a pass from Steve Mortimer and sliced through a gap to put Michael Cronin in the clear. Mick ran wide, drew John Ribot and passed to the debutante Phillip Duke who made a bird of it. He scored in the corner, but 'the Crow's' conversion attempt was astray and Queensland led 5–3 at half-time.

Ten minutes after half-time, Queensland were the beneficiaries of a remarkable error by referee Don Wilson. A scrum packed five metres out from the Queensland line and it was the Maroons' loose head and feed. Mark Murray erred in feeding the scrum and somehow managed to put the ball in the New South Wales second row.

To the amazement of all concerned, and to the southerners' horror, Don Wilson blew his whistle and awarded the Maroons a penalty for an incorrect feed.

But this wasn't the end of it. The ruling upset Blues half-back Steve Mortimer no end. He made his displeasure known to the ref who promptly moved the penalty ten metres downfield for dissent. The Queenslanders were both amused and delighted but the Blues didn't see anything to laugh at. Neither were they amused at what followed. Wally Lewis took the penalty and kicked deep into New South Wales territory. Phil Sigsworth fielded the Lewis kick, which had bounced around the in-goal without going into touch. The defensive line was on him as he picked up the ball and tried to run it into the field of play. Paul McCabe caught him in a solid tackle and, as he did, Sigsworth offended against an unwritten rule as old as Rugby League. He passed the ball in his own in-goal. The intended receiver of the pass was earlier try-scorer Phil Duke. No doubt aware of the golden rule, Duke was so surprised at his fullback's impromptu action that he dropped the ball. Before he could recover either the ball or his composure, a Maroon jumper flashed past underneath him and Wally Lewis had scored the winning try. Wally sealed both the match and his grip on the Man of the Match award, while the names of the two unfortunate Blues would be remembered forever. It would be twenty years before another such blunder occurred in a State of Origin game. The Queenslanders led 8–3 and Mal Meninga's conversion made it 10–3.

There was a fair level of spite in the game, exacerbated no doubt by the result of the referee's error. At one point Wally Lewis had his hand trodden on in a tackle by one of the Blues' forwards. Wally had a fairly short fuse. He rose and hurled the football at the offender's head. The referee saw only the King's reaction and penalised him. Mick Cronin kicked a goal to make the score 10–5 in Queensland's favour and that was how it remained for the remaining twenty-five minutes of some of the toughest defensive football ever played on the Sydney Cricket Ground.

Over the years, the origin and timing of Wally's elevation to the nobility has often been the subject of argument and pub bets and probably the point is moot. However, there is certainly a record of

---

Final result

Queensland 10 defeated New South Wales 5.

Tries for Queensland: Rohan Hancock, Wally Lewis. Goals: Mal Meninga (2).

Try for New South Wales: Phillip Duke. Goal: Mick Cronin.

Crowd: 20,242.

Man of the Match: Wally Lewis.

---

the Queensland champion being described as 'King' in this his second year as Queensland captain. Following Queensland's series-winning victory in the decider of the first Origin series, Lawrie Kavanagh's report in the *Courier-Mail* was headlined 'SCG patrons rise to salute King Wally':

> Queensland, brilliantly led by five-eighth Wally Lewis smashed the might of New South Wales Rugby League with a 10–5 win in the deciding State of Origin game at the Sydney Cricket Ground last night.
>
> In a magnificent effort over the closing stages, with Kiwi referee Don Wilson caning them in the penalties and with little scrum possession, Queensland held on in one of the best defensive displays after losing the scrums 7–11 and with penalties going against them 10–17.
>
> The win gives Queensland the first Origin series 2–1 and restores the prestige of the northern league, drained by the constant stream of players to Sydney over the years.
>
> It was a stunned press box and 20,242 long-faced SCG patrons who watched the home team take a back seat. Forget about any excuses you may hear that this is a second-rate New South Wales team after five changes for injuries. Apart from test men Ray Price and Paul Merlo, the Blues were no match for Queensland. And as for the glamour boys of Sydney, Steve Mortimer and Brett Kenny, they were no match for Queensland half-backs Mark Murray and Wally Lewis. On his performance last night, even the NSW crowd would not begrudge Lewis the Australian five-eighth position for the Test series against New Zealand. And any thinking Australian would certainly not begrudge Lewis if he were named Test captain. On last night's showing, Queensland should be looking at seven or eight positions in the test team.[5]

Wally Lewis failed to make it as Test captain against New Zealand.

Max Krilich, the New South Wales captain, got the nod, but Kavanagh was close to the money regarding selections. In fact, Queensland had six in the run-on Test team: Wally Lewis, John Ribot, Kerry Boustead, Paul Vautin, Rohan Hancock and Rod Morris. Mal Meninga was named as one of the two reserves. Wally was named as vice-captain and won the man-of-the-match award in the first of the two Tests, both of which were won by Australia.

Later in the year, when the Kangaroos left for a tour of Great Britain and France, eleven Queenslanders were selected, and once again Wally Lewis was vice-captain. The other members of the touring party were Kerry Boustead, Greg Conescu, Rohan Hancock, Paul McCabe, Mal Meninga, Gene Miles, Rod Morris, Mark Murray, Rod Reddy and John Ribot. This equalled the greatest number of Queenslanders ever to join a Kangaroo tour, a figure set twenty-six years earlier.

With his men gaining a record representation on the Kangaroo tour and a State of Origin series win, plus a Test man-of-the-match award to the Queensland captain, it would have needed a surgical operation to remove the smile from Senator McAuliffe's face. His long years of planning were at last showing the return he had dreamed of. Most of the team that had won State of Origin honours, and virtually all of its major stars, were still eligible to play in an Under-23 competition. They would be back bigger and better, stronger and faster in 1983.

CHAPTER 4

1983

It's Hard to Be Humble

THE WILL to win exists, or ought to exist, in every sportsman. It is a human quality to be admired. But it reached a new level of functional acceptance with State of Origin Rugby League. The depth of feeling that exists between the Rugby League communities of Queensland and New South Wales is of proportions that exceed those of any normal sporting rivalry by a factor close to infinity.

The achievements of the Maroons in those first three years of State of Origin football brought childhood memories flooding back to the man who stood at the head of Queensland Rugby League. Ron McAuliffe was apt to remind people that the Queensland team had emulated the gallant deeds of that first band of Queenslanders who had subdued the Blues in 1925. Of five matches played that year, Queensland had won four. In the 1980s, it had taken three years to play five matches under the State of Origin principle, but the result had been the same, four out of five. Queensland Rugby League followers could hold their heads high once more.

Fans owed a debt of gratitude to Arthur Beetson. Beetson's example and leadership during that first game in 1980 tapped a chord in the character of every other Queensland player. Memories of years of domination by the Blues tempered their efforts in the same way that the Smithy's hammer tempers steel. A new determination drove them on to win that first game. McAuliffe detected a special quality there, and for the second game he had invited the Big Fellow to both captain and coach the Maroons. Unfortunately, a recurrence of an old injury kept Artie off the field, but he would have crawled over broken glass with a broken leg to take up the coach's job.

When Arthur Beetson joined the Redcliffe Club as an eighteen-year-old in the 1965 season, he came into the care of the club coach, Dick Turner. They were a fortunate pairing, since Turner was a gentleman of deep understanding and experience, well versed in the ways of young men like Artie and understanding of their needs. In his wisdom, Ron McAuliffe decided that if Arthur was to continue as coach, then it might be wise to reinforce the management of the team with a local who was well known to him. For the 1982 campaign he invited Dick Turner to take part, an inspired appointment that would outlast the century.

A self-made man of considerable wealth, Dick Turner was once a lightweight A Grade forward. Dick preferred to play in the second row, but on those occasions when the team was short of a front-rower he never hesitated to oblige. In either position Dick earned the respect of everyone, including several international front-rowers who outweighed him by a considerable margin. He brought to the Queensland State of Origin team an understanding nature and a healthy sense of humour, but his special contribution stemmed from his fierce animosity towards anything in a Blue guernsey.

Queensland won the 1982 State of Origin series two games to one, and scored a total of 36 points to the Blues 32 in the three games played. When a two-Test home series was played against New Zealand in July that year, there were seven Queenslanders among the fifteen selected. The Australians won the first Test 11–8 and they completed the double a fortnight later. Wally Lewis was named Man of the Series after having been Man of the Match in the first game. Wally played five-eighth in both games, and his half-back partner was Steve Mortimer of Canterbury club. In both games their combination was the cornerstone of the Australian attack, but in the second match 'Turvey' Mortimer had a blinder. They were both among the first picked for the subsequent Kangaroo tour of Great Britain and France, and that was as it ought to have been.

Despite having seen his team soundly beaten by the Beetson-coached Maroons, the New South Wales coach, Frank Stanton, was appointed to coach the Australian team for the two Tests against New Zealand. Having won both, he had the inside running for the Kangaroo tour. There were those in Queensland who thought that the winning coach for the State of Origin series ought to have had both jobs, but if this proposal ever surfaced in Sydney it was quickly torpedoed and sank without a trace. In Sydney at that time, the State of Origin games were still considered to be something short of a selection trial. Form in these fixtures was a rough guide only for national selection, whether it be for player or coach. The Stanton appointment was bad news for the eleven Queenslanders who made the Kangaroo tour. It was particularly bad news for Wally Lewis, despite his having been named vice-captain.

On such tours it was customary for there to be three officials appointed to select teams for each game. For the Kangaroo tour of 1982/83, these were Frank Farrington, team manager and president of Newtown Club in Sydney, coach Frank Stanton, of Manly Club, and Tom Drysdale, a Brisbane Rugby League official and the team's co-manager. The southerners were in a two-to-one majority, and when the selectors met. Stanton and Farrington paid no heed to any claims that Wally Lewis or his State of Origin half-back partner Muppet Murray may have had for Test selection. Neither did they give much consideration to the successful test pairing of Mortimer and Lewis, which had engineered two victories over New Zealand. Young halves Peter Sterling and Brett Kenny had starred in the Parramatta side which defeated Manly–Warringah 21 points to 8 in the 1982 Sydney Grand Final and they were first choice as halves for the first Test. English Rugby League was in a parlous state and Australia won the Test by 40 points to 4. Failing injury, such a result secured the positions of every member of the side for the remainder of the tour. Anyone on the outer for the first Test stayed on the outer.

Mal Meninga and Kerry Boustead were the only Queenslanders selected for the first Test in England. Both backed up for the second, and after being named as a reserve Wally Lewis came on at half-time as a replacement for injured Eric Grothe. The result was another massacre, 27–6. With the series well and truly won, Meninga, Boustead, Ribot, McCabe and Morris got a run in the final game, while once more Wally came from the bench after half-time to finish a game that resulted in another flogging for the Poms, 32 points to 8.

The incumbency of Mortimer and Lewis in the Australian side after the two-match win against New Zealand ought not to have been threatened on the strength of a club performance by their rivals, regardless of the importance of the club match in question. If the Farrington–Stanton action was seen by Queenslanders as typical of the New South Wales bias that had always disadvantaged the Maroons, then who could blame them. A loyal New South Welshman, Steve Mortimer was just unlucky. He suffered collateral damage through standing too close to a Queenslander.

The Australians completed the tour undefeated and they were spoken of and written about as world champions, but even before they left Europe the right of this New South Wales–dominated side to the title was being questioned in Queensland and there was talk of a special challenge match to decide the issue. Nothing came of this, of course, although something similar was on the fixture card anyway. When the Maroons met the Blues in the first State of Origin game on 7 June 1983, there were plenty of 1982 Kangaroos in both sides, and the Queenslanders had an opportunity to prove their point.

Over time, Barry Gomersall was to gain a reputation for favouring Queensland in State of Origin games. A careful analysis of his performances fails to demonstrate this, but perhaps the opening phases of the first game of 1983 could have jump-started such a belief.

The game wasn't four minutes old before the New South Wales outside backs were caught offside in the play the ball and Queensland was awarded a penalty. Play restarted twenty-five metres out from the New South Wales' goal line, and on the second tackle Greg Conescu worked the run around with Muppet Murray who gave the ball to Fatty Vautin. Fatty ran ten metres before feeding the ball on to his captain and Wally Lewis scored under the posts. Mal Meninga completed the easiest of conversions and the Maroons were away to a 6–0 lead after less than five minutes of football.[2]

In the 12th minute Darryl Brohman took the ball up for Queensland. Les Boyd was the first New South Welshman to reach him but

---

STATE OF ORIGIN I, 1983
LANG PARK, 7 JUNE

Queensland	New South Wales
Colin Scott	Greg Brentnall*
John Ribot*	Eric Grothe*
Mal Meninga*	Brett Kenny*
Gene Miles*	Phil Sigsworth
Steve Stacey	Chris Anderson*
Wally Lewis (c)*	Alan Thompson
Mark Murray*	Peter Sterling*
Wally Fullerton-Smith	Ray Price*
Paul Vautin	Les Boyd*
Bryan Niebling*	Wayne Pearce*
Darryl Brohman	Geoff Gerard
Greg Conescu*	Max Krilich (c)*
Brad Tessman	Geoff Bugden

Reserves:

Brett French	Steve Ella*
Dave Brown	Ray Brown*

Coaches:

Arthur Beetson	Ted Glossop

Referee: Barry Gomersall (Qld)

* Members of the 1982–83 Kangaroos.

---

he made no attempt to tackle Brohman. Instead he simply ran to one side of the man and smashed him in the face with a cocked elbow. Darryl Brohman's jaw was broken so badly that he was out of the game for the rest of the season, but he played on for more than fifteen minutes and left the field only after strong urging by the team doctor. Gomersall was notoriously liberal in his interpretation of the laws governing rough play. He awarded a penalty for the high shot but Les Boyd remained on the field.[3]

Play resumed and the Blues were penalised for offside, Mal Meninga kicked a goal and the Maroons led 8–0. At the 17th minute of the game Les Boyd demonstrated that he had learned nothing from his earlier escape. Following a breakthrough by Wally Lewis that threw the Blues into panic mode, Boyd hit Bryan Niebling with a swinging right arm, for which he was penalised and banished to the sin-bin for ten minutes. The incident occurred only twenty-five metres out from goal, almost in front, and Mal Meninga added another two points to the score: Maroons 10, Blues 0.

The Queenslanders drew another penalty eight minutes later, and Mal Meninga landed a goal from forty-five metres out. When Les Boyd returned from the sin-bin it was to a team that was down 12–0, and it didn't get any better.

With just eleven minutes until half-time, a Queensland attack saw the ball played just two yards out from the try-line. Wally Lewis was dummy half and as the ball came back to him he noticed that Ray Price was standing a fraction too wide. He drove straight at the famed Blues' defender and scored the softest of tries, right alongside the right-hand goal post. Mal Meninga converted, and Queensland led by 18 points to nil. The game continued to be one of constant dropped ball contrasting with solid tackling, but with just four minutes to go until half-time the New South Welshmen cracked the Maroon defence.

From a ruck ten metres out, Peter Sterling worked the blind and passed to Les Boyd who sent the Parramatta flyer Eric Grothe away to score in the corner. Phil Sigsworth kicked the goal and Queensland's lead was reduced to 12 points, the half-time score 18–6.

The second half was a saga of lost opportunities. Time and again Wally Lewis made breaks for Queensland only to see them fail through bad handling. Brett Kenny and Peter Sterling worked tirelessly for the Blues with equally poor results. Alan Thompson was replaced as five-eighth by Steve Ella after half time and this paid a dividend. Twenty-five minutes into the second half, Ella went to dummy half in a ruck close to the Queensland line. From the play the ball, Ella worked a run around with Peter Sterling and beat two defenders to score close to the posts. Sigsworth converted and suddenly the Maroons were within a converted try of disaster. Sustained, solid defence saw the Queenslanders hold out and then, with less than five minutes to play, the Maroons received a penalty twenty-five metres out. Wally Lewis restarted play with a tap-and-run.

Muppet Murray ran from a ruck and beat second-rowers Pearce and Boyd and his opposite number, Peter Sterling, to touch down under the posts without a hand being laid on him. Mal Meninga added the extras and the game was safely in the Maroons' keeping at 24 points to 12.

Final result

Queensland 24 defeated New South Wales 12.

Tries for Queensland: Wally Lewis (2) Mark Murray. Goals: Mal Meninga (6).

Tries for New South Wales: Eric Grothe, Steve Ella. Goals: Phil Sigsworth (2).

Crowd: 29,412.

Man of the Match: Wally Lewis.

Following the first State of Origin game, an Australian side was selected to play the first of a pair of home-and-away tests against New Zealand. The clear-cut flogging delivered by the Maroons saw something of a revolution. For the Auckland test, and for the first time since 1932, an Australian Test team took the field containing a majority of Queenslanders. As part of this, Wally Lewis regained his rightful place as five-eighth. Kerry Boustead, Paul Vautin, Paul McCabe, Mal Meninga, Dave Brown and Wally Fullerton Smith also ran on wearing the Green and Gold, while Muppet Murray was a reserve in a Test that Australia won 16–4.

Queensland took a few casualties because of this commitment, and a tour to New Guinea by a Queensland residents' side. Paul McCabe, Kerry Boustead and John Ribot were unavailable for Origin II, as was Darryl Brohman. Other than the necessary replacements for this quartet, the Queensland team that met the Blues in Sydney on 21 June was little changed, but the New South Wales selectors had wielded the axe with reckless abandon. Brett Kenny replaced Alan Thompson as five-eighth, while Steve Ella took his place in the centre. In total, there were seven new faces added to the team.

STATE OF ORIGIN II, 1983
SYDNEY CRICKET GROUND, 21 JUNE

Queensland	New South Wales
Colin Scott	Marty Gurr
Terry Butler	Neil Hunt
Gene Miles	Mick Cronin
Mal Meninga	Steve Ella
Chris Close	Eric Grothe
Wally Lewis (c)	Brett Kenny
Mark Murray	Peter Sterling
Paul Vautin	Ray Price (c)
Wally Fullerton Smith	Paul Field
Bryan Niebling	Gavin Miller
Dave Brown	Lindsay Johnson
Greg Conescu	Ray Brown
Brad Tessman	Geoff Gerard

Reserves:

Brett French	Steve Mortimer
Ross Henrick	Stan Jurd

Coaches:

Arthur Beetson	Ted Glossop

Referee: John Gocher (NSW)

It appeared that New South Wales supporters had at last got the message that State of Origin football was something special. More than 21,000 fans turned out at the Sydney Cricket Ground on 21 June to cheer for the Blues and sat through a game that was played in atrocious conditions. Drenching rain had fallen on the Cricket Ground for two days prior to the match, turning the poorly drained arena into a swamp. A 'super sopper' was borrowed from the ground staff at Randwick Racecourse. It worked all day in an attempt to stem the tide, but no implement devised by man was going to make a difference. Nor could anything be done with the huge expanse of cricket pitch in the middle of the ground. The heavy Bulli black soil of which the pitch area was formed had attained a sticky glue-like consistency to a depth of more than fifteen centimetres, and within ten minutes of kick-off all of the forwards and most of the backs carried a generous coating of black muck from head to foot.

Just thirteen minutes after the start, Wally Lewis ran from a ruck and passed the ball to Muppet Murray. Muppet positioned Colin Scott for a pass and the fullback found Mal Meninga running free outside him. Mal side-stepped Brett Kenny, then outpaced Steve Ella and Eric Grothe before he scored in the corner. His mighty touchline conversion made it 6–0 after a quarter of an hour of play. An early try in such conditions as prevailed is often a match winner, a sideline conversion something of a miracle. It was never going to be a high-scoring game, but the New South Welshmen squared the contest ten minutes later.

Following a penalty against the Queensland forwards for holding down in a tackle, Brett Kenny passed the ball to Peter Sterling from dummy half and ran around him before sending it out to Mick Cronin who positioned his winger, Neil Hunt. Hunt had a clear run to the corner and managed to improve his position to provide Mick Cronin with an easy conversion. The players went in at half-time with the score tied at 6 all.

An earlier game between the Queensland and New South Wales under-18s had churned the cricket pitch area into a sullen slush, and the first half of the main game had further liquified the mixture. Handling became a nightmare for both sides. Cronulla forward Gavin Miller was having a great game for the Blues. Halfway through the second half he made a break and passed the ball to Ray Price. Price got the ball to Marty Gurr and the fullback kicked deep. Mick Cronin chased hard, got a boot to the ball, and his lucky mis-kick advanced it almost to the try-line where Steve Ella emerged from a confused scramble to score a try. Mick Cronin's kick was wide of the posts but New South Wales led 10–6.

The Maroons tried hard. Twice they were over the line and the tries were disallowed. On one occasion a Queenslander accidentally ran in front of Wally Lewis for a shepherd, which cost the Maroons a certain 6 points. In the end, the New South Welshmen held on to win.

Final result

New South Wales 10 defeated Queensland 6.

Tries for New South Wales: Neil Hunt, Steve Ella. Goal: Mick Cronin.

Try for Queensland: Mal Meninga. Goal: Mal Meninga.

Crowd: 21,620.

Man of the Match: Peter Sterling.

On 28 June the two teams came back to Lang Park for the decider, and more than 24,000 rabidly vocal Queenslanders turned up to barrack for the Maroons. There was considerable change to the New South Wales side once again, but minimal alterations to the home team.

Queensland opened the scoring early when English referee Robin Whitfield penalised the Blues for a high tackle in the third minute of the game. Following a kick for touch by Wally Lewis, the restart of play took place right on the Blues' 22-metre line. On the third subsequent tackle, Mark Murray worked the run around with Greg Conescu. He drew three tacklers to him before he sent the hooker away to score the first try of the game just two metres from the left-hand goal post. Mal Meninga converted and the Queenslanders led 6–0.

With the game twelve minutes old, the Maroons received a penalty right in front for a Blues failure to play the ball correctly. Meninga made short work of the kick: Queensland 8, New South Wales 0.

Wally Lewis's splendid kicking game and general direction of play kept the Maroons on the attack. The New South Welshmen thought that they had found a path to success down the Queensland left flank. Both Steve Ella and Marty Gurr made breaks down the touchline, but on those occasions when they failed to drop a pass or kick out on the full, committed defence by the Queensland cover snuffed out the incursion. In the 23rd minute of the game a ball knocked on by Steve Mortimer forty-five metres out from his own line was snaffled by Mal Meninga who quickly passed it to Gene Miles. Geno beat two men before sending Steve Stacey away to

STATE OF ORIGIN III, 1983
LANG PARK, 28 JUNE

Queensland	New South Wales
Colin Scott	Marty Gurr
Mitch Brennan	Chris Anderson
Gene Miles	Mick Cronin
Mal Meninga	Steve Ella
Steve Stacey	Neil Hunt
Wally Lewis (c)	Brett Kenny
Mark Murray	Steve Mortimer
Paul Vautin	Gavin Miller
Wally Fullerton Smith	Paul Field
Bryan Niebling	Stan Jurd
Dave Brown	Geoff Bugden
Greg Conescu	Max Krilich (c)
Brad Tessman	Lindsay Johnson

Reserves:

Bruce Astill	Kevin Hastings
Gavin Jones	Ray Brown

Coaches:

Arthur Beetson	Ted Glossop

Referee: Robin Whitfield (UK)

score in the corner. Mal Meninga's kick from the sideline sailed right through the centre of the uprights and the Maroons led 14–0.

The Queenslanders scored again three minutes after the restart when Brad Tessman ran wide from a ruck, drew the defence and passed to Mitch Brennan. The former Souths (Brisbane) flier sprinted away to score in a handy position for Mal Meninga to convert his try: Queensland 20, New South Wales nil.

With Queensland on the attack inside the Blues quarter, and the half-time hooter about to sound, Wally Lewis added insult to the injury that his braves were inflicting and kicked a field goal. The game was virtually over at half-time when Queensland led 21 points to nil.

Converted tries by Mitch Brennan and Dave Brown blew the lead out to 33–0 before the New South Welshmen scored, but the Maroons were far enough in front to coast home. Under the whip from their coach, Ted Glossop, the New South Welshmen scored four tries. Chris Anderson got a hat-trick, but if they imagined a 33–22 score line might help, the Maroons brought them down to earth. First, Bryan Niebling scored an unconverted try, and then, just before full-time, the King floated a huge pass out to Gene Miles which fell short and bounced but Geno picked it up and scored the final try in a canter. The Maroons freewheeled to a comfortable 43–22 victory.

Final result

Queensland 43 defeated New South Wales 22.

Tries for Queensland: Mitch Brennan (2), Gene Miles, Steve Stacey, Dave Brown, Greg Conescu, Bryan Niebling. goals: Mal Meninga (6), Colin Scott. Field goal: Wally Lewis.

Tries for New South Wales: Chris Anderson (3), Steve Mortimer. Goals: Mick Cronin (3).

Crowd: 26,084.

Man of the Match: Wally Lewis.

A Queensland journalist had this to say:

'... the NSW team last night must have been one of their best. But at no stage did it match the mighty Maroons.'[5]

Barry Dick, another Queenslander, described Wally Lewis's contribution to the victory:

Lewis's performance in the crucial opening 20 minutes of last Tuesday night's State of Origin decider at Lang Park defied description. There might have been 25 other players on the field but for that first 20 minutes, only Lewis was on centre stage ... Those who were there should feel privileged to have seen a sporting marvel at work.[6]

And there was also solid praise for the administrative genius who had nurtured Wally Lewis's career, the man who had been responsible for the introduction of State of Origin Rugby League in the first instance:

> Great credit must be given to [Ron] MacAuliffe who, against popular feeling, retained players like Mal Meninga and Lewis for Queensland against huge Sydney offers. McAuliffe has flown in the face of unpopularity because of his stubborn stands against players transferring to Sydney, but last night every Queenslander was proud of the results ...[7]

There was a pop song high on the hit parade at the time which started 'Lord, but it's hard to be humble / When you're perfect in every way'. The songwriter might well have been inspired by a famous McAuliffe quote, 'It's tough to be modest when you are a Queenslander.'[8]

There was one brief and final chapter for Queensland's most successful year since the 1920s. The Queensland Rugby League laid on the end-of-season trip to end all end-of-season trips. A Queensland residents' party was selected for a short tour of England where they played three fixtures against leading clubs. Their opening game against Hull–Kingston Rovers resulted in a narrow loss, 6–8, but the Maroons then went on to defeat Wigan, 40–2 and Leeds 58–2. They conceded only one try in all three games.

The tour party consisted of players Joe Kilroy, Wally Lewis (c), Shane McNally, Mark Murray, Larry Brigginshaw, Shane Benardin, Brad Tessman, Barry French, Cavill Heugh, Wayne Lindenberg, Mitch Brennan, Colin Scott, Bryan Niebling, Greg Dowling, Paul Khan, Gene Miles, Gavin Jones, Trevor Patterson, Steve Stacey, Wally Fullerton Smith and Chris Phelan, coach Arthur Beetson, managers Dick Turner and Kevin Brasch, liaison officer Ted Verrenkamp and trainer Darryl Gateley.

CHAPTER 5

1984

Big Boots to Fill

RON McAULIFFE had every right to feel content. As the 1984 season opened in Australia, there was no doubt as to who was King of the Castle. Eight State of Origin matches had been played in four years and Queensland had won six of them. The Maroons had won both of the two series played and in doing so had scored 136 points to the Blues 70.

The Australian Rugby League's midweek knockout competition was sponsored by National Panasonic in 1984, and in the final a Brisbane side that contained eight of the victorious 1983 State of Origin team defeated Eastern Suburbs 12–11 after eliminating South Sydney 25–18 and Parramatta 14–12. Ron McAuliffe expressed his pleasure: 'The Sydney bandits were silenced when Brisbane accounted for Parramatta at Leichhardt Oval and then followed up with a remarkable win over Eastern Suburbs to win the final for the first time.'[1]

And there was more than just a trophy involved. National Panasonic provided $80,000 in prize money and another $20,000 went to Wally Lewis who was named Player of the Series. He was King Wally indeed and his reputation was further enhanced when he was chosen to captain an Oceania team that played in Paris to celebrate the 50th anniversary of the establishment of Rugby League in France.

There were clear signals from Sydney that the New South Wales Rugby League attitude to the State of Origin series had undergone a vast change because of Queensland's success. The New South Welshmen announced that the Blues 1984 squad would go into camp for intensive training prior to the first game, and there was more. The players selected for State of Origin would be excused from their club duties on the weekend prior to the interstate games.

When the Blues came to Lang Park that season, there was no suggestion anywhere that the New South Wales Rugby League didn't take the game seriously. They were in deadly earnest and they were desperate to win.

The New South Wales team looked strong, and it was under the determined captaincy of Ray Price, who was renowned as a fierce competitor. The Blues were favourites when they ran out into 'The

STATE OF ORIGIN I, 1984
LANG PARK, 29 MAY

Queensland	New South Wales
Colin Scott	Gary Jack
Kerry Boustead	Eric Grothe
Gene Miles	Brett Kenny
Mal Meninga	Steve Ella
Chris Close	Ross Conlon
Wally Lewis (c)	Alan Thompson
Mark Murray	Peter Sterling
Paul Vautin	Ray Price (c)
Wally Fullerton Smith	Wayne Pearce
Bryan Niebling	Noel Cleal
Dave Brown	Craig Young
Greg Conescu	Rex Wright
Greg Dowling	Steve Roach

Reserves:

Brett French	Brian Hetherington
Bob Lindner	Pat Jarvis

Coaches:

Arthur Beetson	Frank Stanton

Referee: Kevin Roberts (NSW)

Cauldron' and the Queenslanders set them off to an auspicious start. The Maroons knocked the ball on inside the first minute, and before the next sixty seconds had expired Queensland and Manly front-rower Dave Brown did the New South Welshmen another favour when he steadied their captain with a short right hook in a tackle, causing the referee to award them the first penalty of the game.

Having observed Mal Meninga's remarkable success with the boot in Origin III in 1983, the Blues selectors chose Ross Conlon in the run-on side for Origin I, 1984. Formerly with Wests, Conlon was a winger with Canterbury and probably no better at his job than any of a dozen or so flankers playing in the Sydney competition. But he was the best and most reliable long-range goal-kicker in the game by at least the length of one of his better kicks. He opened the scoring with a goal from the sideline. The Blues led 2–0, and less than ten minutes later another penalty saw Conlon land one from almost halfway to give New South Wales a 4–0 lead.

From this third restart of play the Maroons penned the Blues in their own half, and when they kicked short on the last tackle Queensland went on the attack. Gene Miles fielded a long pass from Wally Lewis and broke through a Ray Price tackle into the clear. Ten metres from the try-line he gave the ball to Paul Vautin who passed to Greg Conescu. Conescu sent it on to Dave Brown who found that Miles had backed up on the outside. Geno found Paul Vautin on his inside, gave him the ball and Fatty completed the contract with a try near the posts. It was fast, clever football, but the Lang Park crowd was shocked when Mal Meninga missed the easiest of conversions.

The Maroons had squared the score at 4 all, but just two minutes later New South Wales was awarded a penalty for offside. Wally Lewis considered the referee's decision unjust and told him so. Kevin Roberts responded by marching the Maroons back a further ten metres, which was just enough to place the penalty spot comfortably within Ross Conlon's considerable kicking range. He accepted the gift and the score became New South Wales 6, Queensland 4.

With twenty minutes of the first half gone, the Queenslanders were on the attack. From a scrum penalty ten metres from the Blues line, Wally Lewis put up a bomb which came down close to the goal posts. The Blues' fullback, Gary Jack, was jostled as he attempted to take the ball and it went to ground in a welter of arms and legs. Kerry Boustead picked up the ball and scored under the posts. Mal Meninga kicked a sitter, and the Maroons led 10–6.

Shortly after the restart of play, a scrum penalty to New South Wales set up an attack. 'Blocker' Roach was halted only centimetres short of the Maroon try-line, but, after Steve Ella knocked on, a penalty for a loose arm in the scrum set Queensland on the attack from 28 metres out from their own line.

Kerry Boustead made the first break and was tackled just inside the Blues half. Then Chris Close took the ball to within two metres of the try-line. Wally Lewis was in close attendance and from dummy half he 'went the blind' with less than a metre of room in which to move and scored in the corner. It was a brilliant piece of work and took the score to 14–6 in Queensland's favour. Mal Meninga's conversion attempt from the sideline failed to add to the score, and in hindsight it is difficult to understand why Artie Beetson and Wally Lewis persisted with Mal. The star kicker was under a cloud with a groin injury suffered in the Oceania game in France, and it was obvious that this had affected his goal-kicking.

Strong defence led by Paul Vautin, Wally Fullerton Smith and Bryan Niebling kept the Blues in their own territory for most of the remainder of the first half, but the Maroons failed to cross the New South Wales line. With only seconds remaining until half-time, Wally Lewis dropped the ball on his toe thirty-two metres out and calmly potted a field goal, then led his side off the field with the score Queensland 15, New South Wales 6.

Jack Gibson, doyen of Rugby League coaches, was part of the commentary team with Channel 9. At half-time he suggested that if the New South Welshmen were to make a comeback they would have to 'do it now'. The restart of play after half-time gave no indication that they had heard his advice, but defence was solid on both sides and twice in the first ten minutes Wally Lewis failed to rise after heavy tackles. On each occasion the application of the 'magic sponge' seemed to work wonders, but the New South Welshmen were to be the first to draw blood in the second stanza.

Following a penalty, the Blues went on the attack from a tap restart just fifteen metres from the Maroon line. After several attempts at the line from short range, they ran the ball on the sixth tackle. In a movement that is best described as scrappy but effective, the ball went from dummy half Rex Wright to Brett Kenny who straightened the attack before passing to Wright on the run around. The Blues hooker gave the ball to 'Blocker' Roach who put 'Crusher' Cleal through a gap to score untouched under the posts. Ross Conlon converted and New South Wales started to look dangerous at 12–15.

Eighteen minutes before full-time a simple open-side movement saw the Queenslanders score again. From a ruck forty metres out Greg Conescu fed the ball to his half-back, Mark Murray. Murray passed to Wally Lewis who threw one of his trademark long passes to Mal Meninga, cutting out inside centre Gene Miles. Ross Conlon left his wing to help his centre stop Mal, always a two–man task. Mal drew them both and passed the ball to Kerry Boustead. Bowie gave his well-known imitation of a startled gazelle as he headed for the corner to score a try.

Mal Meninga again failed to convert, but Queensland was away to a seven-point lead, 19–12.

The Blues were a beaten side. Frank Stanton had been appointed Australian coach for a Test against a visiting English team. Jack Gibson foreshadowed the composition of the team he would get when he told the television audience, 'I hope they play as well for Stanton as they did for Beetson.'

Five minutes before the hooter heralded a Queensland victory, the Maroons were again across the line. In the simplest of moves from the base of a ten-metre scrum, Colin Scott chimed in from fullback to take the pass from half-back Muppet Murray. Scotty sent it on to Gene Miles, who strolled past Brett Kenny to score under the posts. Mal Meninga converted the try to make the score 25–12. Then, with the seconds ticking down to full-time, the Maroons five metres from the Blues' line, and the ref's count on tackle five, Wally Lewis passed the ball to Bob Lindner who put the neatest of chip kicks into the in-goal for Kerry Boustead to retrieve and complete the second hat-trick of tries to be scored in State of Origin Rugby League. It remained unconverted and the Maroons were home 29

Final result

Queensland 29 defeated New South Wales 12.

Tries for Queensland: Kerry Boustead (3), Paul Vauten, Wally Lewis, Gene Miles. Goals: Mal Meninga (2). Field goal: Wally Lewis.

Try for New South Wales: Noel Cleal. Goals: Ross Conlon (4).

Crowd: 33,662.

Man of the Match: Wally Lewis.

---

points to 12, or, to describe it in a context not entirely apparent in the raw figures, a six tries to one victory.

The Brisbane *Courier-Mail*'s Lawrie Kavanagh reported Queensland Rugby League as having come of age, and added, 'Lewis's leadership, tactical kicking, direction of attack and power in defence make him a cut above all others ...'[2]

The Great Britain team was in Australia, and the first Test was played at the Sydney Cricket Ground just a few days after Queensland's demolition of New South Wales. Maroons filled eight places in the run-on Australian side, and with the appointment of Wally Lewis they also provided the captain. Chris Close was a reserve. That six resident Queenslanders could make the Australian team was a tribute to the Maroons' record in State of Origin, but it was an even greater tribute to the efforts made by Ron McAuliffe to retain young talent within the state. These were great footballers and they would have made the Australian team regardless of where they played their club football, but by retaining them in Queensland McAuliffe had given strength to the local competition, strength which would otherwise have been dissipated among the 'Sydney bandits'.

Rugby League in Great Britain hadn't shown a great deal of improvement since the 1982 tour and Australia had a comparatively easy victory, 25–8.

If there was one thing consistent about New South Wales' selectors it was their axemanship. For Origin II, a third of their Origin I squad got the chop. The selectors got some stick from the Sydney media over the five-eighth position for Origin I, Ella or Thompson.

They avoided further argument by sacking both of them. To pair Brett Kenny with his Parramatta team-mate Peter Sterling may have seemed like a good option. However, they sacked Sterlo and left Kenny in the centres paired with newcomer Andrew Farrar. They then reinstated Steve Mortimer as half and picked his Canterbury team-mate Terry Lamb as five-eighth. Craig Young and Rex Wright also found their careers as Origin forwards cut short and Royce Simmons made his Origin debut as hooker.

In the Queensland side there was a little musical chairs. Mal Meninga took Chris Close's place on the wing and Chris replaced Mal as centre. It is significant that, in this second game of 1984, five of the Queensland side had played in the original State of Origin

---

STATE OF ORIGIN II, 1984
SYDNEY CRICKET GROUND, 19 JUNE

Queensland	New South Wales
Colin Scott	Gary Jack
Kerry Boustead	Eric Grothe
Gene Miles	Brett Kenny
Chris Close	Andrew Farrar
Mal Meninga	Ross Conlon
Wally Lewis (c)	Terry Lamb
Mark Murray	Steve Mortimer
Paul Vautin	Ray Price (c)
Wally Fullerton Smith	Wayne Pearce
Bryan Niebling	Noel Cleal
Dave Brown	Peter Tunks
Greg Conescu	Royce Simmonds
Greg Dowling	Steve Roach

Reserves:

Tony Currie	Steve Ella
Bob Lindner	Pat Jarvis

Coaches:

Arthur Beetson	Frank Stanton

Referee: Barry Gomersall (Qld)

game in 1980. With Alan Thompson's departure, the last of the 1980 New South Wales side had ridden off into the sunset.

On 19 June 1984 Sydney received a deluge that continued into the night. At kick-off time the ground was a quagmire, the water was beginning to pond on the uneven surface and the rain continued to tumble down in buckets. Yet more than 29,000 spectators turned out in raincoats and carrying umbrellas to support the Blues.

Running on the Sydney Cricket Ground that night was like trying to sprint wearing hobbles. Any attempt to swerve or side-step met with disaster, while the coating of mud that quickly formed on the ball rendered it as easy to handle as a wet cake of soap.

But the Maroons were prepared to do or die that night and they gave notice that this was the case when one of the New South Welshmen decided to go the biff on the second tackle of the game. It initiated a chain reaction. Within ten seconds almost every player on the field was involved, and the Queenslanders gave far more than they got. Barry Gomersall, the Queensland referee, observed the mayhem with complete detachment, wearing an indulgent smile. He made no attempt to quiet the fracas, and asked about his attitude later he pointed out that he was paid to referee football matches. There was nothing in his job description about all-in brawls.

The pugilists ran out of puff soon enough. Gomersall awarded a penalty to Queensland for the original punch thrown by New South Wales front-rower 'Blocker' Roach and the game continued with no further outbreaks of fisticuffs. Blues supporters in the stands roared their disapproval of the penalty, and continued to voice their objections as Gomersall awarded four more penalties to the Queenslanders in the next four minutes.

The game was more than ten minutes old before the Blues received a free kick, and it would have been a sitter for Ross Conlon on a dry day — just twenty-five metres out and almost in front of the goal posts. He registered a clean miss. With the Sydney Cricket Ground's sacred turf fast disappearing beneath a rising water table, mud was king and goal-kicking wasn't going to win this game. Nor would tries come easily. Almost every player who received the ball saw it slide out of his grasp at the first solid tackle, and after forty minutes of slipping, sliding, knocking on and chasing the slippery ball the two teams went to the sheds at half-time with the score nil all.

As the teams ran out for the second half, the deluge continued. The ground was awash and two minutes after the restart of play the Maroons forced a line drop-out by the Blues. Noel Cleal took the kick, but when he dropped the ball it stuck in the mud, his foot made passing contact with the top and it skidded away through the mire like a topped drive at golf. It failed to travel the required ten metres and the Maroons were awarded a penalty right in front. Mal Meninga kicked the goal and Queensland led 2–0, a score that might easily have been a winning margin in the conditions that prevailed.

Luck's a fortune. In the sixteenth minute of the second half, with the Maroons on the attack within ten metres of the Blues try-line, Wally Lewis put up a bomb on the sixth tackle. It was intended to come down just short of the try-line under the posts, but such was Lewis's pinpoint accuracy that the descending ball struck the crossbar and bounced back into play. Debutante Maroon front-rower, Greg Dowling, was moving forward to chase the kick when he found the ball coming straight toward him. He flung himself forward and caught it at full stretch on the full, on his fingertips, just centimetres short of the ground in a diving save. His momentum carried him forward and he cast a bow wave like an ocean liner's as he surfed through three or four metres of slush to score under the posts. Mal Meninga sent another one over from close range and the Maroons led 8–nil. With the depth of the Sydney Cricket Ground mud increasing by the minute, this was definitely a winning lead and the Maroons dug deep to defend it. It was the forwards' night, and in a pack that was magnificent Greg Dowling stood out. Playing his first State of Origin game, he was described by Jack Gibson as the find of the year, but he wasn't far ahead of his comrades-in-arms. Paul Vautin, Bryan Niebling, Wally Fullerton Smith, Dave Brown and Greg Conescu all had blinders, and in the backs, Gene Miles, Chris Close and Mal Meninga shouldered a forward's share of the load whenever asked, as the Queenslanders fought like tigers to keep the Blues at bay.

Halfway through the second half the Maroons were penalised ten metres out from their own line, in front of the posts, when Wally

Lewis stole the ball in a ruck. Ross Conlon kicked a goal to bring the score down to 8–2, but that was as close as it got.

With four minutes of play remaining, and the Queenslanders on the attack close to the New South Wales line, Gene Miles ran from dummy half. He was set upon by Noel Cleal, a fresh replacement forward who was helped by Pat Jarvis and Blues fullback Gary Jack, but Miles carried all three over the line as he scored under the posts. Mal Meninga kicked the conversion and it was 14–2. It was still 14–2 a few minutes later when Barry Gomersall called a halt to proceedings. The better prepared, better coached Queensland team won the match, and the 1984 State of Origin series.

Final result

Queensland 14 defeated New South Wales 2.

Tries for Queensland: Greg Dowling, Gene Miles. Goals: Mal Meninga (3).

Goal for New South Wales: Ross Conlon.

Crowd: 29,088.

Man of the Match: Wally Lewis.

When Wally Lewis was handed the award for Man of the Match, he accepted it with great reluctance. He praised his forwards for their role in the win, and singled out Greg Dowling as his personal man of the match.

The Maroons' win saw eleven Queenslanders chosen for the Australian side for the second Test, ten of them in the starting thirteen. The Australians secured the Test series with a hard-fought but inevitable win by 25 points to 8 and then went on to remain undefeated by Great Britain when they won the third test 20–7. The latter Test was only a few days before the final State of Origin game and most of the Queenslanders who played in it had played a lot of football.

The Maroons went into the third game without their half, Mark Murray, without Chris Close or Gene Miles, their champion centres, and without stalwart forwards Paul Vautin and Bryan Niebling, all injured. John Ribot came back into the side, along with Brett French, Ross Henrick and Bob Lindner who had been on the reserve bench for the first two games that year.

The New South Wales side was also greatly changed. Ray Price's Rugby League career came up a game short of his intended lifetime total when he was not selected for what he had planned to be his last Origin game before retirement. Peter Wynn came into the second row. Eric Grothe, Andrew Farrar and Terry Lamb were all unavailable through injury. Brett Kenny moved to five-eighth and Chris Mortimer and Brian Johnston were the new centres. Steve Ella was picked on the bench but contracted food poisoning. He was replaced by Mick Potter from St George. Junior Pearce had been chosen to

---

STATE OF ORIGIN III, 1984
LANG PARK, 17 JULY

Queensland	New South Wales
Colin Scott	Gary Jack
Kerry Boustead	Steve Morris
Brett French	Chris Mortimer
Mal Meninga	Brian Johnston
John Ribot	Ross Conlon
Wally Lewis (c)	Brett Kenny
Ross Henrick	Steve Mortimer (c)
Bob Lindner	Peter Wynn
Wally Fullerton Smith	Noel Cleal
Chris Phelan	Chris Walsh
Dave Brown	Pat Jarvis
Greg Conescu	Royce Simmonds
Greg Dowling	Steve Roach

Reserves:

Tony Currie	Mick Potter
Bob Kellaway	Peter Tunks

Coaches:

Arthur Beetson	Frank Stanton

Referee: Kevin Roberts (NSW)

replace Ray Price as captain but he hurt his knee in a club game. Chris Walsh was promoted to second row and Peter Wynn was the new lock. Steve Mortimer's appointment as replacement captain was a move that had significant consequences.

Referee Roberts was determined to put his stamp on the game early, and when he penalised Queensland in the third minute of the game following some sloppy play, Ross Conlon kicked a goal from right in front to give New South Wales a 2–0 lead. Less than five minutes later Roberts did it again when Wally Lewis was deemed to have stolen the ball. This time the kick was from just outside the 22-metre line, but it was right in front and equally simple for Conlon, who made it 4–0.

With the game a quarter of an hour old, John Ribot was fed the ball by Mal Meninga and broke away in a move that took play more than sixty metres downfield. Mal Meninga ran from dummy half. He was pulled down in a desperate tackle by Steve Mortimer, but when Queensland was awarded a scrum penalty, he tapped the ball and ran, then passed it to Ross Henrick who put it down under the posts. The Maroons' cheers were quickly silenced when Roberts called the final pass forward, but the Queenslanders would not be denied.

They were awarded another penalty shortly afterwards when Ross Conlon held Kerry Boustead back in a chase for the ball. Wally Lewis took the tap restart and passed to Mal Meninga who sent Boustead away. Boustead passed to Bob Lindner who drove through two tacklers to score in the corner. Mal Meninga's prodigious kick from the right sideline struck the left post but bounced forward over the crossbar. Queensland hit the lead, 6–4, but within ten minutes the Maroons suffered a devastating blow. Greg Conescu left the field injured after falling awkwardly in a tackle. Greg Dowling took over the hooking duties, but this was 1984. There were lots of scrums, half-backs weren't allowed to put the ball in the second row, and at least 80 per cent of ball possession depended on the skill of the man in the centre of the front row. Big Greg was a willing amateur. His opposing hooker, Royce Simmons, was a practising professional. With the Blues playing it tight, and their brilliant half, Steve Mortimer, kicking into touch at every opportunity, the Maroons were starved of possession and forced to defend relentlessly. They couldn't keep the Blues out forever, and two minutes before half-time Steve Mortimer worked a simple blind-side move with Brett Kenny and centre Brian Johnston was in for a try in the corner. Ross Conlon's attempt to convert went astray but as the troops left the field at half-time New South Wales led 8–6.

Five minutes into the second half New South Wales captain, Steve Mortimer, was away downfield in a burst that took play to the Queensland quarter-way line. The dummy half lost the ball in the first tackle but the Blues regained possession almost immediately from a Maroon knock on. They played out their set of six tackles, and on the last Steve Mortimer put up a perfect bomb that came down a metre inside the Maroons' goal line, directly under the crossbar. There was a mad scramble of blue and maroon guernseys, and at the end of it Noel Cleal was on the ground with the ball. Roberts signalled a try. Ross Conlon had the easiest of conversions and the southerners looked winners at 14–6.

They went further ahead three minutes later. Attacking from the kick-off, they forced a Queensland line drop-out. Gary Jack fielded the kick and ran it back to the Queensland quarter-way line where the Maroon forwards gave up a penalty for holding him down too long in the tackle. Ross Conlon had no trouble with the kick and it was New South Wales 16, Queensland 6. The Blues were awarded another penalty in the thirteenth minute of the second half, this time for offside, and Conlon kicked his fifth goal for the day to make it 18–6. Three minutes later another disaster struck the Maroons. Dave Brown used an elbow on Steve Mortimer as he made a try-saving tackle. Referee Roberts ordered him to the sin-bin and the Queenslanders were without one of their most effective forwards for the next ten minutes. Before Brown had completed his penance, New South Wales scored again.

In the 26th minute of the half, Wally Lewis lost the ball in a heavy tackle, reefed out of his grasp by Blocker Roach. Brett Kenny picked it up, ran about three steps and sent it on to Brian Johnston who put it down in the corner for a try-scoring double. Ross Conlon's conversion attempt failed when the ball hit a goal post: the Blues led 22–6.

Ten minutes before full-time, Tony Currie made his State of Origin debut as a fresh reserve and was quickly into the game. He initiated a break that saw Greg Dowling reach the New South Wales ten-metre line. Gary Jack safely defused the fifth-tackle bomb, and following the drop-out the new arrival once more ran the ball back. Wally Lewis went to dummy half, spotted Kerry Boustead unmarked wide out and threw a pass thirty metres to the winger, who scored twelve metres in from the sideline. Mal Meninga's kick was successful and the Maroons had closed the gap, but it was New South Wales 22, Queensland 12, and that remained the score until Kevin Roberts blew his whistle for full-time five minutes later.

Final result

New South Wales 22 defeated Queensland 12.

Tries for New South Wales: Brian Johnston (2), Noel Cleal. Goals: Ross Conlon (5).

Tries for Queensland: Bob Lindner, Kerry Boustead. Goals: Mal Meninga (2).

Crowd: 16,559.

Man of the Match: Steve Mortimer.

In what was to be his final report as Chairman of the Queensland Rugby League, Ron McAuliffe wrote: 'Season '84 will go down in the annals of the code as one of unprecedented success on and off the field and will undoubtedly prove a difficult target for players and administrators of the future to match.'[3]

With the tendering of this report, McAuliffe drew a line under a period which was equally as unprecedented as the success of the year past. During the fourteen years of his stewardship of the code in Queensland, Rugby League in Australia had been revolutionised, and it was largely due to the senator. His masterstroke, and the achievement for which he will always be remembered, was the major contribution he made to the introduction of the State of Origin principle to the selection of teams for the interstate series.

State of Origin was a magic wand, Rugby League's elixir of life.

It had regenerated a competition that was in extremis. Success there was in abundance for Queenslanders, success which allowed them to hold their heads high for the first time in forty years. If he had done nothing else, then this alone ought to entitle the senator to Rugby League immortality, but he achieved far more than that.

Had it not been for the tremendous efforts by Queensland teams of the 1970s, inspired and driven as they were by McAuliffe's enthusiasm and love for the game, the interstate series may have perished before the idea of State of Origin jelled and found favour. That this didn't happen is down to Senator Ron McAuliffe.

The senator resigned as Chairman and Chief Executive Officer of the Queensland Rugby League at the end of the 1984 season and such was the size of his boots that it took two pairs of feet to fill them. Bill Hunter, Chairman of the Redcliffe Rugby League Club, was elected to replace him as Chairman of the Queensland Rugby League, but, his position was somewhat different from that of the man who had been called El Supremo.

Ross Livermore was Ron McAuliffe's protege, hired as General Manager of the Queensland Rugby League in 1981. In the four years that he had served the senator, Ross had demonstrated a capacity for hard work and attention to administrative detail that persuaded McAuliffe that this was the man who ought to succeed him as Chief Executive Officer.

Meanwhile, although Ron McAuliffe had resigned all of his positions save one, he did not say goodbye. He remained as Chairman of the Lang Park Trust, and he was retained by the Queensland Rugby League as a consultant. He continued to maintain close contact with his former associates and it was whispered that top Rugby League had not seen the last of him by any means and that the senator had other fish to fry. It was said that he would have a future active role, one related to yet another revolutionary change in the New South Wales Rugby League's arrangements, a change almost as revolutionary as the one that he engineered in 1979.

CHAPTER 6

1985

Southern Breakthrough

THE New South Wales Rugby League expanded from eight teams to ten in 1947 when groups at Manly and Parramatta were invited to enter. In 1967 a club from Penrith and one from Cronulla joined the league, to make it a twelve-team competition. This situation continued for a further fifteen years, when it was decided that a southern expansion was justified. In 1981 a club was formed in Wollongong and entered in the New South Wales Rugby League competition under the regional name, Illawarra. At the same time, a club was formed in Canberra. Both clubs entered teams in all grades in the 1982 competition.

Newcastle was part of the New South Wales Rugby League at its foundation, but it withdrew after only two seasons. The reasons for the withdrawal have not been recorded, but they are fairly obvious. Men with a living to earn worked at least half a day on Saturdays in those days, there was no Sunday sport, and the 200-kilometre journey from Newcastle to Sydney took at least six hours by steam train and ferry.

The 1980s presented a different picture. A super-highway linked the two cities. Travel was no longer a problem and Newcastle was the strongest Australian Rugby League centre outside the two capital cities, Brisbane and Sydney. It was bound to produce a strong side, but if a bye was to be avoided a second candidate was needed, and inspired by the success of State of Origin Rugby League the Blues cast their eyes further north. The New South Wales Rugby League would cross state boundaries. A team from Brisbane would be invited to take part. The eight Brisbane clubs were not so sure that this was a good idea, but the winds of change which had wrought the State of Origin revolution still blew strong. Former Queensland Rugby League supremo Ron McAuliffe agreed with the New South Wales Rugby League that this was progress. He made his plans accordingly, and waited.

In Sydney, Queensland's State of Origin victories were starting to hurt. The Blues' supporters were becoming restless and their failure to win a State of Origin series had made them the butt of pub jokes. Canterbury's supercoach, Warren Ryan, heard a story about an expatriate Queenslander living in Sydney who invited a friend home to watch a State of Origin game. Queensland duly won, and when the final whistle sounded, the host's cat reared up on its hind legs and emulated the Maroons as they did their lap of honour, strutting upright around the lounge room. The visitor was astonished.

'Does your cat do that all the time?' he asked.

'Only when the Maroons win,' he was told.

'What does he do when the Blues win?'

'I've no idea,' his friend replied. 'The cat's only ten years old.'

Eight losses out of eleven State of Origin games played armed the New South Wales team with a terrible resolve to win in 1985, and this was particularly the case with their captain.

Steve Mortimer, of the Canterbury club, had his pride badly dented on the 1982 Kangaroo tour. Since then, he had been engaged in an ongoing battle with Peter Sterling, the brilliant Parramatta half, to work the scrum in State of Origin games. Sterling had displaced him in the first two games in 1983, while Mortimer fed the scrums in the third. In 1984 he had reversed the situation. Sterling was half for the first match of the season while Steve Mortimer took over for the remaining two. Although the Blues lost the series, Steve 'Turvey' Mortimer inherited the captaincy for Origin III when injury forced Junior Pearce to withdraw and the Canterbury half led his side to victory. In 1985 he was appointed Captain in his own right and he took his captaincy seriously. When Turvey Mortimer led his team on to Lang Park on the night of 28 May, he was a man on a mission.

On the other hand, Wally Lewis wasn't having a good year. Wynnum Manly, his Brisbane club, was in financial difficulties and the Sydney media was pressing for Brett Kenny to replace the King as Australian five-eighth. Former Australian captain and local Sydney icon Reg Gasnier wrote in a newspaper column: 'Kenny's English experience has completed his football education and he has the ammunition to blast Lewis out of the game.'

Strong words. And Kenny partnered Mortimer in the first game of the State of Origin series.

The Queenslanders approached the series with confidence, al-

STATE OF ORIGIN I, 1985
LANG PARK, 28 MAY

Queensland	New South Wales
Colin Scott	Gary Jack
Dale Shearer	Eric Grothe
Chris Close	Michael O'Connor
Mal Meninga	Chris Mortimer
John Ribot	John Ferguson
Wally Lewis (c)	Brett Kenny
Mark Murray	Steve Mortimer (c)
Bob Lindner	Wayne Pearce
Paul McCabe	Noel Cleal
Paul Vautin	Peter Wynn
Dave Brown	Pat Jarvis
Greg Conescu	Ben Elias
Greg Dowling	Steve Roach
Reserves:	
Brett French	Steve Ella
Ian French[1]	Peter Tunks
Coaches:	
Des Morris	Terry Fearnley

Referee: Kevin Roberts (NSW)

though the absence of champion centre Gene Miles with damaged knee ligaments must have been good news to the Blues.

Steve Mortimer was well aware that it was Wally Lewis with his imperious long passes who gave the Maroons the edge and he believed that he had a plan to nullify this. Mortimer's club coach that season was Warren Ryan who had the equivalent of a PhD in Rugby League tactics. At Canterbury, Ryan employed a form of sliding defence to place his defenders in a position to outflank the opposition backs before they moved up and in to tackle them. Under the five-metre rule that then governed the depth of the defensive line, this enabled the defending backs to get among the attackers' backline before the ball got past the five-eighth.

Rather than attempt to tackle the hard-running Lewis, Mortimer instructed his defenders to cut off Wally's runners. As soon as he believed he knew which way the Maroon captain would move or pass, he would call 'slide left', or 'slide right'. The Blues' defenders would move like a Tivoli chorus line and Close, Meninga or a forward running wide to take the pass would find himself outflanked and outnumbered by an unbroken defensive line. Perhaps, too, there was a hint of complacency in the Queensland side that night. Playing at Lang Park before a capacity crowd of screaming Queenslanders the Maroons may well have been over-confident to the point where they thought themselves invincible, but that could not be offered as an excuse for what happened.

New South Wales had made six changes to their side. The Queensland players were accustomed to seeing that, but there was one change the importance of which was by no means clear before the game — the introduction of a debutante of special significance. Michael O'Connor came from the Australian Capital Territory and he toured England and Europe in 1977 with the same Rugby Union schoolboy team that contained Wally Lewis. He came to Brisbane and played Rugby Union for a season, was selected for the Wallabies, and played thirteen Tests for Australia before signing to play Rugby League with St George. At Lang Park that night he had the kind of representative debut that is enjoyed by only a fortunate few of those who aspire to greatness.

The players took the field in drenching rain, and, although there was no ponding of surface water as had occurred in Sydney in Origin II, 1984, the ground was extremely greasy and handling was difficult from the start. Players on both sides knocked on constantly, scrums were messy, and New South Wales referee Kevin Roberts handed out penalties with gay abandon, all too often with the unsolicited assistance of a persistent New South Wales' linesman. The game see-sawed with neither side gaining any great advantage, and even when breaks were made, little came of them. Penalties in kicking range gave Michael O'Connor and Mal Meninga limited opportunity to demonstrate their skills and the scores were New South Wales 4 (O'Connor two goals), Queensland 2 (Meninga a goal) when the teams left the field at half-time.

The rain had eased early in the second half, but the conditions underfoot couldn't change and poor ball handling still plagued both sides. However, Steve Mortimer let the Queenslanders make most of the ball-handling mistakes. On the first occasion that the Blues got the ball, he kicked on tackle 2, deep into the Maroons' half. The Queenslanders battled to bring the ball back, but Mortimer's form of umbrella defence restrained the Maroon centres. Too often Wally Lewis found himself kicking on the last tackle from well inside his own half. As soon as the Blues received the ball, they repeated the tactic and again the Maroons found themselves bringing a slippery ball out from inside their own twenty-metre line. Eventually Steve Mortimer found himself in a position to turn a profit. Twelve minutes into the second half a Queenslander knocked on and the ball was recovered by the Blues' forwards. Steve Mortimer received the ball from the dummy half deep in the Queensland half. He gave it to Wayne Pearce, who passed to Brett Kenny, who had Michael O'Connor coming through on the outside flying to place the ball for a try fifteen metres in from the sideline. New South Wales led 8–2, and after O'Connor converted, it was 10 points to 2.

By midway through the second half the Blues had kicked on early tackles twelve times, and the Maroons were becoming very tired of playing football inside their own quarter. Attempting to emulate the New South Wales tactics, in the twenty-third minute Mark Murray kicked deep and was taken in a tackle both late and high by his opposite number. Steve Mortimer was aware that he had sinned.

Television has recorded for posterity the swift, surreptitious glance that he cast at the referee. It was as good as a notarised confession, but he need not have worried. Referee Roberts followed the ball to where it had been taken by Noel Cleal and penalised Wally Lewis for stealing it from him. When Wally asked the referee about Steve Mortimer's social error with Murray, Roberts didn't like his manner and took the mark ten metres closer to the Maroon line for dissent. O'Connor seized the moment and kicked a goal to make the score 12–2 in favour of the Blues.

Five minutes later the Blues scored again, and once more it was O'Connor. In the second half's thirty-fourth minute Brett Kenny made a break down the blind-side and passed to Michael O'Connor, who scored ten metres in from the left sideline. His successful conversion took the score to 18–2 and that was game, set and match. Michael O'Connor had scored two tries and kicked five goals, the entire New South Wales score.

Final result

New South Wales 18 defeated Queensland 2.

Tries for New South Wales: Michael O'Connor (2). Goals: Michael O'Connor (5).

Goal for Queensland: Mal Meninga.

Crowd: 33,011.

Man of the Match: Peter Wynn.

Queensland made only two changes for the second State of Origin game, to be played at the Sydney Cricket Ground on 11 June. New South Wales made just one.

More than 39,000 Blues' supporters turned out to watch, cheer and support Steve Mortimer and his men. After five years of build-up, an uninterrupted sequence of Queensland series victories, and with their team one up and playing at home, the New South Wales Rugby League public had at last accepted State of Origin as the main event that it had become. Brisbane's *Courier-Mail* told the story next morning:

New South Wales buried the State of Origin myth when they sealed the 1985 series with a classy 21–14 win over Queensland at the Sydney Cricket Ground last night.

The victory gave New South Wales success in a State of Origin series for the first time since the system was introduced in 1980 …

The NSW players reacted amazingly — some cried, others were kissed by team officials, and eventually the Blues did a lap of honour surrounded by hordes of supporters …

Queensland took two devastating blows when lock Bob Lindner and fullback Colin Scott were carried off with serious knee injuries [which] ended the Queensland pair's hopes for Australian Jerseys.[2]

It was a classic match in which strong attack by both sides was

---

STATE OF ORIGIN II, 1985
SYDNEY CRICKET GROUND, 11 JUNE

Queensland	New South Wales
Colin Scott	Gary Jack
Dale Shearer	Eric Grothe
Chris Close	Michael O'Connor
Mal Meninga	Chris Mortimer
John Ribot	John Ferguson
Wally Lewis (c)	Brett Kenny
Mark Murray	Steve Mortimer (c)
Bob Lindner	Wayne Pearce
Wally Fullerton Smith	Noel Cleal
Paul Vautin	Peter Wynn
Dave Brown	Pat Jarvis
Greg Conescu	Ben Elias
Greg Dowling	Steve Roach

Reserves:

Tony Currie	Steve Ella
Ian French	Peter Tunks

Coaches:

Des Morris	Terry Fearnley

Referee: Barry Gomersall (Qld)

matched by equally fierce defence. The Maroons had gone to school on the tactics used by the Blues in State of Origin I. Wally Lewis used the tactical kick at every opportunity and he wasn't the only kicker used. Shearer chip-kicked and opened up opportunities several times during both halves and Muppet Murray and Paul Vautin were also used as alternate kickers from time to time. Although the Maroons dominated play for much of the early part of the game, New South Wales were the first to score when their captain, Steve Mortimer, broke the line and cleared away downfield to serve winger John Ferguson, who was tackled five metres short of the try-line. Steve Mortimer was hot on his heels to accept his quick play the ball and immediately skied a bomb from dummy half. His brother, Chris, was in close support and won the in-goal scramble to score a try under the posts. Michael O'Connor kicked the easy conversion and after just eleven minutes of play New South Wales led Queensland by 6 points to nil.

Five minutes later Steve Mortimer again broke away and passed to front-rower Pat Jarvis, who was pulled down on the Queensland 22-metre line. From the play-the-ball, Benny Elias ran towards the left-hand corner of the ground, beat Colin Scott with dummy and step and ran around to score under the posts. It was another simple conversion for Michael O'Connor and the alarm bells were ringing for the Maroons, down 0–12.

Taking the ball from the restart, Gary Jack kicked deep into Maroon territory, the Blues' tactics plain to see: play the game at the Queensland end of the paddock and wait for the Maroons to make mistakes. With the Queenslanders showing a similar distaste for possession in their own half, the game see-sawed. There was a break to this routine in the nineteenth minute. A touch judge rushed on to the field to report Greg Dowling for an over-enthusiastic tackle, but referee Gomersall had his own view of the incident. To the annoyance of the Sydney Cricket Ground crowd, he administered a severe verbal slap on the wrist to Greg, and awarded a penalty to the Maroons for the Blues' provocation, which had apparently upset him.

Shortly after play restarted, Chris Close gained possession of a dropped ball. He beat Ben Elias and Pat Jarvis before passing to Dale

Shearer. Shearer ran twenty metres downfield before the cover defence caught up to him, but Muppet Murray was backing up on the inside and he sent the ball on to Paul Vautin. Fatty drew two defenders, and he gave the ball on to Bobby Lindner who trotted around and placed it under the posts. It was the Maroons first try of the 1985 series. Mal Meninga converted and Queensland was back in the game at 6–12.

Ten minutes before half-time, disaster struck the Maroons. Bob Lindner was tackled into touch and failed to rise. At almost the same time it was found that Colin Scott was down with a leg injury. Lindner rose limping with what was believed to be a corked thigh, but Scott was stretchered off the field, to be replaced by talented utility player Tony Currie. Shortly afterwards, Steve Mortimer conceded a penalty right in front when his tackle on his opposite number, Muppet Murray, was deemed by Barry Gomersall to be too high. Mal Meninga kicked the goal and the Blues' lead was reduced to 12 points to 8.

With half-time only three minutes away and the Queenslanders on the attack deep in the Blues' territory, Steve Mortimer ran behind his second-rower Noel Cleal while trying to run the ball out from his own ten-metre area. He was called for a shepherd, and Mal Meninga placed the ball for a sitter, fifteen metres out and right in front. He missed, and when the hooter signalled the break, the scores remained at New South Wales 12, Queensland 8.

Bob Lindner's injury was worse than at first thought and Ian French took the field in his place after half-time. The second half was barely under way when a scrum erupted in a ferocious exchange between front-rowers Greg Dowling and Steve Roach. As was his practice, referee Gomersall stood aloof from the proceedings, but one of his touch judges made a bold attempt to terminate the fracas. When it was over, Gomersall sent both participants to cool off in the sin-bin for five minutes and repacked the scrum.

Twelve minutes into the second half, Tony Currie put Queensland on the attack with a strong run, and a few minutes later, after an exchange of knock ons, Queensland won a scrum ten metres from the Blues' line. From the first tackle, Ian French broke the line and was over for the Maroons' second try to tie the scores at 12 all. Mal

Meninga's conversion gave Queensland the lead, 14–12, but in the 25th minute Steve Mortimer put up a bomb and was flattened by Chris Close and Greg Conescu. Gomersall deemed the tackle to be late, and awarded a penalty twenty metres out and about five metres to the right of the Queensland goal posts. This was money for old rope for Michael O'Connor, who levelled the scores at 14 all. Nine minutes later he potted a field goal to put the Blues' in front, 15–14.

There followed a classic exhibition of rugged defence from both sides, and with only two minutes to go the Blues gave an Oscar-winning exhibition of organised procrastination as player after player rose like an arthritic octogenarian after each tackle. Then, with the end of play imminent, the brilliant Brett Kenny dived in for the try that sealed the Maroons' fate. It was 19–14, and as the full-time siren sounded, Michael O'Connor's boot made it 21–14.

Final result

New South Wales 21 defeated Queensland 14.

Tries for New South Wales: Chris Mortimer, Ben Elias, Brett Kenny. Goals: Michael O'Connor (4). Field goal: Michael O'Connor.

Tries for Queensland: Bob Lindner, Ian French. Goals: Mal Meninga (3).

Crowd: 39,068.

Man of the Match: Wally Lewis.

It was both the game and the series to New South Wales and the fans went wild. Hundreds of them crowded on to the ground to accompany the players as his team-mates lifted Steve Mortimer on to their shoulders and carried him in a lap of honour around the ground. There would be another game to be played at Lang Park, but it could not alter the series result. At last the Blues could hold their heads high and they reaped their reward when the Australian selectors sat down to pick the side to play New Zealand.

Just seven Queenslanders, John Ribot, Chris Close, Mal Meninga, Wally Lewis, Mark Murray, Greg Conescu and Greg Dowling, were picked. Wally Lewis was named captain, and how could it be otherwise. He had been awarded the 'Adidas' Golden Boot on the unanimous verdict of a panel of international experts hired to select the winner of the trophy. Wally's comment on the award was a measure of the man: 'I am honoured to be the recipient of the award,' he said, 'but it is hard to accept the rating because it is unfair to compare a five-eighth with a prop forward.'[3]

The *Courier-Mail* named John Ribot as the hero of Australia's 26–20 win over New Zealand: 'Ribot, in his final season of Rugby League, scored two tries and kicked a touchline goal to give Australia a 1–0 lead in the three test series …'[4]

Nine Maroons were selected in a party of twenty to travel to the Shaky Isles for the completion of the three-Test series, seven of them resident Queenslanders: Greg Conescu, Greg Dowling, Wally Fullerton Smith, Wally Lewis who went as captain, Mark Murray, Mal Meninga and John Ribot. Paul Vautin and Chris Close, Maroons who played for Manly in the Sydney competition, were also chosen.

After two easy wins in warm-up games against provincial teams the Australians wrapped up the Test series with a 10 points to 6 win by a team that contained eight Maroons. Queenslanders scored all of the points (John Ribot a try and Mal Meninga two goals). However, between victory in the second Test and the selection of the side for the third, four Maroons fell by the wayside. Greg Dowling was dropped for Peter Tunks, Greg Conescu for Ben Elias, Mark Murray for Des Hasler and Chris Close for Steve Ella. With a few strokes of his pen, coach Terry Fearnley succeeded in drawing a solid line of demarcation between Blues and Maroons. Wally Lewis remained in the side as captain, but it was 1982 and England revisited. Fearnley had made the changes without consulting the team captain. And there was yet another problem.

A day or so before the team was announced, Wally Lewis walked into a conference room at his hotel looking for a cloth cap he wore when travelling. He was surprised when he disturbed a tete-a-tete between Terry Fearnley and his vice-captain, Wayne ('Junior') Pearce. On the table, and the focus of their attention, was an Australian Rugby League pro forma used for recording team selections. Names had been inserted in the squares provided and it was obvious that the two men were engaged in earnest consideration of the team for the third Test. This would have been sufficient to offend anyone in Wally Lewis's position, but when it appeared later that the coach had appeared to seek vice-captain Wayne Pearce's guidance in eliminating Wally's Maroon team-mates, while keeping the captain in ignorance of his intention, any chance that the Fearnley or Pearce names would appear on the Lewis family's 1985 Christmas card list went right out the window.

Later, Australian Rugby League president Ken Arthurson was to write of the relationship between captain and coach:

> One of the big difficulties on the tour was the gulf that developed between Fearnley, the coach, and Wally Lewis, the captain. Lewis wasn't in any way close to Fearnley ... [who] worked more closely with the tour vice-captain, Wayne Pearce. It became apparent after the tour that this had got right up Lewis's nose ...[5]

In the circumstances, the president should hardly have been surprised that Wally was so offended. In fact, in the circumstances, Ken Arthurson himself could well have been offended, since any status, authority or influence Wally Lewis may have had as captain derived from his appointment by the executive that Ken Arthurson chaired. In bypassing Lewis, intentionally or otherwise, Fearnley declared a lack of confidence in the people who had appointed him. If the coach had discovered an overwhelming urge to ignore his captain and instead discuss team selections with Junior Pearce, then perhaps he ought to have first spoken to Arthurson and suggested a change of captain. Ken Arthurson was available. He was staying at the same hotel as Fearnley and was in daily contact with the touring party.[6]

There are few secrets among the personnel of a touring football team. The rejection of the Queenslanders by Fearnley, Junior's alleged role in the affair and the snub to their captain poisoned team relationships for the remainder of the tour, particularly since the amended team lost the final Test 0–18. In New Zealand the local media were jubilant and they were also quick to jump on another statistic. In total, the Kiwis had scored 44 points to the Australians' 36 in the three-Test series.

Steve Mortimer and his men had wrapped up the annual interstate series with two straight wins, but following the return from New Zealand there was one more State of Origin game to play. No doubt the Blues hoped to complete a whitewash, but the New Zealand experience suggested that if that ethereal quality, Queensland spirit, had the smallest modicum of substance to it, their chances didn't look all that great.

New South Wales made only three changes to the side that had won the second game. Steve Mortimer had put his cue in the rack. He was replaced as half-back by Des Hasler. David Brooks replaced Noel Cleal in the second row, and Tony Rampling came in as a reserve in place of Peter Tunks. Junior Pearce was the new captain.

For Queensland, Paul Vautin took over the lock position from the

---

STATE OF ORIGIN III, 1985
LANG PARK, 23 JULY

Queensland	New South Wales
Colin Scott	Gary Jack
Dale Shearer	Eric Grothe
Chris Close	Michael O'Connor
Mal Meninga	Chris Mortimer
John Ribot	John Ferguson
Wally Lewis (c)	Brett Kenny
Mark Murray	Des Hasler
Paul Vautin	Wayne Pearce (c)
Wally Fullerton Smith	David Brooks
Ian French	Peter Wynn
Dave Brown	Pat Jarvis
Greg Conescu	Ben Elias
Greg Dowling	Steve Roach

Reserves:

Tony Currie	Steve Ella
Cavill Heugh	Tony Rampling

Coaches:

Des Morris	Terry Fearnley

Referee: Barry Gomersall (Qld)

injured Bob Lindner, and Cavill Heugh was named as a reserve to replace Ian French who moved to second row.

Where any sporting series has been won in 'straight sets' there are always those who will consider the rubber dead and any further contest irrelevant.[6] Not so for the Maroons at Lang Park on 23 July 1985, nor for the Blues. Steve Mortimer's dedication to his mission in May was a pallid shadow of the depth of the Maroons' commitment in July. With Mortimer retired, Junior Pearce was determined to make his mark, and the Blues had publicly declared their intention to achieve a 'whitewash' of the Maroons.

Although he no longer had any official connection with the Maroons, Ron McAuliffe addressed the team in its dressing room before they ran on.

> We're beaten two nil, but it isn't too late to salvage our reputations — not just of the Queensland Rugby League but of Queensland itself. We've had this controversy in New Zealand and we've gone heavy on the coach. But all of this is to no avail and no one will believe us — we'll be regarded as a team of whingers unless you go out on the paddock and do them over.[7]

Do them over — a fine old Australian vernacular phrase and most appropriate in the circumstances. State of Origin III, 1985, was very personal, but the Queensland cause got off to a shaky start when Mal Meninga missed an early penalty from right in front of goal. He made amends ten minutes later, however, when the Maroons received another shot within kicking distance and Queensland led 2–0 after thirteen minutes.

Immediately after the restart, the two hookers, Greg Conescu and Ben Elias, locked horns in a scrum and came out fighting. Since Gomersall refused to acknowledge such activity as relevant to his task, the bout lasted for some time. A touch judge halted play to inform the referee of the disturbance, but Gomersall considered it of little importance. He restarted play with a scrum.

The kicking game was popular in State of Origin games that season, and few sets of six tackles ran their course without a tactical kick from one or other of the experts on both sides. Midway through the first half of football, Colin Scott kicked long from deep in his own half. Dale Shearer gave chase and, with the ball bouncing towards touch, he caught it on the fly. Eric Grothe attempted the cover tackle but all he caught was the breeze of Shearer flying past as he went on his way to score in the corner. Mal Meninga made a brave attempt at conversion, but the ball brushed the wrong side of the right-hand goal post and the Maroons led by only 6 points to nil.

The Queenslanders continued to dominate play, but the determined Blues' defence held them out. There was some more excitement when Wally Lewis and big Blues' forward, Tony Rampling, exchanged punches but neither side troubled the scorer. They went to the break with the score still Queensland 6, New South Wales 0.

Chris Close was hurt during the first half and his place was taken by Tony Currie when the teams returned. Just six minutes into the second half the Queenslanders forced a scrum when Mal Meninga and Tony Currie sheep-dogged a chain-passing movement by the Blues' backline that went nowhere and ended with a wild pass to no one that sailed out over the sideline. The Queenslanders won the scrum and from the first tackle Greg Conescu gave the ball to Mark Murray who drew two men and passed to Wally Lewis. Wally sent a long pass to Mal Meninga. The centre found second-row forward Ian French coming through inside him, gave him the ball and French sprinted thirty metres to put it down under the posts. Mal's conversion gave Queensland a 12–nil lead.

The Blues never stopped trying, but the Maroon defence was impenetrable. Their forwards constantly attacked down the middle but the Maroon forwards, and centres Tony Currie and Mal Meninga, were up to the task. At one point Tony Rampling came through at pace only to run into a Meninga shoulder charge and collapse at the big man's feet. Veteran winger John Ferguson attempted to stop a rampaging John Ribot. He failed to rise after the robust Queenslander simply mowed him down.

Play continued with both sides being forced to defend their try-line. Then with only nine minutes left to play, the Queenslanders broke through. Ian French was having a wonderful game in the Maroon second row in his first outing in a State of Origin run-on side. He broke away from deep inside his own half and ran down the touchline. As the cover got to him, 'Rowdy' Shearer loomed inside. French gave Rowdy the ball and he was in the clear. No one was likely to catch him. Mal Meninga's attempt to convert failed, but with eight minutes left in the game Queensland were safe with a 16-point lead. Just two minutes later Lang Park erupted. From a blind-side movement, Tony Currie drew the defence and passed the ball to an unmarked John Ribot. In his farewell appearance for his state, and with Lang Park in an uproar, the veteran galloped forty metres, beat the cover defence and ran around to put the ball down under the posts.

The Blues gained a consolation try a few minutes later when Brett Kenny ran from a ruck and put Steve Ella over the line with an inside pass. Michael O'Connor kicked the goal and it was Queensland 20, New South Wales 6 when the full-time hooter drew thousands of ecstatic Queenslanders over the fence and on to the playing field.

McAuliffe told the Maroons to 'do them over' and do them over they did. They were totally dominant as they routed the Blues, and the satisfaction felt by the fifteen Maroons was very special.

The *Courier-Mail* told the story the next morning:

> Queensland extracted sweet revenge from New South Wales and Australian Rugby League coach Terry Fearnley when they sent the Blues packing to the tune of 20–6 at Lang Park last night.
>
> The comprehensive nature of last night's victory would not compensate for losing the 1985 series 1–2 but it would have given the four Queenslanders axed by Fearnley before the third test in Auckland a couple of short weeks ago plenty of satisfaction ...
>
> Dowling, Conescu, Dave Brown and Fullerton Smith did most of the heavy work in the middle, while Mark Murray, Wally Lewis, Colin Scott and big Mal Meninga reigned supreme in the backs. Meninga silenced his critics with a block-busting display which gave the Blues' Rugby Union convert, Michael O'Connor, nightmares ... and veteran winger John Ribot absolutely blitzed his opposite number, John Ferguson. The Blues simply had no answer to Queensland's total commitment ...[9]

John Ribot received the thanks of the Maroon Rugby League community and reaped the ultimate compliment after the game

---

Final result.

Queensland 20 defeated New South Wales 6.

Tries for Queensland: Dale Shearer (2), Ian French, John Ribot. Goals: Mal Meninga (2).

Try for New South Wales: Steve Ella. Goal: Michael O'Connor.

Crowd: 18,825.

Man of the Match: Wally Fullerton Smith.

---

when his team–mates and hundreds of supporters lifted him high and carried him from the ground.

CHAPTER 7

1986

A Blue Whitewash

A T THE END of the 1985 season the New South Wales Rugby League decided to include a Brisbane team in its competition. Of course, this couldn't happen without the approval and cooperation of the Queensland Rugby League. There had never been much evidence of a close personal relationship between those who controlled the game in Queensland and their southern neighbours, but in first proposing State of Origin football, and then fighting so hard to have his proposal adopted, Senator Ron McAuliffe had formed a close friendship with two key figures in the New South Wales Rugby League, Kevin Humphreys and Ken Arthurson. Humphreys succeeded to the chairmanship of the Australian Rugby League on the death of Bill Buckley in 1973. According to Ken Arthurson:

> [Kevin Humphreys] was one of the finest administrators rugby league has ever had. With him, alongside Queensland Senator McAuliffe, rests the responsibility for the birth of State of Origin football in 1980 — the jewel in the crown of the modern game.[1]

Kevin Humphreys was out of office by 1985, replaced by Ken Arthurson, but Arko's relationship with McAuliffe was simply a continuum of the Humphreys years and one of the matters frequently discussed was the New South Wales Rugby League's plan to offer a franchise for a Brisbane Rugby League team to join the Sydney competition in 1987.

Dick Turner of Redcliffe Club was heavily involved in State of Origin football from the early days. He favoured the idea.

I thought that anything that would stop the drain of our Queenslanders to Sydney clubs would be good for the game. The Brisbane clubs didn't have the financial clout to do it and this seemed to be the only way it would happen.[2]

At the other end of the scale were those who took a narrower view. One senior club official summed it up: 'Why should we vote for it. If it doesn't happen, Wally and Geno and half of Wynnum will go to Sydney and we'll win the premiership.'[3]

But it was a case of 'when, not if', and two things seemed certain. First, Wally Lewis would be captain of the new club's First Grade side. Second, and even more certainly, Ron McAuliffe would be chairman of the board. It was widely believed that he had resigned from his Queensland Rugby League chairmanship at the end of the 1984 season with just that in mind. Whether this was true or not, his resignation had certainly freed him to put together a syndicate to bid for the franchise.

In the meantime, the prospect of a team playing in Sydney had the effect that Tosser Turner predicted. A lot of footballers, including Wally and Geno, put plans to negotiate with southern clubs on hold and concentrated on their preparations for the first game of the 1986 State of Origin series, due to be played at Lang Park on the night of 27 May.

Despite the fact that Queensland had lost the 1985 series to New South Wales, such had been the magnitude of the victory in the third game, and the fire and determination of the side that won it, that Queenslanders had great expectations of their 1986 team, which contained most of the stars of that epic contest. The series opener was the first occasion on which every seat in the ground was pre-sold a week before the game. Lang Park was packed for the encounter and the crowd got value for money.

The Maroons received an early penalty twenty-five metres out from goal when Wally Lewis ran the ball back straight into a Blues forward who was offside. Mal Meninga kicked the goal from only five metres to the left of the line of the left-hand goal post and

---

STATE OF ORIGIN I, 1986
LANG PARK, 27 MAY

Queensland	New South Wales
Colin Scott	Gary Jack
Dale Shearer	Steve Morris
Mal Meninga	Michael O'Connor
Gene Miles	Chris Mortimer
Chris Close	Andrew Farrar
Wally Lewis (c)	Brett Kenny
Mark Murray	Peter Sterling
Bob Lindner	Wayne Pearce (c)
Gavin Jones	Noel Cleal
Bryan Niebling	Steve Folkes
Dave Brown	Peter Tunks
Greg Conescu	Royce Simmons
Greg Dowling	Steve Roach

Reserves:

Peter Jackson	Terry Lamb
Ian French	David Gillespie

Coaches:

Wayne Bennett	Ron Willey

Referee: Kevin Roberts (NSW)

Queensland led 2–0 after only two minutes of football. Then, following a scrum, the New South Wales attack swept down the field to within ten metres of the Queensland goal line. Following some broken play in which at least ten Blues handled the ball, fullback Gary Jack ran on to a Steve Folkes pass at full speed and scored under the posts. Michael O'Connor's conversion made it 6–2 in favour of New South Wales.

Ten minutes later the Blues scored again. From a ruck close to the Queensland line, Noel Cleal passed to Steve Roach from dummy half. The big Balmain forward made ground before giving the ball to Steve 'Slippery' Morris, who lived up to his name. He slid past grasping hands before handing it on to Peter Sterling who found

Chris Mortimer unmarked and on the burst inside him. Mortimer scored close to the posts and Michael O'Connor had an easy conversion. Suddenly, New South Wales was 12–2 in front.

A superb Meninga penalty from twenty-eight metres out and well wide of the posts reduced the Blues' lead to eight points, and then, just ten minutes before half-time, Queensland went on the attack. From a ruck on the New South Wales 22-metre line, two short passes from Conescu to Murray to Lewis saw the King run the ball and the Blues' backs pay far too much attention to him. He drew two defenders and attracted the interest of at least one other before he slipped a beautiful one-handed pass to Gene Miles. Geno beat two men with pace and strength and at top speed gave Gary Jack no chance at all as he stepped around him to score close to the left-hand upright. Meninga converted and Queensland trailed 10–12, the half-time score.

The Maroons were back in the lead shortly after half-time. Gary Jack fumbled a mid-field bomb which Gene Miles gathered in. Geno ran more than thirty metres and with the cover about to claim him he passed to his Wynnum–Manly colleague Greg Dowling who dived in under the posts. It was 16–12 in favour of Queensland, but a few minutes later Royce Simmonds was dummy half only a metre out from the Queensland line. The Queensland defender on the blind-side moved a fraction to his right just as the ball was played. Simmonds burrowed through the opening, and with the conversion the Maroons were down 16–18.

Five minutes before full-time, Dale ('Rowdy') Shearer ran to gather the ball following a Brett Kenney kick deep into the Queensland half. He was under no pressure and moved casually as he trotted to the ball. Then he knocked it on. There was a ten-metre scrum and the Blues used a tactic as old as Rugby League. The Blues' forwards screwed the scrum to move the Queensland back row to the open side, then Peter Sterling went the blind. The quick-breaking lock Junior Pearce was outside him as he picked up the ball from behind the second row, and with the Maroons back row out of play, the Blues had a clear three on two advantage. Sterling drew the half and passed to Pearce, Pearce drew the winger and sent Andrew Farrar away unmarked to score in the corner. That was the ball game.

Queensland were attacking as the siren sounded, but a mid-field knock on bombed the movement. It was New South Wales 22, Queensland 16, and the Blues were one up in the 1986 series.

Final result

New South Wales 22 defeated Queensland 16.

Tries for New South Wales: Gary Jack, Chris Mortimer, Royce Simmonds, Andrew Farrar. Goals: Michael O'Connor (3).

Tries for Queensland: Gene Miles, Greg Dowling. Goals: Mal Meninga (4).

Crowd: 33,066.

Man of the Match: Royce Simmonds.

Queensland faced the moment of truth for a second year in succession and the Maroons' selectors had serious problems with injuries. For the second State of Origin game at the Sydney Cricket Ground on 10 June, Canberra's Gary Belcher took Colin Scott's place. North Sydney winger Les Kiss replaced Choppy Close, and Darryl Brohman, Cavill Heugh and Brad Tessman replaced Bryan Niebling, Dave Brown and Greg Dowling. Paul Vautin had missed the first game with a broken arm and was still unavailable.

No longer were there any doubts about the interest shown by New South Wales Rugby League fans. More than 40,000 of them filled the stands at the Sydney Cricket Ground to see a battle royal and a try-scoring feast.

The game started at what had become normal pace for State of Origin, one hundred kilometres an hour and with plenty of niggle. Blocker Roach was awarded an early stint in the sin-bin for kneeing an opponent in a ruck close to his own line. Mal Meninga kicked a goal from the penalty and after six minutes of play the Maroons led 2–0.

Sixteen minutes into the game, with Queensland on the attack deep in Blue territory, Brett Kenny dummied his way through the defence and ran thirty metres before throwing an ill-advised pass to a winger who was absent. The ball went into touch and from the

STATE OF ORIGIN II, 1986
SYDNEY CRICKET GROUND, 10 JUNE

Queensland	New South Wales
Gary Belcher	Gary Jack
Dale Shearer	Brian Hetherington
Mal Meninga	Michael O'Connor
Gene Miles	Chris Mortimer
Les Kiss	Andrew Farrar
Wally Lewis (c)	Brett Kenny
Mark Murray	Peter Sterling
Ian French	Wayne Pearce (c)
Gavin Jones	Noel Cleal
Bob Lindner	Steve Folkes
Darryl Brohman	Peter Tunks
Greg Conescu	Royce Simmons
Cavill Heugh	Steve Roach

Reserves:

Peter Jackson	Terry Lamb
Brad Tessman	David Gillespie

Coaches:

Wayne Bennett	Ron Willey

Referee: Barry Gomersall (Qld)

scrum forty metres out the Maroons mounted an attack on the Blues' line. From a ruck, the ball came quickly to Wally Lewis through Greg Conescu and Muppet Murray. Wally drew three men and put Ian French through a gap to score the simplest of tries under the posts. Mal Meninga converted. Queensland had 8 points to the New South Wales' 0, but the Blues were quick to retaliate. Following a break by Steve Folkes, a sweeping movement downfield sparked by brilliant halves Peter Sterling and Brett Kenny put Andrew Farrar away with a clear run to the left-hand corner. Michael O'Connor failed to convert and the score was Queensland 8, New South Wales 4.

A few minutes later a bustling run by Blues second rower 'Crusher'

Cleal took the ball deep into Queensland territory, and from the play the ball Brett Kenny got outside the defence to take a long pass from Sterling and send O'Connor downfield to score in the identical spot. The scores were locked up at 8 all. When O'Connor missed the conversion they remained that way until the Blues snatched the lead with a try by their captain, Wayne Pearce, in which he both started the movement and finished it. Following a scrum on the Queensland ten-metre line, Pearce ran wide on the blind-side, took a pass from Peter Sterling and sent the ball on to winger Brian Hetherington who passed inside to Blocker Roach. Roach broke a tackle before giving the ball on to Chris Mortimer who found Junior Pearce backing up to take the score to 12–8 in the Blues' favour. Mick O'Connor was not having a good night with the boot and it remained 12–8 after his kick missed.

With the scoreboard clock showing thirty-nine minutes and Queensland on the attack, Wally Lewis punted the ball high in the air to descend in the in-goal wide out. There was a confused scramble and Bob Lindner emerged from the melee lying on the ground with the ball safely in hand. Mal Meninga's kick was astray and the two sides went to oranges with the score 12 all.

Just after half-time a Maroon penalty saw the game restart on the Blues' ten-metre line. Greg Conescu took the tap and passed to Wally Lewis who sent a long pass to Gene Miles. Gary Belcher chimed into the back line, received the ball from Miles and immediately chipped it into the in-goal. Les Kiss and winger Brian Hetherington flew high for the ball. Hetherington got his hand to it, failed to hold it, but knocked it back to Les Kiss who scored the try. It was Queensland 16, New South Wales 12.

In the twenty-first minute of the second half, Barry Gomersall found an offside penalty for the Blues thirty metres from the Queensland goal posts and right in front. Michael O'Connor was untroubled to kick the goal and the Maroons lead was down to a bare two points. The Queensland referee was doing his compatriots no favours and the already lopsided penalty count became 6–1 in the Blues' favour when he awarded them a differential penalty for a Maroon scrum offence. The fifth tackle from the restart was close to the Queensland line. Peter Sterling dummied to hoist the bomb and the Maroons defence moved to cover, but Sterlo slipped the ball to his Parramatta partner instead and 'Bert' did the rest. It was a try to Brett Kenny, and O'Connor made the score 18–16.

With only minutes left on the clock, Andrew Farrar made what might well have been the most determined run of the evening. He broke tackle after tackle before passing to his Canterbury team-mate, Chris Mortimer. Mortimer sent the ball on to Brian Hetherington who put Crusher Cleal away to score under the posts. Michael O'Connor converted, the Blues had taken a firm grip on the game at 24–16, but Queensland hadn't finished for the night. Gary Belcher made a brilliant run, beating four men before he ran Dale Shearer into position and gave him the ball. Shearer outpaced the cover defence and dived in for a try. Meninga converted. The Maroons were down 22–24, and at the final whistle the Blues had clinched the series.

Final result

New South Wales 24 defeated Queensland 20.

Tries for New South Wales: Michael O'Connor, Andrew Farrar, Brett Kenny, Wayne Pearce, Noel Cleal. Goals: Michael O'Connor (2).

Tries for Queensland: Dale Shearer, Les Kiss, Ian French, Bob Lindner. Goals: Mal Meninga (2).

Crowd: 40,707.

Man of the Match: Peter Sterling.

Three weeks later, on 1 July, the teams met again at Lang Park. The victorious Blues made just two replacements. Brian Johnston replaced Brian Hetherington on one wing and Eric Grothe came in for Andrew Farrar on the other. Steve Mortimer's business commitments had caused him to retire from representative Rugby League. Peter Sterling remained the half-back and Junior Pearce retained the captaincy.

The Queensland back line remained unchanged. Bobby Lindner reclaimed his lock position, Bryan Niebling returned to the side in the second row and Brad Tessman replaced Darryl Brohman. Ian

STATE OF ORIGIN III, 1986
LANG PARK, 1 JULY

Queensland	New South Wales
Gary Belcher	Gary Jack
Dale Shearer	Brian Johnston
Mal Meninga	Michael O'Connor
Gene Miles	Chris Mortimer
Les Kiss	Eric Grothe
Wally Lewis (c)	Brett Kenny
Mark Murray	Peter Sterling
Bob Lindner	Wayne Pearce (c)
Gavin Jones	Noel Cleal
Bryan Niebling	Steve Folkes
Cavill Heugh	Peter Tunks
Greg Conescu	Royce Simmons
Brad Tessman	Steve Roach

Reserves:

Grant Rix	Terry Lamb
Ian French	David Gillespie

Coaches:

Wayne Bennett	Ron Willey

Referee: Kevin Roberts (NSW)

French returned to the reserves bench and newcomer Grant Rix joined him there in place of Peter Jackson.

Queensland had lost the series, but there was no thought given by either side to this being a dead rubber. Neither team had ever made a clean sweep of the series, and with the first two games under their belt this became the Blues' Holy Grail. The Maroons were equally determined to prevent it and in the early stages of the game it seemed that this would not be a problem.

In tackle three of the second Maroon possession, Mark Murray played the ball fifteen metres out from the Blues' line. From dummy half, Greg Conescu gave the ball directly to Wally Lewis who threw a pass thirty-five metres to Gene Miles standing wide. It cut out four men and hit Geno right on the chest. The pass enabled him to send Dale Shearer away and despite the attention of four cover defenders, Rowdy scored in the corner. Mal Meninga missed the kick at goal and Queensland led 4–0 after only five minutes. It very quickly became 8–0 when Gary Belcher came up into the back line and hit a gap flying as he collected the ball from Miles, who had received another Wally Lewis special. Gary Belcher beat the cover, but four defenders stood in his way and two of them had handholds somewhere on his person as he carried them and the ball over the line to score in the same corner that Shearer had claimed. Commenting on the game, supercoach Jack Gibson remarked, 'Everything's happening off Lewis.'[4]

Twenty-two minutes after kick-off, it was Lewis again with a slick pass to Miles who found Conescu coming up on his inside to take a pass unmarked and score close to the posts. Meninga was having a bad night with the boot. His attempt from almost in front was a shocker, but it was 12–0 to Queensland and the Lang Park crowd was roaring, confident of ultimate victory. The Queenslanders were on the attack again and only fifteen metres out from the Blues' line when Peter Sterling hit Bobby Lindner with a tackle that dislodged the ball. Swooped on by Gary Jack, it went quickly to Brett Kenny, who sent Michael O'Connor away. The speedster scored a length-of-the-field try right under the posts and then converted it. After scoring three tries to one, Queensland found themselves leading by just one converted try, and then suddenly their lead disappeared altogether.

Ten minutes before half-time, from a ruck just inside his own half, Peter Sterling gave the ball to Brett Kenny. There was nothing on as Kenny ran wide but he spotted half a chance. He accelerated to beat Ian French with pace and run inside Les Kiss on the wing to find Wayne Pearce backing up inside. It was 12 all when Michael O'Connor converted Junior's try.

The Maroons struck back quickly when Mal Meninga made a break and sent Les Kiss away for a try, but again the kick missed. It was Queensland 16, New South Wales 12. Then with less than a minute remaining until half-time an incident occurred that decided the footy game.

Following a sustained assault by the Blues, Junior Pearce was pulled down less than a metre from the Queensland line. Big front-rower Peter Tunks was at dummy half and in a hastily contrived Maroon defence Gary Belcher took his place immediately to the right of the marker. The 100-kilogram-plus Tunks lunged at the lightweight fullback and was over the line carrying the ball under his right arm. Quickly realising that the right elbow wasn't going to make it to the try-line, Peter Tunks attempted to transfer it to his left hand but in completing the transfer the ball tumbled forward onto the try-line where he forced it with his left hand.

So near but yet so far …

In later years not even the most biased video referee could have given the Blues the benefit of the doubt, but in 1986 referees had no such assistance. It was a case of 'call it as you see it', and unfortunately for the Queenslanders, and despite plain evidence to the contrary, what Kevin Roberts saw was a try. It was 16 all.

What followed after half-time was a feast of defensive football and frustrated, high-quality attack, a feast provided by both sides. For thirty-five minutes of the second half the score remained even, until Greg Conescu failed to mark up straight right in front of the goal posts. An O'Connor penalty from close range gave the lead to New South Wales at 18–16. With two minutes to go, and desperation prevailing, Queensland looked to be in with a chance. In misfielding a Lewis kick deep into territory, Brian Hetherington appeared to knock the ball forward, but referee Roberts ruled it knocked back. The crowd booed him incessantly for the remainder of the game and then there was an incident that angered them even more. Cavill Heugh dived over the try-line from dummy half under a pile of blue guernseys and appeared to have scored a try. Roberts ruled that he was short of the line. From the subsequent ruck, the ball was kicked into the in-goal and fielded by Brett Kenny. As he dived to secure it he appeared to lose the ball forward. It was pounced on by Greg Conescu who grounded it. As the full-time hooter sounded, he claimed a try, and jubilant Maroons commenced to hug each other and jump up and down, Roberts ignored them and blew the whistle for full-time.

There is no doubt that Queensland were good things beaten. This was particularly galling to their supporters, since they believed that the Blues had prevailed on the back of some controversial refereeing decisions, the Tunks try being decidedly dodgy. However, beaten they were, and New South Wales had achieved a 3–nil whitewash. It was a magnificent achievement after a hard–fought series in which the greatest margin in any game was the six points by which the Blues won Origin I. In Origin III, Queensland scored one more try than New South Wales, but whereas Michael O'Connor kicked three goals to supplement the three tries that they scored, the normally accurate boot of Mal Meninga failed the Maroons and their sixteen points came from four tries.

But Origin III, 1985, revealed one unchallengeable truth about the game, a tenet which would stand the test of time. The series was decided before the game was played and New South Wales had won. Yet without doubt Origin III was the most bitterly contested of all three games and it proved the point that there is no such thing as a dead rubber in State of Origin Rugby League.

Final result

New South Wales 18 defeated Queensland 16.

Tries for New South Wales: Wayne Pearce, Michael O'Connor, Peter Tunks. Goals: Michael O'Connor (3).

Tries for Queensland: Dale Shearer, Les Kiss, Gary Belcher, Greg Conescu.

Crowd: 21,097.

Man of the Match: Brett Kenny.

Despite Queensland's loss of two series in a row, and six games out of the last seven, Wally Lewis was accepted universally in Rugby League as the heart and soul of State of Origin football, and when he was named as the Kangaroos' captain for the English tour, he was the first Maroon to be so honoured since Tom Gorman led the Kangaroos to England in 1929. The 1982 Kangaroos came home in 1983 wearing the title 'The Invincibles', but they were no more invincible than Wally Lewis's 1985 touring party, which set records everywhere it went. In twenty matches played on tour they scored

139 tries and had only 16 scored against them. The British public loved them and their appearance in the first Test at Manchester drew what was then a world Rugby League record attendance of 50,583. But the Queenslanders returned to find a situation where their recent exploits didn't seem to be all that relevant. All eyes were focused on the Queensland Rugby League and its pending decision regarding the entry of a Brisbane team in the New South Wales competition.

Regardless of what means were found to accomplish this, it was accepted as an immutable fact that Lewis would be its captain and there was other outstanding Queensland talent likely to be available. Besides Wally Lewis, seven Queenslanders played Test football for Australia in England that season: Les Kiss, Gene Miles, Mal Meninga, Dale Shearer, Bryan Niebling, Greg Dowling and Bob Lindner. All but Meninga and Shearer were available to form the foundations of a competitive team if the Queensland Rugby League accepted the New South Wales League's offer of a place in their 1987 competition.

Bill Hunter was the chairman of the Queensland Rugby League and he was aware that when the question was asked the vote would be close. Bill was in favour of the proposal but he knew that a tied vote was likely. He had long made up his mind that, if this occurred, he would not use his casting vote as chairman to break the deadlock. When he called for a show of hands, he found that only four of his colleagues favoured the proposal while five voted in the negative. If the chairman had voted according to his convictions, it would have been a five all deadlock and his casting vote would have decided the issue. He abstained in the initial ballot and the motion was lost 4–5. There would be no Brisbane team playing in Sydney in 1987.

The Wynnum–Manly stars Lewis, Dowling and Miles were not the only players who were dwelling on the establishment of the new Brisbane club and the decision created a stampede. Before the first ball was kicked in 1987, fifty-nine Queensland footballers, the equivalent of four football teams, had signed contracts with Sydney clubs. Wally Lewis and star centre Gene Miles declared their intention to join the gold rush and actually flew to Sydney and negotiated contracts with Manly, but Ron McAuliffe had outmanoeuvred them. When they spoke to the Queensland Rugby League about a release, they discovered that the fine print of their contracts contained clauses which related to future options, one of which gave the Queensland Rugby League the right to meet any offer made by a southern football club.

The deals that the King and Geno negotiated proposed two separate payments — a comparatively modest one by the Manly club, and another, larger one to be paid by the club's main sponsor, Kerry Packer, owner of the Channel 9 television network. Under their contracts, the Queensland Rugby League had only to meet the amount that Manly had offered and they were prepared to do this. Wally and Geno protested, loudly, since this was less than half of the total offer, but Ross Livermore pointed out that the Packer contribution wasn't his concern. The contract only required the Queensland Rugby League to meet the Manly offer and any amount promised by Kerry Packer or any of his companies was a legal irrelevance.

The King and his chief courtier were tied to Queensland for another year and it so happened that this was entirely compatible with Ron McAuliffe's business plans.

CHAPTER 8

Birth of the Broncos

IN 1984 Ron McAuliffe resigned from every position he held bar one. He remained as chairman of the Lang Park Trust, a non-elective post to which he was appointed by the Queensland government. Despite his lifelong affiliation with the Labor party, Ron McAuliffe was a close friend of Sir Edward ('Top Level Ted') Lyons, a financier who acted as chief adviser to the rabid anti-socialist premier of Queensland. Sir Edward shared sporting interests and a close friendship with the Labor senator, a political aberration by any measure.[1]

In 1986–87 Ron McAuliffe was also the titular head of a group known as the Norwood–MacKay syndicate, which had been formed with the intention of bidding for a new Rugby League franchise for Brisbane. The Norwood in the syndicate represented money. Alister Norwood was the Principal of Jeans-West, a nationally famous clothing company that had its origins in West Australia. His partner, Jim McKay, was a Victorian sporting entrepreneur and marketing specialist. The two men had been involved in an unsuccessful bid for the licence that established the Bears Australian Rules team in Queensland.[2]

Neither Norwood nor McKay had the kind of background that might inspire the confidence of the Rugby League hierarchy. However, Ron McAuliffe was board chairman, and he intended to involve other prominent Rugby League identities. There would be an appropriate balance of money and expertise within the group.[3]

What this syndicate proposed was a Rugby League club similar to no other in existence in Australia — one that would have no voting members and no social obligations. It would be a privately owned entity employing full-time professional players and conducted purely for profit. In discussing the new venture with his close friend Dick Turner, McAuliffe once said, 'Well, Richard, a man is entitled to make a quid, isn't he.'[4]

Since Richard Turner had made a considerable number of quids during a long career in business, he could not but sympathise with the senator's view.

A second syndicate had been formed by Darryl Van der Velde. A former A Grade second-row forward with Brisbane Souths, Van der Velde was coach of the Redcliffe A Grade team in the Brisbane competition. Later a group composed of three former international footballers, Bob Hagan, John Sattler and Peter Gallagher, also threw its hat into the ring. Barry Maranta, the sports-minded businessman who facilitated the acceptance of the State of Origin principle, and his future son-in-law, Steve Williams, sponsored a fourth syndicate that included Queensland financier Paul Morgan and Brisbane publican and businessman Gary Balkin.

Ron McAuliffe effected a major coup when he persuaded first Gene Miles and then Wally Lewis to join his bidding entity. This made it a very hot favourite, both with the media and with the public. He also had strong reason to believe that he had created difficulties for any other bidder through an arrangement he had made between the Lang Park Trust and Castlemaine Perkins, the makers of Queensland's most popular brand of beer.

The New South Wales Rugby League laid down certain fixed financial parameters that would have to be met by an applicant, and handed these to the Queensland Rugby League, the members of whose committee then had two decisions to make. First they would have to decide whether or not to allow the plan to go forward. If they voted to proceed, there would be a decision to make regarding the most suitable applicant.

Ron MacAuliffe had served as deputy chairman of the Australian Rugby League for many years and he and Australian Rugby League supremo Ken Arthurson enjoyed a long and close association. It is not surprising that Arko quite openly favoured the bid by a syndicate headed by an old friend, the depth of whose commitment to Rugby League and its future was unquestioned.[5] If this alone wasn't sufficient to ensure the acceptance of the Norwood–MacKay bid, then McAuliffe had the declared support of the biggest name in Rugby League, that of Wally Lewis, whose God-like figure was presented to the faithful many times each night in a television advertisement for the senator's other ace-in-the-hole, Fourex Beer and its brewers.

On Castlemaine Perkins' behalf, and for thirty seconds at regular intervals each evening, scenes of Wally preparing for the fray and doing battle with the hated Blues flashed onto television screens throughout Queensland to the accompaniment of an extremely catchy jingle:

> Here's to Wally Lewis, for lacing on his boots,
> Sometimes he plays it rugged, sometimes he plays it cute.
> He slices through their backline, like a Stradbroke Island shark.
> There's glue on every finger, he's the Emperor of Lang Park.[6]

Almost every sports-minded child in Queensland and most of the adults knew the words in full or in part. Wally Lewis was a public idol, and with such support, MacAuliffe's incomparable record of service to the game, and more than adequate finance to support it, the McAuliffe–Norwood–MacKay bid looked to be a racecourse certainty. Arko and the executive of the New South Wales Rugby League had a right to assume, as did most people, that the interests of Ron McAuliffe and his associates were safe in the hands of the senator's northern friends.

But all of the traditional Brisbane senior clubs did not take the same view as Dick Turner of Redcliffe. Most were far from enthusiastic about having a Sydney club operating in their midst. On 23 March 1987 the Queensland Rugby League executive met at Lang Park and once more the proposal was put to the meeting.

Ron McAuliffe struck a major hurdle when he was questioned about his continued involvement with the Lang Park Trust. Asked if he intended to relinquish his position as chairman of the trust in the event of his syndicate obtaining the franchise, he replied, 'I would leave that up to the members of the trust.'

Bill Hunter felt that, with the support of Sir Edward Lyons and

Sir Joh Bjelke-Petersen, the senator would retain his chairmanship of the Lang Park Trust regardless of any opposition, and that this would be, prima facie, a breach of ethics or law, perhaps both, in that it might lead to a conflict of interest.[7] He considered that it would be unwise to allow the process to proceed to a competitive vote to select the franchise holder until this was cleared up. When the motion was put, the nine directors voted 5 votes to 4 to reject the proposal. The chairman abstained and it was lost.

The decision created pandemonium among the media people waiting outside the meeting venue. Surrounded by microphones and cameras immediately following the meeting, Hunter calmly stonewalled the harassing questions of reporters with a four-word statement, 'A vote was taken.'

It could not be the end of the matter. A battle between the Norwood–Mackay–McAuliffe interests and the Maranta–Morgan party ensued as they lobbied the individual Brisbane clubs for their support. This kept the pot boiling and Barry Maranta was as busy as a one-armed paperhanger with dermatitis.

He made an amazing discovery. After he talked to all of the Brisbane club presidents directly, he found that popular assumptions regarding the level of support for MacAuliffe among Brisbane's club officials were optimistic in the extreme.

> As an outsider, I could never have imagined the level of distaste that existed … it threw me … absolutely threw me … we discovered that we had a momentum going for us. Gary Balkin was critical in these discussions. Gary was locked in with Souths, and had a long association with Brisbane Rugby League clubs. We found that MacAuliffe didn't have it all his own way and from there, we gathered momentum.[8]

There was bid and counter bid to the clubs by both syndicates. The final offer by Maranta was that, rather than accept a $2,000,000 lump-sum compensation bid offered by Norwood–McKay, the Queensland Rugby League would be better off with 30 per cent of the profits of the new enterprise. The offer's generosity was enhanced by a condition that saw the Maranta–Morgan syndicate assume sole responsibility for all losses. Maranta also gave an undertaking that his company would match each club's sponsorship raisings on a dollar-for-dollar basis up to a limit of $10,000. As a final sweetener, the Queensland Rugby League was offered seats for two members on the club's board of directors. The total package made the League something more than a 30 per cent financial partner in the enterprise and gave it a voice in company policy, all at no cost and with no financial risk. It was an offer in the Godfather mould, too good to refuse. The Maranta syndicate saw light at the end of the tunnel. In early April there was a dramatic development when the Brisbane Rugby League rescinded its opposition, and then, on 5 April, the Queensland Rugby League executive passed a resolution to once more put the wheels in motion. This time the vote was unanimous, but the MacAuliffe–Norwood–Mackay group was no longer the red hot favourite that everyone had believed it to be.

That the Maranta–Morgan group had a lot going for them was clear to anyone who examined the background of the syndicate's four principals. Maranta's professional expertise in the sporting world was well known. He was the man who stole Greg Chappell, Australia's cricket captain, from South Australia and brought him to Queensland. And he was a former first grade footballer to boot.

Besides being a former first grader and a Bulimba Cup[9] representative, Paul Morgan was the high-profile entrepreneur who raised the money that financed *Crocodile Dundee*, the most successful movie ever made in Australia. Steve Williams was one of Brisbane's brightest young advertising gurus and had been responsible for upgrading the Queensland Rugby League's marketing strategy to make it one of the most successful enterprises of its kind in Rugby League. He was also a former Maroon who played five-eighth for Queensland.

The fourth member of the syndicate was from a family known all over Queensland through its ownership of hotels in Brisbane and in the bush. Gary Balkin, a publican and the son of a publican, was once a flying winger for Brisbane in the old Bulimba Cup competition. He was a life member of Souths and the club's Patron.

On 14 April 1987 the Queensland Rugby League met to make a decision and the executive faced its moment of truth. The three Brisbane delegates had been persuaded by the offer of 30 per cent of the profits, three of the country delegates voted with them, and the Morgan–Maranta syndicate got the nod by seven votes to three. Thus were born the Brisbane Broncos.

There is a touch of sadness in Barry Maranta's view of the result: 'That we won the licence was really a reflection of the fact that the body of Rugby League was voting no confidence in MacAuliffe. As an outsider, I never could have imagined this happening.'[10]

Ron McAuliffe did not accept defeat gracefully and he still had many supporters within the Rugby League hierarchy, so the path trod by the new club was not a smooth one. In setting their financial parameters, the Maranta–Morgan Syndicate planned to support the team that played in the New South Wales Rugby League competition with two teams, a first grade side and another in an age grade, both registered with the Brisbane Rugby League. These plans went sadly awry when the Brisbane Rugby League slammed both doors in their faces. The new club would have to look elsewhere. The Broncos were left with no option but to enter a Reserve Grade side in the Sydney competition and this was an expense for which they had not budgeted.

The rejection of the Broncos by the Brisbane clubs posted a warning that the relationship between the new club and the Queensland Rugby League heirarchy would be difficult, but then there was the 'landlord'. Under the terms of their franchise, the Broncos were committed to play at Lang Park, and since Ron McAuliffe still chaired the Lang Park Trust there was no expectation that the team would be warmly welcomed.

The result didn't cause anyone in Sydney to break out the champagne either. Later, Ken Arthurson was to write:

> My personal belief was that the Jeans-West (Norwood–McKay) proposal was easily the superior of the two. To an extent I was swayed by Ron McAuliffe's view; he was strongly and bitterly against the Broncos' proposal.[11]

'Strongly and bitterly opposed' is a fair description. The new club was to find that its future relationship with every level of higher authority on both sides of the Tweed River would be a little on the cool side, if not downright frosty. This was unfortunate, since, regardless of all else, this new local team was certain to provide the players who would be the foundation of all future Queensland State of Origin sides. There were interesting times ahead for Rugby League.

Meanwhile, there were three State of Origin games to play in 1987, the first on 2 June at Lang Park.

CHAPTER 9

1987

An American Journey

MARK ('Muppet') Murray was one of the pillars on which Queensland's early State of Origin success was built. He earned his first Maroon jumper in a non-State of Origin game in 1981. Ross Henrick was the preferred half for State of Origin that season but Muppet got the nod in 1982 and proceeded to work the scrum in fourteen consecutive State of Origin matches. Tragedy struck in July 1986, when a playful wrestling match at the Valleys' League's club saw a glass broken and a portion of it enter Muppet's left eye. The wound healed, but he was left with permanent double vision and that was the end of his Rugby League career.

Mark Murray's contribution to Queensland football stands adjacent to that of Wally Lewis and his contemporaries who saved Queensland Rugby League from extinction and gave it self-respect. His premature retirement was a savage loss, but the Queensland Rugby League was fortunate in the youngster who replaced him. His selection came as something of a surprise to a lot of supporters and even officials, but it wasn't long before they were to be astounded when they saw how he could play footy.

If Allan Langer had moved to a town where he wasn't known in 1987, the local high school could have rung him in as half for their Under 14 team, no questions asked. Short, boyish, almost child-like in appearance with a light build that belied his great strength, Allan sported a tuft of fair curly hair, that quickly gained him a nickname garnered from a popular television character, A.L.F., short for Alien Life Form. They called him Alf or Alfie and he was an eye-opener.

Injury to Mal Meninga necessitated a change in the backs from the side that had gone down to the Blues in 1986. Peter Jackson came into the centres, the first time he had been selected in the run-on side, and Tony Currie was also moved from the Reserves bench to wing to replace Les Kiss. The forwards also had a different look, being without Wally Fullerton Smith and Bryan Niebling. Ian French came in to lock the scrum, while Martin Bella made his State of Origin debut in the front row. Sydney Souths hard man and second-rower Les Davidson was an inclusion in the front row for the Blues and the New South Wales referee, Mick Stone, was also a debutante.

STATE OF ORIGIN I, 1987
LANG PARK, 2 JUNE

Queensland	New South Wales
Gary Belcher	Gary Jack
Dale Shearer	Andrew Ettingshausen
Gene Miles	Mark McGaw
Peter Jackson	Brian Johnston
Tony Currie	Michael O'Connor
Wally Lewis (c)	Brett Kenny
Allan Langer	Peter Sterling
Ian French	Wayne Pearce (c)
Paul Vautin	Steve Folkes
Trevor Gillmeister	Noel Cleal
Martin Bella	Pat Jarvis
Greg Conescu	Royce Simmons
Greg Dowling	Les Davidson

Reserves:

Colin Scott	David Boyle
Gary Smith	Des Hasler

Coaches:

Wayne Bennett	Ron Willey

Referee: Michael Stone (NSW)

As was fast becoming traditional, Lang Park was packed for the kick-off and the game blew up seconds later when Michael O'Connor took exception to the vigour of a Wally Lewis tackle. The punch he threw didn't bother the King too much, but the penalty that it brought was gratefully accepted. With no Mal Meninga in the side, Peter Jackson was the designated kicker. He hadn't impressed anyone during a hastily arranged practice session earlier in the day, but with this one almost in front he potted it and the score was Queensland 2, New South Wales 0.

The game settled into the hard grafting mode expected in State of Origin, but the crowd rose to their feet and roared twenty-seven minutes after the game started when Tony Currie crossed the line and grounded the ball off a short pass from Allan Langer. Cheers turned to loud boos as the Queenslanders voiced their disagreement with Mick Stone when he ruled a forward pass. Two minutes later their disappointment was compounded. With the Maroons deep in Blues' territory, Crusher Cleal made a bust and passed to Mick O'Connor. With Allan Langer looming in cover defence, O'Connor kicked deep. Alfie turned and chased and it came down to a foot race that could have but a single outcome. Alfie did his best but he couldn't pace it with one of the fastest men in either code of Rugby. O'Connor gathered the ball in and scored under the posts before converting his own try: New South Wales 6, Queensland 2.

There was further Maroon consternation to follow. Tony Currie must have offended the gods of chance, because three times in the first half bad passes to Tony went either to ground or into touch when a better delivery would have seen him score. Then eight minutes before half-time, with the Queenslanders pressing, Gary Jack made a break for the Blues. Tony Currie ran him down and grounded him less than ten metres short of the Maroon try-line. From the ruck, Royce Simmons ran about three paces and sent the ball on to Les Davidson who was having a wow of a game in the Blues' front row despite playing out of position. The Souths second-rower took the ball on the fly and scored the Blues' second try. O'Connor missed the kick, but it was New South Wales 10, Queensland 2.

It seemed certain that this would be the half-time score, but a determined Maroon attack took the ball deep inside the Blues' half and Wally Lewis put on a blind-side move close to the line. Big Greg Dowling came through, took the pass from Wally and scored in the corner. The try remained un-converted and, when the referee called half-time, Queensland went back to the sheds only four points down. The score was 10–6 in favour of the Blues.

In the second half the Blues attacked from the kick-off but it was twenty four minutes before there was any addition to the score. With Noel Cleal held up just short of the line, Peter Sterling acted as dummy half and gave the ball to Brett Kenny. He moved it quickly to Michael O'Connor who had only to bend down and place the ball over the line. He then converted the try from wide out. At 16–6, New South Wales looked to be away to a match-winning lead, but within minutes Wally Lewis weaved his blind-side magic again when he worked the run around with Peter Jackson before he put Dale Shearer away. Rowdy ran more than fifty metres to score. Following his earlier success with a simple conversion, Peter Jackson had produced two bad misses with penalty shots. His captain tore up Jacko's goal-kicking contract and Gary Belcher converted Shearer's try. The Queenslanders were again within four points, and with only four minutes left to play, another Lewis blind-side move put Tony Currie over in the corner, this time for a fair try and the equalising one. It was 16 all.

With both sides desperate to score and only two minutes thirty seconds left in the match, a New South Wales field goal attempt missed. The Queenslanders regained possession from a dropped ball soon after the 22-metre drop-out and put on a move which broke down when Gene Miles failed to take a pass on the Blues' quarter-way line. Snapped up by the Blues, the ball was thrown from man to man in desperate haste. With full-time almost upon them, the Blues kicked long into the in-goal. As the ball was about to trickle over the dead ball line, the flying 'Sparkles' McGaw dived and touched it down, but only the referee, the Blues and the small handful of their supporters who were present at Lang Park believed it was a fair try. Thirty thousand Queenslanders screamed their dissent, certain that Sparkles had touched the ball down either on the dead ball line or in touch. But the referee's opinion was the only one that counted

---

Final result

New South Wales 20 defeated Queensland 16.

Tries for New South Wales: Michael O'Connor (2), Mark McGaw, Les Davidson. Goals: Michael O'Connor (2).

Tries for Queensland: Dale Shearer, Tony Currie, Greg Dowling. Goals: Gary Belcher, Peter Jackson.

Crowd: 33,411.

Man of the Match: Les Davidson.

---

and Michael O'Connor's conscience was clear when he converted the try. New South Wales had won the match 22 points to 16.

With Meninga still on the injured list, an attempt to improve the Queensland team's goal-kicking capability for the second game saw Colin Scott replace Tony Currie on the wing in the run-on side, and the Maroons travelled to Sydney to meet the Blues at the Cricket Ground on 10 June.

Heavy rain fell in Sydney on game day and continued into the night. The Sydney Cricket Ground could well have been renamed the Sydney Cricket Swamp. It was a sea of slush and mud. The rain was still bucketing down when the teams ran out, yet the largest crowd ever to attend an interstate game packed the stands and bleachers for this second game of the 1987 series. With four wins in a row to contemplate, the Blues' supporters eagerly anticipated another New South Wales victory, and nine minutes after kick-off it seemed likely that their dedication might be rewarded.

A Blues' kick landed deep in the Maroon half, struck a patch of mud, skidded without bouncing and was picked up by Dale Shearer. A determined chase by Michael O'Connor, a slippery ball and a solid tackle caused Shearer to lose possession. Andrew Farrar snapped up the ball, took off for the line and scored in good position for O'Connor to convert: New South Wales 6, Queensland 0.

Six points in such conditions have been enough to win many a game. The Blues were handling the mud better than the Maroons, but the slippery ball was difficult to control. Blues' half-back, Peter Sterling, attempted to drop-kick a field goal in the eighteenth minute,

---

STATE OF ORIGIN II, 1987
SYDNEY CRICKET GROUND, 10 JUNE

Queensland	New South Wales
Gary Belcher	Gary Jack
Dale Shearer	Andrew Farrar
Gene Miles	Mark McGaw
Peter Jackson	Brian Johnston
Colin Scott	Michael O'Connor
Wally Lewis (c)	Brett Kenny
Allan Langer	Peter Sterling
Bob Lindner	Wayne Pearce (c)
Paul Vautin	Steve Folkes
Trevor Gillmeister	Les Davidson
Martin Bella	Pat Jarvis
Greg Conescu	Royce Simmons
Greg Dowling	David Boyle

Reserves:

Tony Currie	Paul Langmack
Ian French	Des Hasler

Coaches:

Wayne Bennett	Ron Willey

Referee: Barry Gomersall (Qld)

---

but the ball simply stuck in the slush where he dropped it. Then, in the thirty-third minute of the game, there was a scramble close to the Blues' line. Allan Langer recovered a dropped New South Wales ball and passed to Dale Shearer who scored a try to bring the scores closer. The conversion attempt by Colin Scott was a failure, but Queensland was well in it at 4–6 down. After 40 minutes the score was still New South Wales 6, Queensland 4.

Shortly after play resumed, the two full-backs indulged in a long-range, old-fashioned kicking duel. The crowd failed to appreciate what was almost a lost art. They expressed their displeasure and when Gary Jack sought to end it by sending Brian Johnston away, the winger was absolutely flattened in a tackle by Wally Lewis. This angered New South Wales supporters, several of whom threw missiles at the Queensland captain, but they were even more upset a little later. Gene Miles made a strong run and positioned Greg Dowling for a pass. The Wynnum–Manly front-rower dived over for the try that put Queensland in front. The score was 8 points to 6. Colin Scott's attempt at conversion missed, but with only minutes to go Scott sealed the match for the Maroons when he crossed after collecting a Wally Lewis pass. The try was scored right in the corner, conversion with the mud-heavy ball a hopeless task.

Despite a strong last-gasp attack by the Blues, the Queenslanders held on to win the match. The score was 12 points to 6, but although the Blues finished within a converted try of the Maroons score, this was a comprehensive three tries to one victory. Wally Lewis had no doubt as to his choice for Man of the Match. As the teams strolled off the almost submerged ground, he threw his arm around the shoulder of Alf Langer, drew his head toward him and bestowed a muddy kiss on the crown of the little half-back's muddy thatch. However, his opinion was of no account. To the disgust of the Maroons, and despite their comprehensive victory, the Sydney-based Channel 9 broadcasting team chose the Blues' half-back, Peter Sterling, as Man of the Match.

Final result

Queensland 12 defeated New South Wales 6.

Tries for Queensland: Dale Shearer, Greg Dowling, Colin Scott.

Tries for New South Wales: Andrew Farrer. Goal: Michael O'Connor.

Crowd: 42,048.

Man of the Match: Peter Sterling.

The teams came back to Lang Park on 16 July to play the decider and Queensland again made only one change. Bryan Niebling returned from injury to replace Martin Bella in the front row. As was their habit, the Blues made several changes.

It was the deciding game. The Blues had won the 1985 series,

STATE OF ORIGIN III, 1987
LANG PARK, 15 JULY

Queensland	New South Wales
Gary Belcher	Gary Jack
Dale Shearer	Brian Johnston
Gene Miles	Brett Kenny
Peter Jackson	Andrew Ettingshausen
Colin Scott	Michael O'Connor
Wally Lewis (c)	Cliff Lyons
Allan Langer	Peter Sterling
Bob Lindner	Wayne Pearce (c)
Paul Vautin	David Boyle
Trevor Gillmeister	Les Davidson
Bryan Niebling	Peter Tunks
Greg Conescu	Royce Simmons
Greg Dowling	Phil Daley

Reserves:

Tony Currie	Mark McGaw
Ian French	Steve Folkes

Coaches:

Wayne Bennett	Ron Willey

Referee: Barry Gomersall (Qld)

whitewashed the Maroons in 1986, and at the start of the season they considered themselves to be the best of good things to make it three in a row in 1987. But after two games, the scores were one plays one. Origin II had been an epic, and the Maroons were quietly confident as they ran on to the cheers of a capacity Lang Park crowd.

But motivation is one thing, performance something else, and when first Michael O'Connor and then debutante five-eighth Cliff Lions made long breaks and forced a Queensland line drop-out in the first minutes of play, alarm bells started to ring. In the commentary box, former Maroon Mick Veivers predicted that Michael O'Connor was about to 'cut them to ribbons', but he was quickly forced to change his tune. Five minutes after kick-off the Maroons had the

Blues penned inside their own quarter line, and following a fifth-tackle kick and chase Alfie Langer just missed scoring when the ball beat him over the dead ball line by millimetres.

After Queensland regained possession from the drop-out, Wally Lewis's kick found touch close to the Blues' try-line and New South Wales' hooker Royce Simmons was penalised for feet up in the ten-metre scrum. Greg Conescu took a quick tap and passed to Allan Langer. A chain passing movement ensued. With no pass travelling more than two metres, the ball went from Langer to Greg Dowling then back to Alfie who sent it on to Wally Lewis. Lewis passed to Gary Belcher. Belcher hot-potatoed it to Bobby Lindner who crossed for the try. The Queenslanders led 4–0, and the score was unchanged after Colin Scott's unsuccessful attempt to convert.

The Queenslanders continued to dominate possession, with the Blues' defence equal to the task of restraining them. On those occasions when the Blues did get their hands on the ball, the Maroon defence was equally impenetrable. Seventeen minutes into the first half, with Queensland attacking on the halfway line, Wally Lewis's fifth-tackle kick was charged down by the Blues' captain, Wayne Pearce. Pearce's reflex grab at the ball as it bounced met with success and he quickly sent it wide to Bryan Johnston on the wing. Johnston came inside and as the defence closed in he passed to second-rower David Boyle who ran thirty metres to score under the posts. Michael O'Connor converted and New South Wales led Queensland by 6 points to 4.

From the restart, the Maroons lost control of the ball when the referee awarded an offside penalty to the Blues. The tap to restart took place just inside the Blues' half, but when Les Davidson knocked on, Maroon front-rower Bryan Niebling snapped up the ball and streaked away, to be tackled on the Blues' 22-metre line. Subsequent play saw the Blues trapped in their own in-goal and forced to drop-out from the goal line. On the third tackle, Greg Dowling found himself in possession fifteen metres out from the Blues try-line, surrounded by four defenders. Dale Shearer was in the clear fifteen metres away. He signalled to Greg Dowling who put boot to ball and lobbed a perfect chip kick, exactly where Shearer was able to claim it and touch down. Once again, the conversion kick was astray but the Maroons were in front. It was Queensland 8, New South Wales 6.

Nine minutes before half-time a Michael O'Connor penalty evened the scores at 8 all. Four minutes before half-time Trevor Gillmeister made a break. When he lost the ball in a tackle, Peter Sterling came up with it and put the ball into the air for Michael O'Connor to chase. The tactic worked well. O'Connor made a perfect catch and was about to set sail for the line when the whole thing came unstuck. Referee Gomersall blew the whistle and told him he had been in front of the kicker and offside. This meant a penalty back where the ball was kicked, well within goal-kicking range.

The Maroons had tried a number of kickers that season, but there were no Mal Meningas among them. A number of candidates had demonstrated their wares at training on that very afternoon, and on the strength of the comparative performances Wally Lewis threw the ball to Dale Shearer for the tie-breaker. The phlegmatic Rowdy cooly potted it between the uprights from thirty-five metres out and as the teams left the field for half-time the scoreboard showed Queensland 10, New South Wales 8.

The second half of Origin III was Rugby League on a grand scale, but it was an epic in which not a single point was scored. A measure of the Queenslanders' dominance in the first half can be found in the tackle count. The Blues had been forced to make almost eighty tackles, Queensland just fifty. With such an overwhelming tackle differential, a Blues' collapse in the second half would have been excusable, particularly since the Maroon dominance persisted. But if the first half was an arm wrestle, the second was trench warfare. Each side defended in its own quarter as if their lives depended on it, whereas the no-man's-land between belonged to whoever had the ball at any given time, and like the no-man's-land of a deadly battle it was often littered with the bodies of the fallen. Yet they rose time and time again and hurled themselves back into the fray.

Both sides used their two reserves. Cliff Lyons ran himself into the ground in defence. He was replaced by Mark McGraw after twenty minutes, and a little later Blues' coach Ron Willey sent Steve Folkes out to give David Boyd a spell. On the Maroon side, Gene

Miles had come into the game injured. Midway through the second half he was rested and Tony Currie took his place. A little later, Ian French came on for Bryan Niebling who had been hurt early in the half. Greg Dowling hurt his arm and shoulder badly, but with both reserves already in action he refused to leave the field.

Clinging desperately to their two-point lead, the Maroons had enough possession to win six Rugby League games, but the defence was equally desperate. In the nineteenth minute of the second half, the Queenslanders received a penalty on their own quarter line. Play restarted deep in the Blues' half, and when Tony Currie was grounded on tackle three the ball was less than ten centimetres from the try-line. The Blues' got possession from a knock-on but the Maroons gained a goal-line drop-out when Gary Belcher and Bob Lindner tackled Junior Pearce and drove him back into his own in-goal.

The goal-line drop-out that followed was the first of seven consecutive such kicks as the Queenslanders pinned the Blues to their try-line. The defenders were forced to make more than forty consecutive tackles as the overwhelming flood of Maroon possession saw them driven back into their own in-goal time after time. When the sequence of drop-outs was broken, it was by a gang tackle that sent the Blues' ball carrier over the sideline a metre out from the try-line.

It was a magnificent defence by the Blues, but in the end it did them no good. A score of 10–8 was good enough. With the Blues' still unable to work the ball out of their own half, the hooter sounded the end of the struggle and it was time for the Queenslanders to celebrate. Lawrie Kavanagh told the story in the Brisbane *Courier-Mail* the next morning:

> Queensland grabbed back the Winfield State of Origin championship at Lang Park last night with an heroic second half shut-out of a desperate New South Wales.
>
> Wally Lewis's Maroons ended three years of disappointment in winning 10–8, beating New South Wales in the area in which they were edged out in 1985 and 1986 — by showing superior discipline under the special demands of Origin Rugby League.
>
> The Queenslanders hurled themselves into each other's arms at the siren and went to all corners of the stadium to salute their fans at the end of another magnificent Origin contest.

Pint-sized Alan [sic] Langer won the man of the match award but forwards Trevor Gillmeister, Paul Vautin and Bryan Niebling and fullback Gary Belcher played leading roles ... One jolting tackle by Gillmeister on New South Wales hooker Royce Simmons ... will be long remembered.

Queensland ... were more settled and sharp in attack. Their kicking game was superior and they made better use of the boot ...

Final result

Queensland 10 defeated New South Wales 8.

Tries for Queensland: Dale Shearer, Bob Lindner. Goal: Dale Shearer.

Try for New South Wales: David Boyle. Goals: Michael O'Connor (2).

Crowd: 32,603.

Man of the Match: Allan Langer.

There was one additional Origin contest played in 1987 when the two teams travelled together to Los Angeles to showcase Rugby League to the Americans. The Queenslanders had climbed their mountain and at no point did they take the project seriously in any competitive sense. The State of Origin trophy was safely stowed in the Queensland Rugby League boardroom at Lang Park, and for the Maroons the visit to the United States was their end-of-season outing, the game an exhibition. Castlemaine-Perkins sponsored the Maroons' journey and stocked the aircraft with their product. Once the plane began its flight, Wally Lewis and his men settled down to indulge in a pastime traditional with touring sporting teams. They made an earnest endeavour to drink the bar dry, but they received no cooperation whatsoever from the Blues. Such was the Blues' disappointment at the loss of the State of Origin series that they would go to any length to restore some vestige of their lost pride.

The New South Wales Rugby League hierarchy told their men to prepare for the contest as though it was a deciding test match. The two teams were segregated aboard the aircraft, New South Wales for'ard, Queenslanders aft. Although the Blues' management stopped short of posting armed guards to separate them, fraternisation was firmly discouraged.

Canterbury's chief executive, Peter 'The Bullfrog' Moore, was the Blues' team manager and he and coach Ron Willey kept vigilant watch. Up for'ard, only soft drinks were served.

The excursion cost the Australian Rugby League more than half a million dollars, and since they holidayed in Las Vegas after the football match the Queenslanders, at least, considered the money well spent. Whether the exercise served to lift the profile of the game in America is a moot point. It certainly didn't cause any group in the United States to go out and buy a Steeden football and start playing Rugby League and no one has ever discovered a good reason to reprise the venture.

For the record, Queensland 18 lost to New South Wales 30. The game was played at the Veterans' Memorial Stadium at Long Beach in suburban Los Angeles, and most of the 12,349 slightly bemused Californians who watched the game were college students who had been rounded up at the local UCLA campus and given free tickets.

CHAPTER 10

1988

No Sad Song for the Senator

NINETEEN EIGHTY-EIGHT was the Year of the Horse, and love them or hate them the Brisbane Broncos were here to stay. It would not be an especially brilliant season for the new side. They didn't make it to the semi-finals that year, but the debut of a Queensland team into the New South Wales competition caused a sensation right from the start. In their very first game at Lang Park on 6 March 1988 the Broncos met Manly, and they buried the 1987 Sydney premiers by 44 points to 10. The victory was no surprise to any Queenslanders who knew their Rugby League, nor was the extent of it. True to the predictions that had been made since the first discussions of the New South Wales Rugby League's plans for expansion, the Broncos side was heavily laced with State of Origin talent. Led by the King, the list included Gene Miles, Greg Dowling, Colin Scott, Bryan Niebling, Allan Langer, Greg Conescu and Joe Kilroy.

Nor was it any source of amazement when the new club went on to defeat, in turn, Penrith, Wests, Norths, Parramatta and New-castle, before losing a match to Balmain on 17 April. By the time that the State of Origin sides were selected for the first game of the season, the Broncos had lost a couple more, but they had a 7–3 winning record, and their contribution to the Queensland team was considerable, although there was one significant name missing. Origin I, 1988 was to be the twenty-first such interstate match since the

State of Origin concept was first trialled in 1980. Wally Lewis had played in all twenty games, and captained Queensland in nineteen of them. During Brisbane's 22–25 loss to the Gold Coast Giants on 7 May, the King suffered a badly bruised shoulder in a savage tackle by Ronnie 'Rambo' Gibbs. He would be a spectator for this one, replaced by Peter Jackson of Canberra as five-eighth. The captaincy fell upon the broad shoulders of Paul Vautin, only the third player to captain the Maroons in eight years of State of Origin.

For the first time since the concept was introduced, the New South Wales Rugby League hosted two of the three games in the series. This was also the first New South Wales versus Queensland match ever played at the new Sydney Football Stadium.

Allan Langer's selection for the Queensland side in 1987 had been a matter of some discussion but neither his youth nor his size had proven a handicap. He had done everything asked of him and more and won Man of the Match in the deciding game. But he had done all of that playing alongside Wally Lewis. Jack Gibson had once pointed out that everything happened around the King. With Wally Lewis unable to play five-eighth, no Queensland replacement with any experience of the position at State of Origin level existed. While Peter Jackson was no stranger to Alfie, he had huge boots to fill. So did Paul Vautin, who found himself captain of a side that had been Wally's and Wally's alone for seven years.

As standard operating procedure, the Blues selectors had introduced a number of new faces, starting with the coach. John Peard replaced Ron Willey, and with Gary Jack serving a suspension, Jonathon Docking, the Cronulla fullback, had his first Blue guernsey. Brett Kenny was out for the season with a knee injury and Cliffy Lyons was given his five-eighth spot.

Referees often like to stamp their authority on a game early and it took Barry Gomersall only one minute and twenty-six seconds to penalise the Blues for offside, twenty-eight metres out from their own line and right in front of the goal posts. Gary Belcher kicked the goal and Queensland led 2–0.

In the next ten minutes the Maroons murdered at least three tries and good teams exact payment for such ineptitude. In the thirteenth minute of the game, Michael O'Connor presented the Blues' bill.

STATE OF ORIGIN I, 1988
SYDNEY FOOTBALL STADIUM, 7 MAY

Queensland	New South Wales
Gary Belcher	Jonathon Docking
Alan McIndoe	Andrew Ettingshausen
Gene Miles	Mark McGaw
Tony Currie	Brian Johnston
Joe Kilroy	Michael O'Connor
Peter Jackson	Cliff Lyons
Allan Langer	Peter Sterling
Paul Vautin (c)	Wayne Pearce (c)
Bob Lindner	Steve Folkes
Wally Fullerton Smith	Noel Cleal
Martin Bella	Steve Roach
Greg Conescu	Royce Simmons
Sam Backo	Les Davidson

Reserves:

Scott Tronc	Terry Lamb
Brett French	David Trewhella

Coaches:

Wayne Bennett	John Peard

Referee: Barry Gomersall (Qld)

Crusher Cleal burst through tackles and ran the ball inside the Queensland quarter. From the play the ball, Peter Sterling spotted O'Connor wide and unmarked, threw him a long pass and watched the former Union player stroll over in the corner. The Blues led 4–2 when the try scorer missed the conversion.

Two minutes after the restart of play, Greg Conescu won a scrum against the head fifteen metres out from the Blues' line. Alfie ran the blind and beat Peter Sterling to the corner. The kick was a bit outside Gary Belcher's normal range and it was Queensland 6, New South Wales 4 after the conversion attempt.

Ten minutes before half-time Steve Roach made a charge from close to the Maroons' line and was stopped centimetres short of scoring by Allan Langer, but a Queenslander was penalised for offside in the play the ball. Michael O'Connor kicked the goal to tie the score at 6 all. Three minutes later Allan Langer ran the ball from deep in his own half. Under pressure from the defence, he chip-kicked over their heads. Andrew Ettingshausen came across to recover the ball. Just as he had it almost in hand, the hard-chasing Langer kicked it from his fingertips and chased again. Fullback Jonathon Docking's attempt to collect the ball suffered a similar fate as Alfie caught up with it. The Bronco half-back tapped it forward with his toe, caught it as it bounced and then sprinted over the line to score under the posts. Gary Belcher added the extras and the Maroons went to half-time with a lead of 12–6.

Eight minutes after half-time Greg Conescu worked a dummy half move with Gary Belcher to send Peter Jackson in for the try that made it 16–6. Then with a try by Alan McIndoe which Gary Belcher failed to convert, and another which he scored himself and did convert, the Maroons led 26 points to 6 with seven minutes to go. Late tries by Andrew Ettingshausen and Mark McGaw, both converted by Michael O'Connor, served to make the score look more respectable, but when the final siren sounded a disappointed crowd of Blues' supporters trailed out of the new Sydney Football Stadium in the knowledge that the invaders from the North were off with a 1–0 lead in the 1988 State of Origin series.

With the next game due just fourteen days later, the Blues challenged front-rower Sam Backo's eligibility to play for Queensland. Sam was a late bloomer as representative footballers go. A North

---

Final result

Queensland 26 defeated New South Wales 18.

Tries for Queensland: Allan Langer (2), Peter Jackson, Alan McIndoe, Gary Belcher. Goals: Guy Belcher (3).

Tries for New South Wales: Michae O'Connor, Andrew Ettinghausen, Mark McGaw. Goals: Michael O'Connor (3).

Crowd: 26,441.

Man of the Match: Allan Langer.

Queenslander, born in Ingham, he was recruited directly from Cairns by the Canberra Raiders when that club first joined the New South Wales Rugby League in 1982. He was a veteran in his fifth year of First Grade Rugby League before he attracted the attention of the Queensland selectors. His long association with Canberra gave certain people the impression that he was a New South Welshman, but this was not the case. He earned his eligibility for Queensland in North Queensland during his teenage years and this was easy to confirm. Wally Lewis had recovered from his shoulder injury so Peter Jackson returned to the centres and Tony Currie moved to the wing at Joe Kilroy's expense. 'The Axe', Trevor Gillmeister, returned to the side as a fresh reserve.

STATE OF ORIGIN II, 1988
LANG PARK, 21 MAY

Queensland	New South Wales
Gary Belcher	Gary Jack
Alan McIndoe	John Ferguson
Peter Jackson	Mark McGaw
Gene Miles	Michael O'Connor
Tony Currie	Andrew Ettingshausen
Wally Lewis (c)	Terry Lamb
Allan Langer	Peter Sterling
Paul Vautin	Paul Langmack
Bob Lindner	Steve Folkes
Wally Fullerton Smith	Wayne Pearce (c)
Martin Bella	Steve Roach
Greg Conescu	Ben Elias
Sam Backo	Phil Daley

Reserves:

Trevor Gillmeister	Paul Dunn
Brett French	Des Hasler

Coaches:

Wayne Bennett	John Peard

Referee: Michael Stone (NSW)

State of Origin I, 1988 had been a free-flowing affair with plenty of tries scored, all of them by the backs. Origin II was nothing like that. Very early on, a head-high tackle on Greg Conescu by Blues' prop, Phil Daley, sparked an all-in ruckus and the two chief contestants were banished to the sin-bin by referee Mick Stone. This upset the parochial Lang Park crowd who howled in protest. The fight occurred in that part of the field closest to Lang Park's Fourex can bar. When Wally Lewis's role in the melee caused Mick to suggest that the Queensland captain might also benefit from a spell in the sin-bin, the protest reached a crescendo, with yellow Fourex cans, both empty and full, being hurled at the referee as he quickly ducked out of range. The game had to be stopped while attendants picked up the hardware that littered the ground.[1] Whether it was the rest period thus gained, or an infusion of spirit garnered from their supporters, the Maroons seemed inspired when play resumed. They attacked constantly and although they failed to put the ball over the line Gary Belcher's boot put them in front 4–0. Not long before half-time, a dropped Maroon ball gave the Blues an opening. Michael O'Connor took full advantage. He picked it up and outpaced the defence to score. He converted his own try and at half-time New South Wales led 6 points to 4.

Sam Backo drove through a ruck to score near the posts just after half-time and Queensland led 10–6. Then not long before full-time Allan Langer and Greg Conescu worked a simple reverse pass move and the little half-back crossed for a neat try near the posts. Gary Belcher added the extras and the score at the final siren was 16–6 in favour of Queensland.

Final result

Queensland 16 defeated New South Wales 6.

Tries for Queensland: Sam Backo, Allan Langer. Goals: Gary Belcher (4).

Try for New South Wales: Michael O'Connor. Goal: Michael O'Connor.

Crowd: 31,817.

Man of the Match: Sam Backo.

With two wins under their belt, and the series theirs, the Queensland State of Origin side travelled to Sydney for the third game and they had the opportunity to make history. Up to that point, Queensland had won thirteen games of State of Origin football and New South Wales had won 10, but of the six three–game series completed, New South Wales had won only two and Queensland four. The Maroons were two games up but there was a burr under their saddle. In 1986 the Blues had achieved the first and only 3–0 State of Origin whitewash and they were very chesty about it.

The Maroons wanted that third game.

The Blues scored early after Gary Jack broke away downfield. He found Wayne Pearce in support and the team captain touched the

---

STATE OF ORIGIN III, 1988
SYDNEY FOOTBALL STADIUM, 21 JUNE

Queensland	New South Wales
Gary Belcher	Gary Jack
Alan McIndoe	John Ferguson
Peter Jackson	Mark McGaw
Tony Currie	Michael O'Connor
Joe Kilroy	Andrew Ettingshausen
Wally Lewis (c)	Cliff Lyons
Allan Langer	Des Hasler
Paul Vautin	Paul Langmack
Bob Lindner	Steve Folkes
Wally Fullerton Smith	Wayne Pearce (c)
Martin Bella	Steve Roach
Greg Conescu	Ben Elias
Sam Backo	Steve Hanson

Reserves:

Trevor Gillmeister	Noel Cleal
Brett French	Greg Florimo

Coaches:

Wayne Bennett	John Peard

Referee: Greg McCallum (NSW)

ball down only three metres from the left-hand goal post. O'Connor quickly made it 6–0 and the clock showed that only six minutes had elapsed since the first whistle.

The Maroons quickly struck back. After recovering the ball from a New South Wales error, Lewis and his men took play downfield. After a ruck ten metres out from the Blues' line, Wally Lewis dummied to Tony Currie, went himself and scored in a handy spot for Gary Belcher to convert. The score was 6 all after just eight minutes of play. Shortly afterwards, an offside penalty enabled Michael O'Connor to put the Blues in the lead again, and only two minutes later, with the Blues leading 8–6, a Queensland error saw them score another try. Sloppy passing on the sixth tackle left Peter Jackson to make an awkward clearing kick which was charged down by Ben Elias who pounced on the loose ball. He whipped a pass out to Des Hasler who sent John Ferguson away to touch down in the corner. Michael O'Connor missed the conversion and the score favoured the Blues 12–6.

The Maroons defence lacked cohesion, and they were making a lot of errors in other areas as well. Pearce's men took every advantage of this and some chain passing saw the ball end up with debut forward Steve Hanson who scored under the posts. The game was 24 minutes old, the Blues led 18–6 and Queensland was in trouble. Big Sam Backo came to the rescue. Taking the ball from the dummy half, he broke tackles and ran downfield before he gave it to Allan Langer who scooted away to score. Once more the Belcher boot was up to the job and the Blues' lead was reduced to six points.

With only two minutes to go until half-time, the Queenslanders knocked on while defending within their own ten-metre line. Greg Conescu saved the day by winning a scrum against the feed. After only two tackles, Wally Lewis put the boot to the ball and sent it deep into the New South Wales half where a Blues' error saw a scrum packed down thirteen metres from their line. It was a Maroon loose head and feed with only seventeen seconds to play. After one tackle, ten metres out, Wally Lewis ran the ball wide, passed to Sam Backo running free on his inside and Sam took some weak defence over the line with him as he scored. Gary Belcher converted and the two teams went to oranges with the score at 18 all.

Twelve minutes into the second half Queensland scored again. Alfie chip-kicked — a little punt that dribbled no more than five metres and turned the defence around. He picked it up and speared it straight to Peter Jackson who ran fifteen metres with the cover defence at his heels before he dived over the line amid a welter of arms and legs. He rolled as he hit the ground and from a prone position, reached back over his head and touched the ball down. Belcher's score was four out of four when he kicked the goal to convert. After a passing rush that took play downfield, Benny Elias made a break and got the ball away to Des Hasler who sent Michael O'Connor away to score in the corner. He missed the kick and it was Queensland 24, New South Wales 22, but Sam Backo extended the lead again when he ran up the middle to take an inside pass from Greg Conescu to score his second try alongside the right-hand upright. Gary Belcher made it five out of five and the score was 30–22.

Martin Bella was concussed by a shoulder charge and had to leave the field, replaced by Trevor Gillmeister. The Queenslanders had an eight-point buffer but they weren't done yet. With eleven minutes to go, Joe Kilroy scored a nice try after some good lead-up work between Gillie and Allan Langer. Gary Belcher spoiled his perfect goal-kicking record but the score was 34–22. Then with the game within two minutes of its finish, the Sydney crowd were treated to an 'Alfie special'.

Taking the ball as first receiver, Allan Langer put a beautifully judged grubber kick into the corner. Substitute winger Brett French

---

Final result

Queensland 38 defeated New South Wales 22.

Tries for Queensland: Sam Backo (2), Joe Kilroy, Allan Langer, Wally Lewis, Peter Jackson, Brett French. Goals: Gary Belcher (5).

Tries for New South Wales: Michael O'Connor, John Ferguson, Wayne Pearce, Steve Hanson. Goals: Michael O'Connor (3).

Crowd: 16,910.

Man of the Match: Sam Backo.

outpaced the Cronulla flyer, Andrew Ettingshausen, to dive on the ball for the final try of the game. The Maroons were big winners by 38 points to 22.

To beat New South Wales three out of three had special significance for the team, for the management and for Queensland. It squared the ledger for the 1986 series defeat by New South Wales and there was one Queenslander who took special joy from the Maroons 3–0 whitewash. As one of his Labor colleagues would say about another, later win, it may well have been the sweetest victory of all for Ron McAuliffe. But it was tainted. While he still retained his strong ties to the game, and his deep and abiding interest in the accomplishments of the Maroons, the coming of the Broncos had estranged the senator from some of the people who had previously been closest to him.

In the last years of his chairmanship, and in the first of his consultancy, the Queensland Rugby League was served, and served well, by a triumvirate that was hand-picked by McAuliffe. Wayne Bennett worked for the league in a coaching role, John Ribot served as its development officer, and Wally Lewis was appointed to promote Rugby League among school children. In this year of Queensland's greatest triumph, all three were alienated from their former chief. Ribot was chief executive officer of the Broncos, Bennett was their coach, and the former apple of the senator's eye, Wally Lewis, was the captain of the new club. In 1987 McAuliffe had been disappointed (in fact, enraged) at the failure of his syndicate to gain the franchise. He could live with the departure of Bennett and Ribot to join the enemy in 1988, but the departure of the man who he loved like a son was a savage blow. McAuliffe's and Lewis's was one of the great partnerships of Rugby League.

There is no doubt that time would have healed the wound. Perhaps McAuliffe would have been reconciled to the Broncos, too. Soon after gaining the franchise, the Broncos' chairman, Paul Morgan, told Wally Lewis's biographer, Adrian McGregor, 'It is a travesty that with his knowledge, experience and charisma we don't have him on the board.'[2]

But if a quick reconciliation was ever on the cards, the 'Gunfight at the Powers Corral' served to ensure that the chairman of the Lang

Park trust was unlikely to extend the hand of friendship to his new tenants soon, if ever.

One of the conditions attached to the franchise for the new football team was a requirement that it use Lang Park as its home ground and this posed a problem. The Broncos had negotiated the richest sponsorship ever obtained by a Rugby League club, with Mr Bernie Power who had just introduced his own brand of beer to the Queensland market. What is more, the contract provided for the value of the sponsorship to be increased in proportion to any increase in the sales of Powers Beer. Wally Lewis had terminated his promotional contract with Fourex and the famous television commercials with 'the Emperor lacing on his boots' had disappeared from public view. Instead, the Emperor of Lang Park was featured in a new campaign for the new brewery. People had begun to walk into bars all over Queensland and ask for a pot of 'Wally's Brew' and Powers and the Broncos were doing very nicely.

Castlemaine Perkins had been taken over by Western Australian interests controlled by that famous yachtsman and even more famous fraudster Alan Bond, and to emphasise his transfer of allegiance from the Bond-owned Fourex, each of the King's new television commercials ended with the King sucking down a goodly draught of Wally's Brew direct from the can. As he lowered the container he would exclaim 'Aaahh ... that's better'. Then with a sidelong glance and a mischievous smile at the camera, he would say 'Sorry, Bondie'.

Powers' beer sales soared, but not at Lang Park. The Lang Park trust went beyond simply banning its sale in the bars and kiosks around the ground. Bernie Power wasn't even allowed to give it away to the friends he entertained in his corporate box.

Maranta and his crew were honourable men. They had accepted sponsorship of an unprecedented kind from Bernie Power. They felt they had a duty to leave no stone unturned to promote his product, and they had their own reasons to sell more of it. Prior to the Broncos' first encounter with the historic St George club, which was bound to draw a near-capacity crowd, a Powers advertising man conceived a ruse whereby wider brand recognition might be achieved. At half-time at Lang Park that afternoon, the Brisbane Broncos led St George by 10 points to 8, and when the referee signalled the break Wally Lewis assembled his team at the northern end of the ground where they arranged themselves in suitable poses on the turf, Rugby Union style, to peel and consume their oranges and strew the peels upon the greensward. With the oranges came attendants bearing some wooden stakes and a large roll of calico. They proceeded to drive the stakes into the ground and then to use the roll of calico to screen the players from the view of the crowd. Unrolled, it was revealed to be a large and garish advertisement for POWERS BEER. Aware of the sponsorship controversy, most of the nineteen thousand spectators knew immediately that this was a move that might create a sensation and applauded accordingly. Ron McAuliffe watched the performance from the stand. He didn't applaud, and he didn't say 'Aaaah ... that's better.'

The former League president remained well and truly estranged from his former associates at the Broncos, including Wally Lewis. In time, Bernie Power sold his brewery to Castlemaine-Perkins' major competitor, Carlton United, and Powers Beer became history. Fourex assumed its rightful place as a major sponsor of the Broncos, and perhaps, in time, Ron McAuliffe would have accepted an invitation to join the Broncos board. It seems certain that one would have been offered,[3] but it was never to be. Just seven weeks after the Maroons completed their whitewash of the Blues, Ron McAuliffe was dead of a stroke. An account of his funeral appeared in the Brisbane *Courier-Mail* on 17 August 1988: 'Queensland Rugby League officials said goodbye to Ron McAuliffe yesterday, not with misty eyes and handkerchiefs but with a brass band. That was the way he wanted it.'

Perhaps 'Gunsynd'[4] had a premonition. Ron had discussed the arrangements with Dick Breen, the manager of the Lang Park Leagues Club, less than a week before he fell ill. He told Dick: 'I will leave you some money, and when I go I want you to bring a band in here and put plenty of booze on to blast me away.'[5]

Ron was a long-time parishioner at St Patricks Church in the Valley where he had spent so much of his time. One of Brisbane's larger houses of worship, it was hard pressed to contain the hundreds who attended Ron McAuliffe's funeral and the crowd overflowed into the churchyard. Wally Lewis joined a party of notables as one of his pall bearers.

Supercoach Bobby Bax took teams to more Brisbane Grand Finals than any two coaches put together. He was also an off–course, unregistered Turf Accountant who had done considerable Starting Price business with the senator over the years. Bob wrote in his football column in the *Courier-Mail*:

> McAuliffe's one ambition was to see Queensland beat New South Wales three–nil. Our State of Origin whitewash of the Blues was achieved this season.
>
> He was hellbent on improving the standard here ... McAuliffe was tough, and made tough decisions, but he was never one who had trouble in making a decision and trying hard to make it work.

The *Courier-Mail*'s Sports Editor, Barry Dick, wrote McAuliffe's epitaph:

> RONALD EDWARD McAULIFFE, born Brisbane 25 June 1918. School, St Joseph's (Gregory Terrace). Senator for Queensland 30.6.71 to 30.6.81. Warrant Officer II AIF Middle East, New Guinea. Joint secretary Queensland Rugby League, Brisbane Rugby League, chairman Queensland Rugby League, deputy chairman Australian Rugby League, chairman Rothmans National Sports Foundation, chairman Lang Park Trust.
>
> We would not have had State of Origin football without Ron McAuliffe and for that alone every League supporter owes the man a huge debt. Ron was always good for a quote and he would come up with a little gem like: 'The best committee consists of three people with two away sick.' Or, 'You can't sit on the fence and have your ear to the ground at the same time.' Or; 'All things considered, it is awfully hard to be humble when you are a Queenslander.' And 'Wally Lewis is the high priest of the spectacular ...'
>
> Ron was typical of the men of his generation; men who were born at the end of the First World War and who fought in another. He loved a drink, loved an argument, loved a punt and most of all, he loved company. He was lost without people and he was a marvellous host ... It is not often that you call a man twice your age 'mate', but I will always be proud to say that is what Ron was to me.[6]

CHAPTER 11

1989

Unchallengeable Champions

IT IS A fact of life that the requirements of representative football in general, and the State of Origin competition in particular, severely affect the premiership chances of the Brisbane Broncos every season. Yet, as club policy, there has always been a determination to do everything possible to ensure Queensland's continued domination of the annual State of Origin series.[1] Five Broncos contributed to the 1988 clean sweep over New South Wales, and following the transfer of Peter Jackson and Sam Backo from Canberra to Brisbane during the off-season, there were seven of the 1988 Maroons in the First Grade squad at the club's Red Hill headquarters pre-season 1989. Three of them were among the *Rugby League Year Book*'s five players of the year.[2] Wayne Bennett had coached the Queensland team in 1988, and his record in the State of Origin competition stood second only to that of Artie Beetson. Both coaches were totally committed to Queensland and to the defeat of New South Wales whenever the two sides met.

Far from resenting State of Origin's interference with the Club's premiership campaign, the Broncos coach was a Queenslander who held a strong belief that representative football should always take precedence.[3] However, his loyalty would be severely tested in 1989.

In 1989 the Blues carried a good deal of inexperience within their ranks. There were six debutantes selected in the seventeen to play the first State of Origin game and it was said that the side also lacked leadership. Much blame for this was laid at the door of their 1988 captain, Wayne Pearce, and half-back Peter Sterling. They had apparently placed their club's interest first, and declared themselves unavailable for what threatened to be a disruptive mid-season tour of New Zealand by an Australian team. The League decreed that they were therefore also ineligible for selection for State of Origin. However, Sterling's replacement, Des Hasler, had played twelve Tests for Australia, only six fewer than Sterling, and was equally well experienced at State of Origin level. Pearce's leadership had not prevented a Maroon whitewash in 1988 and his replacement, Cronulla back-rower Gavin Miller, would win the Dally M Player of the Year trophy in 1989.

New South Wales had Laurie Daley, Glen Lazarus, Chris Johns, Bradley Clyde, John Cartwright and Mario Fenech wearing the Blue guernsey for the first time, but since five of the six would, between them, go on to play seventy Tests for Australia, they were pretty fair substitutes for whoever was dropped. Southern officials had boasted for years that New South Wales could easily find two teams good enough to beat the best that Queensland had to offer. This was their chance to prove it and Queensland wasn't far behind the Blues in the debutante stakes anyway.

A media explosion occurred in Brisbane at the start of the season when 1988 reserve grader Kerrod Walters was preferred to international Greg Conescu as hooker at the Broncos for 1989, but the nineteen-year-old had earned his spurs. He also replaced Conescu in the State of Origin side after just thirteen First Grade games. When Michael Hancock ran on to Lang Park on the evening of 28 May 1989, he was the youngest footballer ever to play State of Origin for either state. Of the other replacements, only Shearer could claim great experience at State of Origin level. Trevor Gillmeister played two games in 1987, and was a replacement in one in 1988. Gary Coyne and Michael Hagan were both making their debut. It might also be suggested that Gene Miles was a debutante. After a long career, and sixteen State of Origin games as a centre three-quarter, Miles was about to reinvent himself as a second-row forward.

But the Maroons were not short of leadership. They had it in spades. Wally Lewis was about to play his twenty-fourth State of

STATE OF ORIGIN I, 1989
LANG PARK, 23 MAY

Queensland	New South Wales
Gary Belcher	Gary Jack
Michael Hancock	John Ferguson
Mal Meninga	Andrew Farrar
Tony Currie	Laurie Daley
Alan McIndoe	Chris Johns
Wally Lewis (c)	Terry Lamb
Allan Langer	Des Hasler
Bob Lindner	Bradley Clyde
Paul Vautin	Gavin Miller (c)
Gene Miles	Paul Sironen
Martin Bella	John Cartwright
Kerrod Walters	Mario Fenech
Dan Stains	Paul Dunn

Replacements:

Trevor Gillmeister	Glen Lazarus
Dale Shearer	Greg Alexander
Gary Coyne	Andrew Ettingshausen
Michael Hagan	Chris Mortimer

Coaches:

Arthur Beetson	Jack Gibson

Referee: Mick Stone (NSW)

Origin game, he was leading Queensland for the twenty-third time, and coach Arthur Beetson stood unchallenged as the doyen of Origin coaches.

Jack Gibson was the most highly regarded coach in Rugby League, but he was new to State of Origin. Jack had made a study of American sports coaching and he was an innovator, prepared to try a little gamesmanship. With the home side already on the field and exercising in various ways, Gavin Miller ran out at the head of his team followed by a single player, his five-eighth, Terry Lamb. The two Blues were loudly hooted by the Lang Park crowd, while Gary Jack stood fast at the tunnel outlet at the head of the remainder of the side until the massive chorus of boos for his captain and vice-captain subsided. The fullback then led the remainder on to the field.

Jack Gibson's purpose, if this was his initiative, was something of a puzzle, although it may well have been a ploy to bring good luck. If it was, it worked well. Alan McIndoe knocked-on in his own in-goal fielding the kick-off. This gave the Blues a golden opportunity from a five-metre scrum, but they failed to show a profit. Queensland gained possession from a New South Wales error and quickly moved the ball downfield. A long chase came to nought when Wally Lewis's kick went dead in goal. There was another unusual diversion at this point when the Blues' hooker, Mario Fenech, took the 22-metre tap to restart play. Standard practice was to place the ball on the ground, tap it with the side of the foot, then pick it up and pass it to a runner. Mario didn't do that. He placed the ball on the ground, then stood upright and heeled it back to Des Hasler. Des did a reverse run-around with Terry Lamb, got the ball back and was tackled on the spot where Mario took the tap. This was even more puzzling than the decapitated team run-on before play, but Mario continued to do it all night so no doubt there was some sound, if totally obscure, tactical reasoning behind it.

The Queenslanders continued to attack and after thirteen minutes their patience was rewarded. Wally Lewis made a long break from within his own half and passed to Mick Hancock who took the ball down to the Blues' twenty-metre line before he was tackled. The Blues were penalised for being offside as he played the ball. Allan Langer took a quick tap, threw a thirty-metre pass to his right winger and Alan McIndoe had a clear run to the line. Mal Meninga quickly made it Queensland 6, New South Wales 0.

Midway through the first half, with the Blues attacking inside the Queensland quarter, Mick Stone penalised Gene Miles for lying in the ruck. Laurie Daley's attempt at goal was a shocker, flying metres wide of the posts. Wally Lewis took the 22-metre drop-out and kicked the ball sixty metres downfield to bring play inside the Blues' half, and a dropped ball right on halfway was recovered by Bob Lindner. Bobby gave it to Paul Vautin who beat four men in a magnificent run which ended twenty metres from the line. Fatty's quick play the ball to Lewis went quickly to Allan Langer, on to Tony Currie, then to Mick Hancock who scored within easy kicking distance. Mal Meninga converted. It was 12–0.

Just three minutes after the restart of play, Kerrod Walters made a break downfield before passing to Mal Meninga who was tackled on the Blues' twenty-metre line. Gene Miles made a burst from the play the ball. He passed to Allan Langer close to the line and Alfie produced a trademark short chip and chase into the in-goal where he beat Gary Jack to the ball and scored under the posts. Mal Meninga converted. The Queenslanders were away to an 18–0 lead and there was still more than ten minutes to half-time. The Blues were playing catch up, and had men over near the Queensland try-line when Wally Lewis tackled the dummy half from an offside position. Judged to be a professional foul, this earned him a ten-minute stint in the sin-bin, but with four minutes to go until half-time, twelve Maroons held the Blues pointless until the hooter sounded for the break.

At half-time Artie Beetson gave his troops a simple instruction: 'Don't attempt to play them inside your own quarter, get hold of the ball, kick it away early in the tackle count, then chase it.'

This was sound advice since the Blues launched a determined attack from the kick-off. Nine minutes into the half Terry Lamb put up a mid-field bomb. A nasty misunderstanding between Gary Belcher and Alan McIndoe saw the ball spilled and recovered by the Blues, but they failed to capitalise when their winger was tackled into touch. From the scrum, some magnificent chain passing by both the Maroons' forwards and their backs took play into the New South Wales half, with the full width of the field used in both directions. From a play the ball twenty metres out, Gary Belcher served Wally Lewis from dummy half and then worked the run-around to regain possession. He passed to Allan Langer who found that Wally had doubled around him to take the ball and send it on to Mal Meninga. Mal finished the movement off in style, then turned to face the grandstand. With arms and legs akimbo, he waved clenched fists to celebrate a great try. After fifteen minutes of the second half it was 22–0. The try scorer's attempt at goal failed, but just three minutes later another passing movement saw Bob Lindner beat three players before he gave the ball to Mal who made it a double when he scored wide out. He missed with another conversion attempt but Queensland led 26 points to nil. When play restarted, the Maroon backs were away again. Wally Lewis ran from a ruck and passed to fullback Gary Belcher. Belcher got outside his man and gave the ball inside to Gene Miles who was tackled about eight metres from the line. Falling, he sent a one-handed pass to Bob Lindner who was backing up. The back-rower gave Mal Meninga a relatively easy kick by scoring halfway between the right-hand post and the touchline. The conversion hit a goal post before bouncing over the bar and the Maroons were fireproof at 32–0.

Some loose play by the Queenslanders allowed the Blues to attack again and after a scramble close to the line Andrew Ettingshausen followed a little kick by Des Hasler to touch down. The television replay showed that ET was at least a pace offside when the ball was kicked, but video referees were something for the future and Mick Stone didn't bother to consult his linesman before he awarded the try. Laurie Daley had also discovered where the goal posts were. This time he kicked the goal. It was Queensland 32, New South Wales 6.

Not long before the final siren Michael Hancock matched Mal Meninga's double. Given the ball only five metres out, right on the sideline and with only centimetres in which to move, he bullocked off a determined tackle by his Broncos' team-mate, Chris Johns, and stayed in the field of play long enough to put the ball down in the corner. The kick from the sideline missed and Queensland ran out winners 36 points to 6, the greatest winning margin by either side since State of Origin football commenced.

Final result

Queensland 36 defeated New South Wales 6.

Tries for Queensland: Michael Hancock (2), Mal Meninga (2), Alan McIndoe, Allan Langer, Bob Lindner. Goals: Mal Meninga (4).

Try for New South Wales: Andrew Ettinghausen. Goal: Laurie Daley.

Crowd: 33,088.

Man of the Match: Martin Bella.

Three weeks later the two sides met once more, this time on the Blues' home turf, the Sydney Football Stadium. The Blues selectors made several changes to their run-on side, although there were only four men dropped from the seventeen who contested the first game. Greg Alexander replaced Des Hasler as half, Chris Mortimer replaced his Canterbury team-mate Terry Lamb as five-eighth, Andrew Ettingshausen was in the centre instead of Andrew Farrar, Paul Sironen was out of the second row and Bruce Maguire was in, and Mario Fenech had a new front-rower to support him in Peter Kelly. Of the seventeen who donned Blue guernseys for the first game, Terry

---

STATE OF ORIGIN II, 1989
SYDNEY FOOTBALL STADIUM, 14 JUNE

Queensland	New South Wales
Gary Belcher	Gary Jack
Michael Hancock	John Ferguson
Mal Meninga	Andrew Ettingshausen
Tony Currie	Laurie Daley
Alan McIndoe	Chris Johns
Wally Lewis (c)	Chris Mortimer
Allan Langer	Greg Alexander
Bob Lindner	Bradley Clyde
Gene Miles	Gavin Miller (c)
Paul Vautin	Bruce Maguire
Martin Bella	Peter Kelly
Kerrod Walters	Mario Fenech
Sam Backo	Paul Dunn

Replacements:

Trevor Gillmeister	Des Hasler
Dale Shearer	John Cartwright
Gary Coyne	Brad Mackay
Michael Hagan	Alan Wilson

Coaches:

Arthur Beetson	Jack Gibson

Referee: David Manson (Qld)

Lamb, Andrew Farrar, Glen Lazarus and Paul Sironen made the supreme sacrifice, while Des Hasler and John Cartwright joined Brad Mackay and Alan Wilson on the bench.

With a capacity crowd of more than 40,000 packed into the Sydney Football Stadium, Origin II commenced in ordinary enough fashion — in rather similar style to Game I, in fact. The Blues kicked off and although the man receiving the kick-off didn't knock on, someone else did almost immediately and the Queenslanders were on their own line at once, engaged in desperate defence. They held the Blues out and when they did get their hands on the ball Michael Hancock ran it back into the Blues' half with tremendous determination. From the play the ball, Kerrod Walters fed Wally Lewis who sent the ball on to Allan Langer. Langer found Bob Lindner outside him and Lindner positioned Michael Hancock for the pass before sending him away to score in the corner. Mal Meninga kicked the conversion from the touchline and Queensland led 6–0 after just five minutes of play.

The resumption of play suggested that the Maroons' game plan required them to restart with a knock-on. Sam Backo took the ball from the kick-off and promptly dropped it. Once more desperate defence was the order of the day, until an offside penalty was given against the Queenslanders well within kicking range. Laurie Daley's position as preferred kicker for the Blues became pretty shaky after a disastrous attempt that rose hardly more than a metre off the ground.

Defence by both sides was savage, with players quick to 'bean bag' the tackled man. Following one such tackle just eighteen minutes into the game, Allan Langer failed to rise. It was a body blow to Queensland when the stretcher was called for and Alfie was carried off. He did not return and was replaced by Michael Hagan. There was a brief flare of fisticuffs when Martin Bella swung a punch at Bruce Maguire after being held back during a ruck, and such was the strength of the defence on both sides that a low-scoring game seemed a prospect. Sensing this, Wally Lewis attempted a field goal in the twenty-first minute. He had no luck and the score remained 6–0.

Blues' half-back Greg Alexander, was having an outstanding game, and a quarter of an hour before half-time the Blues seized an opportunity when he skied a mid-field bomb and a gaggle of Maroon and Blue guernseys gathered under the descending ball. Gary Belcher was jostled as he attempted the catch. The ball popped out of his hands and straight into those of Laurie Daley who put it down under the posts for a four-pointer. Laurie's brief kicking career had run its course. Greg Alexander made it six and the scores were tied at 6 all.

With nine minutes remaining until half-time, Mal Meninga went down in a heavy tackle and didn't get up again. He was forced to leave the field with his eye socket shattered. Not long after Dale Shearer took his place there was more consternation in the Queensland camp when Mick Hancock stayed down after a tackle. He had damaged a shoulder joint but he played on.

Sam Backo had made a total of twenty-one tackles in the first half. Paul Vautin hurt his leg early in the game, carried the injury through most of the first half and made almost as many. Trevor Gillmeister took Fatty's place after half-time. Twelve minutes into the second half, with the Maroons in possession in their own half, Gary Belcher cut through at pace and unloaded the ball to Alan McIndoe. McIndoe raced downfield before giving it to Dale Shearer who streaked away. When the cover defence crowded him, Rowdy passed inside to Michael Hagan who quickly put Kerrod Walters through a gap. Kerrod put his ears back and headed for the try-line. Gary Belcher converted his try and Queensland was once more in the lead, 12 points to 6, but just five minutes later Bob Lindner was down with a leg injury. Bobby could only just manage to walk, which was not surprising since he had broken his tibia. At about the same time, Mickey Hancock's damaged shoulder gave up. He left the field, to be replaced by Gary Coyne, and for the good of the team, Bob Lindner gritted his teeth and played on. Coyne moved into the pack, Gene Miles resumed duty as the Maroons centre and Tony Currie moved to the wing. The Maroons were fortunate. After they reshuffled the backs, they still had an international three-quarter line, but Bob Lindner was on borrowed time and Tony Currie had taken a hard knock halfway through the second half.

Fortune favours the brave. Halfway through the second half, Wally

Lewis ran from a ruck almost in front of the New South Wales posts and some fifteen or so metres out. The King dummied to pass left, then ran to his right. He turned Greg Alexander inside out, left Chris Mortimer grasping at nothing and then fended off Laurie Daley and Gary Jack to score a superb try. It was 16–6 and although Gary Belcher failed to convert the try the game looked to be safe in Maroon hands.

With about fifteen minutes left to play, the Blues were on the attack ten metres out with Des Hasler at dummy half. Hasler passed the ball wide to John Cartwright who ran only two steps before he heard Chris Johns call for the ball inside. The Broncos centre's deceptively light build contained great strength and he was very quick. Johns took the ball travelling at top speed and carried two tacklers with him over the line. Alexander converted but 16–12 was never going to be close enough. Bobbie Lindner was gone five minutes before full-time, the wonder of it being how he managed to play more than fifty minutes of football with a broken leg. The Maroons had run out of replacements, but they continued to attack with only twelve men and were still attacking when the siren sounded full-time.

With the 1989 series won, the Queenslanders had recorded seven consecutive wins and completely dominated State of Origin since 1986, but that wasn't enough. Every Maroon, their coach and their management wanted another whitewash and they didn't think they needed to change much to achieve it. Unfortunately, change was inevitable. Allan Langer was out with a broken ankle and Mal

---

Final result

Queensland 16 defeated New South Wales 12.

Tries for Queensland: Michael Hancock, Kerrod Walters, Wally Lewis. Goals: Mal Meninga, Gary Belcher.

Tries for New South Wales: Laurie Daley, Chris Johns. Goals: Greg Alexander (2).

Crowd: 40,000.

Man of the Match: Wally Lewis.

Meninga with a smashed eye socket. A broken tibia certainly doesn't heal in a fortnight, so Bobby Lindner would also see the final State of Origin game of 1989 from the grandstand. Michael Hagan had done nothing wrong as half-back when Alfie was injured, Dale Shearer had filled in adequately for Mal Meninga and Dan Stains was recalled to play second row in Lindner's stead. Kevin Walters, Kerrod's twin, was with Canberra. He and the tried and true Peter Jackson were named as replacements.

The Blues made changes, probably for different reasons. Brian Johnston and Michael O'Connor came into the side and there was a reshuffle of the backline with Andrew Ettingshausen and Laurie Daley dropped from the team. Des Hasler replaced Chris Mortimer as five-eighth and Brad Clyde was dropped for Brad Mackay. Penrith firebrand Mark Geyer moved into the second row with Gavin Miller and the front row was completely reshuffled. David Trewhella replaced Mario Fenech as hooker, while Bruce Maguire moved in to take the place of Paul Dunn. There was also a new referee. Although largely unloved by Queenslanders, the hirsute New South Welshman Greg McCallum was invited to officiate.

It didn't appear, at first, that the changes had done the Blues a lot of good. Origin III, 1989 wasn't two minutes old before Kerrod Walters broke down the right flank from dummy half and threw a pass to Alan McIndoe. The Emerald Express scooped the ball in one-handed and simply streaked away to score just ten metres away from the goal posts. With Mal Meninga away, Dale Shearer was the chosen goal kicker, but he missed this one. It was Queensland 4, New South Wales 0.

Peter Kelly, the new Blues' hooker, had a reputation for violence. On the second tackle after the resumption of play he was called out by Greg McCallum, warned, and penalised for throwing a rather innocuous right hook at Gene Miles.[4] The score remained in the Maroons favour for almost ten minutes during which the game became an arm wrestle, but a smart movement initiated by Greg Alexander from a scrum close to the Maroons' line saw him run to the open, beat noted tacklers Paul Vautin and Wally Lewis and pass the ball to Des Hasler who sprinted away to score under the posts.

STATE OF ORIGIN III, 1989
LANG PARK, 28 JUNE

Queensland	New South Wales
Gary Belcher	Gary Jack
Michael Hancock	John Ferguson
Dale Shearer	Michael O'Connor
Tony Currie	Brian Johnston
Alan McIndoe	Chris Johns
Wally Lewis (c)	Des Hasler
Michael Hagan	Greg Alexander
Paul Vautin	Brad Mackay
Gene Miles	Gavin Miller (c)
Dan Stains	Mark Geyer
Martin Bella	Peter Kelly
Kerrod Walters	David Trewhella
Sam Backo	Bruce Maguire

Replacements:

Trevor Gillmeister	Terry Matterson
Peter Jackson	John Cartwright
Gary Coyne	Phil Blake
Kevin Walters	Alan Wilson

Coaches:

Arthur Beetson	Jack Gibson

Referee: Greg McCallum (NSW)

O'Connor converted and the Blues led 6–4, but there was a swift riposte.

Michael Hagan kicked on a second tackle and there was a footrace between Dale Shearer and John Ferguson. The New South Welshman had five metres start but Shearer caught him, jostled him off the ball and touched it down. The Blues howled interference but either referee Greg McCallum differed or he couldn't hear their complaint for the cheers of the capacity Lang Park crowd. It was a fair try. The Maroons held an 8–6 lead, but a penalty against Gene Miles for being offside provided Brad Mackay with the opportunity to run the ball. He ducked under Martin Bella's tackle and passed to Dave Trewhella who scored the easiest of tries. Michael O'Connor converted, the Blues led 12–8 and this was still the score at half-time.

Five minutes into the second half, young Queensland hooker Kerrod Walters broke away and raced toward the Blues' line. Gene Miles backed up and sent the ball on to Tony Currie who put Hancock away to score. Gary Belcher converted the try. It was Queensland 14, New South Wales 12 and within another four minutes the Maroons did it again. From a fifth tackle play-the-ball close to the Blues' line, Wally Lewis grubbered into the in-goal. In attempting to recover the ball, Australian fullback Gary Jack fumbled. Kerrod Walters had chased the kick and was in position to claim the ball and a try adjacent to the left-hand upright. Shearer's simple conversion was successful. The second half was but eight minutes old and the score was 20–12, but the sight of a physiotherapist removing Wally Lewis's guernsey and applying yards of adhesive strapping to his shoulder was hardly encouraging. The King had started the game with his right forearm strapped to protect a previous injury, and now the new strapping was on his left shoulder.

Despite some solid defence, a Blues' chain passing movement sent Chicka Ferguson away down the right-hand sideline in a magnificent run, but Mick Hancock ran him down and bundled him into touch a metre short of the try-line. Nine minutes later the Queenslanders increased their lead following a wonderful exhibition of football in which the ball went from Paul Vautin to Michael Hagan to Gary Belcher to Gene Miles to Wally Lewis and back to Gary Belcher for the try. Shearer converted and Queensland led 26–12.

On television, veteran broadcast announcer Alan Thomas began comparing the 1989 Queensland side with all of the great football teams he had seen in the past, and as he did so they scored again after Michael Hagen, Gene Miles, Kerrod Walters and The King all handled the ball before Wally threw a one-handed pass over two defenders to Tony Currie who beat two men to score in the corner. With fifteen minutes to go, Queensland led by 30 points to 12.

Gary Jack didn't have a good night. He left the field eighteen minutes before full-time. Phil Blake came on to play five-eighth for the Blues and Des Hasler moved to fullback. Des Hasler celebrated by beating six defenders in a run almost to halfway from his first touch of the ball, but the Blues were in extremis, beyond human aid. Peter Jackson came on to spell Tony Currie and promptly made a forty-metre run downfield before passing to Shearer who was tackled ten metres short of the Blues' try-line. Two tackles later, Shearer ran from dummy half, did a run-around with Wally Lewis and scored under the posts. His conversion of his own try made it Queensland 36, the Blues 12. An unconverted consolation try by Bruce Maguire just before full-time added to the New South Wales score.

Final result

Queensland 36 defeated New South Wales 16.

Tries for Queensland: Dale Shearer (2), Tony Currie, Michael Hancock, Alan McIndoe, Kerrod Walters, Gary Belcher. Goals: Dale Shearer (4).

Tries for New South Wales: Des Hasler, David Trewhella, Bruce Maguire. Goals: Michael O'Connor (2).

Crowd: 32,268.

Man of the Match: Kerrod Walters.

This was Queensland's eighth consecutive State of Origin victory, and the second whitewash of the Blues in succession. The presence of twelve Maroons in the Australian party that left to tour New Zealand during the week after Origin III was hardly a surprise. Neither was it surprising that Maroons dominated selections in each of the three Tests, although it was a source of wonder that Alan McIndoe, the most outstanding winger of the series, failed to find a place in the twenty-man touring squad and equally surprising to Queenslanders that Steve Roach was preferred to Martin Bella as Test front-rower. Bella had been prominent in all three interstate clashes and had a Man-of-the-Match award in one of them. Roach was picked for Australia purely on club form and given precedence in Test selections despite being overlooked for all three New South Wales State of Origin sides in 1989.[5]

CHAPTER 12

1990

No Dead Rubber

WITH A heavy concentration of eligible Queensland talent now in Brisbane, the foreseeable future of State of Origin Rugby League was bound to be tied to that of the Broncos, and in 1990 there was bad news from Red Hill.[1] Wally Lewis had 'done a hammy.' At Leichhardt Oval on April Fools' Day, in a game that the Broncos lost to Balmain, the King strained a hamstring tendon and the injury plagued him throughout the season. He joined the team for the Origin I camp, but after a bizarre televised fitness test which he undertook in the corridor of the hotel, the Queensland Rugby League doctor ruled him out. Michael Hagan took his place.

The King wasn't the only member of the triumphant 1989 side who was unavailable. Sam Backo was also out. So were the brilliant rising stars Michael Hancock and Kerrod Walters and that Rock of Gibralter in defence, Tony Currie. All four had shone in the 1989 series. Les Kiss, North Sydney winger, joined the team, and Tony Currie's centre spot was filled by winger Dale Shearer. A reshuffle of the available forwards saw Dan Stains move to the front row and the talented Walters family produced a couple of replacements. Older brother Steve became the Maroons hooker while Kerrod's twin, Kevin, was picked on the bench. And there was another significant omission. Geno Miles was gone. Exempted from representative football, he would play only club football for the remainder of his career.[2]

Change following a defeat was standard operating procedure for the Blues. However, in 1990 the Blues selectors showed remarkable restraint. They were faced with a new season and could look back at eight consecutive losses. A new half in Ricky Stuart would serve his Canberra club-mate Laurie Daley who was about to stake a proprietary claim to the Blues five-eighth position. Hard man Ian Roberts and even harder man David 'Cement' Gillespie came into the pack. Ricky Walford, the St George flyer, was on the wing and baby-faced half-back Geoff Toovey from Manly made his State of Origin debut on the bench. Of the players selected for Origin I, 1989, only Bradley Clyde and Laurie Daley ran on for the first State of Origin game of the 1990 season.

With the King sidelined, Paul Vautin stepped up to lead the proud Maroons for the second time.[3] They did things differently in the south. If the mantle of the Blues captaincy had been a real robe rather than a hypothetical badge of office, it would have been a shabby and shopsoiled garment indeed as it was draped about the broad shoulders of Balmain hooker Ben Elias, the Blues' ninth captain in ten years.

Had he been alive in 1990, the Immortal Bard might well have been thinking of the Maroons' ball security in Origin I when he had Macbeth cry, 'To throw away the dearest thing he owned / As t'were a careless trifle'.

The game has been described as one of the least eventful State of Origin matches ever played,[4] a fair call in anyone's language. It was a game that featured eighty minutes of desperate defence by the Maroons, defence made necessary by an unbelievable error count. The Queensland side coughed the ball up fourteen times in the first twenty minutes, and by half-time they had committed more than twenty-five unforced errors. In the second half it got worse. It seemed at one point that the knock-on was part of the Queensland game plan, the rule to be followed faithfully rather than the unforgivable exception.

Only one factor saved the Queenslanders from defeat by fifty points. The New South Wales handling was only marginally better. Given the supply of the football that came their way, the Blues ought to have led by at least 24–0 at half-time, but such was the commitment of the Queenslanders to defence that the game was more than thirty

STATE OF ORIGIN I, 1990
SYDNEY FOOTBALL STADIUM, 9 MAY

Queensland	New South Wales
Gary Belcher	Andrew Ettingshausen
Alan McIndoe	Rod Wishart
Mal Meninga	Michael O'Connor
Dale Shearer	Mark McGaw
Les Kiss	Ricky Walford
Michael Hagan	Laurie Daley
Allan Langer	Ricky Stuart
Bob Lindner	Bradley Clyde
Wally Fullerton Smith	David Gillespie
Paul Vautin (c)	Bruce Maguire
Martin Bella	Ian Roberts
Steve Walters	Ben Elias (c)
Dan Stains	Steve Roach

Replacements:

Trevor Gillmeister	Paul Sironen
Mark Coyne	Glen Lazarus
Gary Coyne	Graham Lyons
Kevin Walters	Geoff Toovey

Coaches:

Arthur Beetson	Jack Gibson

Referee: David Manson (Qld)

minutes old before they scored. Movement after movement by both sides ended in a dropped ball or a knock-on, but with half-time only ten minutes away Mark McGaw made a dummy-half run from a Blues play the ball on the Queenslanders' quarter line. He passed to Laurie Daley and doubled around him to receive the ball before passing again to Andrew Ettingshausen, who had chimed into the movement from the fullback position. The pass appeared to be a little more than marginally forward, but referee David Manson didn't think so and ET sent the ball on to Ben Elias, backing up on the inside. Ben Elias's short legs couldn't pace it with the cover defence.

He threw a highly speculative overhead pass to Ricky Walford who was in second gear outside him. Walford caught the ball, changed up and took off. Gary Belcher ran him down close to the line, but as he fell Mark McGaw bobbed up to take a miracle pass and score in the corner. It was 4–0 to the Blues, soon to be made 6–0 when Michael O'Connor converted from the touch line.

This was the only try scored in eighty minutes of football. Ten minutes after half-time Paul Vautin and Ian Roberts engaged in a futile exchange of punches while locked together on the ground. Dan Stain's attempt to sort things out with a rabbit killer to Ian Roberts' neck was detected by a touch judge who rushed in to name Wally Fullerton Smith as the culprit. Regardless of who threw the punch, he wore a maroon guernsey and the Blues were given a penalty right in front of goal. It was a gift of two points for Michael O'Connor, and 8–0 to the Blues. But despite having to chase leather all night, a 9–5 penalty count against them, and more than twenty missed tackles, the Maroons were never out of the game until almost full-time.

Final result

New South Wales 8 defeated Queensland 0.

Tries for New South Wales: Mark McGaw. Goals: Michael O'Connor (2).

Crowd: 41,235.

Man of the Match: Ben Elias.

The Australian Rugby League had made an abortive attempt to interest the Americans in the 'greatest game of all' in 1987, but there had been no substantive missionary work done south of the Murray River since 1951.[5] However, broadcast on television in Victoria, State of Origin football had rated its socks off, and in 1990 the 'Mexicans' would be given the opportunity to see it live and in the flesh. On 30 May, Queensland met New South Wales in Origin II at Olympic Park, Melbourne. Approximately 28,400 Victorians attended and this was just about the ground's capacity.

His hamstring no longer troubling him, the King returned to

claim the Maroons' five-eighth position and for this second game Sam Backo was also back. Wally Fullerton Smith was a controversial omission and Paul Vautin was unavailable through injury. The youthful Broncos' front-rower Andrew Gee made his State of Origin debut from the bench. With one or two exceptions, the Blues selectors seemed content for once. Andrew Farrar replaced Geoff Toovey on the bench, and there was some reshuffling of positions; otherwise the Blues fielded pretty much the same team as the one that had won the first game.

Olympic Park offered a wet surface and a soft and spongy subsoil

---

STATE OF ORIGIN II, 1990

OLYMPIC PARK MELBOURNE, 30 MAY

Queensland	New South Wales
Gary Belcher	Andrew Ettingshausen
Alan McIndoe	Rod Wishart
Mal Meninga	Brad Mackay
Dale Shearer	Mark McGaw
Les Kiss	Graham Lyons
Wally Lewis (c)	Des Hasler
Allan Langer	Ricky Stuart
Bob Lindner	Bradley Clyde
Gary Coyne	David Gillespie
Dan Stains	Bruce Maguire
Martin Bella	Ian Roberts
Kerrod Walters	Ben Elias (c)
Sam Backo	Steve Roach

Replacements:

Trevor Gillmeister	Paul Sironen
Mark Coyne	Glen Lazarus
Andrew Gee	Andrew Farrar
Kevin Walters	Brad Fittler

Coaches:

Arthur Beetson	Jack Gibson

Referee: Greg McCallum (NSW)

covered with grass that was a good deal longer than that to which both teams were accustomed. At the beginning the game produced little but rugged defence and frustrated attack with some bright Rugby League sandwiched between a good deal of slipping and sliding around the strange surface by the two sides. After more than twenty minutes the Blues received a penalty right in front of goal. Earlier, Queensland had been attempting to run the ball out from within their own quarter when Wally Lewis was flattened in back play. The referee failed to detect any infringement, but it seems that Steve Roach might have been a likely suspect, for only five minutes later, when Blocker ran the ball from a ruck, the King hit him with a solid tackle from which the big front-rower emerged with a cut above the left eye. The referee was alerted to Wally's social error by a touch judge, and following a brief question and answer session with both captains McCallum awarded the Blues a penalty. Rod Wishart kicked the goal and New South Wales led Queensland 2 nil.

The Queenslanders were gaining a major share of possession, and they kept the Blues under almost constant attack. A quarter of an hour before half-time a long kick by Blues half-back, Ricky Stuart, was fielded on the halfway line by his Canberra captain, Mal Meninga. Mal set sail and was met by three defenders thirty metres out from the New South Wales try-line. Eventually they wrestled him to ground to play the ball on their twenty-metre line. From dummy half, Kerrod Walters passed the ball to Wally Lewis who spotted Dan Stains running wide. The second-rower caught the ball and immediately sent it on for Gary Belcher, who was coming through at pace. Unfortunately, he failed to spot Ricky Stuart loitering nearby. Stuart snatched the ball from Belcher's outstretched fingertips, then showed remarkable pace for a half-back when he sprinted almost eighty-five metres to score wide out, running away from Maroon winger Les Kiss in the process. Wishart's kick missed and after twenty-seven minutes it was the Blues 6, Queensland nil.

Almost immediately, the Maroons forced a New South Wales line drop-out. With play inside the Blues quarter, Wally Lewis took the ball from dummy half and passed to Mal Meninga. Mal ran through and gave the ball to Bobby Lindner, who had, for all money, scored under the posts when McCallum blew the whistle and called him back, claiming that the Meninga pass was forward. Wally Lewis protested volubly and at length but referees are never wrong and protests don't help once the whistle has been blown. New South Wales 6, Queensland 0 remained the score at half-time.

On the resumption, the arm wrestle continued and the Maroons pressed the Blues constantly with determined attacks in which Meninga and Belcher, Backo and Bella were all heavily involved. With about eleven minutes remaining in the game, Alan McIndoe took off down the left touchline with a tremendous run. Tackled but not held just inside the Blues half, he ran infield and passed to Wally Lewis who sent the ball on to Trevor Gillmeister. Surrounded by New South Welshmen, Gillie threw a pass intended for Gary Belcher, who was running free outside him. The ball was knocked towards the try-line by the hand of a defender, but Belcher ran it down, caught it on a handy bounce and gave it to Les Kiss who raced for the corner to score. Mal Meninga's kick from the sideline was successful and the score was 6–6.

A draw would have been a good result since both sides had fought hard, but this was not to be. With just six minutes of the second half remaining, Wally Lewis tackled Glen Lazarus twenty-five metres out from the Maroons' goal line, right in front of the posts. He failed to hold the big forward who rose and attempted to run. Allan Langer came in as though to tackle Lazarus, but instead he took the ball from him. This was a perfectly legal one-on-one steal but referee McCallum blew the whistle and awarded a penalty to the Blues.[6] Wishart kicked the goal and that put paid to the 1990 State of Origin series. It was the Blues game at 8 points to 6.

With only seconds remaining, the Maroons threw the ball around in desperate fashion in the hope that someone, somehow might make a break, but instead Brad Mackay scored another intercept try for the Blues. Wishart's conversion attempt failed and the score at the final siren was New South Wales 12, Queensland 6.

Minimal change was needed in the Queensland team for Origin III. Mal Meninga was unavailable through injury and Peter Jackson took his place. Steve Jackson joined the reserves. Despite having won the series, the Blues selectors fiddled around with their side without

---

Final result

New South Wales 12 defeated Queensland 6.

Tries for New South Wales: Ricky Stuart, Brad Mackay. Goals: Rod Wishart (2).

Try for Queensland: Les Kiss. Goal: Mal Meninga.

Crowd: 25,800.

Man of the Match: Ricky Stuart.

---

making any apparent difference to its effectiveness. Des Hasler was dropped, his place as five-eighth taken by Brad Mackay, the ninth Blues' pivot to challenge Wally Lewis since he first made the position his own in 1981. Michael O'Connor replaced Brad Mackay in the centres, while Glen Lazarus moved from the bench to replace Blocker Roach in the front row. Blocker became a spectator while Mark Sargent and Greg Alexander joined the side as fresh reserves.

It is great to win the series with two straight State of Origin victories, but, as both sides had discovered, nothing in Rugby League equates to the thrill of a 3–0 whitewash. And there was another incentive. A Kangaroo tour of the United Kingdom and France was in the offing. Green and Gold guernseys were up for grabs. There was no chance of any respite from the grim determination of both sides to win and neither did the fact of the game's irrelevance to the series result deter Queenslanders from turning up to support the Maroons. The teams ran on to Lang Park before a capacity crowd, and the game started at the same hectic pace of the two earlier games.

An offside penalty gave the Maroons a 2–0 lead within five minutes of the opening whistle, but just two minutes later, with the Blues in possession of the football and attacking the Queensland line, Glen Lazarus scored. The Canberra front-rower was making his first appearance in the Blues run-on side, and when his captain, Bennie Elias, was tackled less than two metres out from the Maroons line, he went to dummy half. He dummied to the right and when Kerrod Walters and Martin Bella moved to cover the pass, the big front-rower went straight for the try-line and dived over as they belatedly reversed

STATE OF ORIGIN III, 1990
LANG PARK, 13 JUNE

Queensland	New South Wales
Gary Belcher	Andrew Ettingshausen
Alan McIndoe	Rod Wishart
Peter Jackson	Michael O'Connor
Dale Shearer	Mark McGaw
Willie Carne	Graham Lyons
Wally Lewis (c)	Brad Mackay
Allan Langer	Ricky Stuart
Bob Lindner	Bradley Clyde
Gary Coyne	David Gillespie
Trevor Gillmeister	Bruce Maguire
Martin Bella	Ian Roberts
Steve Walters	Ben Elias (c)
Sam Backo	Glen Lazarus

Replacements:

Steve Jackson	Paul Sironen
Michael Hagan	Mark Sargent
Andrew Gee	Andrew Farrar
Kevin Walters	Greg Alexander

Coaches:

Arthur Beetson	Jack Gibson

Referee: David Manson (Qld)

their direction and attempted the tackle. Rod Wishart's conversion tilted the score 6–2 in favour of the Blues but this soon became 6–4 when Belcher kicked a penalty goal. Fifteen minutes before half-time Sparkles McGaw scored another try in the identical spot to give the Blues a 10–4 lead after Wishart's kick went astray.

The Queenslanders coughed up a lot of ball during the first half, but dogged defence kept them in the game and their determination paid off just before half-time. From a ruck close to the Blues line, Steve Walters passed the ball to Bob Lindner who sent it out to Rowdy Shearer. Shearer quickly hand-balled it on to Trevor Gillmeister and the Axe found Kevin Walters backing up. Walters sent it back inside to Peter Jackson who gave it to Gary Belcher to score right in the corner. With Mal Meninga unavailable to do the kicking, Gary Belcher was 'the best of the rest'. He had kicked two goals, both from fairly easy distances, but touchline conversions weren't really his bag. Knowing this, Wally Lewis relieved him of the responsibility. The King then proceeded to make it look easy, adding the two points with his first ever goal attempt in a State of Origin game. The half-time score was 10–10.

A try on the brink of half-time always lifts a team and demoralises its opposition, but this try, and the identity of the player who had kicked the long-distance conversion, saw the Emperor lead his team to the sheds to an ovation that was deafening, and as they returned, it was to chants of 'Wal … lee, Wal … lee, Wal … lee.' The Maroons had a lot to live up to in the second half and after the restart they quickly penned the Blues in their own half. Then, with strong defence, they kept them there. A measure of the strength of the Maroons defence could be taken from the failure of the Blues backs to make any impression in attack. Michael O'Connor had been the major factor in some of New South Wales' most memorable victories. On one occasion he scored all of the Blues points, but, other than when kicking for goal, his presence in the side was hardly noticed in the first half.

Queensland dominated the second half in both attack and defence, but for a long time bad handling and bad luck let them down when tries seemed certain. Finally, with eleven minutes left in the game, the Maroons' persistence paid off. After yet another Blues line drop-out, State of Origin debutante Steve Jackson dived through a ruck and scored the winning try. Wally Lewis failed to convert, but with the score at 14–10 the Queenslanders dug deep to keep the Blues scoreless for the remainder of the match.

This 1990 series was a disappointment for Queenslanders in that their side was a 1–2 loser, but this last game of the dead rubber demonstrated that, regardless of matches won or lost, State of Origin was contested with each game encapsuled in a place of its own and pride and passion drove both sides. Despite the loss of the series,

Final result

Queensland 14 defeated New South Wales 10.

Tries for Queensland: Gary Belcher, Steve Jackson. Goals: Gary Belcher (2), Wally Lewis.

Tries for New South Wales: Glen Lazarus, Mark McGaw. Goal: Rod Wishart.

Crowd: 31,416.

Man of the Match: Bob Lindner.

Man of the Series: Ben Elias.

thousands of Queenslanders walked away from Lang Park on that June night with their pride in the Maroons undiminished.

CHAPTER 13

1991

Farewell to the King

WHILE Queensland's superiority in State of Origin football was a matter of record during the 1980s, this was seldom reflected in the selection of Australian teams of the era. On 9 May 1991, when the Maroons ran out on to Lang Park for the first State of Origin game of the season, there were eight internationals in the side. But on their heels came thirteen internationals in Blue guernseys, while another four Blues with Kangaroo and Test match credentials walked over and sat on the bench. Every member of the New South Wales squad had worn the Green and Gold. Between them, they had played a total of 105 Test matches.

The eight internationals in the Queensland team had racked up only two fewer Tests than the seventeeen New South Welshmen, but since Wally Lewis and Mal Meninga had played sixty-seven of the total 103, six Maroons shared the remaining thirty-six. The New South Wales internationals outnumbered those in the Queensland side by more than two to one, and against this vast experience was arrayed a team that contained a lock, a fullback and a couple of fresh reserves who were debutantes to the State of Origin arena.

Punting on Rugby League was yet to be legalised, but on the clandestine market the smart money had made the New South Wales team short odds-on favourite to win both the first game and the series. One of the television commentators broadcasting the game called the Blues 'unbelievable favourites'.

STATE OF ORIGIN I, 1991
LANG PARK, 8 MAY

Queensland	New South Wales
Paul Hauff	Greg Alexander
Michael Hancock	Chris Johns
Peter Jackson	Laurie Daley
Mal Meninga	Andrew Ettingshausen
Willie Carne	Michael O'Connor
Wally Lewis (c)	Cliff Lyons
Allan Langer	Ricky Stuart
Gary Larson	Des Hasler
Andrew Gee	Mark Geyer
Mike McLean	Paul Sironen
Martin Bella	Ian Roberts
Steve Walters	Ben Elias (c)
Steve Jackson	Steve Roach

Replacements:

Steve Renouf	Glen Lazarus
Gavin Allen	Mark McGaw
Gary Coyne	David Gillespie
Kevin Walters	Brad Fittler

Coaches:

Graham Lowe	Tim Sheens

Referee: Bill Harrigan (NSW)

It seemed that both sides had a game plan that involved playing in the other team's half. Andrew Ettingshausen received the ball from the kick-off and promptly booted it downfield to Paul Hauff who returned the compliment. There were two or three exchanges until ET kicked short and Michael Hancock picked up the ball and ran with it. There were no more kicking duels and the game settled down to become one of lightning fast play-the-balls, bullocking runs from both backs and forwards, and punishing defence, with 20-year-old Queensland fullback Paul Hauff getting through a mountain of work in the early stages. At one point, after some eight minutes of play, Greg Alexander made a break and was headed for the corner, seemingly try-bound. The lanky Maroon fullback's deceptive pace in cover defence made the Penrith speedster look as though he was wearing lead boots as Hauff scooped him up like a shark swallowing a minnow and bundled him into touch. A little later, when Andrew Ettingshausen kicked through and chased, Hauff beat that noted sprinter to the ball and saved a certain try.

Mark Geyer did little to maintain his reputation as one of the games more feared enforcers and wild men other than in one early incident when he hit Steve Jackson with a high tackle and gave up a penalty within easy kicking distance. When the half-time whistle sounded, there had been no try scored, and Queensland led by 2 points to nil.

Paul Hauff was one day short of his twenty-first birthday. He was playing his first game in a Maroon guernsey, but he handled it like a veteran. Queensland supporters were referring to him as the Rock for his defence, and every time he ran the ball he always beat two or three men. Hauff's performance, and an inspired defensive effort by the Queensland captain, Wally Lewis, were typical of the Maroon team which kept the Blues out for most of the game. With less than fifteen minutes remaining, and the score still 2–zero in Queensland's favour, there came the game breaker.

Martin Bella ran from a ruck fifteen metres from the New South Wales line. He passed to Lewis who drew two men before he sent the ball to Mal Meninga who ran on to the pass at speed about ten metres out. Unstoppable so close to the line, the Maroons' centre simply smashed two would-be tacklers as he went in to score.

Unfortunately, he failed to convert his own try but the Queenslanders led by 6 points to nil. They were able to close the game up and defend their lead successfully until three minutes before full-time. Ranging wide out, and with Michael Hancock closing on him, Laurie Daley grubbered the ball into the in-goal. With Daley in full flight, and Hancock needing to turn and chase, there could be only one winner of the footrace. It was Queensland 6, New South Wales 4, with the kick to come.

Michael O'Connor had kicked 76 goals for New South Wales, and many of them had been from the sideline, but he had to wait to kick number 77. When his attempted conversion went astray, it was the Maroons to kick off with the siren about to sound for full-time and the score Queensland 6, New South Wales 4. The die was apparently cast, but the Blues were to get a second bite of the cherry. When Mal Meninga restarted play, he kicked the ball dead on the full, and a penalty was given to the Blues, to be taken from the halfway line. The siren sounded, before the kick was taken. This made an attempt at goal from the halfway line to tie the game the only feasible option and the ball was thrown to Michael O'Connor. The kick was short, Wally Lewis caught the ball and ran out to be tackled on the quarter line and end the game.

Final result

Queensland 6 defeated New South Wales 4.

Try for Queensland: Mal Meninga. Goal: Mal Meninga.

Try for New South Wales: Laurie Daley.

Crowd: 32,400.

Man of the Match: Wally Lewis.

It may have been a new set of New South Wales selectors, or perhaps the same selectors with a new policy, but contrary to normal practice there was minimal change to the Blues' team for Origin II. Paul Sironen was omitted, Ian Roberts moved back to second row, while Cement Gillespie moved from the bench to join him. Bradley Clyde became lock instead of Des Hasler who went to the bench. There was no place found for Glen Lazarus, and Brad Mackay was picked to replace Brad Fittler in the reserves.

In the Queensland side, Dale Shearer replaced Steve Renouf on the bench and the remainder of the team was unchanged.

Sydney Football Stadium looked splendid as the two teams ran out for Origin II. There was a capacity crowd of more than 40,000, and the field of play glowed emerald green under the floodlights, its brilliance enhanced by the substantial rainfall that Sydney had enjoyed for more than a week. Unfortunately, the emerald green grass was for advertising purposes only. Unlike Lang Park, which

STATE OF ORIGIN II, 1991
SYDNEY FOOTBALL STADIUM, 29 MAY

Queensland	New South Wales
Paul Hauff	Andrew Ettingshausen
Michael Hancock	Chris Johns
Peter Jackson	Laurie Daley
Mal Meninga	Michael O'Connor
Willie Carne	Rod Wishart
Wally Lewis (c)	Cliff Lyons
Allan Langer	Ricky Stuart
Gary Larson	Bradley Clyde
Andrew Gee	Mark Geyer
Mike McLean	Ian Roberts
Martin Bella	David Gillespie
Steve Walters	Ben Elias (c)
Steve Jackson	Steve Roach

Replacements:

Kevin Walters	John Cartwright
Gavin Allen	Mark McGaw
Gary Coyne	Des Hasler
Dale Shearer	Brad Mackay

Coaches:

Graham Lowe	Tim Sheens

Referee: David Manson (Qld)

had been carefully designed to shed water which drained away to leave a firm surface, the new Sydney Football Stadium's drainage system resembled that of a stagnant estuarine swamp.

None of this greatly concerned the players as the Blues kicked off. Although the weather looked threatening, no rain was falling, and the ground, though soft, was playable. While New South Wales supporters had suggested from time to time that Queensland referees were biased, they could hardly have complained about David Manson that night. The Blues were awarded two penalties in the first two minutes of football, both well within Michael O'Connor's consid-

erable kicking range. He missed the first, but his second took New
South Wales to a 2–0 lead. With a wet ball and the ground soft
underfoot, mistakes were plentiful and perhaps frustration was the
cause of the rough stuff that crept into the game. Mark Geyer had
failed to live up to his reputation in the first encounter of the season,
but in the sixteenth minute of this second game he attempted to
redeem himself with a high tackle which flattened Michael Hancock.
Good fortune favoured him since neither referee Manson nor the
linesmen appeared to notice. The Maroon forwards certainly did,
and they filed the information for later reference. Gaps close to the
ruck began to appear in the Blues' line, but after twenty minutes of
play the rain began to fall — heavy, saturating rain — and within
minutes the centre of the ground was ankle deep in water.

From a ruck inside his own quarter, Ben Elias ran wide before
passing to Ricky Stuart. Stuart ran through a gap and almost to the
Queensland quarter-way line before cover defence forced him to
pass to Chris Johns. The Bronco centre put the ball down under the
posts. Despite the rain, it was an easy conversion for O'Connor and
thirteen minutes before half time the score was New South Wales
8, Queensland 0.

Almost from the resumption of play the Maroons struck back.
From a ruck just short of halfway, Allan Langer ran the ball and
passed to Peter Jackson. Jacko made more than twenty metres before
Paul Hauff loomed outside him, took the ball, beat two defenders
and gave it to Willie Carne who sprinted in to score not far from
the sideline. In blinding rain, a tremendous goal kick by Mal Meninga
closed the gap to 8–6 in favour of New South Wales. Ten minutes
later, when the hooter sounded for half-time, this remained the score,
but the first half didn't end without high drama. Just before the siren
sounded, the Queenslanders were awarded a penalty. Steve Walters
ran the ball from the tap restart and was tackled by Mark Geyer,
who first hit him on the chin with a right hook, and then followed
through by bringing his elbow down on the back of the hooker's
neck as he fell. Andrew Gee immediately ripped into Geyer, and
this sparked additional fisticuffs. Wally Lewis and Michael O'Connor
considered it a good time to discuss their differences, and for some
strange reason Ricky Stuart appeared to enjoy a brief exchange with

his captain, Ben Elias. Half-time resolved the situation, but such was the anger of the Queenslanders that David Manson had to ride shot-gun on Mark Geyer, getting between him and the Queensland captain and campdrafting Wally away from the Blues' front-rower all the way off the ground and into the players' tunnel.

Soon after half-time, a high tackle left Allen Langer prone on the turf. Again, no official note was taken of the incident but less than a minute later pandemonium broke out. Paul Hauff ran the ball back from a Ricky Stuart kick and was stopped but not grassed by the Blues' half, who had chased down his own kick. Mark Geyer came in to assist, but he made no attempt to tackle Hauff. In a reprise of the tactic that had cost Les Boyd his career in Rugby League, Geyer ran by and in passing lifted his arm and stunned the tall fullback with a savage blow with his elbow to the jaw.

The referee was unsighted, but the Queenslanders weren't. In they flew, fists flailing, and among the first to get to Geyer was Wally Lewis. Geyer used his discretion. He ran behind the referee. Paul Hauff escaped serious injury, otherwise Geyer's fate may have mirrored Les Boyd's, for his offence was identical. After interviewing all of the usual suspects, Manson awarded a penalty to Queensland, Mal Meninga extracted full value and the scores were all tied up at 8 all.

The Queenslanders remained on the attack. Just twelve minutes after half-time, a ten-metre scrum was called after a Maroon knock-on and Steve Walters won the ball against the head. From a ruck, neat passes from Walters to Langer and then to Lewis preceded a long, bullet-like pass from the King to his winger, Dale Shearer. Rowdy obliged his captain by scoring in the corner. Mal Meninga's kick missed, but the Maroons led 12 points to 8.

The Queenslanders fought hard to protect the lead, but mud, slush and pools of water made it difficult for both sides to retain possession. With full-time looming, the Maroons lost the ball in their own half. It was the final tackle. John Cartwright picked up the crumbs and fed the ball to Bradley Clyde who ran it well downfield before being tackled on the Queensland thirty-metre line. From the play-the-ball, Benny Elias sent Ricky Stuart away. Stuart beat the defence before throwing a long pass to that Maroons' nemesis, Sparkles McGaw. McGaw sprinted for the corner and skidded in for a try to level the scores at 12–12. In the conditions, conversion seemed impossible, but O'Connor struck the sodden ball sweetly, it veered to the right, then swung back like a well-drawn golf shot and sailed straight over the black dot. It would have been a good kick on a good day. In the conditions that prevailed it was miraculous. It won the game for the Blues and took the series to that most intense of all Rugby League contests, a Lang Park decider.

Final result

New South Wales 14 defeated Queensland 12.

Tries for New South Wales: Mark McGaw, Chris Johns. Goals: Michael O'Connor (3).

Tries for Queensland: Willie Carne, Dale Shearer. Goals: Mal Meninga (2).

Crowd: 41,520.

Man of the Match: Steve Walters.

New South Wales selectors had acted with commendable restraint after the loss in Origin I, but this was out of character, as they demonstrated after winning Origin II. Andrew Ettingshausen and Laurie Daley were out of the run-on side for Origin III, as was Cliffy Lyons. They were replaced by Greg Alexander, Mark McGaw and Brad Fittler. John Cartwright replaced his club-mate Mark Geyer[1] in the run-on side and Brad Mackay returned to take the place of Bradley Clyde. Newcomers Craig Salvatori and David Fairleigh were replacement forwards and Brad Izzard was recycled after almost nine years in the wilderness. In the pre-game commentary, the New South Wales pack was described by Gavin Miller as being better balanced than the one that won Origin II.

Queensland stuck with the tried and true.

The Blues early performance suggested that the Maroons may well have had their work cut out for them. The New South Welshmen scored a try before the game was two minutes old. The Maroons received the ball from the kick-off, played out their set of six tackles and kicked deep into New South Wales territory, but after just three

STATE OF ORIGIN III, 1991
LANG PARK, 12 JUNE

Queensland	New South Wales
Paul Hauff	Greg Alexander
Michael Hancock	Chris Johns
Peter Jackson	Mark McGaw
Mal Meninga	Michael O'Connor
Willie Carne	Rod Wishart
Wally Lewis (c)	Brad Fittler
Allan Langer	Ricky Stuart
Gary Larson	Brad Mackay
Andrew Gee	John Cartwright
Mike McLean	Bradley Clyde
Martin Bella	David Gillespie
Steve Walters	Ben Elias (c)
Steve Jackson	Steve Roach

Replacements:

Kevin Walters	Craig Salvatori
Bob Lindner	Brad Izzard
Gary Coyne	Des Hasler
Dale Shearer	David Fairleigh

Coaches:

Graham Lowe	Tim Sheens

Referee: Bill Harrigan (NSW)

tackles the Blues were deep in the Maroon half, and on the fourth tackle five-eighth Brad Fittler put in a grubber kick that ran down the sideline and stopped just inside the in-goal. Chris Johns outsprinted Broncos' team-mate Michael Hancock to the ball and it was New South Wales 4, Queensland 0 with seventy-eight minutes to go. O'Connor's attempt at conversion failed and within three minutes the Maroons took their revenge.

From a ruck just outside the Blues' quarter line, Allan Langer fed the ball to Mal Meninga who found Paul Hauff backing up outside him. He gave the fullback the ball and, with his long legs pumping,

Hauff scored without a hand being laid on him. Mal Meninga missed a relatively easy conversion and the score was 4 all.

The Maroon forwards out-muscled the 'well balanced' New South Wales pack and kept going forward. Then in the nineteenth minute Allan Langer put in what became known as a banana kick. Running towards the left-hand corner, Alfie kicked the ball off the outside of his right foot so that it flew at right angles to his line of travel and went straight down the field. The Maroon chase was enthusiastic and in attempting to gather in the ball the harassed Ricky Stuart got a bad bounce and kicked it straight to Michael Hancock. Mickey didn't wait for an invitation. He put his head down and went for the corner. That made it Queensland 8, New South Wales 4 and it remained that way after Mal Meninga missed another attempted conversion.

Queensland continued to attack and at one point, when Blues' winger Brad Wishart knocked-on attempting an intercept, the Maroons had four successive sets of six tackles within the New South Wales quarter, twice having players knock-on over the line. The Queenslanders continued to gain more than their share of possession, but at half-time the score remained Queensland 8, New South Wales 4.

The Blues came out after the break looking a much better side and they attacked with vigour and persistence. They had their reward after fifteen minutes when Michael O'Connor scored in the corner. Martin Bella, who was in at least as good a position as the referee to know, suggested that the pass to O'Connor was forward. He expressed his view in a sufficiently vigorous manner for Bill Harrigan to lose patience and banish him to the sin-bin for ten minutes. As he walked off, Michael O'Connor missed yet another attempt at goal and the score remained 8 all.

A few minutes later the Queenslanders again threatened the Blues' line. Mal Meninga ran the ball up. He was taken in a tackle by two New South Wales forwards but managed to drop the ball out the back to Allan Langer. Alfie spotted Rowdy Shearer standing wide and unmarked. He threw the ball ten metres to him. Shearer beat the cover defence with blinding pace and then trotted around to score halfway between the goal posts and the sideline. Mal's conversion was the only successful goal kick by either side all night and Queensland led 14 points to 8.

With the Blues next possession, Ricky Stuart was forced to kick on the last tackle from a point just inside his own half. Bob Lindner came on fresh just after half-time. He sprinted forward in an attempt to charge down the kick and got his hands to the ball just as it left the boot, but only with sufficient contact to cause it to fly high into Maroon territory. Craig Salvatori was in a hopelessly offside position until Bobby Lindner touched the ball. It landed in his arms, the referee called play on and Salvo passed it to Des Hasler who outsped the cover defence to score in the corner. Once again, the O'Connor kick missed the uprights. What followed might well be one of the more hectic ten minutes of Rugby League as the Maroons tried to score again to consolidate their position and the Blues attempted to score to either win or draw the match. But the Maroons held on.

Final result

Queensland 14 defeated New South Wales 12.

Tries for Queensland: Paul Hauff, Michael Hancock, Dale Shearer. Goal: Mal Meninga.

Tries for New South Wales: Andrew Johns, Des Hasler, Michael O'Connor.

Crowd: 33,226.

Man of the Match: Martin Bella.

In the end, the 1991 State of Origin series was the ultimate arm wrestle. Each side scored six tries and it all came down to a difference of just one goal kick separating the two sides over three games. New South Wales scored an aggregate 30 points in the series. Queensland scored 32.

But besides being the closest series of State of Origin ever played up until that time, this last match of 1991 was special. It was Wally Lewis's last representative game. It was also his 31st State of Origin game, of only 33 that had ever been played, and he captained Queensland in 30 of them. Wally won more State of Origin Man of the Match awards than any other player, and for more than a decade he dominated Rugby League in Australia as no other player had done, or would do in the 20th century. The King was retiring and Queenslanders would never see his like again. It was a magic night at the Cauldron and a fairytale ending for the King. His wife, Jacqui, and their two small sons came down from the stand to join him and they paraded with him on the field that had been a second home to him from childhood. Lang Park was to be the site of a statue of Wally Lewis, its King–Emperor, but that was for the future. The victorious night of 12 June 1991 was Wally's alone and not a Queensland fan left the stadium until the King and his family had greeted and thanked them. So emotional was the occasion that most of the crowd present, including many a strong man, walked away misty eyed.

CHAPTER 14

1992

A Spirit Worth Bottling

DESPERATE TIMES require desperate measures, and as 1992 dawned, the New South Wales Rugby League's short-term historical perspective presented a desperate picture indeed. The Blues had won only a single series since their clean sweep in 1986, and that by the narrowest of margins. Of the fifteen official games played since then, Queensland had won eleven and New South Wales only four.

Unlike the fabled equestrian in midstream, the New South Wales Rugby League was always ready to swap horses and its collective wisdom held that a new coach might be the answer. In the twelve seasons since State of Origin commenced, the Blues had employed eight coaches while the Maroons had managed to make do with four. For 1992, the Blues appointed coach number 9. Phil 'Gus' Gould had taken Penrith to the Premiership in 1991 and he got the nod for State of Origin '92. It wasn't just the coach who got the chop. Nine of those who played in the final game of the previous season looked in vain for their names among the seventeen chosen for State of Origin I, 1992. The eight survivors were Brad Fittler, Rod Wishart, Brad Mackay, Ben Elias, John Cartwright, Craig Salvatori, David Gillespie and Bradley Clyde.

Some of those omitted were out due to injury, but it was a massive revision by any measure.

The Queensland side had one glaring omission. For only the

second time since the State of Origin series began, Queensland had a new captain. Mal Meninga led the Maroons on to the field. The New South Wales team also had a new leader. Bennie Elias was still in the side, his value as a hooker unquestioned, but he was no longer considered foreman material. Canberra captain Laurie Daley was the tenth to wear the mantle.

Queenslanders were proud of their success, and they had not hesitated to boast that it was largely due to the Queensland Spirit, a rare product distilled from the Queenslanders' indissoluble bond with each other, their fierce pride in the Maroon guernsey, and a

---

STATE OF ORIGIN I, 1992

SYDNEY FOOTBALL STADIUM, 6 MAY

Queensland	New South Wales
Dale Shearer	Andrew Ettingshausen
Michael Hancock	Graham Mackay
Mal Meninga (c)	Brad Fittler
Peter Jackson	Paul McGregor
Willie Carne	Rod Wishart
Kevin Walters	Laurie Daley (c)
Allan Langer	John Simon
Martin Bella	Glen Lazarus
Steve Walters	Ben Elias
Steve Jackson	Paul Harragon
Bob Lindner	Paul Sironen
Trevor Gillmeister	John Cartwright
Gary Larson	Bradley Clyde

Interchange:

Mark Coyne	Robbie McCormack
Gary Coyne	Craig Salvatori
Steve Renouf	Brad Mackay
Gaven Allen	David Gillespie

Coaches:

Graham Lowe	Phil Gould

Referee: David Manson (Qld)

deeply ingrained distaste for anything or anybody wearing sky blue. It was not something that had appeared overnight. It had grown out of the Maroons' early success, and had been nurtured year by year through circumstances that had seen a close-knit group of officials and players grow and develop together as the long-term hard core of the team and its support staff. The sporting journalists had them favoured to win and win easily, but the southern punters didn't agree. Sydney money made the Blues favourites with the bookies.

Gus Gould took all of this as his theme when his team assembled in camp before the first game. He worked hard to persuade his charges to adopt an attitude towards victory similar to that exhibited by the Queenslanders, and he encouraged boozy bonding evenings involving the entire team during the first nights in camp. No doubt this helped, but Gus was not one to ignore first principles, and he did not place all of his eggs in one basket. Very early in the first game, his forwards gave notice that their coach would rely on a less ethereal element for success — the down-to-earth application of some very basic, old-fashioned Rugby League first principles.

In attempting the very first contact of the game, an almighty head-high stiff-arm tackle by lanky Paul Harragon missed by centimetres when it whistled over the head of a shorter Queenslander. Referee Manson was unperturbed by the Chief's indiscretion and, encouraged by this, Paul Sironen came in as second man in the next tackle and pole-axed Steve Jackson with a high shot. Once more, Manson was unsighted. After Jackson was assisted from the field, his feet dragging, the Blues' forwards proceeded to turn on one of the most brutal halves of Rugby League seen since State of Origin was first introduced.

Early in the game, Mick Hancock gave up a silly penalty for 'bean bagging' a tackled player. From the tap restart, Ben Elias worked a simple run-around with Glen Lazarus and put Bradley Clyde away. Clyde headed for the corner and scored about a metre in from the sideline. Rod Wishart converted and, after only eight minutes of play, New South Wales led 6–0.

The big New South Wales forwards were fierce in defence, but the Queenslanders had a fair share of possession and made serious incursions into Blues' territory. Thirteen minutes into the game, with their backs in full flight, the Blues' defence at sixes and sevens, and Meninga about to play the ball, Manson awarded the Maroons a penalty thirty-five metres out and in front of the New South Wales goal posts. The Blues would have been happy to trade two points for a probable six, but Mal Meninga missed the shot at goal.

Through their big men, Harragon, Sironen and Lazarus, the Blues' forwards were gaining the ascendency. Ricky Stuart was out of the team through injury, but his absence was of little consequence. John Simon was playing his first game for New South Wales and doing everything right at half-back but the Maroons continued to throw the ball wide and their fast men kept making substantial gains.

Fifteen minutes before half-time, Dale Shearer ran from fullback and his kick and chase trapped Blues' hooker, Ben Elias, in his in-goal area. The Maroons got the ball back from the line drop-out, and a quick play the ball on the third tackle saw it spread wide to Gaven Allen who found Allan Langer on the inside. Alfie beat two men to plant the ball close to the right-hand goal post and Mal Meninga's kick evened the score at 6–6.

Ten minutes before half-time, Gary Larson took the ball up. He was standing in a tackle, held by two players, when Paul Harragon came over the top with a stiff arm to the jaw and flattened him. He was stretchered off the ground unconscious. He was still bleeding from the ears twenty minutes later and took no further part in the game. While the Newcastle enforcer's action was plain to see both live and on the television replay, none of the officials on the field noticed anything amiss.

Neither did the officials seem to place any great importance on the need to keep the sides apart the five metres that the rules of the day required. For this and other reasons the game was far from being a great spectacle. When the half-time hooter sounded, the scores were still locked at 6 all.

The second half was a reprise of the first. There was a little football now and again and bags of tough stuff in between.

Twenty minutes into the second half Billy Moore tackled Ben Elias; the ball came free in the tackle and went forward off the lock and touched Steve Walters in an offside position almost right in front of the Maroon goal posts. Wishart kicked the penalty goal and New South Wales led 8–6.

With two forwards now non-combatants, and no further replacements available, the Maroon six were doing it tough. When big, fast East Sydney prop Craig Salvatori came on fresh to replace Laurie Daley it became tougher. Six minutes before full-time, the Blues were attacking well inside the Maroon quarter when Salvo ran on to a Ben Elias dummy half pass and bolted for the try-line. Mark Coyne took him in a diving tackle but there was no holding him and he went over the line with the Queenslander hanging on to his legs. After Wishart did the business with his boot, the New South Wales lead was extended. The score, 14–6.

Such was the nature of this savage encounter that an eight-point lead would have been difficult for seventeen fit men to peg back. Two forwards short, it was always going to be beyond the Maroons. Coach Graham Lowe tried to freshen his forwards by moving Mal Meninga into the second row and against medical advice the concussed Steve Jackson returned, but in the end the Maroons were overmatched for muscle. The Blues prevailed.

Final result

New South Wales 14 defeated Queensland 6.

Tries for New South Wales: Brad Clyde, Craig Salvatori. Goals: Rod Wishart (3).

Try for Queensland: Allan Langer. Goal: Mal Meninga.

Crowd: 40,039.

Man of the Match: Ben Elias.

New South Wales coach and selectors had every reason to be content with the result of Origin I. They made only one alteration for the second game of the series. Ricky Stuart had recovered from injury, and despite John Simon having played close to a Man-of-the-Match game on debut, it would be another five years before he was handed his next sky blue guernsey.

Queensland made several changes. Trevor Gillmeister was moved to the bench and Gary Larson to the second row to make room for North Sydney lock Billy Moore. Kevin Walters was also benched in favour of Peter Jackson at five-eighth, while Jacko's place in the centres was taken by Mark Coyne. A newcomer, Adrian Brunker, replaced Willie Carne on the wing, and on the bench Mike McLean made his second last State of Origin appearance and Darren Smith his first.

The second State of Origin game was played at Lang Park on 20 May, and, retired now from representative football, Wally Lewis was a guest commentator with a television station. At the urging of

---

STATE OF ORIGIN II, 1992
LANG PARK, 20 MAY

Queensland	New South Wales
Dale Shearer	Andrew Ettingshausen
Michael Hancock	Graham Mackay
Mal Meninga (c)	Brad Fittler
Mark Coyne	Rod Wishart
Adrian Brunker	Paul McGregor
Peter Jackson	Laurie Daley (c)
Allan Langer	Ricky Stuart
Martin Bella	Glen Lazarus
Steve Walters	Ben Elias
Gaven Allen	Paul Harragon
Bob Lindner	Paul Sironen
Gary Larson	John Cartwright
Billy Moore	Bradley Clyde

Interchange:

Kevin Walters	David Gillespie
Trevor Gillmeister	Craig Salvatori
Darren Smith	Brad Mackay
Mike McLean	Steve Carter

Coaches:

Graham Lowe	Phil Gould

Referee: Bill Harrigan (NSW)

Courier-Mail sporting journalist Lawrie Kavanagh, funds had been raised by public subscription to pay for the casting of a bronze statue of the Emperor of Lang Park and its dedication took place that night. In the break before the big game, a massive crown was wheeled out into the middle of Lang Park. It was coloured royal purple and red and liberally garnished with red and green lights. A policeman attended at the broadcast box and escorted the King down to the ground. He was joined by his wife, Jacqui, and his three children and led out into centre ring. The premier of Queensland made a speech and pressed a button and the larger than life-size statue of Wally Lewis rose slowly, majestically from the centre of the crown. Thirty-three thousand people rose and roared as one.

The presentation of the Emperor's statue had set the tone for the evening, and the Cauldron shook to the crowd's roar as the Queenslanders ran out on to the ground. It trembled again as the Lang Park crowd booed the Blues' entrance. It would have done so earlier for the referee, New South Welshman Bill Harrigan, but he and his linesmen had, very cunningly, run out with the Maroons.

State of Origin II, 1992 was played in the rain. The ground stood up well and, considering the conditions, handling for the most part was excellent in a low-scoring game which, none the less, reached great heights as a spectacle.

The Maroons were determined not to succumb to any intimidatory tactics of the kind that the Blues used in Origin I, and the Queensland forwards went at them from the jump. Within two minutes a Peter Jackson grubber into the Blues' in-goal was scooped over the dead-ball line a hair's breadth in front of the chasers. From the line drop-out the Maroons ran it back and Mal Meninga was over for what appeared to be a fair try. When Referee Harrigan called it back for a forward pass, none of the Queenslanders agreed. Peter Jackson expressed his doubts both eloquently and colourfully and instead of packing a scrum the referee awarded a ground-saving penalty to New South Wales.

The sledging that followed this decision, and a high tackle by Peter Jackson on Paul Sironen, caused a ruck to break up in a general melee, with Bradley Clyde and Martin Bella engaged in single combat at its epicentre. After a brief on-field hearing of evidence, the Blues received another penalty. The ball was kicked into touch and the tap was about to be taken when further expressions of dissatisfaction with the referee led to the Maroons being marched back yet another ten metres before the process was completed.

All of this had taken the Blues almost to the Queensland quarter line and when Bill Harrigan penalised them yet again, this time for failing to retire ten metres for the tap kick, Wishart was within easy kicking range right in front: New South Wales 2, Queensland nil. Peter Jackson and Martin Bella were only two of the thirty thousand Queenslanders present who considered that they were getting a rough deal from Harrigan, but they were the loudest in expressing their view and closest to the referee when they did so. Both were sin-binned and for the next ten minutes eleven Maroons played thirteen Blues. This may have seemed to give the New South Welshmen a tremendous advantage, but the Maroons were on the attack for most of the time that they were two men short. Within two minutes of the return of the malefactors, some smart work on the blind side by Mal Meninga sent Billy Moore over in the corner for a try. Billy got up waving his extended forefinger to the crowd to indicate that it was both his first game and his first try in State of Origin. It would not be the last of either. Wet conditions and a heavy ball saw Mal Meninga's conversion attempt sail just wide of the posts but Queensland led by 4 points to 2.

The game continued without any addition to the score until just before half-time, when crafty Balmain hooker Ben Elias demon-strated how and why he had become known as Backdoor Bennie. Tackled by Allan Langer, he first held the little half-back's guernsey to prevent him from rising. When Alfie did drag himself clear, the Blues' hooker tripped him, causing him to fall back on top of the tackled player. Referee Harrigan didn't see it that way. He penalised Langer for lying in the tackle and Wishart equalised from within easy kicking distance. New South Wales 4, Queensland 4.

What followed was solid defence against determined attack re-gardless of who held the ball, but with few of the distasteful head-highs and second and third tackles that had marred Origin I. Halfway through the second half, Mal Meninga had an opportunity to send

Queensland further ahead. It was an easy angle but almost forty metres out from goal. Mal's kick went wide.

Ricky Stuart twice attempted to kick a field goal, and twice failed. The score remained locked at 4 all until the 38th minute of the second half. A wet and heavy ball and tiring players saw a succession of errors in mid-field. Queensland worked the ball to within field goal range and the least likely candidate took the shot. Alfie Langer had never kicked a field goal in his life. He dropped the ball on to his toe from right in front and it just cleared the crossbar. It took the score to 5–4 and won the game for the Maroons.

Final result

Queensland 5 defeated New South Wales 4.

Try for Queensland: Billy Moore. Field goal: Allan Langer.

Goals for New South Wales: Rod Wishart (2).

Crowd: 31,500.

Man of the Match: Bob Lindner.

Changes to both sides were minimal for Origin III. New South Wales made only one replacement, substituting Tim Brasher for Steve Carter on the reserves bench, but there was one major loss from the Queensland side. The Maroons best cover defender, and also their best yardage man, Bob Lindner withdrew with a hamstring injury. Mike McLean was selected to replace him and came straight into the run-on side.

Paul Hauff had been a sensation for both Queensland and Australia in 1991, but injury had seen him disappear from representative ranks in 1992. This had left Queensland with few options for this most important position. By virtue of his speed and elusiveness, Dale Shearer was one of the finest wingers who ever played the game, but he was blessed with all of the talents and could play at full back as well as he could on the wing. He offered proof of this in the first seconds of Origin III in 1992 when he chased the kick-off and flattened his Broncos' team-mate Chris Johns as he caught the ball.

This set the tone of a game that was very physical throughout.

STATE OF ORIGIN III, 1992
SYDNEY FOOTBALL STADIUM, 3 JUNE

Queensland	New South Wales
Dale Shearer	Andrew Ettingshausen
Michael Hancock	Chris Johns
Mal Meninga (c)	Brad Fittler
Mark Coyne	Rod Wishart
Adrian Brunker	Paul McGregor
Peter Jackson	Laurie Daley (c)
Allan Langer	Ricky Stuart
Martin Bella	Glen Lazarus
Steve Walters	Ben Elias
Gaven Allen	Paul Harragon
Mike McLean	Paul Sironen
Gary Larson	John Cartwright
Billy Moore	Bradley Clyde

Interchange:

Kevin Walters	David Gillespie
Gary Coyne	Craig Salvatori
Darren Smith	Brad Mackay
Steve Jackson	Tim Brasher

Coaches:

Graham Lowe	Phil Gould

Referee: Eddie Ward (Qld)

The Maroons gave as good as they got, and with a fair share of possession early in the game, they penned the Blues up in their own quarter for most of the time. But the educated boot of Ricky Stuart was always there to get his team out of trouble, and once they found themselves in the Queensland half, Stuart, Daley and Ettingshausen were often very hard to handle. After their half-back engineered yet another escape from near their own try-line, the Blues were able to obtain back-to-back sets of six inside the Maroon quarter, and from the third play the ball of the second set Ricky Stuart worked a variation of the old-fashioned run-around and stepped through the

Queensland forwards to score a try. Rod Wishart failed to convert and in the fifteenth minute of the game New South Wales led 4–0.

Thirteen minutes before half-time, with Queensland dominating possession, Allan Langer chased his own kick and was tackled by Bennie Elias and Cement Gillespie less than twenty metres from the Blues' try-line and right in front of the posts. With the Southerners' defence in disarray, a quick play the ball would almost certainly have resulted in a try, but the tacklers lay all over Alfie, gambling a sure two points against an almost certain six. Mal Meninga made the score 4–2. The New South Welshmen were still in front. With a wealth of possession coming their way in the last ten minutes before half-time, the Queenslanders continued to storm the Blues' line, but they still trailed 2–4 as they sucked their oranges.

The second half was only three minutes old when Mal Meninga kicked another penalty goal and the scores were tied at 4 all, but a few minutes later the Maroons were in trouble when Dale Shearer strained a hamstring and had to leave the field. Shearer's contribution as fullback had been magnificent, and his departure removed a major threat to the Blues. Kevin Walters moved into the five-eighth position, Peter Jackson to the centres, Mick Hancock to fullback and Mark Coyne to the wing.

It was a case of dig in and do your best, and for most of the second half the Maroons' best was nearly good enough. A few minutes after Shearer left, a promising move broke down when a simple run-around in the new back line went wrong and resulted in a Blues' penalty for a shepherd. The tap re-start after the penalty kick saw Ben Elias feed the ball to Laurie Daley. Daley ran down the sideline and then kicked. Paul McGregor chased, stooped low and scooped the ball up at full speed before passing it to Daley who was backing up. Daley had Ettingshausen on his hip. He gave him the ball and ET was in for the best try of the game. Tim Brasher had replaced Wishart at half time. A regular kicker for Balmain, he also inherited Wishart's kicking duties, but this time he was unsuccessful: New South Wales 8–Queensland 4.

The Blues scored again after Laurie Daley milked a penalty by deliberately running from dummy half into the back of Darren Smith who was still trying to get onside. The tap restart was just

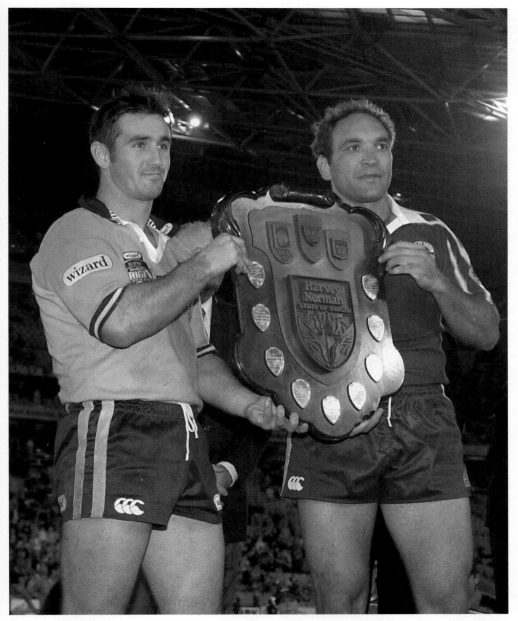

The two skippers, Andrew Johns and Gorden Tallis, after Origin III, 2002. (Action Photographics)

Despite being badly wounded and gassed in World War I, Duncan Thompson became a Rugby League legend in the 1920s as a player and in the 1940s and 50s as a coach. (*Toowoomba Chronicle*)

Mick Madsen was a legendary strong man and front-row forward who first represented Australia in 1928. Mick played his last test in 1936, against Great Britain. (*Toowoomba Chronicle*)

The first Queensland side to beat New South Wales, 1922. Players (not in photo order): E. Fraunfelder, W. Paten, T. Gorman, J. McBrien, W. Spencer, E. S. Brown, J. Bennett, C. O'Donnell, A. Brown, E. Stanley, N. Potter (with ball, captain), J. Johnson, Cyril Connell.

New South Wales team, Brisbane, 23 July 1938. Front row: R. Johnson, Len Dawson, Fred Felsch (captain), L. Maher (manager), A. Stewart, Roy Kirkaldy, R. Thompson. Second row: R. Harrison, S. Goodwin, H. Porter, J. Gibbs, F. Dhu. Back row: R. T. Pierce, H. F. Narvo, A. Norval. The team lost to Queensland 22–36 but won the series 2 games to 1.

Queensland team, Brisbane, 23 July 1938. In front: Ivan Blow, Les Ridgewell. Front row: unknown official, Bill Ryan, Hughie Melrose, Gordon Whittle, Jack Reardon (captain), Jack Stapleton, Col Wright, Ron Cooper, Harry Sunderland (manager). Second row: Jack Gayler, Frank Doonar, Eddie Collins, Les Heidke, Norm Smith, Tommy Rowe, Jack Ryrie, Jack Bates. Back row: Laurie Kearney (visitor), unknown official, Tom Dickson, unknown official, Jack Little, Vic Jensen (QRL patron), unknown official.

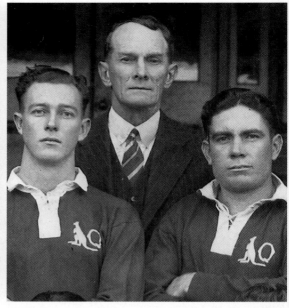

Harry Bath was a 19-year-old second-rower for Queensland in 1945, was signed for Balmain in 1946 and played for New South Wales before his 21st birthday. He signed with the English club Warrington and set records as a try-scoring forward and a goal kicker for ten years.

Herb Steinhort (centre) coached Queensland on many occasions. He is seen here with members of the 1946 Maroons, Bill Tyquin, Kangaroo and Queensland captain and lock forward, and Reg Pegg, who played on the wing for Queensland in the immediate post-war years.

Len Pegg, the older of the two Pegg brothers, played centre for Queensland post–World War II. He played two tests against New Zealand and was a Kangaroo tourist in 1948–49.

Brian (Bull) Davies played 31 games for Queensland and 28 tests for Australia. He spent most of his playing career with Past Christian Brothers in Brisbane. (Nappy Arnold collection)

Jack Reardon, Queensland captain, Australian vice-captain and sports journalist, advocated the adoption of the State of Origin principle as far back as 1964.

Eddie Brosnan represented Queensland and Australia directly after World War II and toured with the 1948–49 Kangaroos. He was Wayne Bennett's uncle, and an inspiration to the Queensland coach during his formative years. (Nappy Arnold collection)

Duncan Hall, the prince of Queensland front-row forwards in pre-Origin times. Fast, tough and totally fearless, Duncan played 23 tests for Australia and was several times named the best Rugby League forward in the world.

Mick Crocker, seen here in a New South Wales guernsey, is an example of the finest Queensland talent that was enticed to play in Sydney prior to the 1980s. Mick played 17 games for Queensland and 12 tests for Australia before moving south to join Parramatta.

Lang Park in 1957. The concrete terraces have been completed, and work is about to start on the Frank Burke stand.

Part of the crowd that attended the first Brisbane Rugby League Grand Final held at Lang Park in 1958. Brothers defeated Valleys 22 points to 7. The north-east corner, site of the notorious can bar, is to the right of the picture.

Wayne Bennett was a flying winger with Brisbane's Past Christian Brothers in the early 1970s. He was one of the players who formed the first live-in training camp organised by Ron McAuliffe. He played for Queensland in pre-Origin times and played for Australia in 1971.

Bill Hunter succeeded Ron McAuliffe as Chairman of the Queensland Rugby League. His decision not to use his casting vote cost the syndicate headed by Ron McAuliffe the Brisbane franchise that later became the Brisbane Broncos.

The Queensland captain, Greg Vievers, talks to the troops in the Lang Park dressing room during a pre-Origin match in 1975. He is watched by coach Barry Muir.

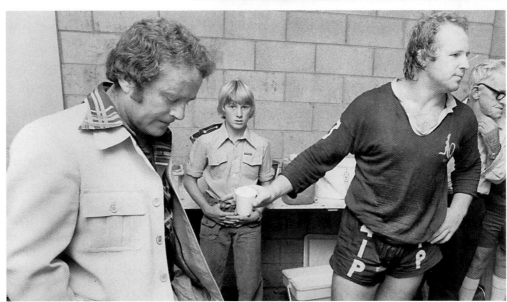

Johnny Lang marks up for the Maroons in a pre-Origin game. Johnny played 19 games for Queensland during the 1970s but was signed by Sydney Easts in 1980 and selected to play for New South Wales. He swapped his blue guernsey for a maroon one for the 1980 Origin game, the first ever played, and became part of history.

Greg Oliphant, Maroon half-back in the first State of Origin game in 1980. Ollie provoked the famous ruckus that was the overture to what this intensely competitive struggle was to become.

Arthur Beetson and Wally Lewis congratulate each other after the Maroons won Origin II, 1984. Arthur Beetson coached the Queensland side in 16 games and they won 11 of them.

Sometimes called The Rock of Gibraltar in consideration of his defence, Tony Currie played 13 State of Origin games for Queensland between 1982 and 1988.

Brett Kenney played a major role in the solitary Blues victory at the Sydney Cricket Ground in 1983.

Brian Johnson sets himself to try and stop Mal Meninga as the big Queensland centre drops his shoulders to bump him off in Origin II, 1984.

A passionate Maroon and a tower of strength in 11 State of Origin games from 1984 to 1987, Greg Dowling strikes a typical pose following a club victory with Brisbane club Wynnum–Manly.

Queensland State of Origin team, 1982. Front row (left to right): Greg Holben, John Ribot, Dick Turner (manager), Wally Lewis (captain), Kevin Brasch (manager), Mark Murray, Brad Backer. Second row (left to right): Daryl Gatley (strapper), John Dowling, Paul Vautin, Rod Morris, Mitch Brennan, Rohan Hancock, Arthur Beetson (coach). Back row (left to right): Paul Khan, Paul McCabe, Gene Miles, Colin Scott, Norm Carr.

Barry Muir and Dick Turner at State of Origin training. Muir's coaching put some starch into the Maroons in the 1970s and paved the way for the State of Origin teams that won those first games and series. He coined the term `cockroach' for the Maroon's rivals from New South Wales.

Three Maroon stars of the 1980s. Gene Miles, Wally Lewis and Allan Langer in a light-hearted moment.

Chris (Choppy) Close is held by Noel Cleal and Chris Mortimer in Origin II, 1985, at the Sydney Cricket Ground. Chris was Man of the Match in the first two State of Origin games. He went on to play 16 games for the Maroons between 1980 and 1986.

One of the most fearsome sights on a 1980s Rugby League field: Maroon and Australian captain Mal Meninga on the charge.

Brett Kenney (left) and Pat Jarvis take it easy in the dressing room after the Blues drew first blood in the 1985 series at Lang Park, 27 May.

Queensland front-rower Dave Brown wraps Benny Elias up in Origin II at the Sydney Cricket Ground, 11 June 1985.

'The King', Wally Lewis, with Ken Arthurson, chairman of the Australian Rugby League, in 1985.

Steve Mortimer led New South Wales to their first series victory at the Sydney Cricket Ground, 11 June 1985. His team-mates lifted him high and most of the Sydney crowd joined in a lap of honour as he was borne from the ground.

Lang Park, 27 May 1986, was the scene of Royce Simmons' (right) night of glory. He scored the first try for the Blues and his dummy-half work won him Man of the Match. Brett Kenney gave him a well-deserved pat on the back.

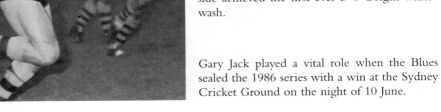

Bitter Origin rivals but Kangaroo team-mates, Wally Lewis and Brett Kenney walk off Lang park arm-in-arm after the New South Wales side achieved the first ever 3–0 Origin white-wash.

Gary Jack played a vital role when the Blues sealed the 1986 series with a win at the Sydney Cricket Ground on the night of 10 June.

Blues fullback Gary Jack flies high for the ball at Lang Park in Origin I, 27 May 1986. Maroon captain, Wally Lewis, moves in to claim him. Greg Conescu comes in as second tackler, watched by Wayne Pearce.

Queenslanders were outraged when four of their number were dropped from the Australian team to play New Zealand in 1985. Following their return, the Maroons' defeat of the Blues in Origin III was twice as sweet. Greg Dowling made the point as Dale Shearer scored yet another try in the 20–6 victory.

Gary Belcher runs the ball out as he takes the pass from Wally Lewis. Peter Sterling closes in for the tackle.

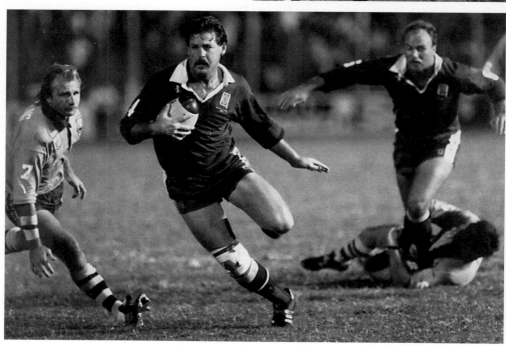

Peter Sterling skies a bomb. Sterling played 13 games as half for the Blues between 1981 and 1988.

Queensland State of Origin team, 2 June 1987. Front row (left to right): Gene Miles, Dale Shearer, Dick Turner (manager), Wally Lewis (captain), Wayne Bennett (coach), Greg Dowling, Allan Langer. Second row: Bob Bateman (manager), Trevor Gillmeister, Greg Conescu, Ian French, Tony Currie, Paul Vautin, Ken Rach (trainer). Third row: Colin Scott, Gary Belcher, Peter Jackson, Gary French, Martin Bella.

Wally Lewis and Allan Langer carry the State of Origin Shield as they do a lap of honour after winning the decider 10–8 in 1987.

Wally Lewis holds the State of Origin shield high following the Maroons' victory at Lang Park in 1987.

Greg Conescu and Tosser Turner at training at the Veterans' Memorial Stadium in Los Angeles in 1987. This attempt to introduce the United States to Origin Rugby League was treated as an end-of-season jaunt by the Maroons who had already won the 1987 series 3 games to nil.

Paul Vautin runs hard and brushes off a Blues defender in Origin II, 1988.

Allan Langer celebrates victory in Origin I, 1988.

Disaster struck in Origin II, 1989, at the Sydney Football Stadium, 14 June. Allan Langer is carried off with a broken leg. Despite a horrific injury toll, the Maroons won the match, 16–12.

Kerrod Walters, Queensland hooker, moves in to claim the ball when Blues fullback, Gary Jack, knocks on in Origin II, 1989.

Sam Backo goes to ground in David Gillespie's tackle as he gets a pass away to Allan Langer. Michael O'Connor moves to block the pass, watched by John Cartwright (NSW) and Trevor Gillmeister, Dan Stains and Gene Miles (Qld).

Wally Lewis worked as a schools liaison officer for the Queensland Rugby League, until the creation of the Brisbane Broncos created a rift between him and his mentor, Senator Ron McAuliffe.

Bob Lindner moves in to claim New South Wales five-eighth Terry Lamb in Origin II, Lang Park, on 31 May 1988.

They were his pride and joy, and his greatest disappointment. Ron McAuliffe (centre) with Wally Lewis (left) and John Ribot in the halcyon early 1980s when Queensland rode high in State of Origin. The men fell out when Lewis and Ribot left the Queensland Rugby League for the Broncos, Lewis as the new club's captain, Ribot as chief executive officer.

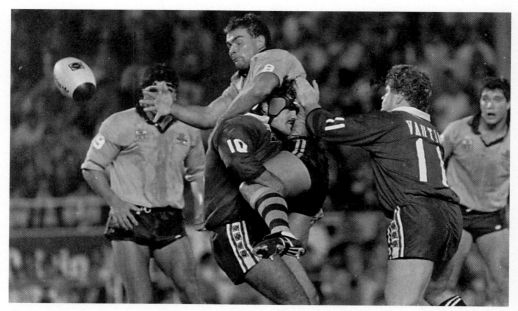

Origin II, Sydney Football Stadium, 14 June 1989. Blues front-rower Peter Kelly (8) gets rid of the ball as he is lifted high by Maroons No. 10, Dan Stains, with some assistance from Fatty Vautin. Mario Fenech (9) and Bradley Clyde (right) are spectators.

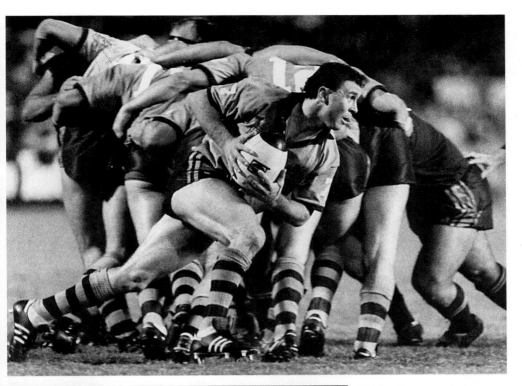

Ricky Stuart made a major contribution to the New South Wales team in 14 State of Origin games from 1990 to 1994. In his initial year as a first grade coach, he guided the Sydney Roosters to a National Rugby League premiership.

Willie Carne carried the ball for Queensland in 12 State of Origin games from 1990 to 1994. His career was shortened by the preference of opposition players to tackle him around the head in both Origin and Club games.

Kevin Walters, Queensland Origin five-eighth, was one of three brothers to share the Origin experience. He played 20 Origin games for the Maroons, 1989–99, and three for Queensland in Super League in 1997. He played 10 tests for Australia.

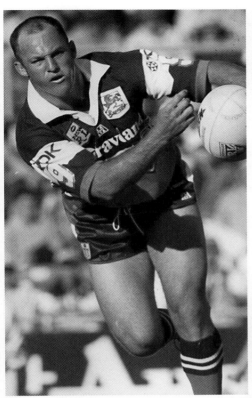

Kerrod Walters, twin brother to Kevin, became the Queensland hooker under controversial circumstances when Wayne Bennett picked him from Reserve Grade to replace Queensland and Australian hooker Greg Conescu. He played six State of Origin games for Queensland from 1989 to 1992 and eight tests for Australia.

Steve Renouf appeared in 11 State of Origin games for the Maroons between 1991 and 1998, as well as two Tri-series games in Super League during 1997. He played 10 tests for the Australian Rugby League and another for Super League.

Michael Hancock played 14 Origin games between 1989 and 1996, the first as an 18-year-old. He played two Tri-series games in Super League and 13 tests for Australia.

Wally Lewis blows up in protest at a Bill Harrigan decision during Origin II at Lang Park on 8 May 1991. Mal Meninga appears uninterested in the outcome.

Julian O'Neill, a brilliant but erratic utility player, appeared in eight State of Origin games and one Tri-series game in Super League. He played in one Super League test.

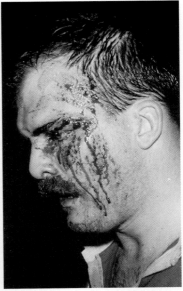

The front row of an Origin scrum is no place for the faint-hearted. Martin Bella leaves the field to have a cut eye attended to during an Origin game at Lang Park.

The picture that inspired the 'blood bin' rule. A jubilant Benny Elias, head swathed in blood-stained bandages, celebrates the New South Wales Origin series win following Origin III at the Sydney Football Stadium, 3 June 1992.

Paul Hauff was a rare talent, but injury forced him out of the game after an all-too-brief career. He played just one series of three games in 1991.

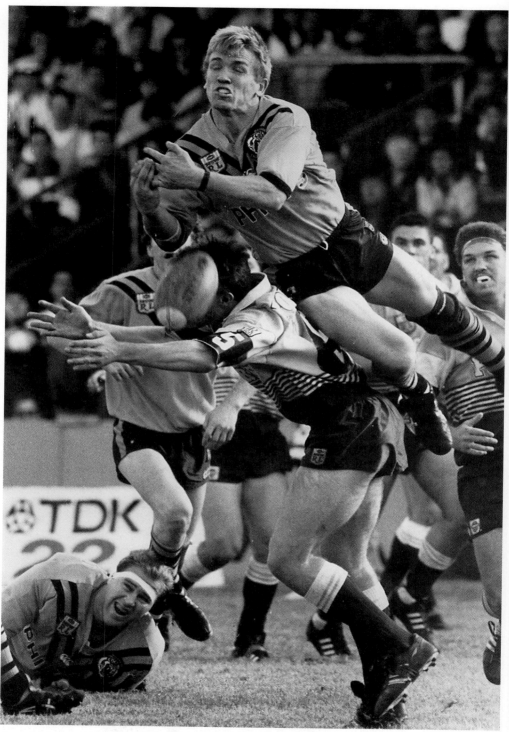

A rare miss by Gary Jack as he soars high in a club game for the Balmain Tigers.

As an 18-year-old teenager, Darren Lockyer signed a three-year contract with the Brisbane Broncos in 1995. Six years later he was a celebrated international player, winner of innumerable Man of the Match awards and vice-captain of the Queensland Origin team.

Probably one of the most feared tacklers in the game, Trevor Gillmeister played 22 Origin games for Queensland. He signed himself out of hospital to captain the side in Origin III, 1995, and led the Maroons to a series whitewash of the Blues.

Chris Walker and his captain, Gorden Tallis, celebrate the brilliant Chris Walker try that sealed the Maroon victory in Origin I, 6 May 2001, at Lang Park. Walker was one of nine Brisbane Broncos in the side that night, many of them debutantes.

Phil 'Gus' Gould, doyen of New South Wales coaches. Gould was in charge of the Blues side from 1992 to 1996 and was recalled to Origin duty in 2002. Of 18 games for which he coached the Blues, they won 10, lost 7 and drew one.

New South Wales supercoach Jack Gibson is one of the finest mentors the game has produced. He had no luck in two years with the Origin, losing four out of the six games played in 1989–90.

Gordon Tallis lines David Barnhill up for a shoulder charge as Brad Fittler and Anthony Mundine close in for a gang tackle, Origin III, 1999.

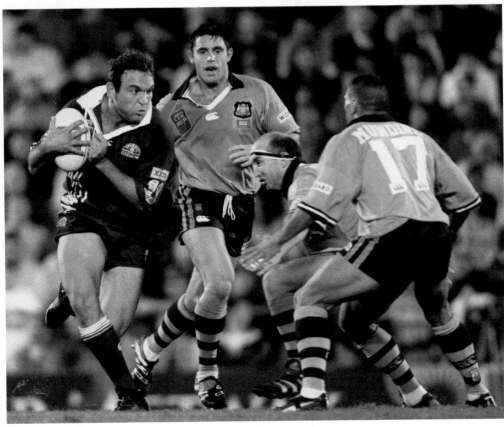

Dane Carlaw is probably the fastest forward in Australia. He stepped around Steve Menzies at full pace on his way to score the equalising try in Origin III, 2002. (Action Photographics)

Darren Smith charges the line in Origin III, 2002. Lockyer looms in support but a Blues' defender already has the ball locked up. (Action Photographics)

Trent Barrett on the charge in Origin III, 2002. The Blues' five-eighth played a major role in both attack and defence in the drawn game. (Action Photographics)

Blues captain, Andrew Johns, attempts to beat Dane Carlaw with step and pace in Origin III, 2002. (Action Photographics)

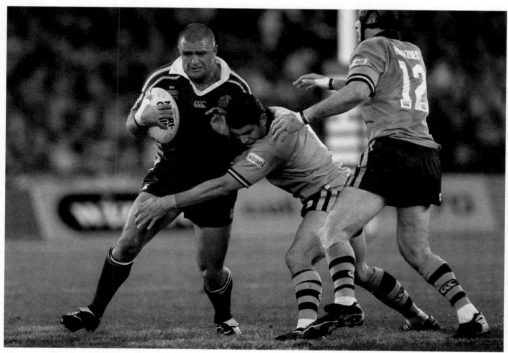

Shane Webcke doesn't get a lot of tries, but he is unlikely to score a more important one than the one he delivered in Origin III, 2002. (Action Photographics)

thirty-five metres out from the Queensland line. Ricky Stuart called for the ball and put up a high bomb. Mick Hancock leapt high for the catch but knocked it straight into the arms of Bennie Elias. The Blues didn't need the six more tackles. From the second tackle, John Cartwright made a diagonal run from dummy half and scored halfway between the goal posts and the corner. Brasher landed the conversion and the Blues were away at 14–4. A little later, Tim Brasher landed a forty-metre penalty goal to make it 16–4 and that was the only addition to the score by either side.

Final result

New South Wales 16 defeated Queensland 4.

Tries for New South Wales: Ricky Stuart, Andrew Ettingshausen, John Cartwright. Goals: Tim Brasher (2).

Goals for Queensland: Mal Meninga (2).

Crowd: 41,878.

Man of the Match: Ricky Stuart.

A visit by the Great Britain side in 1992 saw a great Queenslander take his place in the record books when Mal Meninga captained his country to a Test series win. Perhaps the Australians took the Poms cheaply after the first Test, played at the Sydney Football Stadium, which they won 22–6, for the second was a disaster. Played at Prince's Park, Melbourne as part of a plan to showcase Rugby League in that Australian Rules stronghold, the Australians played 'drop the hanky', using the football as a substitute 'nose wiper'. Thirty-one thousand people watched the Chooms roll over them 33–10.

The two sides met at Lang Park for the decider and Meninga's men prevailed. It was a hard-fought game but the Australians triumphed 16 points to 10, and Mal's name was writ large in the record books. The Brisbane Test match made him the most capped Australian test footballer with 37 tests, one more than Reg Gasnier's former record of 36. He also equalled Keith Holman's record for the number of tests against Great Britain, 14, and his try and four goals gave him a total of 108 points scored in Anglo–Australian Rugby League tests, surpassing both Graeme Langlands record for an Australian, and Neil Fox's overall record. And it was considered quite appropriate that Mal Meninga should win Man of the Match in this his record-breaking Test match.

CHAPTER 15

1993

Mal and the Magic Word

WALLY LEWIS'S long career in representative Rugby League had ended in 1991, but he had continued as captain–coach of the Gold Coast Seagulls. He hung up his boots at the end of 1992, but he continued to coach the Seagulls, and when asked he agreed to become the Maroons' new guide and mentor. The team was little changed. Gary Belcher returned as fullback while Dale Shearer moved to the bench. Steve Renouf replaced Peter Jackson in the centres and Billy Moore was picked as lock. Gary Larson's move to second row displaced Trevor Gillmeister, while Mark Hohn and Andrew Gee were additions to the reserves.

Gus Gould's success in 1992 ensured that he was again chosen to coach the Blues in 1993 and for once the New South Wales team showed some signs of continuity. Tim Brasher's solid game in Origin III, 1992 secured his place. Ian Roberts was back in the team and Paul Harragon displaced John Cartwright in the second row. Andrew Ettingshausen was retained in the side on the wing, replacing Graham Mackay. Chris Johns was also selected but had to withdraw with a strained hamstring. His place was taken by Paul McGregor and there were also one or two changes in the reserves.

There was sensation before the game even got under way. The Channel 9 crew were allowed to take their cameras into the Queensland team's pre-game mid-field huddle, but no one told Mal Meninga that up-close and personal microphones were part of the deal. Mal

STATE OF ORIGIN I, 1993
LANG PARK, 3 MAY

Queensland	New South Wales
Gary Belcher	Tim Brasher
Michael Hancock	Andrew Ettingshausen
Mal Meninga (c)	Brad Fittler
Steve Renouf	Paul McGregor
Willie Carne	Rod Wishart
Kevin Walters	Laurie Daley (c)
Allan Langer	Ricky Stuart
Martin Bella	Glen Lazarus
Steve Walters	Ben Elias
Steve Jackson	Ian Roberts
Bob Lindner	Paul Sironen
Gary Larson	Paul Harragon
Billy Moore	Brad Mackay

Interchange:

Mark Coyne	David Fairleigh
Dale Shearer	Craig Salvatori
Mark Hohn	Jason Taylor*
Andrew Gee	Brett Mullins*

* Were not used in the game.

Coaches:

Wally Lewis	Phil Gould

Referee: Greg McCallum (NSW)

is a great motivator with a first-class vocabulary in the Australian vernacular. Some of the language with which he encouraged the troops that night was quite colourful and of a kind that might offend parents if broadcast before the tiny tots were safely tucked up in their beds. Before the first ball was kicked, Channel 9 switchboards in three capital cities were ablaze with lights as viewers expressed varying degrees of outrage at Mal's pre-game discourse.

With the deafening sound of a capacity Cauldron crowd rolling over the ground, the Blues aimed to first ensure that Queensland didn't score against them. The most obvious way to secure such a result was to kick the ball into the opponents' half at every opportunity and keep it there. The game was a defensive battle from the kick-off and Gus Gould's tactics paid off with an early try. Following a Maroon fumble, Laurie Daley combined with Ricky Stuart to drive play down the field before he fed his fullback, Tim Brasher, who came flying through a gap. Brasher gave the ball to Rod Wishart who scored in the corner. To deafening boos from the partisan crowd, the try-scorer lined up the conversion and put it between the posts. New South Wales led 6–0.

Eighteen minutes into the game, referee Greg McCallum awarded a penalty to the Blues when Queensland hooker, Steve Walters, stole the ball in a tackle. This gave Rod Wishart an opportunity to increase the margin with a kick thirty metres out from the try-line and right in front of the goal posts. He made it 8–0.

The Maroons had more than their share of possession in the first half. They attacked with determination and after about twenty-five minutes of play a penalty in good position enabled Mal Meninga to bring the score closer, but ferocious defence and the educated kicking boot of Ricky Stuart kept the Maroons at bay. Then with less than ten minutes to go until half-time, a Ricky Stuart bomb soared high to come down in the in-goal area near the posts. Gary Belcher flew up for the ball but was almost taken out of play by Andrew Ettingshausen and Tim Brasher. As a result, the ball bounced out of his hands straight into those of the kicker himself. Stuart simply placed it between his feet for a try. The simplest of conversions by Wishart sent the teams to the sheds with New South Wales leading by 12 points to 2.

The Queenslanders were quickly on the attack from the resumption. They drove the Blues back into their own quarter and kept them there. Defence by both sides was fierce, and after one tackle early in the half Paul Sironen left the field with ankle and knee damage, unlikely to return. After only seven minutes of second-half play a powerful run by Bob Lindner sparked a Queensland drive and he played the ball only one metre from the try-line. Just two tackles later, Allan Langer grubbered to the right-hand corner and Lindner ran it down to score the Maroons first try of the match.

The kick sailed wide of the left-hand post, but with a 12–6 scoreline Queensland was looking better.

The second half of football was all Queensland, with the Blues constantly held behind their own 22-metre line, but the New South Wales defence was impeccable. Michael Hancock was renowned for two specialties. He was the man who players hated to tackle. He also had a short fuse. On one of the Blues' rare visits to Queensland territory, Mick was tackled in front of his own goal. Following a bit of niggle by Benny Elias, Mick responded. He pushed the little Balmain hooker on his backside as he got up to play the ball. Wishart extracted full value from the penalty that McCallum awarded and the score was New South Wales 14, Queensland 6.

With thirty minutes of the second half behind them, and the Maroons still on the attack, Steve Walters sent a dummy half pass to his brother Kevin, who quickly hand-balled it on to Allan Langer. Langer beat Brad Mackay before passing to Mal Meninga who ran hard for the line. He seemed to be well covered but he spotted Willie Carne in a better position out wide. He threw a long, high pass to the winger and then watched as Willie drove for the line, carrying Ricky Stuart, Brad Fittler and Tim Brasher on his back. It wasn't Mal Meninga's night with the boot. Mal missed the conversion and it was 14 New South Wales points to Queensland's 10. It remained that way until full-time and the Blues' long run of outs at Lang Park was at an end. Interviewed for television after the game, Bobby Lindner was representative of the whole of the side when he told the interviewer, 'We're dirty on ourselves'. And so they ought to

---

Final result

New South Wales 14 defeated Queensland 10.

Tries for New South Wales: Rod Wishart, Ricky Stuart. Goals: Rod Wishart (3).

Tries for Queensland: Bob Lindner, Willie Carne. Goal: Mal Meninga.

Crowd: 33,000.

Man of the Match: Ricky Stuart.

have been. The Maroons had enough ball that night to win six games of Rugby League. Regardless of the solid defence mounted by the Blues, it was their own bad handling at crucial times and Mal Meninga's loss of goal-kicking form that saw them pull up five points short of victory.

The New South Wales selectors again made minimal changes to their side for Origin II. Ben Elias was out with an injury, replaced by Robbie McCormack, the Newcastle Knights hooker. David Gillespie and Jason Croker replaced Craig Salvatori and Brett Mullins on the bench.

In the Queensland side, the injured Michael Hancock's left wing was occupied by Adrian Brunker. Mark Hohn was picked in Queensland's run-on side for the first time, replacing Steve Jackson who moved to the bench. Trevor Gillmeister came in to the team to join Gary Larson in a reshuffled second row, while Bobby Lindner played lock. Billy Moore was on the bench with Darren Smith and Julian O'Neill, and sad to relate, Mal Meninga had given up goal kicking, at least for the time being. The designated kicker for the evening would be Adrian Brunker.

Queensland had not won at the Sydney Football Stadium since 1989, which may have been why 41,895 Sydneysiders packed the stands for the second Origin game in 1993. They were treated to a feast of Rugby League, with Queensland over for a try within four minutes of the kick-off. At training that year, Broncos' team-mates Allan Langer and Willie Carne perfected a simple move designed to score a try from somewhere inside the opponents' twenty-metre line. From the centre of the field, Alfie would kick the ball so that it landed in the corner of the field, either over or adjacent to the try-line. On the right wing, Willie would first ensure that he remained onside until the ball was kicked, then sprint for the corner. If Alfie's aim was true, then Willie's flying leap in the air would see the ball land on his chest inside the in-goal area where he had but to fall on it or place it for the try.

At the Sydney Football Stadium that night, the move worked perfectly. Television footage clearly shows the winger well onside as the ball leaves the half-back's foot; it depicts his sprint and the leap

STATE OF ORIGIN II, 1993
SYDNEY FOOTBALL STADIUM, 17 MAY

Queensland	New South Wales
Dale Shearer	Tim Brasher
Adrian Brunker	Paul McGregor
Mal Meninga (c)	Brad Fittler
Mark Coyne	Andrew Ettingshausen
Willie Carne	Rod Wishart
Kevin Walters	Laurie Daley (c)
Allan Langer	Ricky Stuart
Martin Bella	Glen Lazarus
Steve Walters	Robbie McCormack
Mark Hohn	Ian Roberts
Trevor Gillmeister	Paul Sironen
Gary Larson	Paul Harragon
Bob Lindner	Brad Mackay

Interchange:

Julian O'Neill	David Fairleigh
Steve Jackson	David Gillespie
Billy Moore	Jason Taylor*
Darren Smith	Jason Croker

* Was not used in the game.

Coaches:

Wally Lewis	Phil Gould

Referee: Eddie Ward (Qld)

for the ball, and finally it shows him circling the cover defence to score halfway between the sideline and the goal posts.

Without appearing to consult his linesmen, Queensland referee Eddie Ward ruled Willie Carne offside and awarded a penalty to New South Wales. It did not look as though it was going to be the Maroons' night. Six minutes after the game started, Gary Larson was finished for the night with a serious leg injury. Fortunately, the reserve bench was flush with good back-rowers and Billy Moore took Larson's place. Moore, Gillmeister, Lindner, Bella, Steve Walters and Mark Hohn were a formidable pack by any measure and they kept the Blues on the back foot throughout the first half, but the Blues had a counter in Ricky Stuart's booming punts downfield.

By way of contrast, Blocker Roach, sideline commentator for Channel 9, described Allan Langer's clearing kicks as pop-guns, but since most of Stuart's kicks were from inside his own twenty-metre line, and Alfie was usually kicking from inside the Blues' half, this presented no problems for the Maroons, whose chief concerns were the tigerish defence of the New South Wales forwards and their own mounting error count.

Queensland could well have been anything from 8 to 12 points up when they finally scored with half-time approaching. With the break looming, Mark Coyne worked a wide blind on the right-hand side of the field. He split the Blues' defence and raced forty metres before feeding the ball inside to Mal Meninga who crashed over, beating both Paul McGregor and Tim Brasher in doing so. Adrian Brunker converted his captain's try and the two teams went to oranges with Queensland leading 6–0.

On the resumption, Alfie Langer tried for an early field goal but missed. Shortly afterwards, Billy Moore anticipated a pass from Laurie Daley to Tim Brasher by a fraction, and was penalised for holding. On the third tackle that followed the tap restart, Laurie Daley scored for the Blues. Rod Wishart's conversion attempt failed and it was Queensland 6, New South Wales 4.

The wisdom of a defender attempting to charge down a clearing kick is often to be doubted. Evidence of this was available just five minutes into the second half when the attempted charge down of a Ricky Stuart kick by Billy Moore resulted in the Queensland lock making just sufficient contact with the ball to place all of the Blues' downtown runners onside but not enough to prevent the ball from flying forty metres downfield to land snugly in Brad Mackay's hands, where he stood unmarked thirty metres from the goal posts. He made haste to score untouched, and Rod Wishart didn't miss with the conversion. Suddenly Queensland was behind, 4–10.

With New South Wales on the attack, Mark Coyne came into a tackle a little too late and lay on the tackled player a little too long. Eddie Ward sent him to the sin-bin for ten minutes, and with

Queensland's twelve-man defence stretched, Andrew Ettingshausen made a long break downfield. Rowdy Shearer ran him down, but from the next tackle Rod Wishart scored under the posts and converted his own try. It was 16–6 to New South Wales. But Queensland never stopped trying and with only a few minutes left in the game Kevin Walters stepped through close defence on the try-line to score next to the posts. Adrian Brunker was never going to miss the kick and it was 16–12.

With the clock ticking down, Mal Meninga made a long break down the right-hand touchline. In his book, Mal describes what happened: 'Across in cover came Blues' Captain, Laurie Daley, and I decided to prop and pass the ball. Soon after, the ball was fumbled, the opportunity lost and the game over.'[1]

New South Wales had won both the game and the 1993 series. Origin II, 1993 was one of the great classics of State of Origin Rugby League, and a game that Queensland ought not to have lost. That the Maroons did lose was due to a number of factors that saw them fail to capitalise on their total domination of the first half. But since the loss was by only four points, it can be laid quite simply at the door of a team that made too many errors.

The teams returned to Lang Park on 31 May for the last game in a dead rubber, but while its status was irrelevant to the outcome of the series, the desire in the Blues for a clean sweep, and that of the Queenslanders to prevent it, ensured that Origin III would be no picnic in the park. There was no suggestion from either side that the occasion might be used to trial new tactics or blood new talent.

Final result

New South Wales 16 defeated Queensland 12.

Tries for New South Wales: Laurie Daley, Brad Mackay, Rod Wishart. Goals: Rod Wishart (2).

Tries for Queensland: Mal Meninga, Kevin Walters. Goals: Dale Shearer, Adrian Brunker.

Crowd: 41,895.

Man of the Match: Tim Brasher.

With Michael Hancock still unfit, brilliant Canterbury winger Brett Dallas replaced Adrian Brunker on the Queensland wing, and at five-eighth Julian O'Neill was preferred to Kevin Walters who was moved to the bench.

In the New South Wales side, Queensland's arch enemy Bennie Elias was back, David Fairleigh moved from the bench to the front row and Terry Hill won his first Blue guernsey off the bench.

It was a New South Wales kick-off before a capacity Lang Park crowd and the portent for Queensland looked good when referee Greg McCallum penalised the Blues for offside after the very first

STATE OF ORIGIN III, 1993
LANG PARK, 31 MAY

Queensland	New South Wales
Dale Shearer	Tim Brasher
Brett Dallas	Graham Mackay
Mal Meninga (c)	Brad Fittler
Mark Coyne	Andrew Ettingshausen
Willie Carne	Rod Wishart
Julian O'Neill	Laurie Daley (c)
Allan Langer	Ricky Stuart
Martin Bella	Glen Lazarus
Steve Walters	Ben Elias
Mark Hohn	David Fairleigh
Trevor Gillmeister	Paul Sironen
Gary Larson	Paul Harragon
Bob Lindner	Brad Mackay

Interchange:

Kevin Walters	Terry Hill
Steve Jackson	David Gillespie
Billy Moore	Jason Taylor
Darren Smith	Scott Gourley

Coaches:

Wally Lewis	Phil Gould

Referee: Greg McCallum (NSW)

tackle. Within a further two minutes the Maroons scored another penalty and this put them on the offensive immediately. They spent almost five minutes attacking the Blues' line before they surrendered possession of the football.

The New South Welshmen seized the opportunity of their first possession and Stuart's boot took them the length of the field. Then, when the Maroons again knocked-on and they regained possession, a Ricky Stuart bomb led to the first points scored in the game. When a huge tackle by Paul Harragon and Paul Sironen on Bob Lindner caused him to lose the ball, the Blues played out a set of six tackles and, on the last, Stuart's kick soared high and came down in the in-goal area close to the Queensland posts. In a scramble in-goal, Brett Dallas had an opportunity to fall on the ball but chose to kick it instead. The ball skidded harmlessly off the side of his foot and the mercuric Andrew Ettingshausen dived on it to score. Wishart converted and after eight minutes New South Wales led 6–0.

A few minutes later Queensland regained possession in their own half. Bobby Lindner beat several Blues in a spectacular downfield bullocking run typical of the man. From the play the ball, Allan Langer hoisted a bomb which Willie Carne retrieved for a try under the posts. Julian O'Neill converted and the scores were tied at 6 all.

Defence was fierce, a normal condition in State of Origin, and, as the game progressed with scores still even, the forwards' tempers appeared to shorten. A trademark third-man stiff-arm tackle on Martin Bella by Paul Harragon set the bells ringing in Bella's head, and in the very next set of six, Bella's get-square led to a one-on-one contest between him and the Chief which was much publicised. This led to boxing becoming more general, and although the story of the Bella versus Harragon heavyweight bout was told and retold for years, it was the view of most of the experts present that the contest between two lighter contestants, 'Boxhead'[2] Steve Walters and 'Backdoor' Benny Elias, was by far the more attractive bout. A men-in-white conference mid-field followed. Despite the urgings of Willie Carne, Mal Meninga and other Queenslanders, Greg McCallum made no signal to the time-keeper and the match clock continued to tick away the seconds and minutes. The four contestants were each given ten minutes to cool it in the sin-bin and the Maroons were awarded a penalty, but by the time that Julian O'Neill's goal netted Queensland two points, and the ball was kicked off to restart play, almost seven minutes had elapsed since McCallum's whistle had signalled the stoppage. Queensland led 8–6, and the twenty-two footballers who continued with the game had all been treated to what almost equalled a buckshee half-time.

Solid defence from both sides saw the status quo retained until just four minutes before the official half-time was declared. Queensland mounted an attack from inside their own half and a forward pass halted play. From the subsequent scrum, and with the clock running down, the Blues threw the ball around as though it was a hot potato. They were fortunate that their passes stuck, and after more than eight men had handled in a scrappy movement, a refreshed Paul Harragon took a perfect pass from Laurie Daley and drove through a gap. Martin Bella and Steve Walters had also enjoyed a seventeen-minute rest period, but both were slow to move to close the gap. They were joined by Kevin Walters and Julian O'Neill in a gang tackle on Harrogan almost a metre short, but, unfortunately for the Maroons, Paul Harragon's arm is a little more than a metre long. Falling, he just managed to lift himself and stretch out to plant the ball over the try-line. The kick by Wishart was successful and the Blues enjoyed half-time savouring the shaky comfort of a 12–8 lead.

The Maroon's second half of football was as determined a passage as they had ever played in State of Origin. They completely dominated the game, but rewards were slow in coming. Time after time Ricky Stuart's boot kept New South Wales out of trouble, and in the forwards Lazarus was outstanding in both defence and attack as first one side and then the other took play end to end. At the seventeen-minute mark, however, Allan Langer made a big break downfield off a Dale Shearer pass. Shearer handled twice in a movement that involved Allan Langer, Mark Coyne and Kevin Walters before Steve Walters beat two tacklers as he dived in low to score. Julian O'Neill was off the field, so that Mal Meninga reprised his kicking role. He converted the Walters try and with twenty minutes of the State of Origin series to go Queensland were again in the lead, 14–12.

Just a few minutes later Darren Smith took off downfield from dummy half and Bob Lindner took a pass from him. Big Scott Gourley thought he had him covered. Ricky Stuart came in from his flank and got a grip on him, but Bobby was too fast, too strong and simply too determined. He fended off Gourley, and with Stuart still hanging on and despite Tim Brasher coming to assist, he was over for a try in a handy position for Mal Meninga to convert. With fifteen minutes until full-time, the Maroons were out to an 8-point lead, 20–12.

With just ten minutes to go, Kevin Walters grubbered into the in-goal. The ball bounced off Andrew Ettingshausen's boot and out into the field of play, there was a mad scramble and Willie Carne was the first to get hold of the ball. A big dive over the line and it was a try to Willie. When Mal's kick missed, it was 24–12 to Queensland. The Blues were tiring fast and the Maroons were in the comfort zone.

The Queenslanders continued to attack, seeking to muster thirty points. The goal posts were ignored when the Maroons were awarded a late penalty right in front of them. Alfie favoured the tap and run, but it brought no reward. Instead, Rod Wishart intercepted the last pass intended for Willie Carne and raced off downfield pursued by Julian O'Neill, Brett Dallas, Willie Carne and Trevor Gillmeister.

Meanwhile, Darren Smith found something offensive in Paul Sironen's manner and hit him with a right hook. Siro responded in kind and the pair attempted to finish what Harragon and Bella had started in the first half. Greg McCallum blew his whistle and soon put a stop to the nonsense. Another men-in-white conference was called, but Wishart and his pursuers failed to hear the signal and a three-or-four-a-side game continued some seventy metres away, with the Blues favoured to score a try. Willie Carne had run Wishart down and the party downfield continued the game for several tackles before they became acquainted with the state of play. By the time it was all sorted out, the siren had sounded. McCallum cautioned every one in sight, threatened to send someone off if they did it again and then blew the whistle for full-time.

So New South Wales won two games out of three and took the trophy home, but from any Rugby League supporter's point of view

---

Final result

Queensland 24 defeated New South Wales 12.

Tries for Queensland: Willie Carne (2), Steve Walters, Bob Lindner. Goals: Mal Meninga (2), Julian O'Neill (2).

Tries for New South Wales: Andrew Ettingshausen, Paul Harragon. Goals: Rod Wishart (2).

Crowd: 31,500.

Man of the Match: Dale Shearer.

---

it had been a cracker of a series, with Queensland unlucky not to win that second game. It was also Bobby Lindner's last series, his last game for Queensland and his last in Australia. He was off to England to see out his career with Oldham.

Bob Lindner played 23 Test matches and 25 State of Origin games in ten seasons and no better Rugby League forward ever wore Maroon or Green and Gold. In the tight stuff he had no peer, and his speed and elusiveness in the open were God-given gifts that were Queensland's pride and joy. The night he finished the game carrying a broken bone in his leg was but the most outstanding of many demonstrations of Bobby Lindner's character, his courage, his loyalty and his commitment to the Maroon guernsey. Aware of all of these things, the Lang Park crowd stayed in the Stadium to farewell him. His team-mates were even more appreciative of his contribution to Rugby League. They lifted him high on their shoulders and chaired him from the field before he strolled around the perimeter and said his goodbyes. Later, at a special ceremony, he was presented with the Wally Lewis medal as Queensland's man of the 1993 series.

CHAPTER 16

1994

Miracle for Mark, Oscar for Bennie

WALLY LEWIS remained as Maroons' coach in 1994, and in his third successive season as New South Wales coach, Gus Gould was seeking a hat-trick.

Apart from the presence of a couple of new interchange players, the Blues were largely the same team that had lost Origin III in 1993. With the exception of David Barnhill, all of them were veterans, most well battle-hardened. The Queensland selectors had made a couple of changes, but Darren Fritz, on the bench, was the only new Maroon.

The five-metre ruck rule had been extended to ten metres for 1994 in the hope that it might give the backs more room to move and open the game up as a spectacle. Perhaps the coaches believed this, but, although both sides made many attempts to pass wide on early tackles, powerful cover defence ensured that the game settled into the same kind of torrid forward battle that State of Origin games had produced under the five-metre rule.

Often it appeared that one or the other side was on top and about to score, but usually there were two or three men in every tackle and when someone did manage to run free, always there was that last tackler coming across in cover. Finally, after eighteen minutes of concentrated defence, a Queensland error gave the Blues a chance. As players converged on the Queensland in-goal in pursuit of a Ricky Stuart bomb, Brad Fittler was spreadeagled while giving chase

STATE OF ORIGIN I, 1994
SYDNEY FOOTBALL STADIUM, 23 MAY

Queensland	New South Wales
Julian O'Neill	Tim Brasher
Michael Hancock	Graham Mackay
Mal Meninga (c)	Brad Fittler
Steve Renouf	Paul McGregor
Willie Carne	Rod Wishart
Kevin Walters	Laurie Daley (c)
Allan Langer	Ricky Stuart
Martin Bella	Glen Lazarus
Steve Walters	Ben Elias
Andrew Gee	Ian Roberts
Trevor Gillmeister	Paul Sironen
Gary Larson	Paul Harragon
Billy Moore	Brad Mackay

Interchange:

Mark Coyne	Andrew Ettingshausen
Darren Smith	David Barnhill
Mark Hohn	Chris Johns
Darren Fritz	David Gillespie

Coaches:

Wally Lewis	Phil Gould

Referee: Bill Harrigan (NSW)

and referee Harrigan deemed Mal Meninga to be at fault. From the tap penalty, Laurie Daley was stopped a metre short of scoring. His lightning quick play the ball to Harragon saw the big Newcastle forward over the line in the midst of three Queenslanders, two of whom claimed to have prevented the grounding of the ball. The referee didn't see it that way. He blew the whistle and pointed to the spot handy to the right of the posts. The Queenslanders considered the try questionable because of the presence of hands between the ball and the ground beneath it, but earlier Laurie Daley's lightning quick play the ball was so effective only because it was made while he was still lying on the ground. As the ball came back from between his legs, his head, shoulder, one knee and one arm were still in contact with the ground. Quite clearly, it ought to have been a penalty to the Maroons, but that was all history.[1] The Blues led 4–0 and after Rod Wishart converted the try they led 6–0.

Field goals seldom enter calculations early in a State of Origin game, but so solid was the defence that Ricky Stuart thought that a point might decide the issue. He attempted a dropped goal in the 24th minute. He missed, but the Maroons continued under pressure and at one point a grubber kick into the in-goal area was saved by Julian O'Neill following a chain passing movement in which the ball went through thirteen pairs of hands. O'Neill's low, raking drop-out was intercepted on the Queensland thirty-metre line by Laurie Daley but a Blues error saw the Queenslanders back in possession. Willie Carne came off the Maroon thirty-metre line and ran the ball sixty metres downfield in the first real sign of attack by the Queenslanders. A New South Wales infringement gave the Maroons an opportunity, and from the third tackle after the tap penalty Allan Langer passed to Kevvie Walters. Walters sent Steve Renouf down the left-hand touchline and backed up to take a pass when the cover came across. The ball then travelled quickly across the field to Allan Langer and on to Steve Walters and Mal Meninga who drew the winger inside before giving the final pass to Julian O'Neill who scored in the corner. O'Neill's attempt at the conversion failed and the Queenslanders were on the board at 4–6, but injuries were taking their toll. In quick succession both Trevor Gillmeister and Julian O'Neill left the field limping. Willie Carne moved to fullback and Mark Coyne took his place on the wing.

The score was unchanged at half-time and for a considerable time thereafter. The Blues were on the attack early in the second half and continued to pound the Maroon defensive line for more than twenty minutes without any joy. Just thirteen minutes before full-time, Laurie Daley put in a little kick and chase on the Maroon forty-metre line. He picked it up on the fly, beat Willie Carne and then gave it to Brad Mackay backing up inside. Mackay cleared out and put it down under the posts. With Wishart out of the game, Graham Mackay took the kick and the score was New South Wales 12, Queensland 4.

The Queenslanders were gone for all money but nobody told them so. With only five minutes to go, Allan Langer ran from dummy half deep in his own half and beat tackles by Laurie Daley and Ben Elias before being brought down on his own forty-metre line by Brad Fittler. He quickly played the ball, which went from Steve Walters to his brother Kevin, on to Willie Carne who chimed into the back line from fullback, and then to Steve Walters who passed to Steve Renouf. In the words of Ray Warren, the Channel 9 commentator, 'Renouf turned on the after burner,' and left grasping Blues' hands behind him as he ran the ball down to the Blues' thirty-metre line where he gave it to Mal Meninga. Meninga found Mark Coyne with debutante Darren Fritz outside him and they both handled before Fritz passed to Willie Carne who scored the try. Mal Meninga converted. It was New South Wales 12, Queensland 10 and the game was taking its toll on both sides. The Blues had also lost their fullback when Tim Brasher was hurt in an attempt to stop Willie Carne.

The Maroons attacked desperately as the clock ran down, but when Ricky Stuart put his clearing kick into touch only twenty metres out from the Queensland goal line, and it lacked less than two minutes to full-time, the punters who had backed the Blues were lining up to collect.

From the scrum, Mark Coyne was caught with the ball and played it on Queensland's forty-metre line. Mal Meninga's dummy half pass went to Allan Langer who sent it on to Kevin Walters. Kevin fed Willie Carne who lobbed an overhead toss to Steve Renouf, still on the Queensland forty-metre line. Steve turned on the turbo charger again and beat three defenders as he sprinted down the left touchline. With cover closing, he passed inside to Mick Hancock who found Darren Smith backing up down the centre. As he was tackled, Darren gave the ball to Alfie and Alfie passed to Mal Meninga. The captain found Mark Coyne outside unmarked. Coyne stepped inside Ricky Stuart and went to ground in the arms of Brad Fittler and the Maroons arch enemy, Benny Elias. Falling, he reached out with the ball and although his arms weren't as long as Paul Harragon's they were just long enough. He plonked the ball down right on the line. The Sydney Football Stadium lapsed into a stunned silence. With only seconds remaining in the game, the Queenslanders had hit the front, 14–12.

It was a magnificent try. Channel 9's Ray 'Rabbits' Warren could not restrain himself: 'It's not a try … it's a miracle.'

Mal Meninga's kicking form had not been great, but he wasn't going to miss this one, and the Maroons defeated the Blues 16–12.

Final result
Queensland 16 defeated New South Wales 12.

Tries for Queensland: Julian O'Neill, Willie Carne, Mark Coyne. Goals: Mal Meninga (2).

Tries for New South Wales: Brad Mackay, Paul Harragon. Goals: Graham Mackay (2).

Crowd: 41,859.

Man of the Match: Willie Carne.

Neither side made any drastic change to their side for Origin II. Renouf was out of the Queensland side, injured, and was replaced by Origin I hero Mark Coyne. In the forwards, Darren Fritz was promoted to the run-on side to replace Marty Bella, also a casualty.

Television ratings had shown that State of Origin Rugby League attracted an army of viewers south of the Murray River, and, in order to capitalise on this, the New South Wales Rugby League was persuaded to sacrifice one of the two 1994 Origin home games to which it was entitled in order to undertake missionary work in the Australian Football League capital, and to carry out this crusade at the AFL Sanctum Sanctorum.

The Blues kicked off before a Melbourne Cricket Ground crowd numbering 87,161.[2] No game of Rugby League in Australia had ever drawn a crowd that came close to this number. However, if it was the intention of the Australian Rugby League to showcase a fast, open, spectacular game, then they forgot to tell the footballers. Thousands of those who attended that night were expatriates from

STATE OF ORIGIN II, 1994
THE MELBOURNE CRICKET GROUND, 8 JUNE

Queensland	New South Wales
Julian O'Neill	Tim Brasher
Michael Hancock	Andrew Ettingshausen
Mal Meninga (c)	Brad Fittler
Mark Coyne	Paul McGregor
Willie Carne	Brett Mullins
Kevin Walters	Laurie Daley (c)
Allan Langer	Ricky Stuart
Darren Fritz	Glen Lazarus
Kerrod Walters	Ben Elias
Andrew Gee	Paul Harragon
Trevor Gillmeister	Paul Sironen
Gary Larson	Dean Pay
Billy Moore	Bradley Clyde

Interchange:

Adrian Vowles	Brad Mackay
Darren Smith	David Barnhill
Mark Hohn	Chris Johns
Gorden Tallis	Ken Nagas

Coaches:

Wally Lewis	Phil Gould

Referee: Graham Annesley (NSW)

Queensland and New South Wales, and there was a very heavy seasoning of Maorilanders in the crowd, aficionados deprived of quality live Rugby League by circumstances of family and employment which caused them to be marooned in the southern sea of Aussie Rules. These were people who understood Rugby League and there is no doubt they enjoyed the dour struggle that was Origin II. However, thousands more were native Victorians drawn by curiosity to come and watch this strange game from the north.

The Blues' forwards dominated the game from the outset. Paul Harragon gave notice of their intention in the sixth minute of the game when he hit Gary Larson with a head-high tackle that failed to attract any form of chastisement from the referee. This set the pattern of play as the big Blues' pack took command of the centre of the ground and made it their own. In his pre-game talk, Gus Gould said nothing about swinging the ball wide and outrunning the Queensland backs. Keep it tight and outmuscle their forwards — that was the plan and the Blues stuck with it all night.

Fortune favoured Queensland early and for the first eight minutes of the game they used a mountain of possession to attack the Blues' line. The Blues absorbed the pressure and once they gained possession they were constantly on the attack. From the fifth-tackle play-the-ball of a set that followed a Maroon line drop-out in the 20th minute of the game, Ben Elias dummied to pass to Stuart for the kick but Glen Lazarus was on the charge and Elias gave him the ball instead. Lazo crashed over the line. Brasher converted the try and less than three minutes later a penalty against the Maroons for raking the ball out in a tackle provided him with another opportunity which he accepted gratefully. The resultant 8–0 in favour of the Blues was still the score when the half-time whistle sounded.

While the Blues continued to play it hard and tight in the second half, whenever they got the ball the Queenslanders attempted to open up the game but had a great deal of difficulty in doing so. Dropped ball and other simple errors plagued the Maroons. Frustration at the constant errors became a factor when Paul Harragon provoked Andrew Gee into pugilistic retaliation in front of goal, inside his own twenty-metre line. After a brief and indecisive bout, the touch judge rushed in, the court assembled and a penalty was awarded to the Blues. Brasher's kick put them into double figures at 10 nil.

A few minutes later Bennie Elias went quickly to ground after a brush with winger Willie Carne and claimed that Willie had clipped him in the head with his elbow in passing. Bennie Elias had Academy Award winning potential in these situations and once more the touch judge halted play for the Blues to be awarded a penalty. The tap restart that followed the penalty was taken about twenty metres out from the Maroon try-line. Ricky Stuart took the ball as first receiver, dummied to run and drew three defenders to him leaving a wide gap. He passed to Paul McGregor who strolled over for the simplest of tries. Tim Brasher's attempted conversion hit the post and bounced back into the field of play, but it was 14–0 and the Queenslanders were gone for all money. For only the second time in fourteen years of State of Origin and over forty games, Queensland bowed down without scoring a point and the form of the two sides suggested that Gus Gould's men had a golden opportunity to achieve a whitewash.

Final result

New South Wales 14 defeated Queensland O.

Tries for New South Wales: Glen Lazarus, Paul McGregor. Goals: Tim Brasher (3).

Crowd: 87,161.

Man of the Match: Paul Harragon.

No footballer had given longer and more effective service to New South Wales than their hooker, Ben Elias, and he was playing in his last series. The Blues wanted to give him a victorious send-off but Bennie was much unloved by the Maroons. They were just as keen to see him leave a loser and they had an agenda of their own. This game would be Mal Meninga's thirty-second game of Origin Rugby League, and his last. The Maroons had provided The King with a victorious farewell in 1991, and they badly wanted to do the same for his successor.

There was minimal change to either team. Renouf was back from injury, pushing Mark Coyne to the bench. Billy Moore replaced Trevor Gillmeister in the second row and former Brisbane Easts utility Jason Smith locked the Queensland scrum.

Andrew Ettingshausen returned to the Blues' wing, and Ian Roberts replaced the injured Glen Lazarus. These were the only changes made by the Blues.

It seemed that so determined were the Maroons to provide their captain with the kind of farewell he deserved that they attempted to score from almost every ruck, and this was their undoing. Knock-

STATE OF ORIGIN III, 1994
LANG PARK, 20 JUNE

Queensland	New South Wales
Julian O'Neill	Tim Brasher
Michael Hancock	Andrew Ettingshausen
Mal Meninga (c)	Brad Fittler
Steve Renouf	Paul McGregor
Willie Carne	Brett Mullins
Kevin Walters	Laurie Daley (c)
Allan Langer	Ricky Stuart
Darren Fritz	Ian Roberts
Steve Walters	Ben Elias
Mark Hohn	Paul Harragon
Billy Moore	Paul Sironen
Gary Larson	Dean Pay
Jason Smith	Bradley Clyde

Interchange:

Andrew Gee	Brad Mackay
Darren Smith	David Barnhill
Mark Coyne	Chris Johns
Gorden Tallis	Ken Nagas

Coaches:

Wally Lewis	Phil Gould

Referee: Bill Harrigan (NSW)[3]

ons, dropped passes and poor selection of options led to chaos. The Blues took full advantage. Just ten minutes after kick-off, Ben Elias intercepted an Allan Langer pass and whipped it out to Bradley Clyde who ran forty metres to score. Tim Brasher converted and New South Wales led 6–0.

The Blues soon scored again, this time after some brilliant work by their captain. From a play-the-ball close to the Queensland line, Laurie Daley stepped around four or five Maroon defenders before placing the ball under the posts. It was an easy kick for Brasher who made it 12–0.

As half-time approached, the Blues' newest addition to the back line, Brett Mullins, intercepted a Maroon pass intended for Michael Hancock. He ran half the length of the field untouched to score under the black dot. Brasher would have sent his side to the sheds with an 18–0 lead, but just before the break Andrew Gee managed to barge over the Blues line, Julian O'Neill converted and at half-time it was New South Wales 18, Queensland 6.

With the second half a quarter of an hour old, Kevin Walters put Steve Renouf through a hole. He outpaced the cover to score in a good position, but a few minutes earlier Ben Elias had potted a field goal for the Blues. After O'Neill's conversion, Queensland still needed to score twice to equalise. It was 19–12 in favour of the Blues.

The capacity Lang Park crowd lifted the Maroons. Two mighty bullocking runs by their captain lifted them even further, but after a serious ankle injury to Willie Carne stopped the game for a few minutes and allowed the Blues to regroup, Brad Fittler kicked another field goal to give his team an 8-point lead.

Fittler struck again soon afterwards. Kevin Walters threw a long, cut-out pass to Mal Meninga. It was ill directed and, moving up in defence, Freddie Fittler had time to alter his line and intercept the ball. No one got near him as he galloped sixty metres and placed the ball under the crossbar. Brasher's conversion made the score 26–12 but the Blues weren't done. Two minutes from full-time Ben Elias delivered his final note of defiance to the Queenslanders when he kicked another field goal. It was the game and the third consecutive series to the Blues, 27–12. For the Maroons to lose by such a margin

---

Final result

New South Wales 27 defeated Queensland 12.

Tries for New South Wales: Brad Clyde, Laurie Daley, Brett Mullins, Brad Fittler. Goals: Tim Brasher (4). Field goals: Ben Elias (2), Brad Fittler.

Tries for Queensland: Andrew Gee, Steve Renouf. Goals: Julian O'Neill (2).

Crowd: 40,665.

Man of the Match: Ben Elias.

hurt — more so when the difference plus a bit was made up of three runaway tries.

For Australian Rugby League 1994 is a landmark year but for all the wrong reasons. It was in 1994 that the slumbering spectre of Super League first reared its rebellious head, although the first recorded use of the magic words was eight years earlier. In July 1986 a Sydney Daily Telegraph journalist wrote:

> Australian Rugby League Supremo Ken Arthurson has proposed a Super League to replace the present mid-week cup competition. Arthurson has suggested a super league comprising four or five teams from Sydney, two from Brisbane, three New South Wales country teams, Queensland Country and Auckland.

The chairman had proposed that teams be amalgamated for the purpose of strengthening the midweek knockout competition. His suggestion was never taken up for this purpose, but those who remembered his proposal would have cause to recall an old biblical quotation: 'He who has sown the wind, shall reap the whirlwind.'[4]

Through his family's controlling interest in the Brisbane *Courier-Mail* newspaper, Rupert Murdoch became a major sponsor of the Brisbane Broncos' club in 1992,[5] but his interest in Rugby League went much deeper. It was his intention that News Ltd, the international media conglomerate that he controlled, would be a major player in Pay Television when it commenced operations in Australia. In America and Europe, sport is the basic diet of Pay TV and if his venture was to succeed in Australia Rupert needed Rugby League as a major drawcard. He had plans for a Super League of about the size suggested by Ken Arthurson in 1986, but as the major all-season regime, and not simply for a midweek knockout competition. He already had a toehold with the sport through a News Ltd subsidiary that had controlled the marketing arm of the Australian Rugby League since 1983 in an arrangement that was very profitable for the League.[6]

Following negotiations, a meeting of all of the clubs was convened in Sydney in February 1995 to hear News Ltd representatives outline their Super League proposal. This, and a subsequent question and answer session, were the sole items on the agenda. However, when the meeting broke for lunch, senior executives of the League rang Kerry Packer, the owner of Channel 9. The Packer interests held the rights to broadcast Rugby League free to air until the year 2000. Senior Australian Rugby League figures sympathetic to the tycoon believed that he had an interest in any proposed change. They invited him to talk to the assembly after lunch.

It has been suggested by some who were at the meeting that the representative chosen to present the News Ltd Super League proposal was something less than diplomatic in his approach to his subject. It is claimed that his sales pitch contained a good deal of criticism of the administration of both the League and its component clubs. However, this point must remain forever moot since Kerry Packer settled the argument in short order, at least for the time being.

The television tycoon told the meeting that his arrangement with the Australian Rugby League provided him with control of Rugby League broadcasts for all forms of television until the year 2000 and no one missed the crux of his speech: 'I would just like you to know that I have a binding contract with you people, and if any of the clubs go against it, I'll sue the arse off you.'[7]

This came as news to most of those present. It also cast some doubt on the Australian Rugby League's good faith in its negotiations with Rupert Murdoch, but the Australian Rugby League officials didn't argue and no one asked Kerry Packer to produce any paper work to prove his claim of virtual ownership of Rugby League in Australia. That would have seemed to have been that, except that Rupert Murdoch decided to start his own Rugby League competition. On 12 March it was reported that nine of the twenty clubs had taken up Kerry's challenge to place their arses in legal jeopardy. They signed up with News Ltd to play in a separate Super League competition in 1996. The resultant split started a conflict that raged for almost as long as World War I. It created factions, some of whose members would bear ill will toward their rivals for a lifetime, and in the short term everyone involved went out and hired job lots of some of Australia's most expensive lawyers and prepared, in Kerry Packer's words, 'to sue the arse off' each other.

For the time being, however, nothing seemed to have changed and the premiership competition continued as normal under the control of the Australian Rugby League. Arko's proposal had back-fired big time. He had proposed twelve teams drawn from Queensland and New South Wales and from both the city and the country. He got Queensland and the country areas involved alright, but instead of twelve 'Super' teams through consolidation, there were twenty clubs, most of them fated to be battlers, all of them considerably short of super quality, weakened as they were by the inevitable dilution of the available talent.

Then, on April Fools Day, Rupert Murdoch and Super League struck in what Arko described as 'The Pearl Harbor attack'.[8] Players from all over the country were signed for a new Super League competition in lightning raids mounted with military precision. Among those signing were the whole of the Brisbane Broncos playing staff and it appeared that the sums for which these contracts were written were more than double that which the best players had received pre–Super League. This swoop was followed by a similar all-out effort by the Australian Rugby League to sign players to contracts for similarly huge amounts, contracts that bound them to those clubs that had remained loyal. Kerry Packer and League sponsors Optus provided what appeared to be unlimited funds for the purpose. In order to reinforce its sales pitch, the League an-nounced that no player who signed with Super League would be considered for representative football.

CHAPTER 17

1995

Fatty Is No Clown

FOLLOWING a run of three consecutive losses, the Queensland Rugby League had asked Wayne Bennett to coach the 1995 Maroons and he had agreed, but the controversy over Super League intervened. While the ban on player selections did not extend to him, Wayne Bennett's position was unique among Australian Rugby League coaches. He was a shareholder in the company that owned the Brisbane Broncos and a member of its Board of Directors. He was totally committed to the club and to its players. When the Queensland Rugby League announced that no Super League player would be selected for the Queensland State of Origin side, he felt obliged to withdraw as its coach.

Seeking a new guide and mentor for the 1995 team, the Queensland Rugby League chose a man whose experience in the highly specialised field of coaching was almost zero. However, his commitment to the cause of the Maroons and his depth of experience in State of Origin football had few equals.

In 1982 Paul Vautin was a member of the first Queensland State of Origin team to play a full three-game series, and in the eight years that followed he was always one of the first players picked. In a nine-year career with the Maroons, his only absence from selected teams had been through injury.

After football, Paul Vautin's had become a household name. Dubbed 'Fatty', or 'The Fat Man', he was familiar to Rugby League supporters through his involvement with national television. He was an integral part of the team that broadcast Rugby League each weekend and he also hosted the high-rating *Footy Show*, broadcast each Thursday night during the Rugby League season on the Channel 9 network. The comical image presented by his activities on the *Footy Show* caused his appointment to coach the Queensland State of Origin side to come as a surprise to some people. However, the real Paul Vautin is no clown. He made this clear at the first meeting of the 1995 Queensland State of Origin team: 'What you see on television, that's what I do for a living and I get paid well to do it ... This is different. I would gladly pay money for the chance to coach Queensland ...'[1]

The team soon discovered that their coach meant what he said, but they had been given a forlorn hope at best. Given Queensland's much smaller player base than that of the Blues, it was obvious to the meanest intelligence that the ban on Super League players would have a far greater effect on the Maroons than it would have on the Blues.

A replacement had to be found for Mal Meninga, now retired, but substitutes were also needed for Mal's natural successor as captain, Allan Langer, for Julian O'Neill and for Steve Renouf, Willie Carne, Michael Hancock and Kevin Walters — almost the entire Maroon back division and internationals to a man. And then there were forwards like Gorden Tallis, Steve Walters, Andrew Gee and that versatile centre–second rower Darren Smith. This was close to being the Maroons' full quota of current and past internationals, all stars and all State of Origin players. Many of those who replaced them were discarded by the experts of the media as 'no-names', a term that was cruelly accurate in some cases.

Matt Sing, a youngster from North Queensland who modelled his game on that of Steve Renouf, was playing his first season of A Grade with Penrith and he was not the least of the unknowns. On the morning that the team assembled at the Park Royal Hotel in Brisbane, Paul Vautin was about to enter the lift when he was accosted by a bare-headed teenager. Dressed in tee-shirt, board shorts and thongs, the lad carried a small kit-bag. He asked the coach where to find the Queensland State of Origin players.

'Sorry, lad,' Fatty said, 'There are no visitors allowed. If you want autographs you can get them later out at training.'

He was taken aback by the response: 'I don't want autographs, Mr Vautin, I'm your new centre. Ben Ikin.'

The Blues were more fortunate. Long prone to change their side at any sniff of defeat, the Blues' selectors had a wide range of State of Origin veterans from which to choose a team.

They had lost Lazarus, the Brisbane front-rower, to Super League, but they were able to replace him with another physically intimidating front-rower in Manly enforcer Mark 'Spud' Carroll. Laurie

---

STATE OF ORIGIN I, 1995
SYDNEY FOOTBALL STADIUM, 15 MAY

Queensland	New South Wales
Robbie O'Davis	Tim Brasher
Brett Dallas	Rod Wishart
Mark Coyne	Terry Hill
Danny Moore	Paul McGregor
Matt Sing	Craig Hancock
Dale Shearer	Matthew Johns
Adrian Lam	Andrew Johns
Tony Hearn	Paul Harragon
Wayne Bartrim	Jim Serdaris
Gaven Allen	Mark Carroll
Gary Larson	Brad Mackay
Trevor Gillmeister (c)	Steve Menzies
Billy Moore	Brad Fittler (c)

Interchange:

Terry Cook	Greg Florimo
Ben Ikin	David Fairleigh
Mark Hohn	Matt Seers
Craig Teevan	Adam Muir

Coaches:

Paul Vautin	Phil Gould

Referee: Eddie Ward (Qld)

Daley and Ricky Stuart were out when Canberra joined Super League, but the Sydney media had been talking for months about the uncanny combination of brothers Matthew and Andrew Johns from Newcastle. The Blues' selectors had the opportunity to showcase them at Origin level. Cronulla's defection left State of Origin stalwart Andrew Ettingshausen out of contention, but there was a wealth of good fullbacks available, and it would not be Tim Brasher's first game for his state in the position.

Queensland was allowed a certain elasticity in the rules of State of Origin in selecting Adrian Lam, a Papua New Guinean, as half. Needs must when the devil drives. That great winger or fullback Dale Shearer was transformed into a five-eighth. St George lock Wayne Bartrim was picked as hooker, but such a jury-rigged team seemed to have little hope against a Blues' side where every man was a specialist in his position. If ever the Maroons' much talked of Queensland Spirit was to inspire its sons, then this had to be the occasion.

And it did.

In the tightest game of interstate Rugby League ever decided, the Maroons stunned the capacity Sydney crowd in an exhibition of sheer guts and commitment that may well have been equalled somewhere but never surpassed. With every man giving everything he had to the team, the tryless Maroons defeated the equally tryless Blues by virtue of a single penalty goal kicked by the erstwhile lock, now a hooker, Wayne Bartrim. This happened in the thirtieth minute of the game. For the remaining seventy-nine minutes, solid, hard-rucking forward play kept the Blues at bay, while inspired defence frustrated them on at least two occasions when a Blues' player crossed the line. In a last-ditch effort Matt Sing got between the ball and

---

Final result

Queensland 2 defeated New South Wales 0.

Goal for Queensland: Wayne Bartrim.

Crowd: 39,841.

Man of the Match: Gary Larson.

the ground in-goal when big Terry Hill looked certain to score. On a second occasion, a desperate tackle took Rod Wishart over the corner post just as he was about to ground the ball over the try-line.

Post-match, Paul Vautin was beside himself. He heaped praise on his team of so-called nobodies, while all over Queensland followers of the game rejoiced in one of Rugby League's magic moments.

For Origin II, Queensland selectors had little room to move. Dale Shearer was unavailable through injury, and they were fortunate in having an equally versatile replacement in Jason Smith. Smith was quite at home at five-eighth and this was the only change made to the victorious Origin I side.

The Blues' selectors applied their normal policy. When in doubt, kick 'em out. Six of the losing seventeen were replaced, and the remainder were reshuffled.

Players weren't the only people blacklisted by the Australian Rugby League. New South Wales' top referees had also defected to Super League, and for the first time in Rugby League history all three 1995 matches were refereed by Queenslanders.

The dour display provided by Queensland and New South Wales at their previous start at the Melbourne Cricket Ground might well have pleased a Rugby League purist, but it was far from being an advertisement for the game, and the crowd that backed up for this second missionary endeavour reflected this. While a fifty thousand plus attendance was beyond the capacity of any ground available in Sydney, it barely half filled the MCG and those who stayed at home were the losers. It was a rattling good game.

A 2–0 loss is hardly sufficient to dissuade a one-eyed fan with money to back his fancy. The replacements in the New South Wales side, such as Dean Pay, Greg Florimo and David Barnhill, were all men of Rugby League substance. In any case, no true Blues' supporter could possibly accept the verdict of Origin I as a true indication of the game. The southern punters sent the Blues out as the hottest of red-hot favourites for Origin II.

It was widely rumoured that the Blues' brains trust considered that there had been too little aggressive spirit displayed by the side that lost Origin I. That they intended to do something about it was made clear when the men-in-blue put the biff on early in Origin

STATE OF ORIGIN II, 1995
MELBOURNE CRICKET GROUND, 31 MAY

Queensland	New South Wales
Robbie O'Davis	Tim Brasher
Brett Dallas	Rod Wishart
Mark Coyne	Terry Hill
Danny Moore	Paul McGregor
Matt Sing	John Hopoate
Jason Smith	Brad Fittler (c)
Adrian Lam	Andrew Johns
Tony Hearn	Paul Harragon
Wayne Bartrim	Jim Serdaris
Gaven Allen	Dean Pay
Gary Larson	Greg Florimo
Trevor Gillmeister (c)	David Barnhill
Billy Moore	Brad Mackay

Interchange:

Terry Cook	Steve Menzies
Ben Ikin	David Fairleigh
Mark Hohn	Brett Rodwell
Craig Teevan	Adam Muir

Coaches:

Paul Vautin	Phil Gould

Referee: Eddie Ward (Qld)

II. With the game less than three minutes old, a scrum broke up in a welter of flying fists. When players attempted to break up the fight, boxing become general, and Eddie Ward and his linesmen had to work hard for almost three minutes to quell the disturbance.

Ten minutes later Mark Coyne scored for Queensland. There was some discussion about the try, with the Blues claiming that there had been a knock-on involved in the movement of the ball to the try-scorer, but Eddie Ward called it a try and there was no going back. Wayne Bartrim converted and it was 6–0 to Queensland. Eight minutes later, a Queensland penalty for offside gave Wayne Bartrim another opportunity: Queensland 8, New South Wales 0. With half-time looming, overheated tempers flared again and a brawl erupted among the forwards. This time Eddie Ward took action. Paul Harragon and Gaven Allen each spent ten minutes in the sin-bin. A little later Wishart added a penalty goal to his tally, and Queensland's lead was reduced to make the half-time score Queensland 8, New South Wales 2.

The Blues staged a come-back early in the second half when Brett Rodwell scored out wide. The try remained unconverted and the Maroons led 8–6, but they went further ahead when Wayne Bartrim landed another penalty goal to give his team a 10 points to 6 lead. Shortly after the restart of play, the Queenslanders scored again when Adrian Lam took a sharp inside pass from substitute Terry Cook and scored wide out. Bartrim missed the conversion, Queensland held a 14–6 lead, and so it remained until five minutes before full-time when the Blues' hooker, Jim Serdaris, scored from a set move and Wishart converted to bring the difference down to just two points.

In the dying minutes the Blues threw everything at the Maroons and almost scored when Steve Menzies was held up over the line. Seconds later, dangerman Tim Brasher came flying to take a pass from Brad Fittler and touched down close to the posts. Roars of delight from the New South Wales supporters turned to howls of rage when Eddie Ward blew the whistle and signalled a forward pass.

Brett Dallas was probably the fastest man on the field that night. From a Maroon play-the-ball on their own twenty-metre line, he

---

Final result

Queensland 20 defeated New South Wales 12.

Tries for Queensland: Mark Coyne, Adrian Lam, Brett Dallas. Goals: Wayne Bartrim (4).

Tries for New South Wales: Brett Rodwell, Jim Serdaris. Goals: Rod Wishart (2).

Crowd: 52,994.

Man of the Match: Jason Smith.

stepped and dummied through tired defence. He broke the Blues' line with the full-time siren sounding and sprinted eighty metres to score under the posts. Wayne Bartrim did the honours and a game that had been delicately balanced with a minute to go became a clear-cut victory to the Maroons.

For the third game, the Queensland side remained unaltered, but the Blues again rang the changes with two recruits new to State of Origin being blooded. David Hall, a North Sydney winger, would play his first and last game for New South Wales, but Geoff Toovey, the game little Manly half-back, would go on to play many.

STATE OF ORIGIN III, 1995
SUNCORP STADIUM, 12 JUNE

Queensland	New South Wales
Robbie O'Davis	Tim Brasher
Brett Dallas	Rod Wishart
Mark Coyne	Terry Hill
Danny Moore	Paul McGregor
Matt Sing	David Hall
Jason Smith	Matthew Johns
Adrian Lam	Geoff Toovey
Tony Hearn	Paul Harragon
Wayne Bartrim	Jim Serdaris
Gaven Allen	Mark Carroll
Gary Larson	Steve Menzies
Trevor Gillmeister (c)	Adam Muir
Billy Moore	Brad Fittler (c)

Interchange:

Terry Cook	Matt Seers
Ben Ikin	David Fairleigh
Mark Hohn	Greg Florimo
Craig Teevan	David Barnhill

Coaches:

Paul Vautin	Phil Gould

Referee: David Manson (Qld)

Origin III, 1995 was the first played at a revamped Lang Park, now named Suncorp Stadium for a sponsor. With a new grandstand, it was capable of accommodating more than 40,000 spectators, and it was packed out for Origin III.

If, at the beginning of the season, a punter had wished to back this bob-tailed Maroon side to win the 1995 State of Origin series 3–0, he could have written his own ticket with any bookmaker in the country. But that is what Fatty Vautin's youngsters were shooting for when they ran on to Lang Park that night and with an early try by Jason Smith, converted by Wayne Bartrim, they gave notice that they just might make it. Their lead of 6–0 was short-lived. A converted try by Tim Brasher brought the Blues level and then, a quarter of an hour before half-time, Rod Wishart crossed in the corner to put the Blues in front, 10–6. It appeared that New South Wales would take this lead into the break, but a minute before the half-time siren was due to sound, Danny Moore stepped inside Tim Brasher to score under the posts. Wayne Bartrim's boot lifted the score to 12–10 in Queensland's favour.

Adam Muir scored just after half-time to put the Blues in front, but within ten minutes the Queenslanders regained the lead. Robbie O'Davis made a long break. There followed a quick play-the-ball and Jason Smith ran from dummy half to feed Brett Dallas with the line open. The red-headed speedster scored untouched between the posts.

It was probably appropriate that the last act of this extraordinary drama should have as its star the unknown youngster who had wandered into the Park Royal in tee-shirt and board shorts. A dropped pass close to the Blues' line was snapped up by Adrian Lam who fired the ball to Ben Ikin. There was nothing in front of the youngster except green grass and the try-line fifteen metres away. Ikin's try was converted by Wayne Bartrim and this brought up the final score, Queensland 24, New South Wales 16.

A clean sweep of a State of Origin series had first been achieved by New South Wales in 1986, but the compliment was returned, in spades, in 1987 and 1988. However, the achievement of this 1995 side of Paul Vautin's transcended anything that had gone before. Deprived of all of the biggest names normally available to the

---

Final result

Queensland 24 defeated New South Wales 16.

Tries for Queensland: Danny Moore, Jason Smith, Brett Dallas, Ben Ikin. Goals: Wayne Bartrim (4).

Tries for New South Wales: Rod Wishart, Adam Muir, Tim Brasher. Goals: Rod Wishart (2).

Crowd: 40,189.

Man of the Match: Adrian Lam.

Man of the Series: Gary Larson.

Maroons, this team of 'second bests', and 'no-names' had achieved what was considered to be the impossible. They were a credit to a state that was proud of them, and no one, especially not those of the Maroon brotherhood who politics had deprived of their places in the team, begrudged them a single moment of the fame and glory that was their right.

CHAPTER 18

1996

Shotgun Wedding

FOLLOWING that first pre-emptive strike by News Ltd to sign players for Super League, a hectic battle was fought for the hearts and minds of Australia's Rugby League community. Rugby League in Australia had been split in a way that could not have been contemplated, and by the end of 1995 Super League was so strong on the agenda that the game almost became secondary to the battle between the two warring factions.

Rupert Murdoch declared Super League a goer. Players were signed, referees and other officials were recruited; there were even new clubs formed and new, extremely colourful guernseys were produced for each of the ten teams that would form the new organisation. Somehow, a major sport that had once sought ways and means of reducing the numbers of its participating clubs from what was considered to be an over-crowded sixteen teams had suddenly been expanded. In 1996 ten teams would contest a Super League competition and a dozen would remain with the Australian Rugby League.

Following the dramatic intervention by Kerry Packer, all twenty clubs then existing had signed loyalty agreements with the Australian Rugby League, but they had not all signed willingly. In the opinion of the expensive lawyers who served Rupert Murdoch's News Ltd, the Australian Rugby League was out of order in demanding such agreements, many of which were signed under duress. As a result, they asked the Federal Court to set these contracts aside. The equivalent of at least a military platoon of lawyers was assembled by each side as they prepared to do battle. The Brisbane Broncos' founding chief executive officer, John Ribot, resigned his position to take charge of Super League. Assured that the legal advice taken by the Murdoch interests was sound, he led the rebel forces into the contest with supreme confidence.

Ken Arthurson, the chairman, and John Quayle, the chief executive officer of the Australian Rugby League, obtained advice from counsel at least as eminent and expensive as those who served Rupert Murdoch. They joined battle equally confident that right was on their side and on 23 February 1996 it appeared that their confidence was not misplaced. Mr Justice Burchett, of the Federal Court, made mincemeat of the News Ltd case. He dismissed it on almost every ground argued. Supporters of the Australian Rugby League celebrated a mighty victory. There would be no Super League in 1996. It looked like the end of the road for the News Ltd venture, but media moguls are possessed of great tenacity, one of the reasons they accumulate such great wealth. When interviewed on television, Rupert Murdoch seemed quite unperturbed. 'Let's call it one nil at half time,' he said, as he announced that his legal people would lodge an appeal to the Full Federal Court.

In 1996 it would be News Ltd lawyers versus Australian Rugby League lawyers in the courts, while for the nonce Mr Burchett's decision created a shotgun wedding of the two parties. Twenty teams would contest the 1996 Australian Rugby League Premiership and all members of all clubs would be available and eligible to play State of Origin football. The sides for Origin I, 1996 were selected on that basis, the outstanding factor in the Queensland case being the retention of 'stop-gap' but miraculously successful coach Fatty Vautin to prepare the Maroons.

By 1996 Rugby League had long since put scrums in the too-hard basket. With loose head and feed going to the non-offending side, the modern hooker is restricted to what was once his secondary duty, to throw a good pass from dummy half. This led to a distinct change in the type of player chosen as 'hooker'. The New South Wales selectors picked Manly and Australian half Geoff Toovey to

STATE OF ORIGIN I, 1996
SUNCORP STADIUM, 20 MAY

Queensland	New South Wales
Robbie O'Davis	Tim Brasher
Brett Dallas	Rod Wishart
Matt Sing	Laurie Daley
Steve Renouf	Andrew Ettingshausen
Wendell Sailor	Brett Mullins
Jason Smith	Brad Fittler (c)
Allan Langer	Geoff Toovey
Tony Hearn	Glen Lazarus
Wayne Bartrim	Andrew Johns
Gary Larson	Paul Harragon
Trevor Gillmeister (c)	Dean Pay
Brad Thorn	David Furner
Billy Moore	Adam Muir

Interchange:

Adrian Lam	Jim Dymock
Michael Hancock	Jamie Ainscough
Alan Cann	Jason Croker
Craig Greenhill	Steve Menzies

Coaches:

Paul Vautin	Phil Gould

Referee: David Manson (Qld)

work the scrums in Origin I in 1996, and teamed him with crack goal-kicking Newcastle half Andrew Johns who played hooker. It was a ploy that worked well.

It was obvious from the first kick-off that the Blues were a more cohesive side than the 1995 losers and they almost scored within two minutes of the start. Andrew Johns' kick to the corner from dummy half was pounced on by Andrew Ettingshausen and the Maroons were saved when referee Manson called the Cronulla flyer offside, a doubtful decision at best. Queensland managed a couple of promising attacks which could have brought up points, but they were a mistake-ridden side, and a couple of early penalties in handy range saw Andrew Johns kick the Blues to an early 4–0 lead. The New South Wales error rate wasn't far behind that of the Queenslanders, but they were making their mistakes in the Maroons' half, well out of penalty goal-kicking range. Then in the 37th minute of play, the lightning fast Andrew Ettingshausen chased a short grubber kick of Freddie Fittler's into the in-goal area, took the ball almost from Michael Hancock's fingertips and scored. Andrew Johns converted his try and the Blues went to half-time leading the Maroons 10–0.

The Queenslanders were forced to defend constantly, but eight minutes into the second half Allan Langer made a break and sent Wendell Sailor away. Wendell gave the ball to Billy Moore who gave it to Steve Renouf who was tackled by Laurie Daley. Interference in the play-the-ball led to a penalty close to the Blues' goal line. Allan Langer took a quick tap and in a flash he was in under the posts. Wayne Bartrim converted and the score was New South Wales 10, Queensland 6.

Unfortunately, the Jason Smith–Allan Langer combination behind the Maroon scrum took time to settle in. The Queensland attack often broke down before it really got going and the Blues had a feast of possession. Most of their attack was blunted by the total commitment of the Maroons to defence, but eventually another Fittler kick into the corner of the in-goal led to a try to Manly second-rower Steve Menzies. The conversion was beyond Andrew Johns' preferred range and when play resumed strong Queensland defence saw the score remain at 14–6 at full-time.

Final result

New South Wales 14 defeated Queensland 6.

Tries for New South Wales: Andrew Ettingshausen, Steve Menzies. Goals: Andrew Johns (3).

Try for Queensland: Allan Langer. Goal: Wayne Bartrim.

Crowd: 39,348.

Man of the Match: Geoff Toovey.

Origin II, 1996 was one of those rare occasions when the New South Wales selectors sent the same side out for consecutive games, but Queensland made a few changes. Julian O'Neill was preferred as five-eighth while Jason Smith went to the bench. When Robbie O'Davis was forced to leave the field in Origin I, Wendell Sailor did sufficient as a replacement to retain the fullback spot in Origin II, and Wayne Bartrim was another casualty when long-serving State of Origin hooker Steve Walters reclaimed his position.

The Queensland Spirit was in evidence at the commencement of the game when the Maroons went straight on the attack and

---

STATE OF ORIGIN II, 1996
SUNCORP STADIUM, 3 JUNE

Queensland	New South Wales
Wendell Sailor	Tim Brasher
Brett Dallas	Rod Wishart
Mark Coyne	Laurie Daley
Steve Renouf	Andrew Ettingshausen
Matt Sing	Brett Mullins
Julian O'Neill	Brad Fittler (c)
Allan Langer (c)	Geoff Toovey
Tony Hearn	Glen Lazarus
Steve Walters	Andrew Johns
Andrew Gee	Paul Harragon
Gary Larson	Dean Pay
Brad Thorn	David Furner
Billy Moore	Adam Muir

Interchange:

Adrian Lam	Jim Dymock
Kevin Walters	Jamie Ainscough
Jason Smith	Jason Croker
Craig Greenhill	Steve Menzies

Coaches:

Paul Vautin	Phil Gould

Referee: David Manson

looked certainties to score in the opening minute. Wendell Sailor sprinted after a trademark Allen Langer grubber but was beaten narrowly by the equally speedy Tim Brasher, and it was the Blues who were first to score. Andrew Johns kicked a penalty goal in the 22nd minute, and New South Wales led 2–0.

Hookers 'Boxhead' Steve Walters and 'Back Door' Bennie Elias had pursued a two-man war for years in State of Origin scrums. Bennie was gone, but Andrew Johns was no shrinking violet and he was quite prepared to carry on the tradition. Shortly after the restart, over-vigorous play in the front row led to Steve Walters serving ten minutes in the sin-bin. With twelve men against thirteen, the Maroons broke a little better than even during his absence. They scored the first try of the match when Steve Renouf chased down an Allan Langer 'bomb'. Julian O'Neill had no trouble with the conversion and Queensland led 6–2.

In the view of the Maroons, this ought to have been the half-time score, but with the break only seconds away Andrew Ettingshausen kicked ahead. As he did so, he was tackled by Julian O'Neill, but Manson ruled the tackle late, and awarded a penalty against the protesting Queenslanders. Nothing is likely to upset footballers more than conceding points on what is perceived to be a bad refereeing decision. A quick tap by the Blues caught the still-protesting Queenslanders on the hop, and Rod Wishart crossed for a try. Johns converted and at half-time the score was New South Wales 8, Queensland 6.

This slender lead brought the Blues back from the break full of vim and vigour. Three minutes after the resumption, Geoff Toovey 'went the blind' from dummy half and fed Brett Mullins who ran in for a try. Again Johns converted and within a few minutes the Blues scored again, or at least this was the view of the referee. When Johns put up a high ball, it was retrieved by Ettingshausen who was credited with scoring a try. However, in a later, more enlightened age the video referee would have clearly seen that he knocked-on in goal. Johns failed to convert, but added two points from a penalty for a head-high tackle by Craig Greenhill on Paul Harragon. Greenhill paid the ultimate price for his misdemeanour, and earned a place in the record books when he became the first State of Origin footballer ever to be sent from the field. But since the incident occurred in the game's sixty-second minute, with the score at 16–6, Craig could hardly be blamed for the Maroons' loss.

New South Wales won Origin II by a margin comprising two controversial converted tries, a total of 18 points to 6, and for the first time ever they went on to play Origin III with the identical run-on side that had won the first two games.

Final result

New South Wales 18 defeated Queensland 6.

Tries for New South Wales: Brett Mullins (2), Rod Wishart. Goals: Andrew Johns (3).

Try for Queensland: Steve Renouf. Goal: Julian O'Neill.

Crowd: 41,955.

Man of the Match: Andrew Johns.

In addition to his historic send-off of Greenhill in Origin II, David Manson also made history in Origin III when he became the first official to referee all three State of Origin games in one season.

Because of the turmoil created by Super League, and with two consecutive losses by Queensland, certain genii of the Sydney media had touted the possibility that State of Origin might be abandoned, but any such rumour was expunged and its bearers silenced when Origin III provided one of the most closely contested exhibitions of bright Rugby League ever seen anywhere.

The Blues dominated a first half of football in which only one try was scored, this wide out by Andrew Ettingshausen off an Andrew Johns bomb. The try was converted by Rod Wishart, and although the Queenslanders had several opportunities to score, they remained frustrated at half-time except for two points from a penalty goal kicked by Willie Carne. Half-time score was New South Wales 6, Queensland 2.

Early in the second half, New South Wales scored again from a bomb when 190 cm Brett Mullins flew high in the air to retrieve a Brad Fittler kick. The conversion by Rod Wishart and a penalty

STATE OF ORIGIN III, 1996
SUNCORP STADIUM, 17 JUNE

Queensland	New South Wales
Wendell Sailor	Tim Brasher
Brett Dallas	Rod Wishart
Mark Coyne	Laurie Daley
Steve Renouf	Andrew Ettingshausen
Willie Carne	Brett Mullins
Dale Shearer	Brad Fittler (c)
Allan Langer (c)	Geoff Toovey
Tony Hearn	Glen Lazarus
Steve Walters	Andrew Johns
Andrew Gee	Paul Harragon
Gary Larson	Dean Pay
Brad Thorn	David Furner
Billy Moore	Adam Muir

Interchange:

Adrian Lam	Jim Dymock
Jason Smith	Jamie Ainscough
Owen Cunningham	Jason Croker
Matt Sing	Steve Menzies

Coaches:

Paul Vautin	Phil Gould

Referee: David Manson (Qld)

goal by Andrew Johns seemed to assure a Blues' victory, with a 14–2 lead. The Maroons came close to scoring when Allan Langer ran off Jason Smith before feeding the ball to Billy Moore, but the pass failed to stick and the Blues looked to be home and hosed. Shortly afterwards, Brad Fittler increased Queensland's difficulties by kicking a field goal: New South Wales 15, Queensland 2.

With less than ten minutes remaining, the Maroons needed two converted tries and a field goal to tie the game. It was a seemingly impossible task, but they never stopped trying, and then suddenly Mark Coyne created a try out of nothing. A miskicked ball took the Blues' defence unawares, and Mark ran it down and scored. The Willie Carne conversion reduced the deficit and the score was 15–8. The 'Queenslander' call was heard and the Maroons lifted. With four minutes left in the game, Matt Sing busted the Blues' line and found Brett Dallas at his elbow. Dallas accepted the pass and left the cover for dead to place the ball between the posts. Willie Carne's aim was true. It was 15–14 and Queensland trailed by a single point.

With the Lang Park crowd in an uproar, and the clock running down, Allan Langer used his well-tried cross-kick ploy, except that instead of Allan to Willie it was Allan to Mark ... Mark Coyne. The former Valleys' centre did the business and the crowd went wild, but in the years before the video referee was introduced to the game, a try scored from a cross-kick was always a chancy proposition, especially if it was scored by a Queenslander. Manson looked at his touch judge for assistance, the linesman signalled that Coyne was offside and the crowd's cheers turned to boos as the referee signalled no try and the Blues gained a clean sweep of the series by virtue of a single point.

Final result

New South Wales 15 defeated Queensland 14.

Tries for New South Wales: Andrew Ettingshausen, Brett Mullins. Goals: Rod Wishart (2), Andrew Johns. Field goal: Brad Fittler.

Tries for Queensland: Mark Coyne, Brett Dallas. Goals: Willie Carne (3).

Crowd: 38,217.

Man of the Match: Steve Menzies.

And so it was 3–0 to the Blues, but in that last game of the season both sides demonstrated clearly that, despite all of the difficulties that faced the game, State of Origin as an institution was alive and well. It would survive regardless of the problems that plagued the administration of Rugby League.

CHAPTER 19

1997

Television General

NEITHER the end of the State of Origin series nor the end of the Rugby League season was the end of Rugby League headlines in 1996. While teams from both sides had contested a single premiership, the parallel legal contest between Super League and the Australian Rugby League continued throughout the season as their teams of lawyers battled it out before the full Federal Court. As both the playing season and September drew to a close, Manly won the premiership, and rumours began to circulate that the Federal Court was about to bring down its decision on the appeal filed by News Ltd. On 4 October, Justices John Lockart, Ronald Sackville and John van Doussa unburdened themselves of the results of their deliberations. The best description of the Australian Rugby League reaction comes from the chairman, Ken Arthurson: 'It was like playing the same team twice, under the same rules but with a different referee, and winning 100–nil one week, and losing 100–nil the next.'

The Full Court had struck down the Burchett decision on almost every count.

Describing his feelings later, Arko wrote, 'I was furious, hurt, bewildered ... I felt as if I had been run over by the Southern Aurora.'[1]

However, neither Mrs Arthurson nor Mrs Quayle ever reared a squib. The Australian Rugby League legal team was instructed to seek leave to appeal to the Australian High Court, but the slings and

arrows of outrageous fortune would get a few more licks in before
they were done with Arko. On 11 November his right-hand man,
'Canon' John Quayle, resigned. Then four days later, he heard from
the High Court. His comment on the news: 'On 15 November, the
High Court took less time than it takes to play a half of football to
knock back our appeal against the Federal Court verdict.'[2]

They were hard days, but there was worse to come.

A wise man once said that in a civil war a good general must
always know exactly when to move over to the other side.[3] In this
context, Kerrie Packer showed impeccable military instincts. His
landmark speech to the meeting in February 1995 had brought on
the war, and his television network had been the public face of the
League establishment during the major battles. Packer interests had
been the Australian Rugby League's main source of support, both
moral and financial, during its prosecution, yet on 17 January 1997
his Channel 9 network completed a deal with News Ltd to televise
Super League matches in 1997.

Ken Arthurson described Channel 9's action as treachery.[4] He
claimed that Kerry Packer 'had stormed in, loaded the gun and
disappeared'.[5]

Arko had had enough. Five days later he resigned from all positions
with the Australian Rugby League.

But big business deals, train smashes, court decisions, treachery
and resignations notwithstanding, Rugby League would be played
in 1997 and with the Federal Court's blessing: at the court's order,
in fact, there would be two competitions. The teams that had signed
with Super League were freed from any obligation to the Australian
Rugby League and would conduct their own competition. The
'loyalist' clubs would proceed under the aegis of the Rugby League
establishment, and with the split in the competition there was a
corollary rift in the supporter base.

But regardless of which side individual supporters favoured, there
was an almost unanimous view that nothing could be allowed to
interfere with the annual State of Origin series. State of Origin
would be played in 1997 regardless, but since it was strictly an
Australian Rugby League promotion it would be played by bob-
tailed Australian Rugby League teams, for there was no way known

STATE OF ORIGIN I, 1997
SUNCORP STADIUM, 28 MAY

Queensland	New South Wales
Robbie O'Davis	Tim Brasher
Brett Dallas	Rod Wishart
Mark Coyne	Terry Hill
Matt Sing	Paul McGregor
Danny Moore	Jamie Ainscough
Ben Ikin	Jim Dymock
Adrian Lam (c)	Geoff Toovey (c)
Neil Tierney	Paul Harragon
Jamie Goddard	Andrew Johns
Craig Smith	Mark Carroll
Gary Larson	Steve Menzies
Billy Moore	Adam Muir
Wayne Bartrim	Nik Kosef

Interchange:

Jason Smith	Dean Pay
Stuart Kelly	David Fairleigh
Jeremy Schloss	John Simon
Tony Hearn	Ken McGuinness

Coaches:

Paul Vautin	Tom Raudonikis

Referee: Kelvin Jeffes (NSW)

that Super League players could be included. It was back to the 1995 drawing board.

The most significant effect of the Super League war was obvious to anyone who was present at Origin I at Lang Park. There were thousands of vacant seats in a stadium that ought to have been packed tight. Statistically, the attendance was down by more than 25 per cent, but the football was up to the usual high standard and the casualty rate was above normal.

Paul McGregor was assisted from the field quite early with what appeared to be a serious arm injury. After a generous application of the magic sponge he returned ten minutes before half-time, and soon afterwards, with the score nil all, the veteran Illawarra centre beat two forwards with a sidestep and scored near the posts. Andrew Johns converted and soon afterwards Rod Wishart landed a long-distance penalty to make the half-time score 8–nil in the Blues' favour.

After half-time the Maroons completely dominated, but without showing a great deal for it. Time and again they attacked the Blues' line and were just as often turned back. The Blues lost Andrew Johns, their tactical kicker of choice, with a leg injury, and for much of the second half Geoff Toovey managed to get his team out of trouble with determined charges downfield from dummy half.

The score remained unchanged until the thirty-minute mark in the second half, when newly appointed Maroon captain, Adrian Lam, charged the line from dummy half and beat the markers to score. Wayne Bartrim did the honours, but that was all there was and New South Wales came home winners by 8 points to 6.

After the match, and without naming any of his players, Queensland coach Paul Vautin described the Maroons kicking game as 'terrible', and some of the grubber kicks as 'shockers'. Despite their coach's criticism of their game, the Maroons did well to hold the Blues scoreless for most of the first half and the coach was proud of the way the side handled itself in the second half.

With only the twelve loyalist clubs able to contribute to both sides in 1997, players from ten clubs were included in the Queensland team and men from eight different teams wore the sky blue. This was also an indication that both states were left with limited room

---

Final result:

New South Wales 8 defeated Queensland 6.

Try for New South Wales: Paul McGregor. Goals: Andrew Johns, Rod Wishart.

Try for Queensland: Adrian Lam. Goal: Wayne Bartrim.

Crowd: 28,222.

Man of the Match: Geoff Toovey.

STATE OF ORIGIN II, 1997
MELBOURNE CRICKET GROUND, 11 JUNE

Queensland	New South Wales
Robbie O'Davis	Tim Brasher
Brett Dallas	Ken McGuiness
Stuart Kelly	Terry Hill
Mark Coyne	Paul McGregor
Matt Sing	Jamie Ainscough
Ben Ikin	Jim Dymock
Adrian Lam (c)	John Simon
Neil Tierney	Paul Harragon
Wayne Bartrim	Geoff Toovey (c)
Craig Smith	Mark Carroll
Gary Larson	Steve Menzies
Jason Smith	Adam Muir
Billy Moore	Nik Kosef

Interchange:

Jamie Goddard	Dean Pay
Jeremy Schloss	David Fairleigh
Julian O'Neill	Matt Seers
Clinton O'Brien	Aaron Raper[6]

Coaches:

Paul Vautin	Tom Raudonikis

Referee: David Manson (Qld)

to move when it came to team changes and few were made for Origin II.

Following his team's clean sweep in 1995, and their failure by a single goal to win in 1996, Paul Vautin had made an incautious undertaking. He had promised to stand down as Queensland coach if his team failed to win the 1997 series. The loss of Origin I, also by the narrowest of margins, placed the Maroons in a sudden-death situation when the ball was kicked off for Origin II. Half an hour later it appeared that Fatty's demise as a State of Origin coach was imminent. The Blues had scored early and they had scored often.

Playing his first game for his state, Western Suburbs only representative, Ken McGuinness, was in for a try after Paul McGregor drew the cover defence and gave the ball to his winger with a clever underarm flick pass. John Simon's attempt to convert went wide. The Blues led 4–0, and in the twelfth minute of the game, with Queensland running the ball out from inside their own twenty-metre line, a dropped pass was snatched up by Nik Kosef who galloped over to score between the posts. John Simon made it 10–0 with his conversion.

The Maroons defended fiercely but the rampaging Blues would not be denied. McGregor broke away and fed the ball to McGuinness. With the cover about to get to him, the Wests winger found John Simon ranging up inside. He gave him the ball and the stocky half-back did the rest. His kick to convert his own try from wide out failed, and after just 30 minutes the Blues led the Maroons 14–0.

But there was no quelling the Queensland spirit. Within five minutes of Simon's conversion, the Maroons scored their first try when Adrian Lam sent Billy Moore down the blind side. Moore drew two men and gave Matt Sing a clear run to the line. Julian O'Neill missed the conversion but Queensland was back in the game, if ever so slenderly, with the score New South Wales 14, Queensland 4.

With points on the board, the Maroons lifted their game, and just three minutes before half-time it was Adrian Lam again who constructed a try. From a ten-metre scrum, he dummied to pass wide to the backs and then gave a short pass to Robbie O'Davis who was on the fly from the fullback position. Robbie scored under the crossbar. Julian O'Neill added the extras and when the two sides went to oranges the gap was only four points: New South Wales 14, Queensland 10.

The gap quickly disappeared. The Maroons came out after the break full of running. Brett Dallas atoned for an earlier error when he side-stepped his opposition winger, Jamie Ainscough, and out-sprinted the cover defence to score in the corner. Again, the conversion failed, but the scores were even. Queensland had a chance to go ahead when Paul McGregor was penalised for a high shot on Matt Sing, but Wayne Bartrim's kick was wide. The scores remained locked at 14–14 until John Simon kicked a field goal with only

---

Final result

New South Wales 15 defeated Queensland 14.

Tries for New South Wales: Ken McGuinness, Nik Kosef, Jim Dymock. Goal: John Simon. Field goal: John Simon.

Tries for Queensland: Matt Sing, Robbie O'Davis, Brett Dallas. Goal: Julian O'Neill.

Crowd: 25,105.

Man of the Match: Paul McGregor.

---

minutes still on the clock. Queensland attempted to manoeuvre for the equaliser, but the only field goal attempt failed. The full-time score was Blues 15, Maroons 14.

Defeat in such circumstances by this narrowest of margins was a hard pill to swallow and slender evidence on which a coach ought to sack himself. Fatty Vautin didn't. He changed his mind and stayed for the third match. Neither would there have been much purpose in making major changes to the team. All seventeen players from Origin II were retained with some minor adjustments.

The Blues had to find a replacement for Paul McGregor, who had scored a two-week suspension for the high shot on Matt Sing. They also recalled Andrew Johns to the hooker position, selected Geoff Toovey as half, and introduced some new blood. Trent Barrett, the young Illawarra five-eighth, replaced Jim Dymock who was dropped from the side. John Simon went to the bench.

While the attendance was well short of the stadium's capacity, it was better than that for either of the previous games. This was encouraging and the Queenslanders ran out on a wet and soggy Sydney Football Stadium determined to regain some of their diminished prestige. They gave notice of this early when Ben Ikin broke the line and tore away for a fine individual try. Julian O'Neill's conversion saw the Blues 0–6 down and forced to kick-off for the second time in four minutes. The Blues found themselves placing the ball on the centre line again ten minutes later after Julian O'Neill ran on to a Ben Ikin pass, scored and converted to put Queensland 12–0 in front after less than fifteen minutes of play.

STATE OF ORIGIN III, 1997
SYDNEY FOOTBALL STADIUM, 25 JUNE

Queensland	New South Wales
Robbie O'Davis	Tim Brasher
Brett Dallas	Ken McGuinness
Mark Coyne	Terry Hill
Julian O'Neill	Jamie Ainscough
Matt Sing	Matt Seers
Ben Ikin	Trent Barrett
Adrian Lam (c)	Geoff Toovey (c)
Neil Tierney	Paul Harragon
Jamie Goddard	Andrew Johns
Clinton O'Brien	Mark Carroll
Gary Larson	Steve Menzies
Jason Smith	Adam Muir
Billy Moore	Nik Kosef

Interchange:

Wayne Bartrim	Dean Pay
Jeremy Schloss	David Fairleigh
Stuart Kelly	Michael Beuttner
Craig Smith	John Simon

Coaches:

Paul Vautin	Tom Raudonikis

Referee: Eddie Ward (Qld)

The Blues took violent exception to Queensland's swift success. In an early skirmish involving both front rows, the two hookers were sent to the sin-bin and placed on report, while Queensland prop, Craig Smith, left the field with concussion.

There were plenty of fisticuffs throughout the evening and a number of penalties as a result. With John Simons kicking a goal from one of these, the Maroons took a 12–2 lead to the sheds at half-time. They went further in front soon after half-time when Mark Coyne ran down an Adrian Lam grubber into the in-goal. O'Neill's conversion took the Maroons out to an 18–2 lead. The

> **Final result**
>
> Queensland 18 defeated New South Wales 12.
>
> Tries for Queensland: Ben Ikin, Julian O'Neill, Mark Coyne. Goals: Julian O'Neill (3).
>
> Tries for New South Wales: Jamie Ainscough, Andrew Johns. Goals: John Simons, Andrew Johns.
>
> Crowd: 33,241.
>
> Man of the Match: Gary Larson.

Blues managed to score twice, but they never looked dangerous, and the Maroons ran out comfortable winners, 18–12.

Super League, meanwhile, conducted its own version of a State of Origin series, but, with a team playing out of Aucklnd and numerous Maorilanders on the playing staffs of other Super League clubs, theirs was a three-cornered contest: a Tri-Series between Queensland, New South Wales and New Zealand. It required a three-way round robin to be played, and at its conclusion the two leading teams played the Tri Series final. Although the New Zealanders fought hard, they lost to both Queensland and New South Wales. Queensland also lost to New South Wales but being the only other winner the Maroons met the Blues in the final at ANZ stadium on 19 May.

For eighty minutes the 35,570 supporters were treated to one of the finest displays of attacking and defensive football ever seen in Brisbane, and at the end of it the score was 22–22. Not a split match between the two sides.

The two teams hurled themselves at each other in desperate defence and threw the ball around in daring fashion in attack. Queensland had dominated in the closing stages of the game, and both Allan Langer and Darren Smith had made desperate but unsuccessful attempts to break the deadlock with a field goal from well out. In the 78th minute, with the ball played only eight metres out from the goal posts and in front, a wrong move saw an opportunity for an almost certain one-pointer squandered, and under rules that were introduced by Super League, they were then required to play an additional ten minutes each way.

The Queensland Super League team was coached by Wayne Bennett, and for the first time in anyone's memory, and probably the only time in his career as a coach, Wayne made his way to the sideline to shout instructions and encouragement to his charges. Such was the level of excitement that the struggle created.

For the first ten minutes of extra time both sides exerted every effort to get the ball over the line, without success. The sides changed ends and continued, and almost immediately Queensland had a chance. Glen Lazarus was penalised for a high tackle on Queensland dummy half Paul Green and Darren Lockyer lined up a shot at goal. It was forty-five metres out from the posts, but it was right in front and well within the fullback's range. It had the legs but it went wide. Fortunately, he kicked it dead. The Maroons got the ball back from a line drop-out, and in the 94th minute Alfie Langer beat more than five defenders before being forced to play the ball eight metres out from the Blues' line. The dummy half pass went quickly wide to Tonie Carroll and the powerful utility carried three tacklers with him as he went to ground in the in-goal. The Maroons started to celebrate. This was the year in which video referees were first used (they were introduced by Super League), but Bill Harrigan didn't bother to call for an opinion. He ruled held up in goal, shocked the Queenslanders into silence, and ordered a ten-metre scrum.

With less than four minutes remaining it was field goal time once more and in the 95th minute Robbie Ross made the first attempt for the Blues. He missed and it was still 22–22.

Queensland restarted play from their twenty-metre line, took the ball the length of the field, and in the 96th minute Paul Green took his shot from thirty-two metres out from goal. It was charged down and within another minute Blues' half, Noel Goldthorpe, was again in position to attempt a field goal. Another miss and the clock ran down with the score still 22–22.

The New South Wales captain, Laurie Daley, seemed to think that New South Wales had won on a countback and the Blues started to celebrate, but referee Bill Harrigan quickly disabused them of this notion. The Super League rule provided that the two captains would now toss for ends, and the loser would kick off for a period of play that would last until someone scored. This was the American style and it was sudden death. Unfortunately for the Maroons, they blinked first.

On the fourth tackle after the kick-off, with the Blues on the halfway line, Steve Renouf gave up a penalty when he dragged Simon Gillies into touch after he had been tackled. This piggy-backed the Blues well into the Maroons' half and with cool precision they manoeuvred play into mid-field to give Noel Goldthorpe a clean shot at goal from the Maroon thirty-metre line. He landed the one that mattered and won the game.

CHAPTER 20

1998

Bean Counters' Nightmare

A S THE MOST extraordinary season of Rugby League football drew to a close, Newcastle Knights defeated Manly in the Australian Rugby League Grand Final, and in Super League the Brisbane Broncos won everything except the *Courier-Mail* Children's Colouring-In Contest, but it was obvious to everyone connected with the game that neither of the combatants could sustain hostilities at the 1997 level of intensity and remain solvent. The Australian Rugby League had shown a ruinous trading loss, despite the financial support of Channel 9 and Optus, and the cost to News Ltd of the Super League season was similarly horrendous.

In addition to the Premiership, News Ltd sponsored a World Club challenge. This involved twenty-two football clubs from Australia, New Zealand and Europe criss-crossing the world as they completed home and away rounds. It ended at Brisbane's ANZ Stadium with the Broncos defeat of the Hunter Mariners in the Cup Final at a cost to the Super League organisation of more than six million dollars.

The total cost of the Super League season was known only to the bean counters at News Ltd and to Mr Murdoch. Apart from the players and one or two coaches who had been signed to ridiculously inflated contracts, no one in Rugby League had made any money, and many of the clubs involved on both sides were on the verge of insolvency. Publicists for both sides were lavish in their praise of the standard of football played and both sides claimed the season to have been successful. However, it was obvious to all who loved Rugby League that the most likely result of another equally successful season would be the bankruptcy of every organisation connected with the game and its disappearance as a major sport. An arrangement had to be made, and it was.

On 7 October Rupert Murdoch and his son Lachlan announced that they were now confident that there would be a single competition in Australia in 1998. Shortly afterwards, one of the News Ltd papers predicted mass redundancies in the Rugby League community to accommodate a single, unified, twenty-team competition with each club committed to a $4,000,000 salary cap. A new organisation would be created to run a new competition, and it would be known as the National Rugby League.

No such upheaval as had taken place could leave the individuals involved unaffected.[1] The rivalries and disagreements that Super League created did not disappear overnight, but there was one aspect of Rugby League that quickly returned to normality. Despite the omission of certain players in certain years, the spirit that drove footballers to give their whole-hearted utmost to State of Origin Rugby League remained untarnished. The now traditional contest would continue without interruption, and with the first game of the series to be played at the Sydney Football Stadium on 25 June, the prospect of reunited teams to contest the 1998 series roused the Rugby League community to a pitch of excitement that had been missing since the break first appeared. And the feeling of optimism was totally justified.

The game started at the pace expected at Origin level, with an early Blues attack being snuffed out by Broncos' fullback Darren Lockyer who fielded an Andrew Johns bomb. Two tackles after the twenty-metre restart, Australian Rugby League loyalist Paul Harragon was penalised for a high shot on Super League winger, Steve Renouf and the Blues versus the Maroons rivalry was back to normal.

From the tap restart, the Queenslanders were quickly inside the Blues' half and Allan Langer put a little grubber into their in-goal. Kevin Walters followed it through for a try alongside the posts,

STATE OF ORIGIN I, 1998
SYDNEY FOOTBALL STADIUM, 22 MAY

Queensland	New South Wales
Darren Lockyer	Tim Brasher
Wendell Sailor	Rod Wishart
Steve Renouf	Terry Hill
Darren Smith	Andrew Ettingshausen
Matt Sing	Adam McDougall
Kevin Walters	Laurie Daley (c)
Allan Langer (c)	Andrew Johns
Shane Webcke	Paul Harragon
Jason Hetherington	Geoff Toovey
Gary Larson	Rodney Howe
Wayne Bartrim	Dean Pay
Jason Smith	Nik Kosef
Peter Ryan	Brad Fittler

Interchange:

Queensland	New South Wales
Steven Price	David Barnhill
Martin Lang	Steve Menzies
Ben Ikin	Matthew Johns
Tonie Carroll	Ken McGuinness

Coaches:

Queensland	New South Wales
Wayne Bennett	Tom Raudonikis

Referee: Bill Harrigan (NSW)

Lockyer converted, and after just six minutes of play Queensland led New South Wales 6–0.

A minute later the Maroons crossed the Blues' line again. Steve ('the Pearl') Renouf broke the line and ran fifty metres to put the ball down under the posts, only to have it declared no try when Matt Sing was penalised for impeding Terry Hill who was in pursuit of Renouf. Since Hill was more than five metres behind Renouf, with no hope of catching him, it was a fairly pedantic ruling by Harrigan. After a linesman ran in and reported Sing for interference, New South Wales was awarded a penalty and for the next ten minutes the Maroons were under siege. Finally, after Lockyer had twice defused bombs in the in-goal, Rod Wishart scored wide out for the Blues. The conversion attempt failed and it was Queensland 6, New South Wales 4.

The Queenslanders continued to attack but the Blues were the next to score when Tim Brasher made a break. The ball went through several pairs of hands before Brasher handled for a second time and scored wide out. Andrew Johns again missed with the kick, but the Blues had a two-point lead, 8–6, and they scored again seven minutes before half-time. Laurie Daley touched down for an unconverted try from an Andrew Johns bomb, and when Johns kicked a 38-metre field goal right on the half-time hooter the New South Wales team went to the break leading by 13 points to 6.

The Blues had been lucky on a number of occasions and their good fortune looked set to continue into the second stanza. Three minutes after half-time, Bill Harrigan awarded loose head and feed to New South Wales after Adam McDougall dragged Wendell Sailor over the sideline. The Blues went on the attack from near the halfway line. Gary Larson's tackle on Laurie Daley a yard from the try-line snuffed out the assault, and shortly afterwards it was New South Wales' turn to scramble in defence. Ten minutes after the break, Tim Brasher made a meal of fielding an Allan Langer grubber into the in-goal and Steven Price scored for the Maroons. Lockyer converted and it was a one-point game, 13–12 in favour of New South Wales.

The Maroons attacked strongly from the restart of play and were ten metres out from the Blues' line on the fifth tackle. Alfie used the grubber again, and this time he followed his own kick and scored under the posts. Again Lockyer converted. The Maroons were back in the lead, 18–13.

It was becoming a game of tit for tat. Five minutes after Queensland took the lead, Brad Fittler put up a mid-field bomb which Adam McDougall fielded. He got the ball to Laurie Daley who spread it wide. Backing up, Brad Fittler took an inside pass from his captain and scored. Johns managed to convert this one and once more New South Wales led by a point, 19–18.

The Queenslanders mounted a sustained attack, but they failed to breach the defence and the Blues scored again six minutes before full-time when Menzies chased a Fittler kick. Andrew Johns was having a bad day out with the boot, but the score was 23–18 after he missed with the conversion. New South Wales looked to have the game sewn up.

With less than two minutes remaining in the game, and the Queenslanders in possession behind their own thirty-metre line, Tonie Carroll kicked long downfield. Ben Ikin chased the ball down and retrieved it. From the play the ball, Darren Smith sent the ball out to Allan Langer who fed it to Darren's brother Jason. Jason Smith passed to Kevin Walters who put the original kicker, Tonie Carroll, into about half a gap. That was all the burly centre needed and he crashed over carrying three Blues with him. Lockyer completed a perfect four out of four score with the conversion, and with the siren sounding the Blues' death knell, Queensland had won Origin I, 1998 by a point, 24–23.

Final result

Queensland 24 defeated New South Wales 23.

Tries for Queensland: Kevin Walters, Steven Price, Allan Langer, Tonie Carroll. Goals: Darren Lockyer (4).

Tries for New South Wales: Rod Wishart, Tim Brasher, Laurie Daley, Brad Fittler, Steve Menzies. Goal: Andrew Johns. Field goal: Andrew Johns.

Crowd: 36,070.

Man of the Match: Allan Langer.

Both sides made changes for Origin II, to be played at Lang Park on 5 June.

The Queenslanders started Origin II like winners and scored a try on their first possession. Following a Maroon kick-off, the Blues were forced to kick after failing to make a significant impression on the Queensland defence. Queensland did better. Gaining possession deep in their own half, the Maroons took the ball to the Blues' ten-metre line in five tackles. From a quick play-the-ball on the sixth, Allan Langer noted that Adam McDougall had left his wing and moved inside. He chipped the ball into the corner on the right

STATE OF ORIGIN II, 1998
SUNCORP STADIUM, 5 JUNE

Queensland	New South Wales
Darren Lockyer	Tim Brasher
Wendell Sailor	Rod Wishart
Steve Renouf	Terry Hill
Darren Smith	Paul McGregor
Matt Sing	Adam McDougall
Kevin Walters	Laurie Daley (c)
Allan Langer (c)	Andrew Johns
Shane Webcke	Paul Harragon
Jason Hetherington	Geoff Toovey
Gary Larsen	Rodney Howe
Gorden Tallis	Dean Pay
Brad Thorn	David Barnhill
Wayne Bartrim	Brad Fittler

Interchange:

Steven Price	Glen Lazarus
Martin Lang	Andrew Ettingshausen
Ben Ikin	Steve Menzies
Tonie Carroll	Nik Kosef

Coaches:

Wayne Bennett	Tom Raudonikis

Referee: Bill Harrigan (NSW)

side of the field. Wendell Sailor was in position to pick it up on the first bounce and in three strides he was over the line. Darren Lockyer's touchline conversion saw Queensland lead 6–0 after just three minutes play.

There was euphoria in the Queensland camp as the record-breaking 44,000-strong Lang Park crowd gave tongue in support of the Maroons, but there was little joy to be had from the remainder of the first half.

The game was only eight minutes old when Freddie Fittler hoisted a bomb which was caught in the field of play by Adam McDougall.

He got the ball away to Rodney Howe who passed to Laurie Daley. Daley found Adam McDougall backing up on his outside to score in the corner. Andrew Johns' poor form with the boot seemed to have followed him to Lang Park and the try remained unconverted. The Queenslanders led 6–4.

When the Maroons ran the ball out from their own line, they found themselves in breach of the law when Bill Harrigan decided that a pass from Allan Langer to Shane Webcke was forward. When the video replay appeared on the big screen, it seemed that he had erred, and the partisan crowd let him know about it. Footballers have to live with such rubs of the green and the outcome of this particular rub was particularly painful. Within two tackles of the scrum that packed on the Queensland forty-metre line, Paul McGregor had scored for the Blues. Andrew Johns' kick was astray but the Blues led 8–6, and Joey Johns atoned for his wayward boot soon afterwards when he ran from the forty-metre line and beat two defenders to carry the ball to the Maroon twenty-metre line. From his quick play the ball, Tim Brasher ran to the blind side and fed Nick Kosef who had Paul McGregor outside him. McGregor was far too big and strong for Matt Sing to stop a metre short of the line and he crossed for his second try. Andrew Johns broke his drought with the boot and the score was New South Wales 14, Queensland 6.

The Queenslanders had difficulty getting out of their own half, and on the few occasions that they did, the movement invariably broke down through poor handling. Six minutes before half-time, a dropped ball by a Queensland centre saw the Blues sweep downfield with the ball spread wide. They were halted on the Queensland ten-metre line, but with the Queensland defence at sixes and sevens Brad Fittler took advantage of a quick play the ball and used his famous sidestep to score just wide of the posts. Andrew Johns added the two points, and when the half-time siren sounded, the score was New South Wales 20, Queensland 6.

The Blues had the game shot to pieces, but although they were in the comfort zone, at no time did they believe that they could rest on their laurels. As former Blues Origin great, Blocker Roach, reminded his television audience just after half-time, Queensland scored eighteen points to win Origin I only a fortnight earlier and no one doubted that they were capable of doing it again. However, five minutes after the game restarted, Freddie Fittler sent a towering bomb high in the air to Matt Sing's wing. Matt knocked-on, and Tim Brasher picked up the crumbs and strolled in for a try. Johns had found his kicking boots by this time and had no trouble making the score 26 points to 6 in favour of the Blues. Any punters present would have wanted very long odds indeed to back the Maroons to come back in this one.

From their next possession, the Maroons swept the length of the field in five tackles but lost the ball on the fifth tackle. There was no try then, but shortly afterwards, still deep in the Blues half, Ben Ikin made a run, passed to Matt Sing who beat three men to score in the corner. With Lockyer off the field hurt, Ben Ikin took the kick and missed. New South Wales 26, Queensland 10.

With Queensland playing catch-up and gaining a glut of possession, there was some spectacular football in the second half but, unfortunately, there were a great number of unforced errors, too. Movement after movement broke down through a dropped ball or a knock-on and the final score of 26–10 was equal to the worst losing margin that Queensland had suffered since State of Origin started in 1980.

With the series poised at one game apiece, the 1998 State of Origin series would be decided at the Sydney Football Stadium on 5 June. Changes to teams were minimal, the only unexpected alteration being made necessary by the withdrawal of Geoff Toovey. In the new-age hooker tradition, he was replaced by a five-eighth, Newcastle's Michael Johns, brother of Andrew.

Final result

New South Wales 26 defeated Queensland 10.

Tries for New South Wales: Paul McGregor (2), Brad Fittler, Adam McDougall, Tim Brasher. Goals: Andrew Johns (3).

Tries for Queensland: Wendall Sailor, Matt Sing. Goal: Darren Lockyer.

Crowd: 44,447.

Man of the Match: Rodney Howe.

STATE OF ORIGIN III, 1998
SUNCORP STADIUM, 19 JUNE

Queensland	New South Wales
Darren Lockyer	Tim Brasher
Robbie O'Davis	Rod Wishart
Steve Renouf	Laurie Daley (c)
Ben Ikin	Terry Hill
Wendell Sailor	Adam McDougall
Kevin Walters	Brad Fittler
Allan Langer (c)	Andrew Johns
Shane Webcke	Glen Lazarus
Jamie Goddard	Matthew Johns
Gary Larson	Tony Butterfield
Gorden Tallis	David Furner
Jason Smith	David Barnhill
Darren Smith	Jim Dymock

Interchange:

Steven Price	Robbie Kearns
Matt Sing	Ken McGuinness
Peter Ryan	Dean Pay
Andrew Gee	Steve Menzies

Coaches:

Wayne Bennett	Tom Raudonikus

Referee: Bill Harrigan (NSW)

Just as they had done in both Origin I and Origin II, the Maroons opened the scoring early in Origin III when Kevin Walters scored seven and a half minutes after the kick-off.

The Queenslanders started in aggressive style and after steadying a Blues assault on the Maroon line Wendell Sailor ran the ball forty metres downfield. From the play-the-ball, eight men handled before Kevin Walters found a gap and beat two tacklers to score in a good position for Darren Lockyer to convert. It was Queensland 6, New South Wales nil.

For the next fifteen minutes, it was all Queensland. Whether defending territorial gains at the New South Wales end of the field, or fending off attacks by the Blues, the Maroons defence dominated completely. On the only occasion that the Blues looked like scoring, a passing movement sent Terry Hill dashing for the corner, only to encounter a gang tackle by at least three Maroons who took him into touch over the corner post.

The Queenslanders maintained the pressure and in the 28th minute Gorden Tallis made a break downfield. Busting tackles and shedding would-be Blues' defenders, he was finally held at the Blues forty-metre line. Standing in the tackle, Gordie looked for support and spotted Ben Ikin flying through on his left. Ben accepted the pass without drawing rein and had gone less than five metres before he realised that he was alone and running free. Wearing a broad smile, and with one arm raised in triumphant salute, the North Sydney youngster ran untouched to the try-line and placed the ball under the posts. Lockyer's simple conversion increased the Maroons' lead to 12–0.

On the Queenslanders' first possession after the restart, a Maroon knock-on returned possession to the Blues from a scrum at the Queensland thirty-metre line. From the first subsequent tackle, Andrew Johns threw a long, cut-out pass to Terry Hill who ran for the corner but then passed to his flank man, Ken McGuinness, who had come inside him. Despite the attention of two defenders, the Western Suburbs winger got the ball down for a try. Andrew Johns' kick failed, and despite valiant attempts to score by both sides, it was Queensland 12, New South Wales 4 at half-time.

Shortly after half-time Darren Lockyer left the field after a clash of heads with a team-mate in a tackle. The Maroons were fortunate in having one of the game's best fullbacks playing on the wing. Robbie O'Davis took Lockyer's place and the Maroon dominance of the game proceeded, unchecked by the loss of their star custodian. In the first twenty-five minutes of the second half, play was contained almost entirely within the Blues' half, and Allan Langer's grubbers into the in-goal forced no fewer than seven Blues' goal line drop-outs. However, the Maroons attacking movements continually broke down. Alfie lost patience with sending others to try to score. From a play-the-ball about ten metres out, Allan Langer celebrated his

30th State of Origin game when he beat at least three defenders with a jinking run and scored under the posts. Darren Lockyer had returned to the fray after treatment, and he converted his captain's try: Queensland 18, New South Wales 4.

There are no more loyal Blues' supporters than the Channel 9 commentators, Ray ('Rabbits') Warren and former Blues Origin great Peter Sterling, yet by the 70th minute they had surrendered. Following a Blues' set of six, which started inside the Maroons' ten-metre line and finished when Wendell Sailor defused a Brad Fittler bomb, they agreed publicly that although there had been occasions when teams had overcome a 14-point lead to win a State of Origin game, this was not going to be one of them.

Jason Smith added a smidgen of icing to the Maroons' celebratory cake when he kicked a field goal as the crowd counted down to the siren and the Maroons took the series with a 19–4 win in Origin III.

Final result

Queensland 19 defeated New South Wales 4.

Tries for Queensland: Kevin Walters, Ben Ikin, Allan Langer. Goals: Darren Lockyer (3), O'Davis. Field goal: Jason Smith.

Try for New South Wales: Ken McGuinness.

Crowd: 38,952.

Man of the Match: Shane Webcke.

Following their defeat in Origin II by a record-equalling score, the Maroons cherished the series decider win, and its fifteen-point margin, but above all they cherished the part played in the whole series by Kevin Walters. Kevin Walters' wife, Kim, was as strongly attached to his Rugby League career as was the player himself. They had been in love since their school days and he lost her to cancer during that 1998 season. During her last days, Kim was well aware of her circumstances, but she was proud of her husband and she urged him to continue to play for her sake and for that of the three small sons who were her legacy to him. He dedicated the whole of his season to her, and to her memory. It was probably fitting that he should play such an important role and score the first try in a series win that had a unique importance for him and for his club, the Brisbane Broncos. Through both its origins and its heavy involvement over the years, the Brisbane Broncos had a special, even a proprietary, interest in State of Origin football, and the year of the formation of the National Rugby League was significant. Later that season they would win the first National Rugby League Premiership and, despite the club's four premierships in eleven years, 1998 would be the first occasion on which the Broncos would win the premiership in the same year that the Maroons won the State of Origin series.

CHAPTER 21

1999

Score First, Score Early

IN 1999 Allan Langer played for Australia against New Zealand in Sydney on Friday night, 23 April. He flew to Townsville the next morning and on Sunday night he backed up for the Brisbane Broncos against the Cowboys. With the team struggling, he left the field before full-time and announced his retirement from the game. When the side was selected for State of Origin I, 1999, Alfie was replaced both as half-back and as captain by Adrian Lam. After one of the shortest retirements on record, Alfie announced a come-back, but not in Australia. He signed to play two seasons with Warrington. He intended to see out his career in England.

The Maroons had trounced the Blues in Origin III, 1998 after losing Origin II by a record-equalling margin in the only game played at their home ground that season. They were determined to repay their supporters by winning the opener at Lang Park in 1999. It wasn't easy, although they did open the scoring. With the game less than four minutes old, a penalty gave Matt Rogers an opportunity to exercise his goal-kicking talents. Queensland led 2–0.

Although members of both teams were responsible for spilling far too much ball, a great number of these errors were the result of fierce defence and solid gang tackles. When Glen Lazarus was too slow to rise after completing one of these in the thirteenth minute, Rogers got another shot at goal and made the most of it. Queensland 4, New South Wales 0.

STATE OF ORIGIN I, 1999
SUNCORP STADIUM, 26 MAY

Queensland	New South Wales
Robbie O'Davis	Robbie Ross
Wendell Sailor	Darren Albert
Matt Sing	Laurie Daley
Darren Smith	Terry Hill
Matt Rogers	Matt Geyer
Kevin Walters	Brad Fittler (c)
Adrian Lam (c)	Andrew Johns
Shane Webcke	Jason Stevens
Jason Hetherington	Craig Gower
Craig Greenhill	Rodney Howe
Gorden Tallis	David Barnhill
Chris McKenna	Bryan Fletcher
Jason Smith	Nik Kosef

Interchange:

Steven Price	Glen Lazarus
Martin Lang	Luke Ricketson
Ben Ikin	Ryan Girdler
Tonie Carroll	Anthony Mundine

Coaches:

Mark Murray	Wayne Pearce

Referee: Bill Harrigan (NSW)

Anthony Mundine was playing his first State of Origin game for the Blues. He came on as a replacement about ten minutes before half-time and scored his one and only State of Origin try after Terry Hill got outside Matt Sing, stepped inside Robbie O'Davis, and passed Mundine the ball with the line wide open. His try under the posts was converted by Ryan Girdler. When the half-time siren sounded, the score was New South Wales 6, Queensland 4.

Queensland went straight on the attack at the resumption and quickly forced the Blues to drop out from their goal line. The movement that followed broke down for yet another forward pass, but in the 13th minute after half-time a penalty against Glen Lazarus, once more for holding down a tackled player, gave Matt Rogers yet another opportunity, this time from just outside the twenty-metre line and fifteen metres in from touch. His aim was true and it was all square at 6 all. Ten minutes later Gorden Tallis drew a penalty for a high tackle and it was well within Matt Rogers' kicking range. The Cronulla winger raised the flags. It was Queensland 8, New South Wales 6.

The Queenslanders dominated possession in the second half and were constantly on the attack. They failed to score a try, but on one of the Blues' rare excursions into the Queensland half, the Maroons gave up a penalty right in front of goal. Girdler put the ball over the bar and with eight minutes to play New South Wales drew level, 8–8.

With only one try scored in seventy minutes, both captains sought other means to get their side home and field-goal attempts became the fashion. Andrew Johns got in good position and took his shot but pulled it wide of the right upright. On the fifth tackle, from wide on the Blues' forty-metre line, Adrian Lam drop-kicked the ball toward the posts but it was a gross speculator which landed well short.

Finally, the Maroons got it right. They gained field position and, despite never having kicked a field goal in his life before, Matt Rogers was the chosen sharpshooter. From just to the right of the posts, and less than twenty metres out, his stab kick was perfect: Queensland 9, New South Wales 8.

With the clock indicating less than two minutes to go, Freddie Fittler fired a shot goalward and missed. From the subsequent

---

Final result

Queensland 9 defeated New South Wales 8.

Goals for Queensland: Matt Rogers (4) and one field goal.

Try for New South Wales: Anthony Mundine. Goals: Ryan Girdler (2).

Crowd: 38,093.

Man of the Match: Jason Hetherington.

twenty-metre tap, Matt Sing took off downfield, running the ball over halfway to give his team space in which to hold the opposition beyond field-goal range. From the play-the-ball, Jason Smith put a grubber into touch on the New South Wales twenty-metre line. The Blues had just fifty seconds to win the scrum and run the ball eighty metres. It was always going to be an impossible task but they never got started. While the scrum was packing, the two hookers had a disagreement that led to fisticuffs, and by the time the referee settled the matter the siren had sounded. Queensland had scraped home by a single point.

STATE OF ORIGIN II, 1999
STADIUM AUSTRALIA, 9 JUNE

Queensland	New South Wales
Robbie O'Davis	Robbie Ross
Wendell Sailor	Adam McDougall
Matt Sing	Ryan Girdler
Darren Smith	Terry Hill
Matt Rogers	Matt Geyer
Kevin Walters (c)	Laurie Daley
Paul Green	Andrew Johns
Shane Webcke	Mark Carroll
Jason Hetherington	Geoff Toovey
Craig Greenhill	Rodney Howe
Gorden Tallis	Nik Kosef
Chris McKenna	Bryan Fletcher
Jason Smith	Brad Fittler (c)

Interchange:

Steven Price	Michael Vella
Martin Lang	Luke Ricketson
Ben Ikin	Ben Kennedy
Tonie Carroll	Anthony Mundine

Coaches:

Mark Murray	Wayne Pearce

Referee: Stephen Clark

For four State of Origin matches in a row the Maroons had scored first and scored early, but not in Origin II, 1999. Forty-two seconds after Stephen Clark blew his whistle to start the game the Blues were in for a try. It was the fastest ever recorded in a State of Origin game.

The Maroons kicked off before a record crowd of 88,336, over a thousand more than had attended Origin II at the Melbourne Cricket Ground in 1994. On their fourth tackle of the game the Blues spread the ball wide. Toovey's dummy half pass to Andrew Johns was hot-potatoed to Laurie Daley. The Queensland defence was compressed in expectation that New South Wales would play it up the middle and there was space out wide. Laurie Daley drew Matt Sing and passed to Ryan Girdler who was able to get inside Darren Smith. Girdler ran fifteen metres and sent the ball wide to Robbie Ross who galloped thirty metres to score under the posts. Girdler converted the try and with just eighty seconds of the game elapsed New South Wales led 6–0. Origin II was five and a half minutes old before the Queenslanders got their first touch of the football. They drove the length of the field in five tackles before Rogers chased Jason Smith's chip-kick to the corner on the sixth to take Robbie Ross into touch in goal.

Heavy rain at the outset developed into a drenching downpour and it was not a night for fast, open football. However, the new stadium had an excellent drainage system and the surface stood up very well despite being saturated. Both sides were adventurous. They used plenty of ball movement. A desperate Robbie Ross tackle on Gorden Tallis stopped a certain try in the 16th minute. There was a Blues' infringement from the subsequent play-the-ball, however, and Matt Rogers brought the scores closer together: New South Wales 6. Queensland 2.

In the 20th minute Matt Rogers saved the day after Robbie Ross could have scored when he kicked a loose ball through and put it into the in-goal with a second well-judged soccer kick. Then, at the 25-minute mark, Jason Hetherington made an effective break for Queensland. He stepped and bumped his way downfield, broke tackles and passed to Kevin Walters on the Blues' forty-metre line. Kevin gave the ball to Jason Smith who drew two men before putting a long pass on to Matt Rogers' chest. Rogers scored in the corner. He converted his own try from the touchline and Queensland led 8 points to 6. The Maroons were looking good. They continued to attack. Nine minutes before half-time Jason Hetherington was over the line, but referee Clark ruled that he was held up and there was no try.

With the Blues in possession, Brad Fittler skied a bomb to the corner and it came down just outside the Maroons' try-line. Robbie O'Davis fumbled the catch. Since he was squarely facing his own goal line at the time, it would have been extremely difficult for him to have knocked the ball on, but in referee Stephen Clark's judgment he had achieved this miracle. From the ten-metre scrum, a New South Wales, attack developed and when Wendell Sailor knocked-on attempting an intercept on the Blues' fourth tackle, this extended into a second set of six tackles. On about the eighth consecutive tackle, with the ball spread wide, Andrew Johns picked up Laurie Daley on an angled run and the Canberra captain scored close to the posts. Girdler converted and the two sides went to half-time with the score favouring New South Wales 12 points to 8.

Not long after half-time, Rogers left the field limping. He didn't come back and there were other casualties on both sides. Andrew Johns was limping badly and in the 60th minute a heavy tackle on Mark Carroll by Jason Hetherington and Gorden Tallis left him inert on the ground, out cold. He left the field on rubbery legs supported by two trainers. Robbie O'Davis was incapacitated in a tackle by Geoff Toovey and left the field in the medicab, then late in the game Adam McDougall was off to seek treatment for a leg injury.

Meanwhile, play moved end to end, but while there were several close shaves there was no change to the score. With seven minutes to play Matt Geyer looked to be in for a try but Terry Hill's pass that sent him clear was ruled forward. A gang tackle on Robbie Ross on his twenty-metre line appeared to cause him to drop the ball. A scrum in good field position might have seen the Maroons accomplish something against a tiring defence, but after a disputed call from a linesman Stephen Clark ruled the ball stolen.

Despite their well-known reputation for coming home in the dying seconds of the game, the Maroons remained frustrated, and

---

Final result

New South Wales 12 defeated Queensland 8.

Tries for New South Wales: Robbie Ross, Laurie Daley. Goals: Ryan Girdler (2).

Try for Queensland: Matt Rogers. Goals: Matt Rogers (2).

Crowd: 88,336.

Man of the Match: Laurie Daley.

---

in the end the record crowd that braved the drenching rain watched a forty-minute scoreless arm wrestle, with the Blues holding on to win by the half-time score of 12 points to 8.

Darren Lockyer and Adrian Lam rejoined the Maroons for Origin III and Lam resumed the captaincy. Brad Fittler was out of the New South Wales side through injury, and it was probably appropriate that Laurie Daley should lead the Blues in this his last State of Origin appearance.

Just as it had with Origin II at Stadium Australia, drenching rain at Lang Park marred Origin III as a spectacle, but Queensland were on the attack from the kick-off. State of Origin crowds had almost become accustomed to seeing an early score in these games, and it almost happened again when a blind-side move from the twenty-metre line saw Robbie O'Davis tackled over the corner post. The Maroons continued to attack and for the first ten minutes of the game the ball never left their opposition's half of the field. Conditions underfoot were atrocious. The ball was often caked with mud and hard to hold and the Blues had great difficulty in putting together the set of six tackles that might get them out of trouble.

But as often happens in what appear to be one-sided affairs where the dominant team fails to score, the underdog bit first. The 11th minute of the game saw New South Wales awarded a penalty. This piggy-backed them into the Maroon half, and for the first time in the game by either team they decided to spread the ball. Andrew Johns noticed that the Maroons were short of defenders on the right side of the field, but his pass to Laurie Daley almost hit the ground before the five-eighth plucked it off his toes and passed to Terry

STATE OF ORIGIN III, 1999
LANG PARK, 23 JUNE

Queensland	New South Wales
Darren Lockyer	Robbie Ross
Wendell Sailor	Adam McDougall
Tonie Carroll	Ryan Girdler
Darren Smith	Terry Hill
Robbie O'Davis	Matt Geyer
Ben Ikin	Laurie Daley (c)
Adrian Lam (c)	Andrew Johns
Shane Webcke	Mark Carroll
Jason Hetherington	Geoff Toovey
Craig Greenhill	Rodney Howe
Gorden Tallis	David Furner
Chris McKenna	Bryan Fletcher
Jason Smith	Nik Kosef

Interchange:

Steven Price	Ben Kennedy
Martin Lang	Luke Rickertson
Brad Thorn	Michael Vella
Paul Green	Anthony Mundine

Coaches:

Mark Murray	Wayne Pearce

Referee: Stephen Clark (NSW)

Hill. Hill drew Wendell Sailor from his wing and gave the ball to Matt Geyer who scored in the corner. Ryan Girdler faced a daunting task with the conversion and it failed, but New South Wales led 4–0. Several semi-tropical thunderstorms had struck Brisbane during the afternoon and more than 100 mm of rain had fallen on Lang Park before game time. Light rain was falling when the teams ran on and became heavier as the game progressed, but at the 25-minute mark there was a breakthrough. Paul Green came on to replace an injured Jason Hetherington as dummy half, and from a play-the-ball less than ten metres out from the Blues' try-line he left three would-be tacklers lying on the ground as he stepped his way through the Blues' forwards and scored alongside the right upright. Queensland snatched a 6–4 lead when Darren Lockyer converted the try.

A few minutes later, with New South Wales in possession, Jason Smith flattened big Manly front-rower Mark Carroll, who took offence at such violence and charged back to retaliate. Stephen Clark's on-the-spot investigation resulted in a Blues' penalty, which Ryan Girdler transmuted into two points to level the scores, 6–6.

Six minutes before half-time, a promising New South Wales attack broke down on the Maroon twenty-metre line when Ryan Girdler knocked-on. The Queenslanders might well have gone ahead just two minutes later when Matt Geyer made a similar error on his own try-line. Neither referee Clark nor his linesmen spotted the infringement. Clark awarded New South Wales a twenty-metre tap restart. With the ball travelling from man to man like a hot potato, the Blues gained good field position in the fifth tackle, and with the crowd counting down to half-time, Laurie Daley missed with an attempt at a field goal. So the two sides sucked their oranges with the score at 6 all, the whole job to do over again, and just forty minutes in which to do it.

When the Blues kicked off to start the second half, Gorden Tallis ran the ball back thirty metres and initiated a movement that saw Jason Smith's kick on the fifth tackle take place on the New South Wales twenty-metre line. Matt Geyer fielded the kick in goal and earned a twenty-metre restart, but on the second tackle a knock-on put the Queenslanders on the attack from a scrum on the Blues' thirty-metre line. Four minutes after the restart, Adrian Lam ran to the line from a play-the-ball and drew defenders before sending the ball out to Ben Ikin. Ben held the pass up momentarily to make space for Darren Lockyer flying through on his outside. He gave him the ball and watched the fullback do the business. Darren Lockyer missed the simplest of conversions but Queensland was back in the lead, 10–6.

The Maroons continued to attack from the restart, with the result that for the first twenty-one minutes of the second half the Blues were inside the Queensland half only twice: once when they chased the kick-off to start play, and again when they restarted play after the Queensland try. But they held the Maroons to just the four second-half points although they never stopped attacking.

In the 67th minute Paul Green was penalised for a high tackle on Michael Vella, and after the kick for touch, play was restarted on the Maroons' thirty-metre line. The Blues were held for five tackles and Laurie Daley put up a high bomb on the fifth. The rain had developed into a torrential downpour and Daley's kick disappeared into the descending torrent as it soared high into the in-goal. With rain almost blotting out his vision, the always reliable Robbie O'Davis made his first error of the evening when he knocked-on.

Two tackles later there was a confused scramble in the goal mouth, with Blues' passes going through at least six sets of hands without any observable effect. Finally, front-row forward Rodney Howe put boot to ball and fluked a chip-kick in perfect position in the corner. Matt Geyer was quick off the mark to claim it, score the try and even the scores at 10–10. Ryan Girdler missed the conversion and, with full-time approaching and tries so hard to score, it was odds on that the game would end in a draw.

There was some confusion about what would occur if the scores were level, probably due to recent memory of the exciting means by which the tie was broken in the 1997 Super League Tri-series, but there was no confusion in coach Mark Murray's mind. Queensland held the State of Origin trophy. New South Wales needed to score to win the series; Queensland didn't.

For nine minutes the Maroons pinned the Blues in their own half. An apprehensive thrill ran through the grandstands when Laurie Daley split the Queensland defence and took the New South Wales

---

Final result

Queensland 10 drew with New South Wales 10.

Tries for Queensland: Paul Green, Darren Lockyer. Goal: Darren Lockyer.

Tries for New South Wales: Matt Geyer (2). Goal: Ryan Girdler.

Crowd: 39,371.

Man of the Match: Wendell Sailor.

attack into the Queensland half. Three tackles later they were on the Maroons' ten-metre line, but although they were within easy field-goal range they panicked. With Daley, Johns and Toovey in the side, all competent with the drop-kick, the dummy half could not find a kicker. He threw the ball wildly and it went to ground. Queensland recovered it. Gorden Tallis ran the ball out to the Queensland thirty-metre line, and when the siren sounded Wendell Sailor had taken it out of harm's way and into Blues' territory.

CHAPTER 22

2000

Thou Shalt Not Steal

LAURIE DALEY played his last State of Origin game in 1999, as had Mark Carroll, and Anthony Mundine had departed from Rugby League to seek fame and fortune in another field. They had to be replaced, and there were other changes to the Blues' team for Origin I, 2000. David Peachey replaced Robbie Ross at fullback, Brett Kimmorley was half-back, and his team-mate from Melbourne, Scott Hill, made his Origin debut off the bench, where Terry Hill joined him, replaced in the run-on side by St George–Illawarra's Shaun Timmins.

The Queensland selectors made few changes. Paul Bowman of the North Queensland Cowboys and Russell Bawden from Melbourne were both new to State of Origin Rugby League, but the team was largely the one that drew the final game of the 1999 series.

The Maroons were on the attack from the time they chased the kick-off. Inside five tackles they had forced the Blues to drop out from their own line. Before the game was three minutes old, Gorden Tallis was over the line in a welter of tacklers but failed to ground the ball. The Queenslanders continued to attack and gained a penalty when Bryan Fletcher hit Adrian Lam late and high after he had kicked the ball. Lam left the field with his arm slung in his guernsey, usually a certain sign of a shoulder injury, and Paul Green took over as half-back.

With almost ten minutes of the game gone, the Blues were yet

STATE OF ORIGIN I, 2000
STADIUM AUSTRALIA, 10 MAY

Queensland	New South Wales
Darren Lockyer	David Peachey
Wendell Sailor	Adam McDougall
Paul Bowman	Ryan Girdler
Darren Smith	Shaun Timmins
Matt Rogers	Jamie Ainscough
Ben Ikin	Brad Fittler (c)
Adrian Lam (c)	Brett Kimmorley
Shane Webcke	Robbie Kearns
Jason Hetherington	Geoff Toovey
Martin Lang	Rodney Howe
Gorden Tallis	David Furner
Brad Thorn	Bryan Fletcher
Jason Smith	Ben Kennedy

Interchange:

Steven Price	Scott Hill
Tonie Carroll	Terry Hill
Russell Bawden	Michael Vella
Paul Green	Jason Stevens

Coaches:

Mark Murray	Wayne Pearce

Referee: Bill Harrigan (NSW)

to set foot in Maroon territory. A penalty for a Queensland offside infringement got them in position to restart play from their own 35-metre line and their attack surged downfield. There was another Queensland infringement and Ryan Girdler took a penalty kick from less than twenty-five metres out and some fifteen metres to the left of the posts to give New South Wales a 2–0 lead.

When play restarted, the Maroons were on the attack immediately when the kick receiver, Ben Kennedy, knocked-on. A promising movement developed from the subsequent scrum but it broke down when Ben Ikin dropped a pass forward. The Blues mounted a substantial attack from within their own half after a failed charge down helped them to drive downfield. In the 14th minute Ryan Girdler ran off Freddie Fittler and crossed in the corner, only to find that the referee had ruled the last pass forward. On the first tackle after the scrum was won by Queensland, Ben Ikin ran over halfway before putting boot to ball to kick it deep so that it trickled into the in-goal. There was a footrace to claim the ball, in which the placings were Matt Rogers first, Darren Lockyer a close second, and Blues' Adam McDougall a distant third. By this time rain had made life difficult for goal kickers and Rogers missed the conversion, but the Queenslanders were in front, 4–2.

New South Wales was back in front seven minutes later. Scott Hill fed the ball to Brad Fittler from a quick play-the-ball and Fittler found Ryan Girdler with a long, cut-out pass. The centre ran wide and drew the winger to give Adam McDougall a clear run to the line. It was not a great night for kickers but New South Wales led 6–4.

Fears that Adrian Lam had sustained a serious shoulder injury were allayed when he returned to the field. The Maroons had dominated play from the outset, but they found the going tough when it came to scoring points. Then seven and a half minutes before half-time, Adrian Lam crossed for the simplest of tries when he ran from dummy half and left Terry Hill grasping fresh air as he scored well to the right of the posts. Rogers missed another conversion, but the persistent two-point margin had shifted in the Maroons' favour: Queensland 8, New South Wales 6.

The Queenslanders continued to attack and in one burst Gorden Tallis and Jason Hetherington took the ball more than sixty metres downfield in the space of two tackles. The Blues helped by missing more than twenty-five tackles in the first half, but there was no luck in the Queensland camp. Wayne Pearce's Blues went to half-time extremely grateful to be only two points behind. No doubt they were also cheered by the sight of Wendell Sailor leaving the field apparently concussed after a late-first-half clash of heads with Darren Lockyer.

Just after half-time it looked as though the Queenslanders' luck had changed. Big Brad Thorn smashed through an attempted tackle by Brad Fittler and tore away downfield before passing to Jason Hetherington who was tackled ten metres from the try-line. Adrian Lam ran from dummy half and dived in for the try through the attempted tackle of the same man who had missed Brad Thorn, Brad Fittler. Rogers converted this one and Queensland had cleared away to an 8-point lead. Following the second tackle after the restart, Lockyer ran the ball from first receiver when he was hit with a driving tackle by Robbie Kearns and dropped the ball. David Furner pounced, picked it up, passed to Brad Fittler who gave it on to Ryan Girdler. Girdler ran for the corner and, with the cover closing, dropped the ball behind him where it was picked up by Adam McDougall who put it over the line. Despite their domination of the game, the Maroons found themselves back to just a 2-point lead, 14–12, after Ryan Girdler converted the try.

For the next quarter of an hour the Queenslanders were under siege and they suffered casualties. Jason Smith was concussed from a Rodney Howe head-high tackle. A clash with a team-mate while making a tackle left goal kicker Matt Rogers lying on the ground, apparently unconscious, and Darren Lockyer was felled by a late tackle. But a big run by Tonie Carroll took the Maroons deep into the Blues' half and, when Bill Harrigan penalised the Blues for offside almost in front of their posts, Darren Lockyer kicked a goal. Queensland led 16–12.

Wendell Sailor returned to replace the injured Matt Rogers. When Adam McDougall looked likely to score in the corner, Wendell ran him down and put him into touch just as he was about to place the ball over the line. But the Queenslanders were having no luck. When Ben Ikin was discovered down and hurt in back play, the video replay showed quite clearly that it was due to a whack behind the ear with David Furner's elbow, but none of the officials had seen the blow that flattened him.

With the Maroons on the attack on the Blues' forty-metre line, Adrian Lam's pass to Ben Ikin was intercepted by Scott Hill. Hill was collared but he got an inside pass away to David Furner who knocked the ball forward before being taken out of play. What happened then was on all fours with the notorious refereeing error by which New Zealand referee Don Wilson decided the 1982 State of Origin series. Television replays confirmed that the knock-on was plainly apparent to everyone around Furner. Some of the Queenslanders adjacent slowed their pace, anticipating the inevitable whistle. No whistle. Terry Hill knocked-on as he retrieved the ball and backhanded it to David Peachey. Still no whistle. Peachey ran hard to his left and picked up Ryan Girdler who beat the cover defence and thought that he scored in the corner. Bill Harrigan thought so too. Gorden Tallis didn't, said so, and appeared to use some rather colourful language in stating his case. Harrigan ordered Gordie to the sin-bin for ten minutes. However, the Queensland captain hadn't finished his submission for the prosecution. When he persisted, Bill withdrew his offer of the sin-bin and sent him off instead. It was 16 all and Queensland a man down for the remainder of the match.

In the 75th minute of the game the Maroons managed to get good field position for a field goal but the Adrian Lam kick went wide. Then in a brief period of rapid ball movement, desperate Maroons grabbing at the football twice managed to restart the Blues' tackle count, and after some spectacular passes were thrown and caught, David Peachey put the result of Origin I beyond doubt with a try in the corner. Girdler's attempt at goal failed, and it was New South Wales 20, Queensland 16.

In due course Gorden Tallis was called before the judiciary. He drew a conviction, but when the circumstances were explained to the good men and true who sat in judgment they considered the Maroons' deprivation of his services following his send-off to be sufficient punishment. He was available for Origin II. The Queens-

---

Final result

New South Wales 20 defeated Queensland 16.

Tries for New South Wales: Adam McDougall (2), Ryan Girdler, David Peachey. Goals: Ryan Girdler (2).

Tries for Queensland: Adrian Lam (2), Matt Rogers. Goals: Darren Lockyer, Matt Rogers.

Crowd: 61,511.

Man of the Match: Adam McDougall.

land selectors recalled Julian O'Neill to replace the injured Ben Ikin. Wendell Sailor was also unfit for the match, and Matt Sing replaced him on the wing. The Blues' team was also left largely intact. Tim Brasher replaced David Peachey, Andrew Johns came into the side on the bench, and a reshuffled back row saw David Furner move to the bench and Scott Hill lock the scrum.

There was no sign early in Brad Fittler's 25th State of Origin game for New South Wales that anything extraordinary would cause it to be any more memorable than many earlier games. Queensland scored early when Robbie Kearns first surrendered possession with

---

STATE OF ORIGIN II, 2000
LANG PARK, 24 MAY

Queensland	New South Wales
Darren Lockyer	Tim Brasher
Matt Rogers	Adam McDougall
Paul Bowman	Ryan Girdler
Darren Smith	Shaun Timmins
Matt Sing	Jamie Ainscough
Julian O'Neill	Brad Fittler (c)
Adrian Lam (c)	Brett Kimmorley
Shane Webcke	Robbie Kearns
Jason Hetherington	Geoff Toovey
Martin Lang	Rodney Howe
Gorden Tallis	Ben Kennedy
Brad Thorn	Bryan Fletcher
Jason Smith	Scott Hill

Interchange:

Steven Price	Andrew Johns
Tonie Carroll	David Furner
Russell Bawden	Adam Muir
Paul Green	Jason Stevens

Coaches:

Mark Murray	Wayne Pearce

Referee: Bill Harrigan (NSW)

a knock-on and then gave up a penalty when he failed to mark up correctly as Adrian Lam played the ball. Matt Rogers kicked a goal and Queensland led 2–0.

There had been rain during the day, light rain fell during the game, and handling errors made it difficult for both sides to get out of their own half when in possession. As time passed without a further score being registered, defence became more vigorous. Rodney Howe was penalised at least twice for head-hunting, and his score ought to have been higher. Adam McDougall lifted a knee as Julian O'Neill made a front-on tackle. This went undetected by the match officials, a phenomenon that severely taxed the comprehension of the Channel 9 team who were unanimous that he ought to have been penalised and reported. Geoff Toovey suffered serious damage to a rib cartilage in another fierce exchange.

The score remained 2–0 until the 32nd minute, when, despite heroic defence by the Blues, a Queensland passing rush took play deep into the right side of the Blues' half. With the Queensland back line running free, and a try a distinct possibility, Shaun Timmins tackled Paul Bowman without the ball, right in front of the posts. Matt Rogers said, 'Thanks, very much,' and potted the penalty goal to give Queensland a 4–0 lead.

Following the restart, a knock-on inside the Queensland twenty-metre line saw the Maroons forced to mount a desperate defence as the Blues launched raid after raid on their line and forced line drop-out after line drop-out. Julian O'Neill drove them back each time with his fifty-metre drop-kicks. During the ten minutes before half-time, the Blues were seldom more than two or three tackles out of the Maroons' twenty-metre zone, but the Queenslanders held. Half-time score was Queensland 4, New South Wales 0.

Two minutes into the second half the Maroons almost scored when Paul Bowman put a grubber into the in-goal. A desperate chase by Matt Rogers was foiled by Tim Brasher when he placed one foot over the dead-ball line and scooped the football into touch.[1] As the ball was taken out to the twenty-metre line for the restart, Maroon lock Jason Smith was being chaired from the field with a serious leg problem.

The Queenslanders hung in well, despite the highly motivated

Blues' endeavours to score, but in the sixth minute of the second half it appeared that Brad Fittler had tired of watching his team's movements break down. Darren Smith gave up a penalty for interference and this piggy-backed the Blues to the Maroons' twenty-metre line. The second subsequent play-the-ball was on the fifteen-metre line. From first receiver, Freddie Fittler ran to his favoured left side, then beat the defence with a big step off his left foot to score a try alongside the posts. Ryan Girdler converted and New South Wales was in front, 6–4. Just four minutes later the Queenslanders struck back.

From a ruck on the Blues' twenty-metre line, Darren Smith ran from dummy half before passing to Tonie Carroll. Carroll got the ball away to Adrian Lam who broke a Rodney Howe tackle and passed to Gorden Tallis. Tallis easily smashed through a tackle by Shaun Timmins and scored. Matt Rogers kick was successful, and the Maroons were back in the lead, 10 points to 6.

After half-time Andrew Johns played dummy half and in the 59th minute of the game he ran the ball on the last tackle. He broke the line before passing to Adam Muir who quickly unloaded to David Furner. Furner drew two tacklers before passing to Shaun Timmins who ran through a gigantic hole in the right-side defence to score. Ryan Girdler converted Timmins try from a wide angle, and with sixty-one minutes gone the Blues went to a narrow lead, 12 points to 10. The Blues then put the game out of the Maroons reach when they stacked on 12 more points in the next four minutes.

Freddie Fittler and Andrew Johns were involved in a movement that put Scott Hill in for his first State of Origin try in the 63rd minute. Ryan Girdler converted: 18–10. Then from the restart of play Andrew Johns burst through again and passed to Ben Kennedy who tore downfield before he gave the ball to David Furner who scored out wide. Ryan Girdler made it 24–10.

With full-time looming, and in the 79th minute, the Blues struck again. With the Maroons throwing the ball about like a hot potato on the Blues' twenty-metre line, Ryan Girdler intercepted and sprinted away. When the cover threatened him, he passed to Adam McDougall and ran around him to take the next pass inside and score wide out. His attempt at a conversion was taken after the siren.

Final result

New South Wales 28 defeated Queensland 10.

Tries for New South Wales: Brad Fittler, Shaun Timmins, Scott Hill, David Furner, Ryan Girdler. Goals: Ryan Girdler (4).

Try for Queensland: Gorden Tallis. Goals: Matt Rogers (3).

Crowd: 38,796.

Man of the Match: Tim Brasher.

It missed, to leave the final score New South Wales 28, Queensland 10.

Prior to 2000, the largest winning margin by a Blues' team in twenty years of State of Origin Rugby League was the 18 points to 2 scored at Lang Park in 1985. This was equalled in 1998 at the same venue when the Blues won by 26 points to 10. The 18-point margin in the Blues 28–10 win in Origin II set a new mark.

Wendell Sailor was again available for Origin III, but Matt Sing remained in the run-on side, replacing Darren Smith at centre. Smith moved to Lock. Ben Ikin was also back. Chris McKenna was in the second row. Brad Thorn was moved to the bench and was joined there by Craig Greenhill. For once, there were no alterations to the Blues' side.

For the first fifteen minutes of Origin III, Queensland was well in it. In the 8th minute of play a strong downfield foray by the Maroon forwards culminated in a dummy half run by Jason Hetherington on the fifth tackle. He was tackled less than a metre out from the line.

A few minutes later a penalty piggy-backed the Maroons deep into Blues' territory. From the tap that restarted play, the ball went to Julian O'Neill. Darren Smith called for the ball but neither he nor O'Neill had noticed Ryan Girdler coming through at pace. The Penrith centre snapped up the intercept and ran sixty metres to score untouched. He converted his own try and the score was New South Wales 6, Queensland 0. It was at about this time that things started to unravel for the Maroons.

From a ruck deep in his own half, Blues' captain Brad Fittler

STATE OF ORIGIN III, 2000
STADIUM AUSTRALIA, 7 JUNE

Queensland	New South Wales
Darren Lockyer	Tim Brasher
Wendell Sailor	Adam McDougall
Paul Bowman	Ryan Girdler
Matt Sing	Matthew Gidley
Matt Rogers	Jamie Ainscough
Ben Ikin	Brad Fittler [c]
Adrian Lam [c]	Brett Kimmorley
Shane Webcke	Robbie Kearns
Jason Hetherington	Geoff Toovey
Martin Lang	Jason Stevens
Gorden Tallis	Ben Kennedy
Chris McKenna	Bryan Fletcher
Darren Smith	Scott Hill

Interchange:

Julian O'Neill	Andrew Johns
Tonie Carroll	David Furner
Brad Thorn	Adam Muir
Craig Greenhill	Michael Vella

Coaches:

Mark Murray	Wayne Pearce

Referee: Bill Harrigan (NSW)

kicked deep and wide to his left. Ryan Girdler ran the ball down and quickly gave it to his winger, Adam McDougall. Adam Muir had just come on the field as a fresh replacement and backed up inside as McDougall drew the cover defence. McDougall's pass left Muir with nothing to do but run. He placed the ball under the posts, Girdler did the honours and the New South Wales' lead was extended to 12–0.

The Maroons sought to recover a grip on the game when Tim Brasher fumbled a high kick to the in-goal by Lockyer. Brasher moved to recover the spilled ball but Matt Rogers had followed the kick at top pace and his hands touched the ball down inches before Brasher's touched it. Rogers' kick was good. The Maroons were again within 6 points of the leaders after twenty-five minutes of play, but it wasn't their night. A mighty cross-field kick by Freddie Fittler was chased by Adam McDougall. He failed to reach the ball in time to make the catch, but the fortuitous boot that he got to it sent the ball flying high into the in-goal where it was fielded by Lockyer who was promptly tackled by McDougall who had followed his soccer kick at top pace. Lockyer had the ball tucked under his arm when he was tackled, and when he landed on his back it bounded high in the air. It was rounded up by Girdler who forced it and claimed a try. Once again Girdler's aim was true and it was 18–6 to the Blues.

In what was fast becoming a very high-scoring half of football, Queensland scored in the 30th minute from an Adrian Lam kick to the right corner. The ball was gathered in by Matt Sing. He gave it to Darren Smith who sprinted down the right touchline to score. The try remained unconverted and it was New South Wales leading, 18–10.

A penalty at the 36th minute for interference, given right in front of goal, provided Ryan Girdler with another opportunity to score points and the Blues went to the break leading the Maroons 20 points to 10. To add to the Maroons' woes, they lost their five-eighth, Ben Ikin, in the first half and were told at half-time that he had a suspected broken leg and would not be back.

Within four minutes of the restart of play, the Blues scored again after the Queenslanders were forced to kick on the fifth tackle on their own forty-metre line. The kick was short and the Blues gained possession less than ten metres inside their own half. Two tackles saw the ball being played well inside Queensland territory. Freddie Fittler ran off a dummy half pass and broke the line. Andrew Johns had only just come on to the field and Fittler's pass on the Maroons' twenty-metre line was his first touch of the football for the match. He had only to run the twenty metres to touch down under the posts. Ryan Girdler made it 26–10.

The Blues' tails were up. During the next thirty minutes they wore a path to the Maroon try-line. Girdler scored his third try in the 54th minute of the game and converted it to make the score New South Wales 32, Queensland 10. He increased the margin to 38–10 in the 59th minute when he converted Gidley's try. Fletcher scored six minutes later and again Girdler did the honours. At 44–10 the score was becoming embarrassing for the Queenslanders and the partisan crowd at Stadium Australia was chanting for fifty. Five minutes later they got their wish when McDougall scored a try. With the conversion, Ryan Girdler was within striking distance of Dally Messenger's all-time point-scoring record, which had stood since 1911, and the score was 50 points to 10.

With only two minutes left in the game the Queenslanders managed to reduce the margin when their captain, Gorden Tallis, stood wide on the blind side to take a pass from Adrian Lam. He beat three tacklers to reach out and place the ball on the line for a try. Matt Rogers kicked the goal and it was New South Wales 50, Queensland 16.

With the siren sounding, Matt Gidley was the last of eight players to handle in a razzle-dazzle movement which saw him score in the corner. Ryan Girdler converted from the touchline. His kick sealed the game at the State of Origin record score of 56–16, and made a major contribution to a stack of records that were broken that night:

- The forty-point margin was the greatest ever achieved in a State of Origin game.
- 56 was the highest score ever achieved in a State of Origin game.

From an individual perspective:

- Ryan Girdler's three tries gave him a share in the record for most tries in a State of Origin game, along with Chris Anderson and Kerry Boustead.[2]
- His ten goals were the most ever kicked in a State of Origin game.
- His 32 individual points were the most ever scored by a player in a State of Origin game and appear to equal Dally Messenger's mark for the most ever scored in an interstate match of any kind.[3]
- His 52 points in the 2000 State of Origin series were easily a record for an individual.

Final result

New South Wales 56 defeated Queensland 16.

Tries for New South Wales: Ryan Girdler (3), Matt Gidley (2), Adam Muir, Andrew Johns, Bryan Fletcher, Adam McDougall. Goals: Ryan Girdler (10).

Tries for Queensland: Darren Smith, Gorden Tallis, Matt Rogers. Goals: Matt Rogers (2).

Crowd: 58,767.

Man of the Match: Ryan Girdler.

There is no nice way to describe the performance of the Maroons in Origin III, 2000. With the single exception of the defeat of New South Wales by a Queensland side in Newcastle in 1925 by 56 points to 23[4] this was a far worse defeat than the Maroons had ever inflicted on the Blues.

Neither the footballers who played that night nor the veteran team that managed the Maroons could have imagined such a result. They flew back to Brisbane deep in thought, determined to find a means to do better. And the football was not their only concern. In Sydney that season Paul Vautin and Peter Sterling, the two stars of the *Footy Show* at Channel 9, had encouraged First Grade Rugby League players to lairise by offering prizes for the best American–style post–try celebration, a choreographed performance by the try–scorer. This spilled over into the State of Origin arena when the Blues got fairly up the collective noses of the Maroon establishment with a production apparently sponsored by Sydney City, Freddie Fittler's club. It showed signs of being rehearsed in State of Origin camp and involved Bryan Fletcher using the football as a dummy hand grenade, accompanied by a mock collapse on the ground by the other twelve Blues as they pretended to be blown away.

If this grotesque performance was insufficient, then the Blues coach poured a little additional fuel on the fire when he was interviewed after the game. Following an especially saccharine effusion regarding the skill and bravery of his charges, he added, 'The scary thing is that I think this side has a lot of improvement in it

... you're seeing the dividends now, and I think you'll see them in the future.'[5]

The Queenslanders had their own ideas about the Blues' immediate future, and while they licked their wounds they plotted the downfall of this highly touted young flock of *Blata Orientalis*.[6]

CHAPTER 23

2001

'Grab Your Boots and Mouthguard, Alf'

THE offensive performance provided by New South Wales at Stadium Australia during and after the record win in Origin II, 2000 grossly offended Queenslanders everywhere, and from the oldest veteran on the management team to the newest initiate to the Brotherhood of the Maroon Jersey the 2001 Queensland State of Origin camp oozed resentment at the exhibitionist high jinks of the gloating Blues. One prominent former Origin great described the exercise as 'an uncouth exhibition by a team of posers and lairs'.

But while anger may be a useful tool to motivate a team, it won't help a bit if they can't play football, and to bridge the gap between Origin III, 2000 and Origin I, 2001 drastic action was needed. The last Maroon coach to win a series was Wayne Bennett, whose record at State of Origin level was matched only by that of Artie Beetson. When asked about preparing the 2001 side, Bennett agreed to do so, but he laid down conditions regarding selection procedures, coaching procedures and the need for an ongoing campaign through the Institute of Sport to develop the new talent required to maintain strength and continuity in future State of Origin sides.

Following some reorganisation to meet the new coach's requirements, highly respected former star players Gene Miles and Des Morris were appointed selectors. Wayne Bennett brought with him his own support staff, and he insisted on retaining veteran managers Chris Close and Dick Turner. Former Origin greats Gary Belcher and Steve Walters were also drawn into Bennett's close circle of advisers and aides. Of the seventeen Maroons who lost Origin III, 2000, only five took the field in Origin I, 2001. Some of the missing players were unavailable because of injury, a couple had sought greener pastures with English League clubs or in Rugby Union, but it was not who had gone but who had replaced them that startled the Rugby League community. Six of the selected run-on side, and all of the four interchange players for Origin I were debutantes and most of the seventeen had strong bonds with the coach. Nine of the debutantes were members of Bennett's 2001 Brisbane squad and two of the veterans wore premiership rings that they had won with the Broncos.

With such a strong one-club contingent and the presence in camp of such State of Origin icons as Close, Miles, Belcher and Steve Walters, bonding sessions were largely redundant. It was a strongly unified, focused group of footballers who accepted the accolades from the Caxton beer garden as the bus brought them to Lang Park for the 33rd State of Origin game to be played at the Cauldron, and the last before the sacred turf was torn up to make way for a new stadium.

Finally, as they stripped and made ready for the fray, the greatest Former Origin Great of them all came to wish the team well. They listened in awed silence as Wally Lewis, veteran of thirty-one State of Origin games and Queensland captain in thirty of them, told the players in a few short words what it means to be a Queenslander, and in a brief but moving ceremony he presented each Maroon with his 2001 guernsey.

Following the profound bath that they had given the Maroons in 2000, the New South Wales selectors saw no need for drastic change. There was a winning coach in charge, and thirteen 2001 Blues had previously played in a State of Origin side, most of them experienced veterans.

Bill Harrigan blew the whistle for time-on and the Maroons kicked off. Youth and enthusiasm were present in generous measure when the young Maroons' first five tackles forced the Blues to kick from well inside their own half on the sixth. Darren Lockyer fielded the ball inside his own thirty-metre line and broke two tackles before

STATE OF ORIGIN I, 2001
LANG PARK, 6 MAY

Queensland	New South Wales
Darren Lockyer	Mark Hughes*
Lote Tuqiri*	Jamie Ainscough
Paul Bowman	Matthew Gidley
Darren Smith	Michael Devere*
Wendell Sailor	Adam McDougall
Daniel Wagon*	Brad Fittler (c)
Paul Green	Brett Kimmorley
Shane Webcke	Jason Stevens
Kevin Campion*	Luke Priddis*
John Buttigieg*	Robbie Kearns
Gorden Tallis (c)	Bryan Fletcher
Petero Civoniceva*	Nathan Hindmarsh*
Bradley Meyers*	Jason Croker

Interchange:

Chris Walker*	Trent Barrett
Chris Beattie*	Michael Vella
Carl Webb*	Ben Kennedy
John Doyle*	Rodney Howe

Coach:

Wayne Bennett	Wayne Pearce

Referee: Bill Harrigan

* Debutantes.

he put Lote Tuqiri away. Lote tore down the touchline, and as the cover closed in he found Lockyer backing up inside him to take the ball and score under the posts. Lockyer converted his own try and with less than three minutes on the game clock Queensland led 6–0.

The Blues came back strongly. John Buttigieg was penalised for lying too long on a tackled player, and after the kick the tap restart on the Maroons' thirty-metre line sparked a strong New South Wales attack that put Matt Gidley over the line. Gidley had managed to cross on four occasions in Origin III, 2000 but on one occasion he dropped the ball and the other three were ruled held up over the line. He had no early luck in Origin I, 2001 either. He fumbled the ball and dropped it, providing Queensland with a twenty-metre tap restart. The Maroons didn't waste their opportunity. The play-the-ball on the fifth tackle was on the New South Wales ten-metre line, just to the left of the goal posts. Darren Smith acted as dummy half, ran strongly to his right and stepped around Robbie Kearns to score close to the posts. Lockyer made it two out of two and the score was Queensland 12, New South Wales 0.

The 56–16 flogging was but a memory. The Maroons were playing against the same team, who had trained under the same coach, but it was a different ball game, although halfway through the first half New South Wales closed the gap slightly. Matt Gidley managed, at last, to both cross the line and ground the ball, in this case five metres in from the sideline, to make it 12–4 to Queensland. Ryan Girdler's kicking boot had been unerring in 2000, but he missed his first for 2001 and Queensland retained an 8-point lead.

A few minutes before half-time Paul Green put Queensland on the attack with a 40–20 kick[1] that went into touch inside the Blues' ten-metre line. Young Bronco Carl Webb had just come on from the bench in his first State of Origin game. On the third tackle the Queenslanders were awarded a penalty and Webb took the ball as first receiver from a tap restart twelve metres out from the Blues' try-line. The strongly built youngster ran hard towards the corner and bumped off or fended five tacklers before crossing the line carrying the last two, Jason Croker and Matt Gidley, on his broad back. Lockyer's attempt at a conversion was wide of the posts but the Maroons went to half-time with a 16–4 lead.

The Queenslanders forfeited a fair proportion of the experience in their ranks when Darren Smith failed to return to the field after half-time, and early in the second half it appeared that the Blues might make a comeback when Brett Kimmorley put Bryan Fletcher away. The Easts second-rower pulled out of a tackle by the lightweight Paul Green and was over the line, but a strong tackle by Darren Lockyer and Daniel Wagon caused him to drop the ball.

In the 45th minute John Doyle drove hard from dummy half,

broke through and stormed downfield. Lockyer ran off him and made thirty metres or more before being tackled, but Doyle stayed with him to take an inside pass and score under the posts. Lockyer added the extras. At 22–4 the Maroons were well away and before the Lang Park crowd had settled back in their seats another of the debutantes scored.

From the restart that followed Doyle's try, a Maroon knock-on saw a scrum form on the Queensland thirty-metre line. When Brett Kimmorley threw a wild pass from the base of the scrum, it was snapped up by Lote Tuqiri who ran to the halfway mark before passing to Chris Walker. Walker gave it to Petero Civoniceva who was tackled on the Blues' thirty-metre line. From the play-the-ball, John Doyle's pass from dummy half was quickly handed on to John Buttigieg and the big man crashed through to score adjacent to the posts. Darren Lockyer's kick took the score to 28–4.

From a play-the-ball six minutes later, John Doyle found Chris Walker running the angle to his right and gave him the ball. Walker had all of the forwards beaten for pace and scored. Once more Lockyer raised the linesmen's flags.

At half-time Wayne Bennett had warned his charges against becoming excited about their 14-point lead. He told them to go out and win the first fifteen minutes of the second half and go from there. With the clock showing the second half a quarter of an hour old, they had scored more than a point a minute and led 34–4.

It was the Blues who scored next when their captain, Freddie Fittler, intercepted a Maroon pass on the Queensland forty-metre line and sprinted the sixty metres to score. Bronco centre Mick Devere kicked the goal and the score was 34–10. Devere also gave the last pass in a movement that saw the Blues score the final try of the game, by Trent Barrett, in the 75th minute. Mick converted the try. The full-time score was Queensland 34, New South Wales 16 and the Maroons had achieved a 58-point turnaround. The victory went a long way towards wiping out the memory of that June night in Sydney in 2000. The Maroons were back, and, playing his first game as captain of Queensland, Gorden Tallis had led by outstanding example. He was by far the best forward on the field and his choice as Man of the Match surprised no one.

Final result

Queensland 34 defeated New South Wales 16.

Tries for Queensland: Darren Lockyer, Darren Smith, John Buttigieg, Chris Walker, Carl Webb, John Doyle. Goals: Darren Lockyer (5).

Tries for New South Wales: Matthew Gidley, Brad Fittler, Trent Barrett. Goals: Mick Devere (2).

Crowd: 38,909.

Man of the Match: Gorden Tallis.

Only three changes were made in the Queensland team for Origin II, all of them because of injuries and one of them a major blow to the Maroons. Gorden Tallis was out, hurt playing for the Broncos against the Northern Eagles on 20 May.[2] The two North Queensland heroes, John Buttigieg and John Doyle, were also casualties of the week-to-week club battle.

Two of their replacements had never played State of Origin before. Tallis's place was taken by yet another young Bronco, Dane Carlaw. North Queensland half-back Nathan Fien took John Doyle's place and he was also playing his first State of Origin game. Russell Bawden, who replaced John Buttigieg in the front row, had a good deal more first grade experience than most of the team, and had played in Origin I and Origin II in 2000.

The Queenslanders were on top early in Origin II with more than 60 per cent of ball possession in the first twenty minutes, but they failed to take sufficient advantage of this. New South Wales did no better and for the first half hour play ebbed and flowed with frequent errors on both sides but no tries. At the 30th minute a single penalty goal and a lead of 2–0 were all that the Queenslanders had to show for such domination. Then a Maroon mistake gave the Blues the first real try-scoring opportunity of the game.

Less than ten minutes before half-time John Doyle's replacement, Nathan Fien, kicked from dummy half on the last tackle and the ball went out on the full. This gave the Blues scrum feed and loose head on the Maroons' thirty-metre line. Trent Barrett, the St George five-eighth, had been selected to play half-back. Big and strong, he

STATE OF ORIGIN II, 2001
STADIUM AUSTRALIA, 10 JUNE

Queensland	New South Wales
Darren Lockyer (c)	Mark Hughes
Lote Tuqiri	Jamie Ainscough
Paul Bowman	Matthew Gidley
Darren Smith	Ryan Girdler
Wendell Sailor	Adam McDougall
Daniel Wagon	Brad Fittler (c)
Paul Green	Trent Barrett
Shane Webcke	Jason Stevens
Kevin Campion	Luke Priddis
Russell Bawden	Mark O'Meley
Dane Carlaw	Bryan Fletcher
Petero Civoniceva	Adam Muir
Bradley Meyers	Luke Ricketson

Interchange:

Chris Walker	Michael Vella
Chris Beattie	Matt Adamson
Carl Webb	Andrew Ryan
Nathan Fien	Craig Gower

Coaches:

Wayne Bennett	Wayne Pearce

Referee: Bill Harrigan (NSW)

ran to the blind from the restart and served Luke Ricketson who beat Daniel Wagon with a dummy and scored in a handy position for Ryan Girdler to convert. New South Wales led 6–2, and that remained the scoreline at the end of what was, for a State of Origin game, a dull half of football.

New South Wales went further ahead four minutes after half-time. Jamie Ainscough tackled Darren Smith as he attempted to run the ball out from his own ten-metre line. As Ainscough made the tackle, his right hand knocked the ball forward on to the ground. The referee ordered 'play on' as no attempt was made by the tackler to play at the ball. Jamie Ainscough pounced on it and ran fifteen metres to place it over the line. Ryan Girdler converted and suddenly New South Wales led 12–2.

In the 47th minute Wendell Sailor knocked-on. The ball was picked up by Craig Gower. Referee Harrigan played the advantage rule. He called 'play on' and Gower lost the ball in a tackle by Wendell Sailor. Harrigan ordered a scrum and indicated that the scrum feed and loose head belonged to Queensland. Freddie Fittler protested loudly. He approached the referee and argued that there had been no advantage accrue to the Blues.[3] In doing so, his delivery was at least as vehement, although perhaps not as colourful, as the famous speech made by Gorden Tallis at Stadium Australia on 10 May 2000. Since there is an unwritten law in Rugby League that referees never change their minds, it came as a shock and a surprise to most people watching when Harrigan reversed himself and gave the scrum feed and loose head to New South Wales. This is the sort of thing that might be seen in a game between two pick-up sides of school children being refereed by one of their mothers, but even in those circumstances it would have been controversial. For Australia's number one referee to first hold a committee meeting with the players and then change his mind in response to a Captain's protest was simply breathtaking. More than thirty years of experience at the top level made Ray Warren the doyen of television Rugby League broadcasters. He spoke for every educated Rugby League follower watching when he told his audience, 'I've never seen that before.'[4] The most famous of all Sydney Rugby League radio and television broadcasters and former New South Wales representative, Frank Hyde, watched the game on television. He was another who said that such a reversal was beyond his previous experience.[5]

Of course, the Blues gained possession in prime field position. Trent Barrett scored a converted try on the fourth tackle following the scrum. There is probably no circumstance which so affects a Rugby League team as a perception that the ranks of the opposition have swollen from thirteen men to fourteen. The advantage gained from the reversed decision became the point upon which the game swung irretrievably in the Blues favour, and the Queenslanders were seething, their anger exacerbated when the television replay of

Barrett's try was repeated in slow motion on the big screen. Bill Harrigan awarded the try without calling for the video and the slow-motion replay plainly showed that in the act of scoring Trent Barrett appeared to lose control of the ball. And it got worse. From the restart, Freddie Fittler scored off an inside pass from Trent Barrett. In the space of seven minutes the Maroons had gone from being 2–12 to 2–20 down due to two tries, one of which left an extremely sour taste in Queensland mouths. Ryan Girdler's conversion made it New South Wales 22, Queensland 2 and the game was gone on the strength of a couple of controversial refereeing decisions.

In the 71st minute of the game Chris Walker ran off a Paul Green pass from dummy half on the New South Wales ten-metre line. With a strong run from the left of the ruck, across towards the right-hand corner of the field, the speedster was unstoppable and scored. Darren Lockyer reduced the Blues' lead to 22–8 but the gap opened again when Freddie Fittler scored wide out close to full-time. Ryan Girdler's kick failed and the Maroons lost Origin II, 2001 by 8 points to 26.

Final result

New South Wales 26 defeated Queensland 8.

Tries for New South Wales: Brad Fittler [2], Jamie Ainscough, Trent Barrett, Luke Ricketson. Goals: Ryan Girdler [3].

Try for Queensland: Chris Walker. Goals: Darren Lockyer [2].

Crowd: 70,249.

Man of the Match: Trent Barrett.

As the 2001 State of Origin series approached its climax, those responsible for the Maroons' performance faced a crisis. Led from the front by Broncos' inspiring captain Gorden Tallis in Origin I, a team of brilliant young Queenslanders had run on to Lang Park and thrashed New South Wales to the tune of 34 to 16. New South Wales selectors had made a few changes for the second game, but the side didn't look much different from the one that these youngsters had steamrollered. Perhaps they could have been excused if they had gone into Origin II firmly believing that they were ten foot tall and bulletproof and then perished through over-confidence, but their loss at Stadium Australia was probably due more to the absence of their captain than to any other factor.

Wayne Bennett knew that he didn't lack quality forwards. He had guided the careers of most of them and he knew that every one of these youngsters was well worthy of the Maroon guernsey that he wore. To beat New South Wales by 18 points had lifted them to the skies. But from 36–16 to 8–26 is a long way down. The young maroons had hit rock bottom but it would serve no purpose to make wholesale changes in the hope of a better result. Bennett was aware that he had the cream of the crop and that their salvation had to come from within. Something else was needed to reinvigorate the team.

Mathematically, the answer seemed simple. If a leader with an aura equally as potent as that of Gorden Tallis could be found to replace him, then all might yet be well. Wayne Bennett and his henchmen believed that there was just such a player available, one whose very name was synonymous with both State of Origin and leadership. What was more to the point, he might jump at the chance to prove it.

It was decided that Allan Langer must come home.

Wayne Bennett rang a phone number in Warrington, UK, and put the question to Alfie. He didn't have to be asked twice. Provided his club would allow it, and provided the Queensland selectors picked him, he would be happy to return to play again for the Maroons.

There developed a covert operation that the CIA might envy, right down to the strategic leaking of misinformation. Shortly after the Queenslanders returned from Sydney, confidential leaks to selected media people suggested that a former Queenslander might be brought home from England, but they were steered toward either Steve Renouf or Tonie Carroll as the target. Alfie's arrival in Brisbane came as a complete surprise to everyone outside Wayne Bennett's circle, and the Queensland selectors saw no need to make any other change to the side that had lost Origin II.

Because work had commenced on the redevelopment of Lang

STATE OF ORIGIN III, 2001
ANZ STADIUM, 1 JULY

Queensland	New South Wales
Darren Lockyer (c)	Mark Hughes
Lote Tuqiri	Jamie Ainscough
Paul Bowman	Ryan Girdler
Chris Walker	Matthew Gidley
Wendell Sailor	Adam McDougall
Daniel Wagon	Brad Fittler (c)
Allan Langer	Brett Kimmorley
Shane Webcke	Jason Stevens
Paul Green	Luke Priddis
John Buttigieg	Mark O'Meley
Brad Meyers	Bryan Fletcher
Petero Civoniceva	Adam Muir
Darren Smith	Andrew Ryan

Interchange:

Carl Webb	Craig Gower
Kevin Campion	Michael Vella
Dane Carlaw	Matt Adamson
John Doyle	Steve Menzies

Coaches:

Wayne Bennett	Wayne Pearce

Referee: Bill Harrigan (NSW)

Park, Origin III was played at the Broncos' home ground, ANZ Stadium. Many of those who had championed the alterations to Lang Park had criticised the Broncos' home ground for its lack of atmosphere for big games. However, none of the 50,000 people who attended the suburban stadium that night complained of the atmosphere. When Allan Langer followed acting captain Darren Lockyer on to the field and the crowd gave voice to their joy at seeing him once more in Maroon, the noise at ground level was deafening and the opening was typically State of Origin. The ball went to John Buttigieg and he knocked-on.

From the ensuing scrum, Paul Bowman allowed Ryan Girdler to get outside him; Wendell Sailor took Girdler's dummy, the Penrith centre handed off Darren Smith with a perfect old-fashioned 'don't argue', and just thirty-eight seconds after Bill Harrigan signalled time on, Ryan Girdler scored a try, shaving 4 seconds off Robbie Ross's 1999 record. He then proceeded to convert it with a kick from the sideline.

In 1999 a similar stroke of good fortune had set New South Wales up for a 12–8 half-time lead, a lead which they successfully defended in a hard-fought second half. From the second kick-off they sought to repeat their earlier triumph. They threw everything at the Maroons and for a time they looked the goods. The Queenslanders missed more than ten tackles in the first seven minutes of play and for a brief period the Blues razzle-dazzle had them on the back foot. But Allan Langer steadied the ship. Alfie set the example. He stood in the first line of defence and did twice his share of the hard yakka. In possession, he drove his forwards on in attack, while his educated kicking game frustrated the Blues.

Brad Fittler's men strove mightily to consolidate their early advantage, but support from the record ANZ crowd was almost overwhelming in both its volume and tone and Lockyer's men held them out. Then, in the 11th minute of the game, Queenslanders were rewarded with a slice of Maroon magic. Lote Tuqiri took the ball on his own thirty-metre line and stepped and wove his way past four pairs of grasping Blues' hands deep into their half. As the cover defence closed on him, he spotted a mop of red hair out of the corner of his right eye and passed to Bradley Meyers who had Chris Walker inside him. Meyers drew his man and gave the ball to the Warwick Flyer who accelerated and left any possible tackler struggling in his wake as he crossed in the corner. This gave Walker the distinction of scoring a try in each of the three State of Origin games in 2001. Lockyer's kick was unsuccessful, but the Maroons were well and truly back in the game, trailing the Blues 4–6.

Both sides were committed to savage defence, and when Paul Bowman and Darren Smith's tackle on Blues' fullback Mark Hughes landed him on his head, Bill Harrigan awarded a penalty. Any advantage that might have accrued was quickly negated. Shane

Webcke smashed Jason Stevens in a tackle. The ball flew out and was pounced upon by Paul Green, the half-back who was the Maroons' hooker.

Two tackles later, John Buttigieg was almost over near the posts. When he played the ball, Allan Langer passed it to Darren Smith who sent the ball on to Paul Bowman. Bowman squared the debt he owed for Girdler's try when he neatly stepped around Freddie Fittler and then drove for the line carrying Adam Muir around his hips and planted the ball for the try. Lockyer again failed to convert but Queensland was in the lead, 8–6. The commentators were full of praise for Allan Langer's bravura performance and deservedly so. He led the attack, he was everywhere in defence, and his tactical kicking was devastating.

The Blues managed to square the ledger in the 20th minute when Darren Smith was penalised for stealing the ball in a tackle. Girdler's penalty goal brought the score to 8–8. This gave the Blues some encouragement. However, a highly touted young forward from the Northern Eagles, Mark O'Meley, was having a bad night with his hands. When a Civoniceva tackle caused him to drop the ball for the fourth time, the Maroons went on the attack In the 27th minute they trapped Brett Kimmorley on his own line under the posts. When the pass he threw to avoid being carried into the in-goal was ruled by Bill Harrigan to have been deliberately thrown forward, the two points were accepted with grace by Lockyer and the Maroons led 10–8.

Three minutes after the Blues restarted play, Allan Langer left their markers grabbing at air as he ran from dummy half, sent the ball to Daniel Wagon who found big Bronco second-rower Dane Carlaw coming through, as fast as any winger. Carlaw accepted the pass and dived over to touch down right alongside the right-hand goal post. Lockyer converted. It was 16–8, the Queenslanders had an 8-point cushion, and ANZ Stadium was in an uproar. One commentator claimed that the wave of emotion that swept the former Commonwealth Games venue had risen to tsunami proportions.[6]

Seven minutes before half-time, Darren Lockyer ran the ball back from his own twenty-metre line, beat one man and put boot to the ball to send it far downfield. Lote Tuqiri and Chris Walker joined him in what became a footrace to see who scored the try. Walker outpaced his captain and the winger, took the ball on the first bounce and scored in almost the same place as he had scored the first try. Lockyer had found the range. In thirty-eight seconds the Blues had scored a too-easy converted try and led 6–0. Just forty minutes later the Maroons sat down to suck their oranges in contentment as they contemplated a lead of 28 points to 8.

In his half-time commentary on Channel 9, former successful State of Origin coach Gus Gould excoriated the Blues' forwards. He claimed that on a scale of one to ten for pride and passion they didn't register on the meter, but perhaps he overlooked the exhibition of skill as well as pride and passion which he had seen from the young Queenslanders.

Junior Pearce read the riot act to his forwards at half-time and the Blues came out determined to do better, but they over-read the situation and went straight into panic mode. While they played touch football in a wild attempt to catch up, Alfie and the Queenslanders played the full-on tackle game and stopped them dead. Wendell Sailor was magnificent in this, his last State of Origin game, and once the ball changed hands Brad Meyers gained yards as though he was a money-hungry miser being paid by the metre. The Maroons lost their best yardage man seven minutes into the second half when Shane Webcke suffered a leg injury. He was replaced by rookie Bronco Carl Webb who had played only a handful of first grade games.

During the first half Allan Langer had been like the fabled Old Half Back who never dies … he just kept passing away. But early in the second half he started to run the ball. Fourteen minutes after half-time Alfie took a pass from John Doyle who had picked up a dropped ball. Langer ducked under an Adam Muir head-high tackle and stepped around two more forwards. Caught from behind and turtled, he went down on his back half a metre short of the line, but his arms were free and he lifted the ball back over his head to plant it point down on the try-line. To the Queenslanders watching, this was fairytale stuff. The crowd went wild and the ground shook as they cheered and pounded the seats and gangways of ANZ's metal stands. Shortly afterwards, Paul Bowman made it a double when he stepped both Freddie Fittler and Ryan Girdler before handing off O'Meley to place the ball over the line. Lockyer missed with the conversion attempt and it was Queensland 36, New South Wales 8.

The Blues struck back within three minutes. Standing wide, front-rower Jason Stevens ran on to a pass that was probably intended for the winger. The Queensland defence was caught on the wrong foot. Stevens scored, and when Girdler converted the score was only slightly more respectable at 36–14.

With eight minutes to play, Carl Webb showed what he was made of when he took the ball up from deep in his own half, beat three tacklers and ran to the opposition twenty-metre line before unloading to a flying Darren Lockyer who scored wide out. Once more he was off target with the kick and it was Queensland 40, New South Wales 14.

Final result

Queensland 40 defeated New South Wales 14.

Tries for Queensland: Darren Lockyer (2), Chris Walker (2), Paul Bowman (2), Allan Langer, Dane Carlaw. Goals: Darren Lockyer (4).

Tries for New South Wales: Ryan Girdler (2). Goals: Ryan Girdler (3).

Crowd: 49,441.

Man of the Match: Darren Lockyer.

The siren that signalled a Queensland victory could scarcely be heard for the tumult in the stands. The crowd of 49,441 was a record for a State of Origin game in Queensland, and as the Queenslanders made their way around the tartan track that borders ANZ stadium, none of them had left the ground. They stayed to cheer their heroes, and they saved a special kind of greeting for the Man of the Hour. At 35 years of age, the experts had expected that Allan Langer would run for forty minutes before being spelled, possibly fifty. But the little champion had played the entire eighty minutes of the game and at the end of it he looked as though he would be happy to play eighty more.

Allan Langer did his state proud. His was the ultimate individual Maroon performance, but that is hardly surprising, as Alfie is the ultimate Maroon. He passed, he ran, he kicked long, he chip-kicked short and in defence, he tackled like a demon. He put in his unique banana kicks and grubbers and he scored the best try on a night when good tries were common. In short, Alfie did it all. At the end of the season, Chris Walker wrote for the *League Year Book*: 'Alfie was guiding us around the paddock and taking the game by the scuff of the neck.'

The scuff of the neck indeed.

How true, how very true, and a well-balanced Queenslander called Scotty McGuigan wrote a poem about it:

THE GREATEST PHONE CALL EVER MADE
This story's of a phone call
The Greatest ever made,
To the Greatest bloody half-back
That ever bloody played.
Wayne Bennett called up London
Said, 'Alf ... we need you back.
So grab your boots and mouthguard, mate,
And don't take long to pack.'

'Mate, we need you back down under
In the good old Sunshine State.
A simple "yes" is all I want,
I've no time for debate.
The Origin is all locked up
The score is one plays one ...
At home we got them easy, mate,
But in Sydney, we got done.'

'See ... we missed big Gordie's bustling runs
We had Buttigieg suspended,
Doyle, of course, had not come back,
His crook leg hadn't mended.
What we need is your experience.
So here's what we might do.
Just listen very closely, mate,
I've got big plans for you.'

'Lockyer's shoulder's healed just fine.
He says it passed the test.
He'll run and pass and find the gaps
And give the Blues no rest.
Young Walker's in the centre,
He can really hit the toe.
When he runs off Lockie's hip
It's "Which way did he go?"

Petero and Shane will lead the charge.
We've got youngsters full of fight,
Wendell and Lote are on the flanks,
So outside we're alright.
Paul Green will be our hooker.
Smithie locks the scrum.
If you come back and strut your stuff,
We'll sit them on their bum.'

With those words, Wayne paused to hear
Alf Langer's brief reply.
'My gear is packed. Done as you spoke,
Now, what time do I fly.'
So Alfie came, and Alfie played.
He chip-kicked, dummied, passed,
The Cockroaches got properly done ...
Out played ... out bloody classed.

To make our day, Alf scored a try.
It was just about our best.
Down south they saw how half-backs rate
THERE'S ALF ... THEN THERE'S THE REST.
So for all of you who missed the game,
And missed the TV call,
The final score was Queensland heaps
And New South ... BUGGER ALL.

CHAPTER 24

2002

Revenge of Dad's Army

WITH FIT half-backs qualified to play for Queensland as scarce as hens' teeth, the unheralded return of Allan Langer to help win the deciding State of Origin match in 2001 was electrifying. It was also as necessary to victory as it was unexpected. At State of Origin time, the Queensland Rugby League was totally dependent on the two Queensland-based National Rugby League teams for certain key personnel and a horrific run of injuries had left both the Brisbane Broncos and the North Queensland Cowboys short of specialist half-backs. Alfie's triumphant return saved the Maroons' day.

But in the little wizard's moment of triumph, Alfie made his position clear. That was all there was. On his return to England he asked for a release from the remainder of his contract with Warrington. He had invested in property at Caloundra, on Queensland's Sunshine Coast, and he intended to settle there and enter the restaurant business. Feeding tourists would be a full-time job. Someone else could feed the scrums. But at the commencement of the 2002 season the half-back situation at the Brisbane Broncos was unchanged. It remained critical. When Wayne Bennett suggested to Allan Langer that he might like to help out pro tem — play a few games for the Broncos just to fill in — Alfie went out and bought a new pair of boots. When fixtures commenced, his few games stretched into a few more, then a few more, and there was inevitable speculation about yet another State of Origin appearance. Although Alfie said neither yea or nay to those who asked him his intentions, they seemed clear enough to those who were familiar with the rules. The truth was that his indecision was, of itself, an invitation to the Queensland selectors to pick him.

When Alfie signed a standard National Rugby League contract to turn out again for the Broncos, he was automatically committed to play representative football if selected unless he asked for an exemption on the basis of his long service to the game.[1] Alfie had not asked. Until and unless he did, the selectors' were duty bound to consider him.

In Sydney, State of Origin selections were made that year in a flurry of fuss and feathers. Wayne Pearce had described the skill level and dedication of his victorious 2000 team as 'scary' and he predicted a long era of Blues domination by the youngsters who had humiliated the Maroons in Origin III. What a difference a few months can make. The 40 points to 14 defeat suffered by the Blues at ANZ stadium in 2001 had been extremely embarrassing both to the Blues and to their coach. Junior Pearce was no longer coach and, with the exception of Bryan Fletcher, Jamie Lyon and Mark O'Meley, new faces abounded among the youngsters who would take the field in 2002. Gus Gould was recycled as coach and Andrew Johns inherited the captain's well-worn robes of office. He would lead a new side, eight of whom had never played State of Origin Rugby League before.

The Queensland selectors were inclined to stick to the tried and true, and just before the three wise men were due to meet, Alfie declared that he would play if selected. There was absolutely no chance that he wouldn't be, and having picked a 35-year-old veteran, the selectors were not about to strain at a few only slightly younger players: Andrew Gee, aged 32, Darren Smith, 32, and Kevin Campion, 30. A Sydney newspaper published photos of this famous four with their faces superimposed on World War II military dress, labelled them 'Dad's Army', and compared them unfavourably with the tenderfoot Blues whose youthful virtues were described in glowing terms.

In terms of players with big match experience, the Maroons

STATE OF ORIGIN I, 2002
AUSSIE STADIUM, SYDNEY, 22 MAY

Queensland	New South Wales
Darren Lockyer	Brett Hodgson
Lote Tuqiri	Timana Tahu
Chris McKenna	Jamie Lyon
Darren Smith	Matthew Gidley
Clinton Schifcoske	Jason Moodie
Shaun Berrigan	Trent Barrett
Allan Langer	Andrew Johns (c)
Shane Webcke	Mark O'Meley
Kevin Campion	Danny Buderis
John Buttigieg	Luke Bailey
Gorden Tallis (c)	Ben Kennedy
Petero Civoniceva	Steve Simpson
Dane Carlaw	Luke Ricketson

Interchange:

Andrew Gee	Braith Anasta
Chris Walker	Bryan Fletcher
Carl Webb	Nathan Hindmarsh
John Doyle	Michael Vella

Coaches:

Wayne Bennett	Phil Gould

Referee: Bill Harrigan (NSW)

outnumbered the Blues by a factor close to two to one. Of those Queenslanders who ran on to the Aussie Stadium on Wednesday night, 22 May, only Clinton Schifcoske and Shaun Berrigan were wearing Maroon for the first time. Almost a year earlier, twelve of the Queenslanders had taken part in the dismantling of New South Wales at ANZ stadium in Brisbane in Origin III, 2001. Only three of that defeated band of Blues took the field in Sydney.

One of those who had been absent in Brisbane a year earlier was the new Blues captain. Widely described as the best Rugby League player in the world,[2] Andrew Johns declared his intention to dominate the 2002 series, and if his performance in Origin I was any indication, then it seemed likely that he might just do that. His long kicking game was quickly shown to be superior, and after three minutes the Blues were inside the Queensland quarter with tackles up their sleeve.

Following a strong run by second-rower Ben Kennedy, and a play-the-ball inside the ten-metre line, New South Wales' new fullback, Brett Hodgson, broke away and passed to Matt Gidley, a late inclusion in the team. Gidley scored in the right-hand corner with just three minutes forty-six seconds showing on the game clock. Andrew Johns completed a magnificent conversion from the touch-line and it was New South Wales 6, Queensland nil.

The Maroons struck back eight minutes later after their forwards had driven deep into New South Wales territory. Allan Langer took a pass from dummy half. He spotted a gap on the Blues' right flank and threw a twenty-metre pass to Chris McKenna. The Cronulla utility made no attempt to catch the ball. He simply tapped it out to his winger, Lote Tuqiri. With two tacklers trying to push him into touch, Tuqiri slammed the ball down for a try a split second before he was bundled over the corner post. Clinton Schifcoske was the chosen kicker, but with a stiff breeze blowing straight down the field the ball was wafted wide of the posts: New South Wales 6, Queensland 4.

As expected, the game was a clash of the forwards, but the lighter Blues pack held their own against the Queenslanders. At the same time they managed to quarantine Allan Langer, cut off his runners and limit his opportunities to penetrate the solid defensive line that they presented.

At the 23-minute mark the Maroons were again in a scoring position. Allan Langer ran to the left from a ruck twenty metres out and then put in a banana kick which came off the right side of his boot and trickled toward the Blues' line. Dane Carlaw sped in pursuit. Had he picked up the ball cleanly, he had only to fall over to score. He knocked-on and what followed was a disaster for Queensland.

A downtown kick by Andrew Johns was chased by Parramatta centre Jamie Lyons. He was favoured by the bounce of the ball, plucked it out of the air at waist height and found Jason Moodie running through at top pace inside him. Moodie headed for the corner, was tackled, and gave the ball plenty of air as he threw it behind him to be picked up by Jamie Lyons backing up. Lyons scored a try just inside the corner flag. A second mighty kick from the sideline by Andrew Johns added the extras and New South Wales led Queensland 12–4.

After Clinton Schifcoske kicked off to restart play, the Blues' forwards rucked the ball back to their forty-metre line and Andrew Johns kicked high and long on an early tackle. In a frightful mix-up, three Queensland backs who were in the vicinity of the ball's point of impact let it bounce and New South Wales regained possession. From the second subsequent play-the-ball Brett Hodgson took off from well behind the ruck and with impeccable timing was on Danny Buderis's hip just as the dummy half turned to look for a runner. He ran unimpeded to Darren Lockyer, and as the fullback closed in to tackle him he found his captain calling to his right. Andrew Johns accepted the pass, and ran another fifteen metres to plant the ball under the posts. The two points for the conversion were a gift at that distance, and after twenty-eight minutes New South Wales led Queensland by 18 points to 4. A penalty within kicking distance five minutes later saw Johns increase the gap and the Queenslanders were down 4–20 with the clock showing six minutes until half-time.

With the clock ticking off the final minute of the first half, Tallis tackled St George five-eighth Trent Barrett. He then took a position marking Barrett. In doing so, he stood on the mark at the point where the player was tackled. In rising, Barrett made contact with the marker. He managed to rise, however, and he played the ball. Then he used both hands to push Gorden Tallis away.

Somehow, referee Harrigan saw an offence in this, and awarded a penalty against the Queensland captain for interference with the play-the-ball. When Gorden questioned the decision, there was no further discussion and Harrigan displayed ten fingers and ordered him to the sin-bin. The Maroon captain went quietly.

From the tap restart of play after the penalty kick, Andrew Johns kicked a field goal to make the score 21–4. It was half-time, and for the Maroons the game was gone.

With half-time behind them, and without their captain, twelve Queenslanders held the Blues scoreless for ten minutes but then, with Tallis only just back on the field again, Andrew Johns made a break from a ruck. Once again, Brett Hodgson was at his elbow, took the pass and carried the attack deep into Maroon territory. From the play-the-ball, Danny Buderis passed to Trent Barrett who sent a long pass out to Timana Tahu on the right wing. Tahu scored in the corner untouched. With Andrew Johns limping from a caulked leg, Hodgson attempted to convert the try. The kick missed and the score was New South Wales 25, Queensland 4.

After Tahu's try, not even the most optimistic fan gave the Maroons a hope at 25–4, and with the game safely in hand, Andrew Johns left the field to a standing ovation. Allan Langer had suffered a severe bout of influenza during the week of the pre-Origin camp and he was also nursing a thigh injury. Wayne Bennett could see no point in risking him further in a lost cause. He was replaced shortly after Johns left. There was no ovation for Alfie. The Sydney crowd was dead silent as he walked to the bench.

With both half-backs spectators, the game wound down as the players did little more than go through the motions. The Queensland defence managed to frustrate the Blues, and ten minutes before full-time, on a sixth tackle, Trent Barrett kicked another field goal: New South Wales 26, Queensland 4.

With just four minutes left in the match, and Queensland on the attack deep inside the Blues' half, a grubber kick by Shaun Berrigan went into touch in goal and a ten-metre scrum was ordered. In a last-ditch attempt to put more points on the board the Maroon forwards put on a giant shove as Trent Barrett fed the scrum. Such pressure is totally unexpected in what passes for a scrum in the Rugby League of the new era. The New South Wales pack disintegrated as the Queenslanders drove through them, but unfortunately the result was not quite as intended.

Somewhere in the Maroon and Blue confusion that had passed for a set scrum, a foot connected with the ball and drove it clear of the scrum and back to where Brett Hodgson stood, just inside his own touchline. He picked it up and ran down the open side of the breaking scrum where ninety metres of open country beckoned

---

Final result

New South Wales 32 defeated Queensland 4.

Tries for New South Wales: Matt Gidley, Jamie Lyon, Andrew Johns, Tinana Tahu, Brett Hodgson. Goals: Andrew Johns (4), Brett Hodgson. Field goals: Andrew Johns, Trent Barrett.

Try for Queensland: Lote Tuqiri.

Crowd: 55,421.

Man of the Match: Andrew Johns.

---

him. Lock forward, Dane Carlaw, and Chris McKenna gave chase but by the time they took up the pursuit Hodgson had ten metres start. He beat them to the try-line by at least eight and scored in a handy position for his conversion of his own try. With the hooter about to sound full-time, it was New South Wales 32, Queensland 4.

The New South Wales selectors made just four changes for Origin II. Matthew Gidley moved into the centres to replace Jamie Lyon, Braith Anasta took the place of the injured Trent Barrett, Nathan Hindmarsh moved in to second row and Scott Hill was the new man on the bench. Ben Kennedy was omitted.

The Maroons had let themselves down in Origin I. They knew it and so did the selectors. This was the year 2000 revisited and it seemed that the massive new Stadium Australia was bad, bad news for the Queenslanders. In five visits to Stadium Australia, the Maroons had lost five times, mostly by big scores. But considering the result of the 2001 series, this latest disaster would seem to have been 'against the run of play' and not something that would cause the selectors to panic. Only two changes were made to the losing side. Justin Hodges, the former Bronco prospect who had signed with the Sydney Roosters, replaced Clinton Schifcoske on the wing and Kevin Campion, who had played out of position as hooker in Origin I, gave way to specialist dummy half PJ Marsh, his fellow New Zealand Warrior. Given a second chance, there was an air of steely determination about the Maroon crew which went into camp to prepare for the return game at ANZ.

STATE OF ORIGIN II, 2002
ANZ STADIUM, 5 JUNE

Queensland	New South Wales
Darren Lockyer	Brett Hodgson
Lote Tuqiri	Timana Tahu
Chris McKenna	Jamie Lyon
Chris Walker	Shaun Timmins
Justin Hodges	Jason Moodie
Shaun Berrigan	Braith Anasta
Allan Langer	Andrew Johns (c)
Shane Webcke	Mark O'Meley
PJ Marsh	Danny Buderis
Chris Beattie	Luke Bailey
Gorden Tallis (c)	Nathan Hindmarsh
Dane Carlaw	Steve Simpson
Darren Smith	Luke Ricketson

Interchange:

Andrew Gee	Scott Hill
Travis Norton	Bryan Fletcher
Steven Price	Steve Menzies
Chris Flannery	Michael Vella
	Matthew Gidley*

Coaches:

Wayne Bennett	Phil Gould

Referee: Bill Harrigan (NSW)

* Travelling reserve.

The Queenslanders kicked off and it became clear early that Gus Gould's game plan called for Andrew Johns to kick toward the left where there was a concentration of inexperience. There was no instant reward for this, and with the Queenslanders' first possession, Gorden Tallis and his cohorts demonstrated that they could gain ground and hold it. The Blues second set of tackles saw Andrew Johns forced to kick on the fifth from his own thirty-metre line, but when Justin Hodges allowed a Johns bomb to find the green grass just outside the try-line, a flying Shaun Timmins caught the ball on the first bounce and forced it in goal. The home side celebrated a try, but a linesman told the referee, Harrigan, that Timmins was in front of the kicker. The result was both a penalty for the Maroons and a salutory let-off.

The Blues were again denied a try when Andrew Johns put in a grubber from the Maroons' ten-metre line. It was followed through by Luke Bailey who forced the ball. Unfortunately he, too, was offside when the kick was made. Two minutes later a scrappy Maroon movement broke down when a pass to no one went into touch. But the Queenslanders made no mistake in the twenty-first minute. Allan Langer orchestrated a back-line movement which culminated in Chris McKenna's perfect round-the-corner one-handed pass to Lote Tuqiri who beat Jason Moodie easily and scored five metres in from the touchline. His attempt at conversion failed, but the Queenslanders led New South wales 4–0.

In the 25th minute Allan Langer fielded a Johns bomb just outside his own try-line but was called offside by Harrigan. This resulted in a close-range New South Wales attack which was held comfortably for four tackles. Andrew Johns' grubber into the in-goal on the fifth was fielded by Justin Hodges. Cornered by the chasers, Hodges threw a poorly directed pass in Darren Lockyer's direction. This was a mortal sin, on a par with that of Phil Sigsworth, the fullback who cost New South Wales the 1982 series with a similar in-goal pass.[3] The ball went wide over Lockyer's shoulder and then to ground where it was pounced on by Braith Anasta for a fair try almost under the posts. Andrew Johns kick put New South Wales in front, 6–4.

Some measure of balm was applied to the Queenslanders' disappointment when their kick-off was taken on the full over the dead-ball line by Parramatta winger Jason Moodie. The penalty on the halfway line put the Maroons on immediate attack inside the Blues' ten-metre zone, where they held possession for more than three full sets of tackles before a McKenna pass to Lote Tuqiri put the big Fijian winger over for a second try in the corner. Again he missed the conversion. The score was Queensland 8, New South Wales 6.

New South Wales rookie fullback Brett Hodgson left the field

while Tuqiri was taking the kick. He had an injury to his ribs and
what later turned out to be a punctured lung. He would not be
back, and with rain falling the task of pegging back any sort of a
lead would not be easy. In the 37th minute, with the Blues attacking
inside the Maroons' twenty-metre line, Andrew Johns put up a bomb
that landed just short of the Maroon line in the right-hand corner.
Timana Tahu caught the ball and was claimed by Chris McKenna.
The ball came loose and bounced into the in-goal where it was
forced by Steve Menzies. Menzies claimed a try, but the video referee
detected a knock-on. A disappointed band of Blues crept off to
half-time with the score still 8–6 in the Maroons' favour.

The beginning of the second half was a reprise of that of the first,
with both sides completing several sets of six that featured solid
defence. Then in the 46th minute Jamie Lyon coughed up the ball
in a tackle with the ball bouncing free more than ten metres to
Allan Langer. Alfie picked it up on his own forty-metre line and
passed to Darren Lockyer who took a tackle on the Blues' forty-metre
line. Alfie was there for a quick play-the-ball and passed to Berrigan
who found the 'Raging Bull' at his hip running at his top and
screaming for the ball. Tallis sprinted the thirty or more metres to
the line and Moodie's tackle was only a token, last-ditch effort, with
the Queenslanders' captain well and truly over the line for a fair try.
Lote Tuqiri's conversion attempt was good and the Maroons led by
14 points to 6.

A Queensland knock-on gave the Blues a scoring opportunity.
When a penalty was awarded a metre from the line and in front of
the posts, Andrew Johns opted for the certain two points and the
score became 14–8. The Queenslanders did their opposition another
favour when the kick to restart play went out on the full. The penalty
from halfway put the Blues on the attack, and when Steve Menzies
picked up a loose ball and dived over the line, they celebrated a try,
only to be disappointed once more by the video replay which showed
that the second-rower had knocked-on.

In the 57th minute the Maroons were in possession on the New
South Wales twenty-metre line. P J Marsh fed the ball to Allan Langer
from a ruck and Alfie drew Andrew Johns in as he ran to the line.
He held up the pass until both Johns and the cover were committed

and then passed to Dane Carlaw who was at top speed as he took the ball. Carlaw was simply too big, too strong and too fast for the defenders, who fell off him as he scored halfway between the right-hand goal post and the sideline. Lote Tuqiri converted his try and the Queenslanders led 20 points to 8 with just twenty-one minutes to play.

With a 12-point lead, the Maroons were in the comfort zone. But they were suddenly startled out of it. With the Blues in possession inside the Queensland twenty metre line, Andrew Johns grubbered into the in-goal for Justin Hodges to field. Forced to run across field in the face of a line of advancing defenders who followed the kick, the winger spotted Darren Lockyer standing wide. To the horror of Queenslanders watching everywhere, he reprised his earlier disaster. This time the ball was wet. As he made to pass it, it slithered out of his hands and trickled along the ground at the feet of Blues winger, Timana Tahu, who reached for the ball but failed to apply downward pressure. However, the ball went backwards to Luke Ricketson, the lock forward, who forced it and claimed a try. Andrew Johns had an easy conversion kick and a comfortable lead of two converted tries was suddenly reduced to a fragile 6 points: Queensland 20, New South Wales 14.

Justin Hodges would be talked about for decades, his name etched even deeper in State of Origin history than that of Phil Sigsworth. He was called to the bench and took no further part in the game, his place taken by fellow Rooster, Chris Flannery.

Soon afterwards, Andrew Johns received the ball from a ruck mid-field on the Queensland thirty-metre line. With the Maroons defence compressed in anticipation of an attack down the centre, the three quarters found an overlap and they spread the ball wide. Quick passes saw the ball go to Shaun Timmins who scored wide out. Andrew Johns' conversion struck the left-hand goal post and rebounded into the field of play and the game was poised on a 2-point difference. Queensland 20, New South Wales 18 with just ten minutes of play remaining.

There had been more than 70 minutes of hectic football, and players were beginning to show signs of wear, but the pace didn't slacken. In the 77th minute Darren Lockyer beat two men with a dummy and crossed the line untouched. Unfortunately, Chris Walker had shepherded two defenders running a decoy and a penalty to the Blues was the net result.

With two minutes to go, the Maroons gained possession through an intercept by Travis Norton. At the end of the set of six tackles that followed, a chip-kick by Lockyer was knocked-on by Jason Moodie on the Blues' ten-metre line. It was the Maroons' loose head and feed. Allan Langer fed the scrum, picked up the ball and passed it to Shaun Berrigan who was tackled ten metres from the try-line. Lote Tuqiri acted as dummy half and ran through Danny Buderis and Scott Hill to score under the posts, his third try for the night.[4] The full-time hooter sounded as he was lining up his successful kick to convert and Queensland had defeated New South Wales, 26–18.[5]

Final result

Queensland 26 defeated New South Wales 18.

Tries for Queensland: Lote Tuqiri (3), Gorden Tallis, Dane Carlaw. Goals: Lote Tuqiri (3).

Tries for New South Wales: Braith Anasta, Luke Ricketson, Shaun Timmins. Goals: Andrew Johns (3).

Crowd: 37,989.

Man of the Match: Chris McKenna.

With the series poised at 1 plays 1, the media made much of statistical material that they considered relevant. Only three deciding State of Origin games had been won by teams which had lost Origin I. The media also made a great deal of the Maroons' record at Aussie Stadium. Five starts, five losses. But two of the three deciders in question had been won by the Queenslanders, and they weren't superstitious about Aussie Stadium. Wayne Bennett and Gorden Tallis settled down to the task of preparing the Maroons to defy such precedents.

The New South Wales selectors seemed to put their ANZ defeat down to bad luck, although it is difficult to imagine any side complaining of the sort of luck which had produced two such tries

as they scored off Hodges' errors. The Blues lost Mark O'Meley
when he had his jaw broken in a club game. He was replaced by
Dragons' prop, Jason Ryles, and the return of Trent Barrett saw Braith
Anasta displaced. These were the only changes for Origin III.

Justin Hodges' omission from the Queensland side for Origin III
was hardly a surprise. He was replaced on the wing by another
recruit for 'Dad's Army' in Robbie O'Davis, making his twelfth
Origin appearance at the age of 29. Eighteen-year-old Bronco Brent

STATE OF ORIGIN III, 2002
AUSSIE STADIUM, 26 JUNE

Queensland	New South Wales
Darren Lockyer	Brett Hodgson
Lote Tuqiri	Timana Tahu
Chris McKenna	Matthew Gidley
Chris Walker	Shaun Timmins
Robbie O'Davis	Jason Moodie
Shaun Berrigan	Trent Barrett
Allan Langer	Andrew Johns (c)
Shane Webcke	Jason Ryles
PJ Marsh	Danny Buderis
Petero Civoniceva	Luke Bailey
Gorden Tallis (c)	Steve Menzies
Dane Carlaw	Steve Simpson
Darren Smith	Luke Ricketson

Interchange:

Andrew Gee	Scott Hill
Travis Norton	Bryan Fletcher
Steven Price	Nathan Hindmarsh
Brent Tate	Michael Vella
	David Peachey*

Coaches:

Wayne Bennett	Phil Gould

Referee: Bill Harrigan (NSW)

* Travelling reserve

Tate replaced Chris Flannery on the bench. Petero Civinoceva returned from injury to replace Chris Beattie in the front row. These changes brought the total number of Brisbane Broncos' players in the side to a record 11.

Queensland kicked off. The Blues made no mistakes in their first set of six. Neither did the Maroon defence, and Andrew Johns' fifth-tackle kick was taken from just inside his own half. The Queenslanders ran the ball back and threw an early scare into New South Wales players and supporters when Chris Walker made a break down the right side.

In the seventh minute there was a mad scramble for a dropped ball on the Blues' twenty-metre line. Dane Carlaw emerged with the prize. Two tackles later, Darren Smith played the ball just ten metres out. PJ Marsh's dummy half pass went to Shaun Berrigan who served Lockyer. Darren Lockyer dropped the ball on the toe and with perfect placement put it into the left-hand corner of the Blues' in-goal. Lote Tuqiri easily won the race to score the first try in Origin III. However, he failed to convert. It was Queensland 4, New South Wales 0.

Just four minutes later, following a referee's call of '6 again' after Lote Tuqiri knocked-on in an unsuccessful attempt to intercept, Steve Menzies took an inside pass from Trent Barrett and scored twenty metres wide of the right-hand goal post. Andrew Johns conversion was good and New South Wales led 6–4.

The Maroons defence was savage. In the 14th minute Brett Hodgson sought to break away down the Blues' right flank. Gorden Tallis collared him some sixteen or seventeen metres inside the sideline. The Queensland captain then used a technique similar to a hammer thrower's as he swung the hapless fullback in circles until his momentum was sufficient to pitch him over the sideline and more than two metres into touch.

In Origin II, PJ Marsh had made a difference with his dummy half play and the New South Wales defence targeted him. In the 18th minute a Queensland penalty resulted from a big hit by Trent Barrett on the little dummy half, a hit delivered long after PJ had kicked the football. From this possession, Queensland attacked and two minutes after the penalty Dane Carlaw took the ball inside the

Blues' ten-metre zone. From dummy half, PJ Marsh sent the ball to Allan Langer who put Shaun Berrigan through a hole in the defence to score a very soft try. It was not Lote Tuqiri's night with the boot and again he failed to convert, but Queensland led 8–6.

In the 27th minute of the game, with the New South Welshmen in possession on their own forty-metre line, Andrew Johns played the ball to Danny Buderis who passed to Trent Barrett. The Blues' five-eighth was quickly into stride. He ran through attempted tackles by Dane Carlaw and Chris Walker then straightened up for the try-line. With only Darren Lockyer to beat and men in support, he passed the ball to Jason Moodie who was unchallenged to touch down under the posts. Andrew Johns made the four points into six and New South Wales took the lead, 12 points to 8. In the 32nd minute PJ Marsh took a hospital pass from Darren Smith and was flattened by Trent Barrett, whose task it seemed to be to target the tough little hooker. PJ was forced to leave the field with what was later found to be concussion, but referee Harrigan ruled a knock-on for the dropped ball.

On the cusp of half-time, a speculator kick by Andrew Johns would have seen Blues' forward Steve Menzies score had he connected with the ball. He didn't. It was claimed by Shaun Berrigan as the hooter sounded and the two teams went to oranges with the score favouring New South Wales 12–8.

Andrew Johns kicked off for the Blues to start the second half. The fifth tackle found the Maroons on their own forty-metre line and Darren Lockyer ran the ball before he passed to Chris Walker. Walker chip-kicked and, chasing hard, Gorden Tallis got in a soccer kick as it landed thirty metres out from the New South Wales try-line. Leader of the chase was Allan Langer. As Jason Moodie rounded up the ball on his own try-line, Alfie was all over him to force the drop-out from the goal line. There was a turnover almost on the Blues' line after the next set of six tackles, but the Queenslanders regained possession and continued to attack from good field position, helped immeasurably by the Blues' poor kicking game.

In the 56th minute Andrew Johns ran from a ruck in his own half and dummied to kick. When the Maroon tacklers held off, he scooted into open space before unloading to Trent Barrett who found Steve Menzies inside and sent him away. Menzies was tackled inside the Queenslanders' ten-metre line, and from dummy half Buderis passed wide to Timana Tahu who dived over in the corner. Unfortunately for the Blues, he lost control of the ball in grounding it and drew a 'NO TRY' from the video referee. The Maroons were allowed to restart with a tap on the twenty-metre line.

New South Wales regained possession on their own forty-metre line but Andrew Johns immediately knocked-on and returned the ball to the Maroons. Three tackles later, Shane Webcke took an inside pass from Allan Langer. He didn't bother to sidestep Brett Hodgson but simply strode over the top of him and scored ten metres wide of the posts. Tuqiri kicked this one. There were just twenty minutes left in the 2002 State of Origin series and the Maroons were in front, 14 points to 12.

In the 68th minute Jason Moodie kicked out on the full. That put the Maroons on the attack from the scrum win. On the fourth tackle, Darren Lockyer kicked and followed through to fly high and snatch the ball from Brett Hodgson's hands. Then, with an athleticism unsurpassed in Rugby League, he executed a perfect full pike, and placed the ball between his descending feet, less than ten centimetres inside the dead-ball line.

Bill Harrigan was uncertain about whether Lockyer's feet had come to earth without touching the dead-ball line and he asked the video referee for a ruling. Mr Chris Ward was the appointed video referee and he found no fault with the position of Darren's feet but did not immediately inform Bill Harrigan of this. This was the same Mr Ward who achieved his fifteen minutes of infamy when he decided the winner of the 1999 Grand Final by awarding a penalty try to the Melbourne Storm. He was about to earn his full shining hour in the spotlight.

While more than three million Australians watched enthralled on national television, he proceeded to have the incident replayed in slow motion, seeking fault with the grounding of the ball. In all, seven replays of various camera angles were exhibited. Not even the Channel 9 crew, with its majority of Blues' talent, could find fault with the grounding and neither could the vast majority of the public who watched the performance, but in the end Mr Christoper Ward did[6] and the red 'NO TRY' signal appeared on the screen.

A 20–12 scoreline would have been a comfort at that point in time but the Maroons still led. They needed only to defend their 2-point lead for eleven minutes to win and they weren't about to allow the vagaries of the video ref to upset them. As holders of the State of Origin trophy, the Queenslanders would retain possession if they drew the game. Andrew Johns' men needed at least a try if he was to mount the podium.

With ten minutes to go, the courageous PJ Marsh was hurt again and led concussed and stumbling from the field by two trainers. Then, with the clock counting past the six-minute mark, the Blues played the ball on their own forty-metre line. From Danny Buderis the ball went to Andrew Johns who passed to front-rower Jason Ryles. Running like a three-quarter, Ryles sent it quickly on to Shaun Timmins. Timmins made ground before he passed to Jason Moodie who outsprinted the cover to score a try in the corner. Andrew Johns landed the conversion from the sideline and the men in blue guernseys hugged each other as they contemplated certain victory. The score, New South Wales 18, Queensland 14.

Wayne Bennett considers a short kick-off to be more a parlour trick than a serious Rugby League tactic, but four points down and less than three minutes to play is desperation time and desperate measures were in order. Darren Lockyer had practised a short kick-off using a grubber to put the ball into touch just over the ten-metre line without the opposition touching it. His execution was perfection and Allan Langer fed a scrum in the centre of the halfway line.

The Queenslanders worked the ball downfield but turned it over at the end of six tackles leaving the Blues in possession on their own twenty-metre line. The Blues played it safe. It was no time for any fancy stuff. The clock had passed the two-minute mark and all that was needed was five good hit-ups by the forwards with a good kick into touch on the end of the sixth. The Maroon defence ensured that the kick on the sixth was taken well inside the New South Wales half and it did not find touch. It was fielded by Darren Lockyer on his own thirty-metre line. He ran it and then passed to Brent Tate who gave it on to Allan Langer. Langer gave the ball to Lote

Final result

Queensland 18 drew with New South Wales 18.

Tries for Queensland: Lote Tuqiri, Shaun Berrigan, Shane Webcke, Dane Carlaw. Goal: Lote Tuqiri.

Tries for New South Wales: Steve Menzies, Jason Moodie, Shaun Timmins. Goals: Andrew Johns (3).

Crowd: 75,484.

Man of the Match: Allan Langer.

Man of the Series: Shane Webcke.

Tuqiri who was tackled on the halfway line. He was on his feet immediately to play the ball back to Shaun Berrigan who had Darren Smith running off him. Darren Smith found that Allan Langer had doubled around outside him. Alfie drew the defence to him before he gave the ball to Dane Carlaw, coming on at pace. Carlaw simply shrugged off an attempted tackle by Jason Moodie and took off. One of the fastest forwards in the game, he beat any cover defence that may have been coming across and there was only Brett Hodgson in front of him. The lightly built Hodgson was already carrying a full set of stud marks and bruises acquired when he tried to stop Shane Webcke twenty minutes earlier. Dane Carlaw provided him with a matching set as he strode over the top of the fullback and grounded the ball. Tuqiri's attempt to convert from the sideline would have provided a Maroon victory, but the Queenslanders didn't need one. A score of 18–18 was good enough and, just as they had in 1999, the Maroons retained the trophy on the strength of a drawn game.

EPILOGUE

Motivational Material

EVEN AS Lote Tuqiri placed the ball to attempt to convert Dane Carlaw's try, the Blues' majority on the Channel 9 broadcast team were bewailing the situation. While the scoreboard would show a draw if he missed the conversion, the Blues were the losers and this did not sit well in the land of Blatta Orientalis. Next morning, Sydney's tabloid press joined the outcry and the shock jocks on talk-back radio had a field day. Media of all descriptions reflected deep southern discomfort with a situation that lacked an extra-time provision such as that used to break a tie in Grand Finals. Their cry was taken up by disappointed Blues all over their state, while north of the Tweed River Queenslanders asked hypothetically, 'Would the Blues' protests be quite as loud were they the holders of the trophy?'

The protesters were ignoring history. The interstate series that was State of Origin's precursor was once played over four matches and series drawn at two games each were not uncommon. It is unlikely that a need to resolve a drawn series was contemplated at the time the rules for State of Origin were written. If there was discussion, then there were sound reasons why such an arrangement would have received short shrift from the Sydney clubs.

State of Origin Rugby League was born at a time when the New South Wales Rugby League establishment and sporting media were clamouring for the abandonment of interstate competition alto-gether. Kevin Humphreys had needed to use muscle to drag dis-senting Sydney clubs kicking and screaming into consensus to even trial the concept. Club officials could not see beyond the possibility of the damage that interstate competition might do to the local Sydney competition and to their individual clubs' premiership chances through injury to star players.

Much was made of the tied 1997 Super League Tri-series final, which continued for a record 105 minutes before a decision was reached. This was a spectacular oddity, but not an example to be pursued over a three-game series. At the State of Origin level of intensity, eighty minutes is probably the maximum dose for even the fittest footballer. Both the health of the players and the demands of club matches a few days later enter the extra time equation. This is particularly the case for a club such as Brisbane, which necessarily contributes a major proportion of any Queensland State of Origin team.

But there is a further consideration. It is only by coincidence that both of the drawn State of Origin games occurred in Origin III. A drawn game may occur at any stage and lead to a tied series. Extra time would have to be used to decide Origin I or Origin II, should either be tied at the eighty-minute mark. While unlikely, it is also possible that all three games in a series would be affected.

In the aftermath of Origin III, 2002, none of this meant a thing to the now twice-shattered Blues. The system used to resolve the Super League Tri-series in 1997, ridiculed by supporters of the Australian Rugby League at the time, was the flavour of the month in Sydney in 2002. Trevor Gillmeister provided the Queensland viewpoint in his weekly newspaper column: 'We don't make the rules, we only play by them.'[1]

Managing director of the Queensland Rugby League, Ross Livermore, further stirred the Sydney pot when he announced that, since video referee Chris Ward's error in Origin III had so plainly robbed the Maroons of victory, the 2002 series would be recorded on the trophy as a win for Queensland.[2]

Twenty years of State of Origin football took place before the first drawn game occurred. It took only three years to produce the next, but it may take another twenty, thirty or even more to produce another. In any case, and just as it had done since 1908, the New South Wales Rugby League would use its numbers to decide the matter. With both drawn games having advantaged Queensland, it was long odds on that change would come, and that it would come sooner rather than later.[3]

In the meantime, winners were grinners. The attitude of the average Maroon fan towards the drawn game was probably best expressed by a caller who rang to congratulate Wayne Bennett on retaining the trophy. He said that watching the Blues squirm and listening to their anguished cries for the system to be changed gave him far more pleasure than any he might have derived from a clear-cut series victory. He claimed that the media uproar in Sydney and earlier comparisons by southern media between certain Maroons and 'Dad's Army' recalled to him those famous words of Lance Corporal Jones as he flourished his rifle with bayonet fixed in that wonderful television comedy with whose characters the Sydney media compared Allan Langer and company: 'They don't like it up 'em sir ... they do not like it up 'em.'[4]

Bennett's caller recommended that Blues' players and their supporters take a cold bath and seek solace in the words of an ancient Japanese Samurai, '... to endure great pain with fortitude and in silence builds character in the warrior'.

But football fans and officials are neither stoics nor Samurai. While vengeance on the field of play must wait until 2003, there were other opportunities. Three weeks after Origin III, a one-off Test match was due to be played against the old enemy, England, at Aussie Stadium. For some weeks the media constantly raised the question of the Australian captaincy. Would it be Andrew Johns or Gorden Tallis?

Of course, it was no contest. Andrew Johns was named as captain.

Seventeen men were to be picked to play the Poms, and following their undeniable dominance of the State of Origin series it was confidently expected in Queensland that at least four or five Maroon forwards would get a guernsey and Darren Lockyer and Lote Tuqiri would be the first backs picked. At least eight Maroons was considered an acceptable share of the seventeen places. When the side was announced, there was disbelief north of the Tweed. Gorden Tallis and Shane Webcke were in, Gordie as vice-captain, and so were Lote Tuqiri and Darren Lockyer. Chris McKenna, Man of the Match in Origin II, also made it, and to the surprise of almost everyone Brent

Tate, with about twenty minutes' experience in State of Origin Rugby League, got a seat on the bench. But if that was a surprise, the selection of Willie Mason of Canterbury and Jason Stevens, the vetern Cronulla prop, was astonishing. Neither of these players had donned a State of Origin guernsey in 2002.

The state of English Rugby League was such that regardless of the options taken by the Australian selectors, they would have needed to be both reckless and stupid and probably drunk as well in order to pick a team that would be beaten. But they did succeed in one area. The failure to select such outstanding Queenslanders as Shaun Berrigan, Dane Carlaw, Travis Norton, Petero Civoniceva and others in the Australian team deeply offended the Maroons.

The decision to select the two Sydney club players who had previously been overlooked by the Blues' selectors was said to have been made by Mr Colin Love, a New South Welshman and president of the Australian Rugby League, who was able to call on the Australian coach, Chris Anderson, another New South Welshman, for advice.

Asked about this by the media, Chris brushed off the Queensland criticism with a joke. 'Queensland was a great state, but God must have had a sense of humour. He filled it with Queenslanders.'

The Queensland versus New South Wales attitude, Us and Them, was first lifted to a higher competitive plane when Barry Muir described the Blues as cockroaches. As long as those most heavily involved, like Chris Anderson, express themselves so colourfully, this competitiveness will remain vigorously alive and will continue to flourish as it drives this most intense of sporting contests in The Greatest Game of All.

Notes

In the Beginning

1. The Queensland team consisted of:

Eric Fraunfelder

Billy Paten   Tom Gorman   Jim McBrien   Bill Spencer

E. S. 'Nigger' Brown

Cyril Connell (snr)

Jim Bennett

Charlie O'Donnell   Arthur Brown

Ernie Stanley   Norm Potter (c)   Norm Johnson

The New South Wales team consisted of:

F. McMillan

J. Flattery   L. Street   O. Quinlivan   C. Blinkhorn (c)

D. Hodgins

D. Thompson

A. Oxford

E. Evatt   F. Ryan

E. McGrath   L. Armstrong.   J. Watkins

Queensland tries: T. Gorman, W. Spencer, A. Brown, L. Stanley,
W. Paten. W. Paten 5 goals. New South Wales tries: A. Oxford, J. Flattery (2).

2. From Ipswich: Eric Fraunfelder, Jim McBrien, Billy Paten, Jim Craig (c), Joe
Hunt, Arthur Brown and Pat Parcells. From Toowoomba: Tom Gorman, 'Nigger'
Brown, Bill Spencer, Jim Purcell and Ces Broadfoot. From Brisbane: Ces
Aynesley, Arthur Henderson, Tom Tierny, Jim Bennett and Joe Jackson. Cyril
Connell represented North Queensland, while vice-Captain Norm Potter was
from Central Queensland.

3. Author's conversations with sons and namesakes of Cyril Connell and Billy
Paten, February 2002.

4. Barry Muir coached the Queensland team to a rare win in 1975 when his

team lost the decider in the three-game series by a single point. He inspired his charges by referring to the enemy as 'just a bunch of cockroaches'.

5. Barry Muir first saw the light of day in northern New South Wales. However, both of his parents were keen surfers who spent most of their weekends and holidays on Queensland's Gold Coast. Barry claims that it was during one of these visits that his conception took place, making him a Queenslander.

1. Decline and Fall

1. Between 1922 and 1934 the Maroons met the Blues on 39 occasions. Queensland won 23 of these encounters, New South Wales 15. One was drawn. Sixteen games were played between 1922 and 1926, of which New South Wales won only 3.

2. A staunch supporter of Rugby League all his life, McAuliffe attended a high school that was a member of the Greater Public Schools association and played only Rugby Union.

3. Second-row forward Les Heidke, from Ipswich, was playing his first Test match, and with the side reduced to ten men, he played as an extra back. Three of the backs were also Maroons. Fred Laws played centre, Joe Wilson was on the wing and Heck Gee played half. Of the ten men afield, seven were Queenslanders.

4. In 1954 a copy of the Brisbane *Courier-Mail* cost three pence, the approximate equivalent of 3 cents, and the Australian dollar was worth ninety American cents. In the year 2002, it is worth about 35 American cents. Using these parities as a measure of inflation over the last half of the 20th century, £17,000 in the 1950s probably had the purchasing power of a 21st century million dollars.

5. Of 37 games played, New South Wales won 25, Queensland 12.

6. Harry Bath returned to Australia in 1957 aged 32 and played three premiership winning seasons with St George during that club's period of greatest success. At one time he held the Sydney club goal-kicking record with 108 two-pointers in a season, while also holding the record in England where he kicked a massive 173 goals during the 1952–53 season.

2. The Union Whiz Kid

1. *Courier-Mail*, 4 June 1964. A soccer star born in Glasgow, raised in Australia and married to a Swedish woman, could change his name to Wung Foo and sign to play for a club in Outer Mongolia, yet still remain eligible to play for Scotland. Such rights and obligations had never been part of the Australian sporting tradition. In Australia, footballers were eligible to play for that state in which they were registered and for no other, regardless of their origins.

2. Leon Larkin became well known in Brisbane when he was appointed manager

of the new Sheraton hotel when it opened. He went on from there to become the Sheraton Group's European manager.

3. The first recorded representative game of Rugby League between teams selected on such a basis was staged by the Australian Army. A two-game State of Origin Rugby League series was played by army sides at Empress Augusta Bay on Bougainville in 1945. Queensland defeated New South Wales in both games.

4. *League of a Nation*, edited by David Headon and Lex Marinos, ABC Books, 1996. Article by Hugh Lunn, p. 62.

5. Conversation between author and Senator McAuliffe, Lang Park, 1979.

6. Sydney *Daily Mirror*, 2 July 1980.

7. *League of a Nation*, Lunn, p. 64.

8. In 1980, and for some time thereafter, a try was worth only three points.

9. This tackle was later selected for use as publicity in connection with an advertising campaign that used the slogan 'State against state, mate against mate'. It took on a life of its own when it was described as the cause of the brawl that erupted after the Olifant–Wynn–Beetson confrontation. This has long been claimed to be the incident that bonded the Maroons together behind their captain. In fact, the Queenslanders were well and truly bonded by the time Artie tackled Mick Cronin. The Maroons led 18–5 with twenty minutes to go when Artie Beetson's fairly innocuous tackle on Cronin took place.

10. As a schoolboy, Chris Close spent most of his holidays with a family friend, a grazier on the South Burnett, and joined in the normal activities on the property. This included the treatment and clearing of timber. His host claimed that Chris would arrive on the job full of enthusiasm, pick up the tomahawk used in poisoning timber, give a few chops and look for a shady tree to sit down. He named him Chop Chop, which was shortened to 'Choppy', and the nickname stuck.

11. *Courier-Mail*, 7 June 1982.

3. A Friendly Referee

1. Conversation between Dick Turner and author, 31 October 2001.

2. Ibid.

3. *Courier-Mail*, 17 May 1982.

4. Barry Gomersall's eccentricities, such as his habit of ignoring fisticuffs on the field and his flamboyant hand signals, demanded that he receive a nickname, 'Grasshopper' seemed appropriate and it stuck, although the donor of the pseudonym is unknown.

5. *Courier-Mail*, 23 June 1982.

4. It's Hard To Be Humble

1. Former Origin Greats. An organisation exclusive to players and officials who have worn the Maroon in State of Origin competition.
2. The value of a try was increased from three points to four at the end of the 1982 season.
3. Darryl Brohman played for Penrith in the Sydney competition. His club demanded that Les Boyd be cited. The judiciary handed Les a full calendar year's suspension and he was out for a season and a half. His career went down the gurgler and he never played representative football again.
4. There was an ironic twist to the scoreline. Chris Anderson's name went into the record books as the first player to score three tries in a State of Origin game. Unfortunately, he scored them on a losing side.
5. *Courier-Mail*, 29 June 1983.
6. Barry Dick, 'Sportsview', Brisbane *Sunday Mail*, 2 July 1983.
7. *Courier-Mail*, 22 June 1983.
8. Ron McAuliffe in a television interview following the third State of Origin game, 28 June 1983.

5. Big Boots to Fill

1. Max Howell and Reet Howell, *The Greatest Game Under the Sun*, Leon Beddington for the QRL, 1989, which quotes 'Financial Statements and Review of Records 1984'.
2. *Courier-Mail*, 30 May 1984.
3. *The Greatest Game Under the Sun*, p. 302.

6. Southern Breakthrough

1. Ian and Brett French were the first brothers to represent Queensland in State of Origin Rugby League.
2. *Courier-Mail*, 12 June 1985.
3. *Courier-Mail*, 20 June 1985.
4. *Courier-Mail*, 19 June 1985.
5. Ken Arthurson, *Arko*, Ironbark Press, Sydney, 1997.
6. Ibid.
7. In Davis Cup tennis, a winning side almost always rests its stars and uses the final match or matches of a dead rubber to give experience to its second string.
8. Adrian McGregor, *King Wally*, University of Queensland Press, St Lucia, 1987, p. 193.
9. *Courier-Mail*, 24 July 1985.

7. A Blue Whitewash

1. Ken Arthurson, *Arko*, Iron Bark Press, Sydney, 1997. p. 86.
2. Conversation with author, 12 November 2001.
3. Adrian McGregor, *Wally and the Broncos*, University of Queensland Press, St Lucia, 1989, p. 208.
4. Channel 10 television broadcast.

8. Birth of the Broncos

1. Sir Edward Lyons was much in demand with people seeking favours from the Bjelke-Petersen government. His nickname was derived from the assurance that he always gave his clients that representations on their behalf would be made at 'the top level'.
2. The Australian Football League issued a franchise to a syndicate headed by corporate fraudster Christopher Skase in 1986 and the 'Brisbane' Bears were established on Queensland's Gold Coast. The club struggled until 1996 when it merged with the struggling Melbourne club, the Fitzroy Lions, and established its headquarters at Brisbane's Gabba ground. The Brisbane Lions played their first AFL game in 1997, and became serious competition for Rugby League in Queensland when they won consecutive AFL Premierships in 2001 and 2002.
3. There was a wide belief, never confirmed, that Ross Livermore of the Queensland Rugby League would join his former president to become chief executive officer of the new entity once a licence was granted.
4. Conversation with author, 11 November 2001.
5. Ken Arthurson, *Arko*, Iron Bark Press, Sydney, 1997, p. 86.
6. Adrian McGregor, *King Wally*, University of Queensland Press, St Lucia, 1987, p. 170.
7. Conversation between Bill Hunter and the author, 14 November 2001.
8. Taped conversation between Barry Maranta and author.
9. The Bulimba Cup, sponsored by Queensland Breweries, was contested annually between the cities of Brisbane, Ipswich and Toowoomba for more than forty years. Selection was a much prized honour which fell not far short of the Maroon guernsey itself. First won by Toowoomba in 1925, competition for the trophy was abandoned when the Bulimba Brewery was taken over by southern interests. Brisbane won the trophy for the last time in 1972. In all, it was won 19 times by Brisbane, 16 times by Toowoomba, and 11 times by Ipswich.
10. Jack Gallaway, *The Brisbane Broncos*, University of Queensland Press, St Lucia, 2001, p. 19.
11. Ken Arthurson, *Arko*, Ironbark Press, Sydney, 1987, p. 182.

10. No Sad Songs for the Senator

1. Some New South Wales officials later claimed that the Queensland ball boys

who assisted in picking up the cans simply dumped them back over the fence for the later use of the marksmen in the crowd should they want to renew the attacks on Mick Stone.

2. Adrian McGregor, *Wally and the Broncos*, University of Queensland Press, St Lucia, 1989.

3. Conversation between the author and Brisbane Broncos' board members.

4. Gunsynd, the great racehorse known as the 'Goondiwindi Grey' and Ron McAuliffe often shared the headlines of the sporting pages and it was inevitable that the silver-haired chairman would acquire this nickname.

5. *Courier-Mail*, 17 August 1988.

6. Ibid.

11. Unchallengeable Champions

1. There were and always have been one or two exceptions to this rule within the Broncos playing staff. Since the club recruited Australia wide, there were always to be found those among their players who were fully eligible Blues.

2. The three were Michael Hancock, Tony Currie and Kerrod Walters. *Rugby League Yearbook*, David Middleton (ed.), Lester-Townsend Publishing, Sydney, 1989, p. 7.

3. Conversation with author, 25 November 2001.

4. Peter Kelly is famous for early penalties. In an Anzac Day game in Sydney between his club, Canterbury Bankstown, and St George, he was sent off for a high tackle so early in the game that he was back in the dressing room before the bugler who played the last post had found his seat in the grandstand.

5. Belcher, Hancock, Currie, Meninga, Shearer, Lewis, Vautin, Kerrod Walters and Backo all played in the three Tests. Stains played in three provincial games, and Jackson and Bella in two each.

12. No Dead Rubber

1. The Brisbane Broncos purchased the Western Suburbs Old Boys' clubhouse at Gilbert Park off Fulcher Road, Red Hill, an inner western Brisbane suburb. The club was sited on council land and the Broncos also acquired a lease of the adjoining football oval. The original clubhouse was developed into a modern poker machine club and a gymnasium and other facilities were erected in a separate building.

2. In what might well be described as a palace coup, Wally Lewis was relieved of his captaincy at the Brisbane Broncos and Gene Miles was installed in his place. One of the reasons for this had been Miles' decision to declare himself unavailable for any future representative football. The explosion that this caused in the media created great public relations problems for the Broncos, but, since Wally's injury ruled him out of the game, it wasn't allowed to interfere with preparations for Origin I.

3. In light of events that occurred later in the 1990s, one point of significance in what was otherwise a game easily forgotten was the choice of Paul Vautin to captain Queensland in the absence of Wally Lewis.

4. Paul Malone, *ALF*, Random House, Sydney, 1997, p. 91.

5. In the late 1940s and early 1950s, former Canterbury–Bankstown five-eighth Bobby Jackson established a Rugby League competition in Victoria, and in 1951 the Australian Rugby League promoted a match in which an 'Australian 13', comprising Sydney and Brisbane internationals, plus Bobby Jackson and a couple of locals, played a touring French team. Players from New South Wales were Clive Churchill (c), W. Dickason, K. Woolfe, J. McLean, G. Hawick, Jack Rayner and Ernie Hammerton. Players from Queensland were Noel Hazzard, Ken McCaffery, Brian Davies (v-c) and Gordon Teys. Players from Victoria were Bobby Jackson, Jack Balmain and Bernie Pease. Of the 'Victorians', Jackson and Balmain were former Sydney first graders and Bernie Pease was a Queenslander. All three were in Melbourne for work commitments.

6. Although Greg McCallum always claimed that he had called 'held' before Allan Langer stole the ball, the controversy over this episode led to a clarification of the rules, which now preclude a player from stealing the ball in other than a one-on-one situation.

13. Farewell to the King

1. Mark Geyer was cited for striking Paul Hauff with the elbow and was suspended for five weeks.

15. Mal and the Magic Word

1. Mal Meninga (with Alan Clarkson), *Meninga: My Life in Football*, Harper Sports, Sydney, 1995.

2. 'Boxhead' is a generic name for a hooker and appears to be exclusive to Queensland. Its first recorded use was to dub Dennis Jackwitz, the Ipswich hooker who represented Queensland in 1955–56.

16. Miracle for Mark, Oscar for Bennie

1. Rule 10 (b): No part of a tackled player's person other than his feet should be in contact with the ground when he releases the ball (Laws of the Game as published in 2002 Media Guide by the NRL).

2. At the time, this was easily a record for a game of Rugby League in Australia, but it was well short of the World Record, which was for a crowd in excess of 100,000 for a Cup Final played at Odsal, in England.

3. Bill Harrigan was the referee of choice of the Queensland Rugby League.

4. The Holy Bible. Hosea, Chapter 8, Verse 7.

5. The *Courier-Mail* and its subsidiaries are owned by the Murdoch family company, Cruden Investments, and not News Ltd.
6. From an enterprise that Ken Arthurson described as being a 'joke' in the 1970s, the marketing arm returned a profit of $700,000 to the League in 1991.
7. Ken Arthurson, *Arko*, Iron Bark Press, Sydney, 1987, p. 202.
8. Ibid., p. 210.

17. Fatty Is No Clown

1. From Paul Vautin's address to the players at his first training session.

19. Television General

1. Ken Arthurson, *Arko*, Iron Bark Press, Sydney, 1987, pp. 254–55.
2. Ibid., p. 257.
3. Henry Reed (1914–86) in an unpublished play, 'Not a Drum Was Heard'.
4. Arthurson, op. cit., p. 228.
5. Ibid., p. 229.
6. Both coaches made an alteration to the selected run-on side. Paul Vautin substituted Wayne Bartrim for Jamie Goddard. Tom Raudonikis removed debutante hooker Aaron Raper to the bench, and went into Origin II with John Simon as half, and the selected half and Blues captain, Geoff Toovey, as hooker. Aaron Raper sat on the bench for the whole of the game, his services not required, much to the public annoyance of his father, Rugby League 'immortal' John Raper, who was also a New South Wales selector.

20. Bean Counters' Nightmare

1. Several footballers from Super League and the Australian Rugby League factions featured in the Birthday Honours in 2002, six years later. In dealing with these, both of the media organisations involved lauded those so honoured who belonged to their own faction, and ignored the others.

22. Thou Shalt Not Steal

1. This manoeuvre had become fashionable after 'supercoach' Warren Ryan identified a loophole in the rules of the game during one of his weekly broadcasts on ABC radio. The practice had always been within the rule which said that if the moving ball touched a player who was in touch that the ball was dead and the scrum feed and loose head would be awarded against the team of the last man to touch it. Warren told his nationwide audience about it, coaches seized upon the practice, and players were quickly trained to place a foot in touch and straddle the line while they scooped the moving ball dead.
2. Lote Tuqiri joined this elite band when he scored three tries for the Maroons in Origin II, 2002.

3. When Messenger set the record, tries were worth only 3 points. He kicked the same number of goals as Girdler, but scored four tries, one more than Ryan Girdler. In real terms, measured in tries and goals, the Messenger record still stands.

4. The Newcastle victory was won by a Queensland team that included five players who had been non-playing reserves in two Sydney games. The New South Wales team included five Newcastle players to add local interest. Strictly speaking, it was not an official part of the 1925 series.

5. Wayne Pearce at the post-game press conference.

6. The name by which the common, dark brown household cockroach is known to science.

23. 'Grab Your Boots and Mouthguard, Alf'

1. Under a rule introduced in the late 1990s, the loose head and feed for the subsequent scrum goes to the attacking side when a ball kicked from inside a team's forty-metre line finds touch inside the defending side's twenty-metre line, thus providing them with possession in a strong attacking position.

2. Adam Muir felled big Gordie with a head-high tackle, and although the effects of this wore off, a cat scan taken during his treatment revealed a genetic narrowing of the spinal canal in the neck. This required surgery and the Queensland captain was out for the remainder of the season.

3. The referee had adjudged the Blues to have an advantage when they gained possession. His call, 'Play on', ought to have negated any possibility of a retrospective consideration of the matter.

4. First employed to describe Rugby League in the early 1970s by Channel 10, Ray Warren transferred to Channel 9 as their chief caller when that station took over the service. In 2001 he claimed the longest service as a television Rugby League broadcaster of any one then active in the industry.

5. Telephone conversation between Frank Hyde and the author, 4 July 2002. Born in 1915, Frank Hyde's experience in Rugby League as player, referee, commentator and long-time observer dates back to the early 1930s.

6. A tsunami is a gigantic tidal wave that is created by an undersea earthquake or by volcanic activity. Tsunamis can reach heights in excess of 100 metres and overwhelm whole coastal populations.

24. Revenge of Dad's Army

1. When he left for England in 1999, Allan Langer had played 31 games of State of Origin football. Peter Sterling (13 appearances) and Wayne Pearce (15) were both excused from State of Origin Rugby League by the New South Wales Rugby League, while Gene Miles was excused by the Queensland Rugby League after 19 games. All three continued to play with their clubs.

2. On page 16 of the Origin II program, Andrew Johns' accomplishments are

listed: Churchill Medal winner, Grand Final captain, captain of New South Wales, 16 State of Origin games and 16 Tests for Australia. At that point in his career, Allan Langer had captained his club to four premierships, played 32 State of Origin games and appeared in 22 Tests and two World Cup campaigns.

3. See Chapter 3.

4. This try elevated Lote Tuqiri into a very elite group. Only three other players had ever scored three tries in a State of Origin game: Chris Anderson, 1983, Kerry Boustead, 1984, and Ryan Girdler, 2000.

5. Lote Tuqiri also made history by scoring the try that lifted Queensland's gross score in State of Origin games to more than 1000 points.

6. According to press reports, his opinion was backed by senior NRL referee, Mick Stone, who was watching the game from the video referee's box (*Courier-Mail*, 28 June 2002).

Epilogue

1. *Sunday Mail*, 30 June 2002.

2. *Courier-Mail*, 1 July 2002.

3. Between 1908 and 2002, Queensland met New South Wales 285 times in 95 interstate series. During that time there were 9 drawn series, and 10 drawn games. In one year, 1974, two of a three-game series were drawn. There have been just two drawn games and two drawn series since State of Origin Rugby League was introduced. At an informal post-season meeting of chief executive officers and coaches, there was overwhelming support by Sydney clubs for change and not just for State of Origin games. Under the new 'golden point' rule, extra time will be used to break a draw, with the first team to score declared the winner. However, a time limit on the overtime period will mean that drawn games will remain a possibility.

4. *Dad's Army*, a BBC television production.

Appendix I

STATE OF ORIGIN RECORDS

Games played: 66
Won by Queensland: 33
Won by New South Wales: 31
Drawn: 2 (Queensland retained the trophy after both draws.)

Record crowd: 88,336 at Stadium Australia, 9 June 1999

Biggest win (Blues): New South Wales defeated Queensland 56–16 at Stadium Australia, 7 June 2000
Biggest win (Maroons): Queensland defeated New South Wales 36–6 at Lang Park, 23 May 1989

Three tries in a match:
  Chris Anderson (NSW), Lang Park, 28 June 1983
  Kerry Boustead (Qld), Lang Park, 29 May 1984
  Ryan Girdler (NSW), Stadium Australia, 7 June 2000
  Lote Tuqiri (Qld), ANZ Stadium, 5 June 2002

Most goals in one match: Ryan Girdler, 10, at Stadium Australia, 7 June 2000
Most points in one match: Ryan Girdler, 32 (3 tries, 10 goals), Stadium Australia, 7 June 2000

Record club representation: Brisbane Broncos — 11 players in Origin 1, 2001. (For Queensland: Darren Lockyer, Lote Tuqiri, Wendell Sailor, Gorden Tallis, Petero Civoniceva, Shane Webcke, Chris Walker, Bradley Meyers and Carl Webb. For New South Wales: Luke Priddis and Michael De Vere)

Most Man of the Match awards: Wally Lewis (Qld), 8

Youngest player: Ben Ikin (Queensland), 18 years and 83 days, 15 May 1995
Oldest player: Allan Langer (Queensland), 35 years 319 days, 26 June 2002

First Queensland-based New South Wales players: Chris Johns and Terry Matterson (Brisbane Broncos), 23 May 1989
Other Queensland-based New South Wales players: Glenn Lazarus and Michael Devere (Broncos), Tim Brasher (North Queensland Cowboys)

Most appearances as captain, New South Wales: Brad Fittler, 16
Most appearances as captain, Queensland: Wally Lewis, 30

Players who appeared in twenty games or more:
For New South Wales Brad Fittler, 29, Andrew Ettingshausen, 27, Laurie Daley, 23, Rod Wishart, 22, Andrew Johns, 20, Tim Brasher, 20, Paul Harragon, 20
For Queensland: Allan Langer, 34, Mal Meninga, 32, Wally Lewis, 31, Dale Shearer, 26, Bob Lindner, 25, Gary Larson, 24, Paul Vautin, 22, Darren Smith, 22, Trevor Gillmeister, 22, Martin Bella, 21, Greg Conescu, 20, Gene Miles, 20, Kevin Walters, 20

Send-offs: Only two players have been sent off in State of Origin games and they were both Queenslanders — Craig Greenhill, Sydney Football Stadium, 3 June 1996, and Gorden Tallis, Stadium Australia, 10 May 2000.

Appendix II

THE BLUES
1980–2002

	Years	App	Res	T	G	FdG	Pts
Adamson, Matt	2001	2	0	0	0	0	0
Ainscough, Jamie	1996–2001	9	3	2	0	0	8
Albert, Darren	1999	1	0	0	0	0	0
Alexander, Greg	1989–1991	4	2	0	2	0	4
Anasta, Braith	2002	1	1	1	0	0	4
Anderson, Chris	1980–1983	4	0	3	0	0	12
Ayliffe, Royce	1982	1	2	0	0	0	0
Bailey, Luke	2002	3	0	0	0	0	0
Barnhill, David	1994–1999	4	5	0	0	0	0
Barrett, Trent	1997–2002	4	1	2	0	1	9
Blake, Phil	1989	0	1	0	0	0	0
Bowden, Steve	1981	1	0	0	0	0	0
Boyd, Les	1981–1983	3	0	0	0	0	0
Boyle, David	1987	2	2	1	0	0	4
Brasher, Tim	1992–2000	20	1	3	9	0	30
Brentnall, Greg	1980–1983	4	0	1	0	0	3
Brooks, David	1985	1	0	0	0	0	0
Brown, Ray	1983	1	2	0	0	0	0
Buderis, Danny	2002	3	0	0	0	0	0
Buettner, Michael	1997	0	1	0	0	0	0
Bugden, Geoff	1983	2	0	0	0	0	0
Butterfield, Tony	1998	1	0	0	0	0	0
Carroll, Mark	1995–1999	7	0	0	0	0	0
Carter, Steve	1992	0	1	0	0	0	0
Cartwright, John	1989–1992	5	3	1	0	0	4
Cleal, Noel	1984–1988	11	1	3	0	0	12
Clyde, Bradley	1989–1994	12	0	2	0	0	8
Cooper, Bob	1980	1	0	0	0	0	0

Conlon, Ross	1984	3	0	0	10	0	20
Coveney, John	1982	2	0	0	0	0	0
Croker, Jason	1993–2001	1	4	0	0	0	0
Cronin, Mick	1980–1983	6	0	1	14	0	31
Daley, Laurie	1989–1999	23	0	6	1	0	26
Daley, Phil	1987–1988	3	0	0	0	0	0
Davidson, Les	1987–1988	5	0	1	0	0	4
Devere, Michael	2001	1	0	0	2	0	4
Docking, Jonathon	1987–1988	2	0	1	0	0	4
Dowling, Gary	1981	0	1	0	0	0	0
Duke, Phil	1982	1	0	1	0	0	3
Dunn, Paul	1988–1989	2	1	0	0	0	0
Dymock, Jim	1996–1997	3	3	1	0	0	4
Eadie, Graham	1980	1	0	0	0	0	0
Edge, Steve	1980	1	0	0	0	0	0
Elias, Ben	1985–1994	19	0	1	0	2	6
Ella, Steve	1983–1985	3	5	3	0	0	12
Ettingshausen, Andrew	1987–1998	24	3	7	0	0	28
Fahey, Terry	1981–1982	2	0	0	0	0	0
Fairleigh, David	1991–1997	1	9	0	0	0	0
Farrar, Andrew	1984–1990	5	2	3	0	0	12
Fenech, Mario	1989	2	0	0	0	0	0
Ferguson, John	1985–1989	8	0	1	0	0	4
Field, Paul	1983	2	0	0	0	0	0
Fittler, Brad	1990–2001	27	2	7	0	2	30
Fletcher, Bryan	1999–2002	9	3	1	0	0	4
Florimo, Greg	1988–1995	1	3	0	0	0	0
Folkes, Steve	1986–1988	8	1	0	0	0	0
Furner, David	1996–2000	6	2	1	0	0	4
Gerard, Geoff	1983	2	0	0	0	0	0
Geyer, Mark	1989–1991	3	0	0	0	0	0
Geyer, Matt	1999	3	0	2	0	0	8
Gidley, Matthew	2000–2002	6	0	4	0	0	16
Gillespie, David	1986–1994	5	10	0	0	0	0
Girdler, Ryan	1999–2001	7	1	7	27	0	82
Gourley, Scott	1993	0	1	0	0	0	0
Gower, Craig	1999–2001	1	2	0	0	0	0
Grothe, Eric	1981–1986	9	0	3	0	0	10
Gurr, Marty	1983	2	0	0	0	0	0
Hall, David	1995	1	0	0	0	0	0
Hambly, Gary	1980	1	0	0	0	0	0
Hancock, Craig	1995	1	0	0	0	0	0
Hanson, Steve	1988	1	0	1	0	0	4
Harragon, Paul	1992–1998	20	0	2	0	0	8
Hasler, Des	1985–1991	6	7	2	0	0	8
Hastings, Kevin	1983	0	1	0	0	0	0
Hetherington, Brian	1984–1986	1	1	0	0	0	0

Hilditch, Ron	1981	1	0	0	0	0	0
Hill, Scott	2000–2002	2	3	1	0	0	4
Hill, Terry	1993–2000	12	2	0	0	0	0
Hindmarsh, Nathan	2001–2002	2	2	0	0	0	0
Hodgson, Brett	2002	3	1	1	0	0	6
Hopoate, John	1995	1	0	0	0	0	0
Howe, Rodney	1998–2001	7	1	0	0	0	0
Hughes, Mark	2001	3	0	0	0	0	0
Hunt, Neil	1983	2	0	1	0	0	4
Izzard, Brad	1982–1991	2	2	2	0	0	6
Jack, Gary	1984–1989	17	0	1	0	0	4
Jarvis, Pat	1984–1987	6	2	0	0	0	0
Jensen, Barry	1981	1	0	0	0	0	0
Johns, Andrew	1995–2002	16	2	3	22	2	60
Johns, Chris	1995–2002	7	2	3	0	0	12
Johns, Matthew	1995–1998	3	1	0	0	0	0
Johnston, Brian	1984–1989	8	0	2	0	0	8
Johnston, Lindsay	1983	2	0	0	0	0	0
Jurd, Stan	1983	1	1	0	0	0	0
Kearns, Robbie	1998–2001	4	1	0	0	0	0
Kelly, Peter	1989	2	0	0	0	0	0
Kennedy, Ben	1999–2002	4	3	0	0	0	0
Kenny, Brett	1982–1987	16	1	2	0	0	8
Kimmorley, Brett	2000–2001	5	0	0	0	0	0
Kosef, Nik	1997–1999	7	1	1	0	0	4
Krilich, Max	1982–1983	5	0	0	0	0	0
Lamb, Terry	1981–1989	4	4	0	0	0	0
Langmack, Paul	1987–1988	3	1	0	0	0	0
Lazarus, Glen	1989–1999	13	6	2	0	0	8
Leis, Jim	1980	1	0	0	0	0	0
Lyon, Jamie	2002	2	0	1	0	0	4
Lyons, Cliff	1987–1991	6	0	1	0	0	4
Lyons, Graham	1990	2	1	0	0	0	0
McDougall, Adam	1998–2001	11	0	4	0	0	16
Mackay, Brad	1989–1995	10	7	3	0	0	12
Mackay, Graham	1992–1994	4	0	0	1	0	2
Martin, Steve	1980	0	1	0	0	0	0
Matterson, Terry	1989	0	1	0	0	0	0
McCormack, Robbie	1992	1	1	0	0	0	0
McGaw, Mark	1987–1991	10	3	6	0	0	24
McGregor, Paul	1992–1997	14	0	4	0	0	16
McGuinness, Ken	1997–1998	2	2	2	0	0	8
McGuire, Bruce	1989–1990	5	0	1	0	0	4
McKinnon, Don	1982	1	0	0	0	0	0
Melrose, Tony	1982	1	0	0	2	0	4
Menzies, Steve	1995–2002	5	9	3	0	0	12
Merlo, Paul	1982	1	0	0	0	0	0

Miller, Gavin	1983–1989	5	0	0	0	0	0
Moodie, Jason	2002	3	0	1	0	0	4
Morris, Steve	1984–1986	2	0	0	0	0	0
Mortimer, Chris	1985–1989	8	1	2	0	0	8
Mortimer, Steve	1982–1985	8	1	2	0	0	7
Muggleton, John	1982	2	0	0	0	0	0
Muir, Adam	1995–2001	9	4	2	0	0	8
Mullins, Brett	1994–1996	5	0	4	0	0	16
Mundine, Anthony	1999	0	3	1	0	0	4
Nagas, Ken	1994	0	2	0	0	0	0
Niszczot, Ziggy	1982	2	0	2	0	0	6
O'Connor, Michael	1985–1991	19	0	11	42	1	129
O'Meley, Mark	2001–2002	4	0	0	0	0	0
Pay, Dean	1994–1998	8	4	0	0	0	0
Peachey, David	2000	1	0	1	0	0	4
Pearce, Wayne	1983–1988	15	0	3	0	0	12
Potter, Mick	1984	0	1	0	0	0	0
Price, Ray	1981–1984	8	0	0	0	0	0
Priddis, Luke	2001	3	0	0	0	0	0
Rampling, Tony	1982–1985	2	1	0	0	0	0
Raudonikis, Tom	1980	1	0	1	0	0	3
Ricketson, Luke	1999–2002	4	3	2	0	0	8
Roach, Steve	1984–1991	17	0	0	0	0	0
Roberts, Ian	1990–1994	9	0	0	0	0	0
Rodwell, Brett	1995	0	1	1	0	0	4
Rogers, Steve	1980–1982	4	0	0	0	0	0
Ross, Robbie	1999	3	0	1	0	0	4
Ryan, Andrew	2001	1	1	0	0	0	0
Ryles, Jason	2002	1	0	0	0	0	0
Salvatori, Craig	1991–1993	0	5	1	0	0	4
Sargent, Mark	1990	0	1	0	0	0	0
Seers, Matt	1995–1997	1	3	0	0	0	0
Serdaris, Jim	1995	3	0	1	0	0	4
Sigsworth, Phil	1981–1983	3	0	0	2	0	4
Simmons, Royce	1984–1988	10	0	1	0	0	4
Simon, John	1992–1997	2	2	0	2	1	5
Simpson, Steve	2002	3	0	0	0	0	0
Sironen, Paul	1989–1994	11	3	0	0	0	0
Sterling, Peter	1981–1988	13	0	0	0	0	0
Stevens, Jason	1999–2001	5	2	0	0	0	0
Stone, Robert	1980	0	1	0	0	0	0
Stuart, Ricky	1990–1994	14	0	3	0	0	12
Tahu, Timana	2002	3	0	1	0	0	4
Taylor, Jason	1993	0	2	0	0	0	0
Thompson, Alan	1980–1984	5	1	0	0	0	0
Timmins, Shaun	2000–2002	4	0	3	0	0	12
Toovey, Geoff	1990–2000	14	1	0	0	0	0

Trewhella, David	1989	1	1	1	0	0	4
Tunks, Peter	1981–1987	7	2	1	0	0	4
Vella, Michael	1999–2002	0	10	0	0	0	0
Walford, Ricky	1990	1	0	0	0	0	0
Walsh, Chris	1984	1	0	0	0	0	0
Wilson, Alan	1989	0	2	0	0	0	0
Wishart, Rod	1990–1998	22	0	5	23	0	66
Wright, Rex	1984	1	0	0	0	0	0
Wynn, Graham	1980	1	0	0	0	0	0
Wynn, Peter	1984–1985	4	0	0	0	0	0
Young, Craig	1980–1984	4	1	0	0	0	0

THE MAROONS

1980–2002

	Years	App	Res	T	G	FdG	Pts
Allen, Gaven	1991–1995	5	3	0	0	0	0
Astill, Bruce	1980–1983	–	2	0	0	0	0
Backer, Brad	1980–1982	3	0	1	0	0	3
Backo, Sam	1988–1990	7	0	3	0	0	12
Bartrim, Wayne	1995–1998	8	1	0	11	0	22
Bawden, Russell	2000–2001	1	2	0	0	0	0
Beattie, Chris	2001	1	2	0	0	0	0
Beetson, Arthur	1980	1	0	0	0	0	0
Belcher, Gary	1986–1993	16	0	4	16	0	48
Bella, Martin	1987–1994	21	0	0	0	0	0
Berrigan, Shaun	2002	3	0	1	0	0	4
Boustead, Kerry	1980–1984	6	0	5	0	0	19
Bowman, Paul	2000–2001	6	0	2	0	0	8
Brennan, Mitch	1981–1983	4	0	3	2	0	11
Brohman, Darryl	1983–1986	2	0	0	0	0	0
Brown, Dave	1983–1986	9	1	1	0	0	4
Bunker, Adrian	1992–1993	3	0	0	1	0	2
Butler, Terry	1983	1	0	0	0	0	0
Buttigieg, John	2001–2002	3	0	1	0	0	4
Campion, Kevin	2001–2002	3	1	0	0	0	0
Cann, Alan	1996	0	1	0	0	0	0
Carlaw, Dane	2001–2002	3	2	3	0	0	12
Carne, Willie	1990–1996	12	0	5	3	0	26
Carr, Norm	1980–1982	2	2	0	0	0	0
Carroll, Tonie	1998–2000	2	6	1	0	0	4
Civoniceva, Petero	2001–2002	4	0	0	0	0	0

Name	Years						
Close, Chris	1980–1986	9	0	2	0	0	6
Conescu, Greg	1981–1988	20	0	2	0	0	8
Cook, Terry	1995	0	3	0	0	0	0
Coyne, Gary	1989–1992	2	9	0	0	0	0
Coyne, Mark	1990–1997	13	6	4	0	0	16
Cunningham, Owen	1996	0	1	0	0	0	0
Currie, Tony	1982–1989	8	7	3	0	0	12
Dallas, Brett	1993–1997	10	0	4	0	0	16
Dowling, Greg	1984–1987	11	0	4	0	0	16
Dowling, John	1982	3	0	0	0	0	0
Doyle, John	2001–2002	0	3	1	0	0	4
Fien, Nathan	2001	0	1	0	0	0	0
Flannery, Chris	2002	0	1	0	0	0	0
French, Brett	1983–1988	1	7	1	0	0	4
French, Ian	1985–1987	3	7	3	0	0	12
Fritz, Darren	1994	2	1	0	0	0	0
Fullerton Smith, Wally	1983–1990	12	0	0	0	0	0
Gee, Andrew	1990–2002	7	8	1	0	0	4
Gillmeister, Trevor	1987–1996	14	8	0	0	0	0
Goddard, Jamie	1997–1998	3	1	0	0	0	0
Green, Paul	1999–2001	4	3	1	0	0	4
Greenhill, Craig	1996–2000	3	3	0	0	0	0
Hagan, Michael	1989–1990	2	3	0	0	0	0
Hancock, Michael	1989–1996	12	1	5	0	0	20
Hancock, Rohan	1980–1982	6	0	1	0	0	3
Hauff, Paul	1991	3	0	1	0	0	4
Hearn, Tony	1995–1997	6	1	0	0	0	0
Henrick, Ross	1981–1984	2	1	0	0	0	0
Hetherington, Jason	1998–2000	8	0	0	0	0	0
Heugh, Cavill	1985–1986	2	1	0	0	0	0
Hodges, Justin	2002	1	0	0	0	0	0
Hohn, Mark	1993–1995	3	6	0	0	0	0
Holben, Greg	1982	0	1	0	0	0	0
Ikin, Ben	1995–1999	7	7	3	0	0	12
Jackson, Peter	1986–1992	14	3	2	1	0	10
Jackson, Steve	1990–1993	5	4	1	0	0	4
Jones, Gavin	1983–1986	3	1	0	0	0	0
Kellaway, Bob	1982–1984	0	2	0	0	0	0
Kelly, Stuart	1997	1	2	0	0	0	0
Khan, Paul	1981–1982	4	0	0	0	0	0
Kilroy, Joe	1988	2	0	1	0	0	4
Kiss, Les	1986–1990	4	0	3	0	0	12
Lam, Adrian	1995–1990	11	3	4	0	0	16
Lang, Martin	1998–2000	3	5	0	0	0	0
Lang, John	1980	1	0	0	0	0	0
Langer, Allan	1987–2002	34	0	11	0	1	45
Larson, Gary	1991–1998	24	0	0	0	0	0

Lewis, Wally	1980–1991	31	0	7	1	2	30
Lindner, Bob	1984–1993	22	3	7	0	0	28
Lockyer, Darren	1998–2002	13	0	4	20	0	56
Marsh, PJ	2002	2	0	0	0	0	0
McCabe, Paul	1981–1985	5	0	0	0	0	0
McIndoe, Alan	1988–1990	9	0	3	0	0	12
McKenna, Chris	1999–2002	6	0	0	0	0	0
McLean, Mike	1991–1992	4	1	0	0	0	0
Meninga, Mal	1980–1994	32	0	6	69	0	161
Meyers, Bradley	2001	3	0	0	0	0	0
Miles, Gene	1982–1989	19	1	6	0	0	23
Moore, Billy	1992–1997	15	2	1	0	0	4
Moore, Danny	1995–1997	4	0	1	0	0	4
Morris, Rod	1980–1982	4	0	0	0	0	0
Murray, Mark	1981–1986	14	1	1	0	0	4
Niebling, Bryan	1983–1987	9	0	1	0	0	4
Norton, Travis	2002	2	0	0	0	0	0
O'Brien, Clinton	1997	1	1	0	0	0	0
O'Davis, Robbie	1995–1999	11	0	1	1	0	6
O'Neill, Julian	1993–1997	6	2	2	9	0	26
Oliphant, Greg	1980	1	0	0	0	0	0
Phelan, Chris	1981–1984	2	0	0	0	0	0
Price, Steven	1990–2002	0	10	1	0	0	4
Quinn, Graham	1982	1	0	0	0	0	0
Reddy, Rod	1980	1	0	0	0	0	0
Renouf, Steve	1991–1998	9	2	2	0	0	8
Ribot, John	1982–1985	8	0	3	0	0	10
Rogers, Matt	1999–2000	5	0	3	12	1	37
Ryan, Peter	1998	1	1	0	0	0	0
Sailor, Wendell	1996–2001	14	0	1	0	0	4
Schifcoske, Clinton	2002	1	0	0	0	0	0
Schloss, Jeremy	1997	0	3	0	0	0	0
Scott, Colin	1980–1987	16	2	1	2	0	8
Shearer, Dale	1985–1996	21	5	12	9	0	66
Sing, Matt	1995–2000	14	1	2	0	0	8
Smith, Alan	1980	1	0	0	0	0	0
Smith, Craig	1997	2	1	0	0	0	0
Smith, Darren	1992–2002	15	7	2	0	0	8
Smith, Gary	1987	0	1	0	0	0	0
Smith, Jason	1994–2000	13	3	1	0	1	5
Stacey, Steve	1983	2	0	1	0	0	4
Stains, Dan	1989–1990	4	0	0	0	0	0
Tallis, Gorden	1994–2002	12	2	3	0	0	12
Tate, Brent	2002	0	1	0	0	0	0
Teevan, Craig	1997	0	3	0	0	0	0
Tessman, Brad	1983–1986	4	1	0	0	0	0
Thorn, Brad	1996–2000	6	2	0	0	0	0

Tierney, Neil	1997	3	0	0	0	0	0
Tronc, Scott	1988	0	1	0	0	0	0
Tuqiri, Lote	2001–2002	6	0	5	4	0	32
Vautin, Paul	1982–1990	20	2	2	0	0	7
Vowles, Adrian	1994	0	1	0	0	0	0
Wagon, Daniel	2001	3	0	0	0	0	0
Walker, Chris	2001–2002	5	0	4	0	0	16
Walker, Bruce	1982	1	0	0	0	0	0
Walters, Kerrod	1989–1991	6	0	2	0	0	8
Walters, Kevin	1989–1999	11	9	3	0	0	12
Walters, Steve	1990–1996	14	0	1	0	0	4
Webb, Carl	2001–2002	0	4	1	0	0	4
Webcke, Shane	1998–2002	15	0	1	0	0	4

Index